KINGS, KILLERS
AND KINKS IN THE COSMOS

Treading Softly With Angels Among Minefields

Other books by Robert Egby.

Cracking the Glass Darkly – AuthorHouse 2008

The Quest of the Radical Spiritualist – Three Mile Point Publishing 2009

INSIGHTS: The Healing Paths of the Radical Spiritualist 2010

PICTURE ON THE COVER:

A PHOTO OF DEATH AND A BOWTIE: A spirit voice urged the author to take a "general view" of a killing in Cyprus. It shows the slain body of a man named Bonici, surrounded by his fiancé Drosoulla, Cyprus Mail editor Brian Wright, British Army officer Major Dick Stuckey. But the general view also showed Nicos Sampson, a journalist standing on the right of the Major. The spirit suggestion only became apparent when some months later, the journalist was arrested as an E.O.K.A. killer group leader. This picture was splashed on the front pages of most British dailies. The bowtie? Bonici, A sales manager at an upscale store on Murder Mile sold this bowtie to the author. Bonici showed him how to tie it before hurrying off to meet his love for lunch. A few minutes later, he was dead, a victim of the Cyprus Emergency. Sampson was sentenced to death -- for carrying a gun, reprieved, and returned to an independent Cyprus to run a newspaper. He also became de facto President of Cyprus for a few days.

KINGS, KILLERS
AND KINKS IN THE COSMOS

Treading Softly With Angels Among Minefields

An Autobiography

Robert Egby

Three Mile Point Publishing
Chaumont, NY

Kings, Killers and Kinks in the Cosmos:
Treading Softly with Angels Among Minefields

Copyright © 2011 Robert Egby

Published by:
Three Mile Point Publishing
26941 Three Mile Point Road
Chaumont, NY 13622

www.threemilepointpublishing.com
Phone: 315-654-2060

Book formatting and cover design by Kimberly Martin

First Published:
Three Mile Point Publishing
February 2011

ISBN: 978-0-9832404-0-2
Library of Congress Control Number: 2011920115

Printed in the United States of America

ACKNOWLEDGMENTS

I would like to express my deepest appreciation and thanks to the following for their invaluable assistance in the creation of this book.

On Planet Earth: Betty Lou Kishler and Ken Kishler for proof-reading and advice.

For valuable information to stir memories, Bridget Hole, the Maidenhead historian; Alan Grace, the curator of British Forces Broadcasting Service; Sandra McFarlane of the SkyTrain Construction Project; and various sources. Know that you are all appreciated.

In the Spirit World, my devoted companions Chang, Paul and Isabel and Barbara, plus a lot of old friends dropping by and reminding me of people, places and events.

I would like to express deep appreciation for some incredible help along the way from David Hand the animator and film director-producer of G B Animation, Moor Hall, Cookham; also Stuart Crombie, sound man at Moor Hall; photographers Dennis Oulds of Central Press Photos, Fleet Street, London and Larry Burrows, photographer of Time-Life; Joe Alex Morris Jr., of United Press International; Iacovos Iacovides, publisher of the Cyprus Mail; Patrick Young and Isabel Corlett of the Vancouver Psychic Society; Tom Passey, dowser extraordinary; and Barbara Thurman of the San Francisco Spiritualist Society and President of the National Spiritualist Association of Churches.

And of course I would also like to express love and appreciation to my Great-grandmother Elen Egby, the Seer of Reading who foretold my life and advised me to tread softly...

And to the Spirit I call "Goddess" and the "Voice" for looking after my Being.

In their own unique way, each of these people gave me the education and drive to tread softly through the darkness of ignorance and suffering and embrace the Light and Freedom of Cosmic Peace.

INTRODUCTION
FOR AN ENQUIRING CHILD
IN SOME DISTANT TIME

In spite of my preference for living in the Eternal Now, there is a lot to be gained from learning from the Past, particularly one's own journey in the current life. It was only when I started to re-read what I had written that I realized my life has been guided, governed, prodded and pushed by a series of phenomena commonly known as "kinks."

Einstein's critics talked about kinks in Space-Time Theory, and planners, production managers and others routinely talk about working the kinks out of charts and projects. But as a spiritual pilgrim I would suggest a kink in etheric terms is "an unusual turn of events or phenomenon that reflects a sudden, mysterious, unexplainable change in the flow of Universal or Cosmic Energy."

It's not something that happens "out there." It is a phenomenon that occurs in just about everyone's life but many fail to notice or even give such things credence. It is only when one reviews one's track record on Planet Earth that the kink phenomenon becomes obvious

If someone had said "You're going to go carol singing and meet a cartoon producer who will change your life," I would at a tender age respond: "You're nuts!." Or someone might have declared: "While you are in the desert you will produce a show that will put you into broadcasting." Or "You will be an accredited war correspondent at age twenty-four."

Or the most way out suggestion: "You will walk with both kings and killers."

First and foremost, I never imagined it or even wanted it. So, who or what was writing the script? Who was pulling the strings? What force, what energy put me onto an Italian steamship heading for Beirut and led me into a special relationship that haunts me to this day?

Some people might suggest it is Fate or Kismet. I have no idea. But one thing is certain, I have lived a complex, fascinating, peculiar life and the kinks did not show up until I began to review my life story.

Why does anyone write an autobiography? For fame? Fortune? Hardly. To make a record for students of twentieth century history? There's an element of truth here. For my own children who missed me because I was "out chasing some news"? Perhaps there's another element of truth here because they probably have no idea of what I was doing when I was not with them. Sadly to my kids I am a stranger.

But is not this the case with many offspring? The knowledge I have of my own father and mother is abysmally deficient. I know even less of my four grandparents, and when it comes to my eight great-grandparents, apart from a brief reference of Great-grandfather Harry Egby in the "Strait Times" in Singapore in 1931, I know nothing. Regarding my Great-grandmother Elen, the Seer of Reading in England, I have only a fleeting memory because she gave me tea and performed a strange psychic reading that became embedded in my mind. This ancestor-gap is tragedy of high cultural proportions. We become thrilled when we discover a string of names and birth places of our ancestors, but that is just a list without much depth. We joyously promote our social contacts on the Internet, but have little or no knowledge of the people who created us. What were their lives, their preferences, their habits good and bad, their likes and dislikes? What made them laugh? It is worthy of note that through social networks on the Inernet, we know more about people on the other side of the world than our immediate neighbors. We live in an age of spacial detachment.

So I am wondering about the children of my children's children. Could it happen that one day in some distant year, on some distant world, a growing child endowed with a high level of curiosity might ask his mother: "My genealogy teacher says I had a great-great-grandparent named Robert. How can I find out something about him?

And his mother will perhaps answer: "If you search the digital archives of the parent planet, you may find his book.

A short while later the child will joyously proclaim, "I found it! I found it! Now, what is a kink in the Cosmos?"

Mother laughs. "What prompted your teacher to mention your great-great-grandparent?"

"I don't know," says the child. "The teacher did say she felt she was being pushed to mention this to me."

"Aha!" says mother, a degree triumphant. "There's been another kink in the Cosmos."

It is for that kid, who is still not even distant twinkles in my great-grand-children's minds that this book is written. And kid, know that you are loved.

Robert Egby
Chaumont, NY
January 2011

CONTENTS

A definition:
Kink in the Cosmos – An unusual turn of
events or phenomenon that reflects a sudden,
mysterious, unexplainable change in the flow
of Universal or Cosmic Energy.

1

THE EARLY YEARS

THE WAY I HEARD IT I was born at 6:10 a.m. on Sunday, February 14th 1932 in the reign of King George V, a notable year for the Royals because it was the first time a British monarch used the radio, or "wireless" as it was then known in England, to broadcast a Christmas Day message to the populace of the realm. Some 2.7 million people were unemployed, seven million were on the dole, and the year saw violence in rioting hunger marchers.

The year was also notable because Aldous Huxley published "Brave New World," while Japanese invaders captured Shanghai, President Doumer of France was assassinated, Hitler's National Socialist Party, after the general elections, was now the largest in the Reichstag, John Cockroft and Ernest Walton split the atom again (Rutherford did it ten years earlier). Little did I know then, that negative energies were jelling for wild times that would change the Planet in my lifetime.

Dad – Robert Gordon Egby – was born on Christmas Day 1904 and felt he had been deprived of a lot of birthday goodies. An electronics engineer, he loved inventing things and making electrical gadgets work. In his heyday he came over as a movie star. As such he also loved flirting with women and was a familiar figure at Skindles and the Showboat, an upper-class lido by the River Thames, all hangouts for the rich and famous. Dad was neither, but he was a good looking flirt and got on with just about anybody.

FATHER: Robert Gordon Egby pictured in his later years.

Mum – Emily Mary Douglas – a young, elegant lass, met Dad at the Maidenhead indoor roller skating club which was part of the famous Hippodrome. Somehow she got pregnant. Initially Dad refused to marry Mum, but "Granny Nellie" - her real name was "Ellen" Egby - exerted matriarchal pressure by threatening to cut off financial life support to her eldest son. This spelled disaster for Dad who happened to be one of those 2.7 million unemployed. He desperately needed money to purchase a Matchless motorcycle with the excuse "so I can get a

MOTHER: Emily Mary Douglas pictured as a teenager. Married the author's father Robert Gordon Egby in 1931.

job." In reality he wanted to be one of the boys who spent weekend jaunts in Dorset and Sussex with his friends. One was a man called Pimm, the other was T.E. Lawrence, the British Army officer and author of Arabia fame and "Ten Pillars of Wisdom." Strangely, both died in tragic motorcycle accidents.

The place where I first saw the light of the world was at the aging brick Nursing Home, situated among a few pines at the bottom of Castle Hill in the ancient Borough of Maidenhead. It was destined for destruction in the 1970s when the Borough fathers chose to place a huge intersection there and split the ancient town. The Nursing Home was also the birthplace of S. Peter Dance. Peter came into the world on February 3rd 1932 – some ten days before me – and has been in and out of my life for almost eight decades.

Dad bought the house at 36 Edith Road, Maidenhead with financial assistance from his mother, my grandmother whom I called "Granny." It cost £5,000 or $25,000 in 1933. (U.S. dollar was devalued in that year). A comfortable bungalow, brick and stucco, with a roof that resembled a pyramid from which protruded two brick chimney stacks. The front door was inset, and flanked by two bay windows. A hallway divided the house, two bedrooms on the east side and a sitting room, kitchen and a "front" room on the west.

Two vibrant apple trees dominated the back garden, along with a lawn and a busy vegetable garden which was Mum's domain. Black and red currant bushes were her pride and joy from which she made succulent pies and jams, a rhubarb plot and my favorite, a gooseberry bush. "Goosegogs" as I called them, were crunchy sweet and delicious. Beyond the back garden was a meadow where the owners occasionally let horses roam, and on the far side was a stand of tall, very old trees known as "Grey's Alley." Many a couple would walk the narrow pathway on a summer's evening and suddenly disappear into the bushes. I was totally innocent in those days and figured they were just playing games.

Dad built three structures at Edith Road. Two were concrete goldfish ponds, one in the back and the other in the front. Neither was conducive to healthy goldfish, mainly because concrete yielded lethal toxins, a point made in advance by Mr. Halifax our next-door neighbor. It was something Dad did not wish to hear, but when 1936 came, and with it my sister Sheila, Dad yielded to Mum's concern that fishponds could be dangerous to a toddler, and reluctantly filled both of them with earth, so we had two instant flower beds full of marigolds every year. Accompanying Dad's reluctance was a distinct wave of anger.

SKELETON IN THE CLOSET

Mum's parents lived at a place called "Flint Cottage" at Taplow, a village on the east side of Maidenhead and the River Thames. The tiny cottage flanked the A-4 highway, also known as the Bath Road. It had a working well in the garden which provided water, and at the back were wheat fields and a small farm where granddad worked. Before World War II they had an old black dog called Jippa, and so, in my small years I referred to mother's mother as Jippa-granny.

Mother, Sheila and I took the Thames Valley red double-decker buses to visit Jippa-granny. Even in those young years, a visit to Flint Cottage was a journey back in time. The inside walls were carefully and meticulously papered with flowery images and the wooden furniture was stark but made comfortable with heavy cushions. Granddad would come from the fields, sweaty and sunburned, push off his mud-caked, leather boots and wash his head and arms under the pump-tap in the kitchen. He always wore a black leather belt that seemed to hold his slender, work-worn figure together.

Jippa-granny was always a lady. She gave us tea in lovely cups and saucers of fine Dresden china, and always gave me two shortbread biscuits. Even today, whenever I delight in shortbread cookies, I sense her energy.

Mum had two sisters. One was several years older, a dour woman who lived in a Kensington apartment in London with her husband known as Uncle Billy. The other was Eydie who married Jack Daniels, a baker and confectioner. Eydie had three children and suffered several bouts of tuberculosis. Sadly, she crossed into Spirit shortly after the war and so did a baby daughter. Mum had several brothers with whom I lost count. Ernie and his family lived a few miles away in Windsor while Jack worked at a distinguished club in London, Whites Gentlemen's Club, which dated back to the 1690s. It was Jack who used to visit Mum and together they would walk along Grey's Alley and into the thicket. Mum had many things on her mind, but she never ever revealed them to me or my sister Sheila in those early years. I sensed it was her deteriorating relationship with Dad. For starters, after 1937 when we all went to Hayling Island, he never accompanied us anywhere.

But there was something else that overshadowed her life. Years later I discovered her so-called "skeleton in the closet." Apparently, her mother – we called her Jippa-granny – had come from a higher class of family that lived in the Manor at a sleepy little village between Newbury and Oxford. The young Jippa-granny, whose maiden name was Annie Reeve, had fallen in love with one of the farm laborers and insisted on marriage. The family promptly disowned her and hence the shadow in my mother's life. Mum's self-esteem was never what it should have been. She was a wonderful mother and worked hard to keep my father, my sister Sheila and I fed during the war years.

DANGER ON THE AIRFIELD

Dad with his Matchless had secured a job at Miles Aviation at Woodley, near Reading and was doing what he enjoyed, working as an electronics engineer on aircraft. Strangely, he had an aversion to flying and never in his life flew on a commercial airliner. Woodley, as an aviation center, came into being in 1932 with the arrival of F.G. (George) Miles who along with Philips and Powis produced the Miles Hawk Trainer, a two-seater, double control aeroplane which subsequently became the Miles Magister.

Dad worked on the team that created the Miles Aerovan, one of the first practical boxcar aircraft. Experts said it changed the face of aviation design. In its history a number of distinguished aviators visited the aviation center including Charles Lindbergh and Amy Johnson. It was at Woodley airfield in 1931 that a young 21-year-old Royal Air Force Officer Douglas Bader performed a low level flying stunt, crashed and lost both legs. He went on to become a World War Two heroic fighter pilot and was credited with downing 22 enemy aircraft. Dad told me that Bader, while flying the Miles Master in the early war years, flew into Woodley airfield several times, and always looked at the area where the crash occurred. "You only do that lesson once," he said with a grin.

For Dad it was not easy working at Woodley. In September 1939 the war started and everything changed. Gas masks were issued, air raid shelters were built, brick and concrete "blast" walls were built outside office windows, air raid drills were frequent, and food became short and was eventually rationed along with petrol. Several times the airfield was strafed by German fighters. On one occasion a Dornier 17 dropped a bomb on the airfield, damaging several aircraft. "I was checking some electronic parts in an aircraft and saw the Jerry coming. I've never run so fast in my life. I took shelter behind a sandbagged wall, and then when it was all over, I realized I was inside a fuel bunker. I couldn't sleep for several nights after that."

One project upon which Dad spent many hours working involved prototypes of aircraft voice recorders, which ultimately became known as the famous Black Box used in most commercial aircraft today. Test pilots urgently needed a device that would record their voices during tests, but would be fireproof and crash-proof. Someone had created a fireproof box and it was now Dad's job to create a recording device that would fit inside and work under arduous circumstances.

Dad had a workshop at the side of the house and worked for months getting a stabilized recording arm to work over a spinning metal disk. He needed a voice, so he organized a stool, placed me on it with a microphone and had me read parts of books, newspapers and handwritten notes. It was the first time I had heard my voice. It was 1942 and I was ten years old, and little did I think then that the microphone would play such an important role in my later life and still does to this day. There is no written record of what happened to Dad's experiments or work on the flight recorder. Miles Aviation closed down after the war and Dad ran a small smoke-shop in Henley-on-Thames. Woodley is still a high spot in aviation tradition. It is the home of the Museum of Berkshire Aviation.

WARTIME RADIO HAM:
Father was a member of the Radio Society of Great Britain, inducted in November 1944 when Society members listened on the air waves for information on Germany.

While writing this book, I found Dad's membership card in the Radio Society of Great Britain. It says he was "elected a Corporate Member of this Society" on November 13th 1944 and his BRS number was 9160. So he was an Amateur Radio Operator. That makes sense. He loved radio and electronics. Further research reveals that some Society members assumed volunteer work with Britain's MI8 – Military Intelligence – and regularly scanned the air waves for information on the Germans. Whether Dad did that I cannot say, but it would be the sort of stuff he would enjoy.

THUNDERING ELEPHANTS IN THE SKY

The war years were memorable, not because they were pleasant, far from it, but because they were different. My early schooling was at Alwyn Road, an elementary establishment between Pinkneys Green and Maidenhead and I used to walk there and back, a mile or so. Someone once brought a Spitfire aircraft and displayed it in the school yard to encourage families to help the war effort by buying savings bonds. The guns fascinated me, and I wondered how an aircraft could fly and shoot bullets at the same time.

A week later I found out. On a Saturday, some friends and I walked into Maidenhead. Someone gasped and pointed. Grey elephants floating in the sky! A Thames Valley bus conductor told us: "That lot is barrage balloons. Keeps the Huns away." It was an enormous flotilla of silvery-grey barrage balloons floating in the skies over the Slough and Langley industrial areas about six miles away. As I found out later, each balloon was about 60 feet in length and 25 feet across, and was attached to a steel cable. They could be winched up to an altitude of about 5,000 feet.

I always thought of them as big, thundering elephants. Operated by a special squadron of the Royal Air Force, the strategy was to prevent low-level aircraft attacks, thereby reducing elements of surprise and accuracy of bombing. The cables created severe psychological effects on enemy pilots, especially if the balloons were hidden in the clouds and they were flying low, they could not see the killer cables until the last few seconds before they sliced through the airplane.

Some months later, I was still ten years old and idling myself in the back garden when a large grey figure caught my eye against the trees of Grey's Alley. A barrage balloon! It had broken loose! My mind switched into high gear and I raced across the field. The balloon was drifting slowly, only about a couple of hundred feet up. Its steel cable was dragging like a huge tail across the field, hissing ominously as its weight cut through the tall grass. A voice echoed in my head. "It's too big. Too big! Let it go." My mind rejected the advice and I tried grappling with the cable but it was too thick for my small hands. I ran further along the cable towards where it was hanging down and tried to pull it back. It pulled itself right out of my hands. Disillusioned, I knew the cable was too big for me to handle. Another idea. I attempted to sit on the cable. Another voice – a real shrill, demanding voice – screamed across the field.

"Bobbie. Get back here this instant! Do you want to get killed?" It was mother, perched on the rhubarb hill at the end of the garden. So ended my encounter with a barrage balloon. It had been ripped from my grasp. It was a power and I had lost it. I felt annoyed, a growing irritation that became a smoldering anger. Mother was over-protective. "You're just like your father, Bullheaded," she said, the day after the barrage balloon incident. She would always post-analyze things next day or sometimes days and weeks after they happened.

A MORRISON SHELTER IN THE BEDROOM

Dad was a frustrated man, perhaps because of Mum's way of handling life, so he took out his irritations on anyone in his environment. He was quick to anger, terribly impatient, and his whiplash tongue lost him many friends. I feel that his relationship with Mum, which had never been great to begin with because of pressures from Granny Egby, steadily deteriorated over the years. This is why when her brother Jack came from London, they would go walking on the thicket for what must have been therapy chats. When he was not angry or impatient, he was a lovable father and one that I admired.

Mother always feared the worst. Ever since my illness at age six, she had been overly protective, at least, that's the way I saw it. When the war came in 1939 her fears seemed to grow. My sister Sheila had arrived in 1936 and was now four years old. Mother had a habit of walking with Sheila into the front garden and standing by the gate. She would gaze down Edith Road as if expecting something bad. It came one day. Some men delivered a Morrison shelter.

Designed for homes that did not have basements, the Morrison shelter looked like a steel table, but it had walls of steel mesh and its foundation was a metal lath mattress. It resembled a heavy steel box. Dad liked it and put it all together in the back bedroom. Mum called it "an iron coffin." The Morrisons created an excellent safety record in the blitz and after the war many families kept them. The designer, Cambridge University engineering professor John

Baker received an inventor's award. He also gathered a knighthood and later a baron's title.

Mother made the shelter as cozy as possible with warm blankets and pillows, but no one used the shelter, and in the early days of the war Sheila and I used to sit on top of the Morrison's roof and play games. Even at night we slept in our own beds, until one night something happened.

I had been asleep and the wail of the sirens brought me to full consciousness. As the sirens faded a new, ominous drone became apparent. A heavy, throbbing engine sounded threatening. Then the whistling started. A long, warbling, howling whistle. A tremendous explosion shook our world. I heard windows being blown out. Mum rushed into the bedroom. "Bobbie...Sheila...into the shelter. Quickly!" We needed no second urging, and scrambled into the shelter. Mum crawled in beside us. Dad was nowhere to be seen. It was at this time that I felt a tinge of fear, but fear of what I did not know. Death? I had never seen anyone die.

A second whistle. It seemed to last a long time, then suddenly it stopped. Sometime later Dad came in and announced there had been two bombs. One had exploded right by Grey's Alley. The other had failed to explode in the field beyond. Dad was an ARP (Air Raid Precautions) warden and he and a neighbor, a Mr. Gee, armed with flashlights, set off across the field to inspect the damage caused by the Luftwaffe. It was dawn when they returned and the police and the army people were arriving. When I look back on that evening, there was no time at which I felt scared. Excited? Yes. But Mum trembled and cried at the same time. I think my excitement and self-confidence that all would be well, was the influence of the woman, the Greek Goddess I had encountered just before the war.

Those were the only bombs that fell on our home at Pinkneys Green during the war. Others came near. One Saturday afternoon the Luftwaffe bombed the St. Martin's Jam Factory in downtown Maidenhead. Dad took me on his motorcycle to have a look. Everything was sticky chaos. One street was covered with marmalade. It got on people's shoes and dogs were having a field-day licking up the stuff.

WATCHING THE THOUSAND BOMBER RAIDS

Sometimes events became laughable, sometimes they just got plain grim. Sometimes my sister Sheila and I would get blankets, spread them on the lawn and watch the evening sky at dusk, and notice the emerging network of stars and planets twinkling in the growing darkness. During summer nights of

1943 and 1944 the beauty of the Cosmos was disturbed by the drone of aircraft. We could just make out the black dots against the darkening sky. "Thousand bomber raids," Dad told us. "Telling old Jerry we mean business." We tried counting the planes but there were too many.

One evening, July 18th 1944, a prolonged explosion shook our bungalow. It seemed to last several seconds. Windows rattled. We rushed out into the garden. The night sky over Maidenhead Thicket was ablaze with light. "Sounds as if one of the bombers has blown up or crashed," said Dad.

"How could that be?" asked Mum.

"Heaven knows," exclaimed Dad as he ran off to check with the Air Raid Wardens office. He returned to say a bomber had crashed in Carpenter's Wood at Burchetts Green near the Henley Road.

Next morning, eager to discover things, my school pal from up the road, David Warren and I cycled over to the woods. We had explored the area several times on bike treks so we were well aware of pathways. The place where the crash occurred was on a slight hill, filled with an undergrowth of small bushes and tall trees. Some trees were brutally sheared off at mid-trunk; other stumps were charred and still burning. They stood like silent sentinels. Pieces of metal were scattered over a vast area through the trees. At twelve years old I could only stare at the devastation. David kicked at a brown boot lying among the shrubs. It slid sideways to reveal part of a leg still inside. I felt nauseous, unable to believe the carnage. We both picked up small pieces of metal as souvenirs and cycled quietly home. Dad said the plane had been a Halifax bomber from 578 Squadron, RAF.

We later found out that six crew members had died in this tragedy, not over Germany, but right here at home in England. It seemed a strange irony. They say a rear gunner parachuted to safety, but according to Maidenhead historian Bridget Hole, he was never found or identified.

A footnote to this story: On July 18th 1998, fifty-four years to the date of the crash, a memorial was established in Carpenter's Wood and dedicated to the crew. Various dignitaries attended the event. Bridget who was there wrote: "As the dedication began, those of us present were startled by a sudden shaft of brilliant sunshine which came through the trees and across the glade and onto the memorial. A fitting tribute to the brave airmen."

Somewhere along the pathways of my early life I lost that piece of metal, that souvenir, but the memory of that evening survives. In those days heading into my teenage years I announced several times that I would never join the Royal Air Force or fly in a bomber. As fate or the Universe would have it I did both.

DOODLEBUGS IN THE SKY

Just after D-Day and the allied landings in France, Germany launched a new terror on England. The V-1 flying bombs which we called Doodlebugs were sent to areas all over southern England. A doodlebug was a monoplane without a pilot. With a wingspan of 18 feet, the 26 feet long aircraft would fly at an altitude of several hundred feet above the countryside. If you could hear the distinctive sound of the pulsing hum of the jet as it zoomed along at some 400 mph you were considered safe. It was when you heard the engine suddenly cut out as the plane approached that you dived for the air raid shelter.

We were tested one Saturday afternoon. I was now twelve years old. Pinkneys Green is at an elevation higher than downtown Maidenhead, so we could see the doodlebug flying towards us. Dad yelled out: "It's coming in very low!" Mother went into hysterics and screamed at my eight-year-old sister Sheila and me to "Go inside! Get in the shelter!" She scooped up my four month old sister Diane from the black and silver pram and ran into the house. Sheila disappeared, but Dad and I stood in the garden watching. It was exciting and too good an opportunity to miss. We were both "irresponsible" as Mum decided afterwards. So, we watched the V-1 coming in. Dad estimated it missed our chimney stack by some 50 feet. Some minutes later we heard an explosion from the direction of Marlow. Thinking back now, I must have been nuts, but there again it was being nutty that got me into strange adventures in my adult life.

Sometimes I slept over at Granny Egby's house which adjoined my grandfather's auto repair business and petrol station. It was called Highway Garage and flanked the A4, the Bath Road. Frederick Egby was a likable man, but rarely said much. He was a dedicated worker. His son, my Dad's brother Gordon worked in the garage when not driving taxis, and everyone pumped the petrol. I say "pump" because that was how petrol was dispensed in the war years. You pulled a wooden handle back and forth. Cars that had frequented the highways prior to 1939 seemed to disappear. People left them jacked up and covered in their gardens. Some people had cars and had petrol ration cards because they were part of the essential services. Dad, working for Miles Aviation was able to operate his motorcycle.

SPECIAL CALLERS AT THE GARAGE

Highway Garage was an unusual place, and you never knew who was going to pull up at the petrol pumps. Tom Arnold the West End producer came through frequently, as did Queen Wilhelmina of the Netherlands who stayed for part of the war at the nearby Stubbings House on the Henley Road beyond Maidenhead Thicket. The Queen always popped out of the car to talk to Granny. They seemed to have something in common. They both did not like where they were. Granny always had a desire to return to Nottingham and Barton-on-Trent, the places of her childhood, and the Queen, well, that was obvious.

One frequent visitor was the debonair Ivor Novello whom Granny worshipped, even when he was caught, found guilty and sentenced to eight weeks in prison for violation of misusing petrol coupons. He served just four. Novello was one of the "greats" in British show business composing songs, singing and acting. He wrote the evergreen wartime song "Keep The Home Fires Burning." In spite of his criminal record, Granny never stopped adoring Ivor who lived at Redroofs in Littlewick Green between Maidenhead and Reading. He died in 1951.

MEETING GREAT-GRANNY EGBY

There was one woman visitor to Granny Egby's who totally impressed me and I only met her three times. A tall, slender woman dressed entirely in black – a full length dress, a bodice, enclosing a blouse, with a shawl wrapping her shoulders – all in midnight black. She tied her hair in a bun, and wore a large black floppy felt hat from which protruded several shiny black ostrich feathers. This was Great-Grandmother Egby from Zinzan Street in Reading and she was somewhere in her eighties. Her face was beautifully white, like Florentine sculptured marble, and her dark brown eyes observed from under heavy hairy eyebrows.

HENRY EGBY: This is the only known photograph of my Great-Grandfather, the poet, composer and song writer.

Elen had been married to Henry Egby, better famously known as a poet and a composer as Harry Egby. When The Royal Princess Charlotte of Wales' Royal Berkshire Infantry Regiment was leaving Reading for the killing fields in northern Europe, a singer named Bert Welfare sang great-grandfather's song "The Goodbye of the Berkshires." The chorus went this way: "Goodbye Lou, Sue, Mary-Jane and Liza, By the left quick march, we are off to thrash the Kaiser, Soon he'll get another big surpriser, from Good King George's loyal Berkshire Boys." It must have sounded great in 1915 and when Granny Egby of Highway Garage related it to me one day, I can't for the life of me wonder why his song and his name both stuck in my head. But they did. Years later it dawned on me that somehow I had inherited his energy for music and creativity. While writing this book I searched diligently for anyone who had copies of his song. Then I found a copy—in the British Library at St. Pancras in London. But I also discovered two other works by Harry Egby. A song called "War Babies" written in 1915. He also wrote some poems in "Rhymes and Romances of Reading Abbey" published in 1922.

Elen Egby hailed from Chelsea in London. She was a character, a real kink in the Cosmos. Someone claimed that the Reading Mercury newspaper once ran a story that suggested she had had a brief relationship with the ailing Robert Louis Stevenson, the Scottish novelist who wrote "Kidnapped" and "Treasure Island." I have nothing to authenticate this, but there is other talk that Elen took into her care and raised as her own, a child illegitimately spawned by an heir to a famous Berkshire company. Perhaps someone will investigate this one day and reveal the truth.

A SEER PREDICTS MY LIFE

There were two fundamental traits I discovered about my Great-Grandmother. One, she was of Romany gypsy stock and two, she was a seer. This metaphysical quality came through loud and clear one day in the spring of 1945 when World II was drawing to a close. Grandfather Fred took me to Elen's basement apartment on Zinzan Street while he went off to meet some automobile business cronies. Elen gave me some honey-sweetened tea and afterwards casually reviewed the residual tea leaves. As she peered across the brim of the cup, her dark eyes danced, almost mischievously as she watched my curiosity filled face. I had just turned thirteen and Elen was, as I discovered later, coming up to her mid-eighties. Now I realize, when she came to perform the teacup reading as a seer, she had switched energies to a Universal Consciousness. It was an energy that I would embrace later in my life, but now I simply sat agog, almost transfixed trying to understand. Her voice was soft, almost a whisper, sounding like a breeze causing aspen leaves to tremble.

"You will have many travels and walk many paths. Unusual gates, doorways will open and take you on many adventures. You will work with the light and heal with sound, and you will help people understand God. But before that you will hurt people, even loved ones, until you set yourself free. You need to set yourself free, but not before you are in the West. It will happen in the West and in the deserts surrounded by mountains you will find the energy of the spirits and you will come through the darkness into the light. The road ahead is yours. Tread softly."

The words were etched in my head. "Set yourself free." It was many years before I came to understand what she was talking about. Before we left Elen suddenly cried: "Let me see the scar just above your left knee." Surprised that she knew, I obediently pulled up my long khaki shorts and showed her the mark on the inner side of my left knee. Her long, delicate fingers gently touched the reddish mark. "The Spirits told me about your sickness that occurred some years ago just as the war was starting. It is well now, but you will carry the scar for the rest of your life to remind you of your spiritual connection. You didn't know I chat with Spirits, did you?" She gave a short laugh, then sighed briefly as I shook my head.

"Bobbie, we will meet again one day and I will be dressed in white."

Somehow I loved this strange, elegant lady dressed in black with a hat brimming with black ostrich feathers. But I had absolutely no idea what she was talking about.

Nobody told me when a year later she died. Perhaps they could not figure out why I should care. But Elen knew.

A BATTLESHIP AT FALMOUTH

The scar on my left knee? That involved a kink in the Cosmos and it occurred when I had achieved seven years in the present life. Mum had a good friend in the ancient harbor town of Falmouth in Cornwall near to the south-west tip of England. Nestled on the River Fal, Falmouth Harbor for many ships is the Gateway to the Atlantic.

Ethel Scribbins, a tall, happy, chatty lady had recently moved from Maidenhead to run a vacation Victorian-boarding house. Dad no longer accompanied Mum on holidays, so she brought Sheila and me to the Scribbins House for two weeks, August 12th to 26th 1939.

The beaches at Falmouth comprised fine golden sands that seemed to stretch for miles, especially when the tide was out. The waters of the English Channel swept in twice a day bringing fresh seaweed. We learned to hang up strips and predict weather conditions. If the weather was fine, the seaweed would be dry, if rain was in the forecast, it would turn moist. Sheila and I made wreaths around our necks. Mum promptly decried them as "Filthy," and ordered us to take them off. Whenever she could Ethel joined us on the beach for long chats with Mum.

One day a massive ship loomed on the horizon and anchored off, perhaps a mile at sea. "That's the Iron Duke," Ethel told us. "It's a battleship." It was another in the growing number of omens that war was looming. It was not just any old battleship, but one of the Dreadnought Class from World War One here for a review at Weymouth and then departing for Scarpa Flow. I discovered many years later that a cousin of mine, John Egby of All Saints Avenue, was serving on the ship and he later died at sea. The presence of the Iron Duke bothered our mother. She worried about everything.

One morning while we were playing in the sand, I suddenly felt something sharp slice across my ankle. I failed to notice anything serious until Sheila cried out: "Look Mum, Bobbie's bleeding! Bobbie's bleeding!" It had been part of a glass bottle, as sharp as a razor. The women rushed over. One wrapped my foot in a large picnic napkin. Ethel, a big woman, picked me up and carried me a couple of blocks to her house. By the time we got there, the white napkin was totally red. Ethel seemed to know what to do. She washed the cut and then covered it with a pad. "Hold it there," she ordered, and then raced off to the local chemist's shop to return with a bottle of antiseptic. "Iodine," she said dabbing it on my ankle. My lungs were ready to burst. I screamed so much that Mum thrust a cushion over my face. I'm surprised I lived. Mum detested loud noises.

By the time we caught the train home, I had a bandaged foot but I was walking or at least limping around. The date was August 24th. A couple of weeks later, I was wandering around Granny Egby's raspberry patch. The sitting-room window was open and I could hear a man's weak, gutless tones on the wireless..."and consequently this country is at war with Germany." It was September 3rd, 1939.

I wondered what war was all about. Nobody took time out to explain it and I could not imagine war, or whatever it was, coming to our town. But Mum understood and she never stopped talking about it. She was a born worrier. Dad took refuge from her worries in his workshop. No one ever imagined what would happen next, least of all me.

A DEATH CALL AND A GODDESS

While war was on everyone's mind, something more dangerous was happening in my body. One morning I woke up and started screaming. My legs were covered with huge, ugly blisters the size of small marbles and I felt awfully dizzy and very sick.

Physicians made house calls in those days, thank God! Dr. Vernon Cadogan who operated a clinic at the bottom of Castle Hill, came with his black bag, took one look at me and announced: "Septicemia! Your boy has septicemia. Blood poisoning!"

He and my mother stood by the bay window as if they were on stage and I was not supposed to hear. "We've had several cases in the area over the last few years. It's usually fatal and the best we can do is have him stay in bed and take sulphur tablets. There is no positive treatment for septicemia."

Mother was shaking. "You...you mean Bobbie is going to..." she staggered through the question, and finally said "..die?"

Cadogan shrugged. "You might try prayer. Some people say it works."

Later, Mom told me that her fears for my life had been enhanced in November when she heard that a famous Canadian doctor, Norman Bethune serving in the Sino-Chinese War, had died of the very same thing – septicemia. I stayed in bed for weeks, gradually losing weight and daily taking the yellow sulphur drugs. By Christmas 1939 my weak and fragile form was up and about. I still have the blister scar on my left leg. But I digress. Let us go back to the day the doctor came.

It was right after Cadogan delivered his doom and gloom prediction, that a spirit appeared. I thought I was dreaming. I had read a comic book recently and they said you can see through spirits, so I figured she was a spirit. Her energy felt kind and warm. I sensed she was a Greek goddess. Some time later, when I was still recuperating, Dad brought me a picture book on the history of ancient Greece, and I figured the spirit in my room that day was Aphrodite, the Greek goddess of love. They mentioned some island I had never heard about – Cyprus. Anyway the picture looked like her, but this one in my room had soft flowing robes all in pure white.

The lady spirit informed me in a clear firm voice: "You're not going to die, Bobbie. You will get well." It was a statement. No ifs, ands or buts. You will get well! I often wonder if it was her energy that drew me to the Mediterranean in my early adult years. Her voice came back many times in my life and I often wondered if I would ever learn her name. For now, she was the Goddess.

RATION CARDS AND SHOPPING

The war years in Britain were something else. Food was rationed and we had ration cards. The government took over the old Hippodrome and the skating rink, where Mum met Dad. It became a busy regional ration card center. We learned to use evaporated milk in our cups of tea. Coffee disappeared altogether and the Camp firm came up with a coffee substitute made from chicory that blooms with blue, lavender and white flowers in the hedgerows of Europe and North America. Some people made hot drinks from acorns.

Mum did the grocery shopping at the Co-op shop on King Street, struggling to the Thames Valley bus stop with two or three bags of food. We did not have a car. I do not think Mum ever drove a car in her entire life.

Britons had ration cards right up until 1954, nine years after the war ended. Granny Egby with her contacts, somehow secured eggs and bacon and sometimes extra sausages and chocolate and passed them on to us. Soda pop, my prewar favorite was "Tizer, the Appetizer," disappeared from the shops. Clothes and shoes were rationed too. I recall my first pair of pants, grey flannel trousers, a pair that Dad never used. They felt baggy but comfortable. Ice cream? Up until 1940 we used to get Wall's in Woolworth's. They were cylindrical blocks that the server perched on biscuit cones. Then one day, they disappeared too and did not return until sometime after the war.

Candies and sweets? One day I lost my candies ration card and Mum made me go downtown and apply for another. Two weeks later, I accidentally found the "lost" card in the lining of my coat. I never told Mum, but I secretly used it for months, getting one penny Nestlé chocolate bars. Somehow I felt guilty as that chocolate melted in my mouth. However, the guilt only lasted as long as the candy.

For entertainment at home we had an old wind-up gramophone and a large superheterodyne wireless set embedded in a very ornate wooden cabinet. Mum had some Richard Tauber records and frequently played those and always mentioned that he had one lung. Tauber was an Austrian tenor who fled Europe and became a British citizen. "You are my heart's delight" and "We'll gather lilacs in the Spring again," were two of his 78 rpm disks that mother enjoyed. "Lilacs" was also recorded by Ivor Novello, so Granny Egby liked that version as well.

Every window in the house was shuttered as nightfall approached, and thick heavy curtains draped the interiors. The wartime home had two distinct but contrary sensations: a protected sanctuary and a prison. On cold nights

Mum had a coal fire burning in the small fireplace. Even coal was rationed. A man with an old horse and cart used to bring it in bags.

DAD CREATES AN EARLY TV SET

During the evenings of the war years I used to rest on the carpet by the wireless and listen to the BBC which was our window on the world. Apart from the news, I always enjoyed their great plays on "Saturday Night Theatre." The big comedy favorite among us all was "ITMA" which stood for "It's That Man Again" with Liverpool comedian Tommy Handley. I enjoyed the humor, but more, the funny, peculiar voices made their mark on me. Maurice Denham and Jack Train did some of the voices, and then, with a little practice I discovered I had the ability to imitate them. Granny Egby enjoyed getting me to perform. Little did I know then, but that ability was a gift that was going to get me into radio and change my life.

After the war, Dad, an electronics engineer, gathered surplus radar equipment and built a television. It featured a four inch screen and for some months we used to sit goggle-eyed at the "Test Pattern" put on by BBC Television when it resumed broadcasting at Alexandria Palace in 1946. It was weird. Dad's television, with its old radar screen designed to retain radar blips, had built in limitations. An actor would walk across the screen and leave an impressive but distracting trail of light. It was fine as long as the actors stood still.

When I was twelve I got a job handling the horses and carts as they gathered the harvest of wheat sheaves at Fanny Headington's farm. Labor was in short supply. Many younger farm workers had gone into the armed forces. There were two older men, a Mr. Freemantle and another man who loaded the sheaves and I ensured the horses pulled the cart to the right place. I always remember those enormous, beautiful creatures. To my eyes they resembled the medieval war horses that carried knights in heavy armor into battle. "Colonel" and "Jolly" could well have modeled for Peter Paul Rubens. They had the stature, but now the fire in their big eyes was mellowed with age. But working with those fine creatures was a joy. Granny Egby always gave me lumps of sugar to give the horses when she knew I was going to work.

A lot of kids my age were hired to help gather the potato harvest which was back-breaking work. Dad lent me a pair of his old trousers to protect my knees. A boy named Cecil Mace, whose grandparents lived at a cottage on Fanny Headington's farm, frequently worked with me and in the winter we made a hideout in the top rafters of the large wooden hay-barn and listened to the patter of rain and the wind rustling through the cracks and broken parts of the barn. The days, even with rain falling, seemed endless and we often talked about what we would do when we "grew up." Cecil wanted to be a fireman and I wanted to be a train driver.

For a while I got into the "train numbers" fraternity. Young kids, fascinated with steam trains would buy books for six-pence from a Mr. Allan who, every week, stood in the Maidenhead Station foyer. He came in on a train, stood there for an hour peddling books, then caught another train to another station. Anyway, every Saturday myself and some other kids would sit on railway embankments watching the great steam trains of the Great Western Railway hurtle by, carrying passengers destined for Plymouth, Exeter, Taunton, and places in the west country. We marked off the numbers as they sped by. Sixty-miles an hour, they said. Wow! It boggled my mind. I loved trains, especially the Kings and Castles classes and somewhere inside I had a deep desire to work on trains.

MY RADICAL NATURE AT SCHOOL

My days at school were close to being a disaster. Mom and Dad went into depression over my lack of academic skills. The elementary school was on Alwyn Road and the secondary school – Americans would call it high school – was at Gordon Road which was closer to Maidenhead. Mathematics and English utterly depressed me, but I thoroughly enjoyed history and geography. They also taught religion in those days. I tormented teachers by asking obscure questions such as: "How did Adam live for 930 years?" and "Where did Adam's sons, Cain and Abel get their wives from?"

Bible studies at Gordon Road really puzzled my innocent mind. Mr. Clough, one of my last teachers at Gordon Road, who knew my grandmother, commented: "I really do not know what I did to God to have your grandson in my class." She relished telling people that story. She seemed to get a kick out of it.

It was at Gordon Road that I almost killed someone. I bought a flashy pocket knife that looked almost like a commando machete. A chap I used to get on quite well with, Norman Cameron, wanted to see it and tried to take it out of my hand, and I pulled away at the wrong time. The blade sliced his arm and blood was everywhere. Luckily teachers were nearby and took over. The police arrived at home and Dad, who was celebrating the arrival of my sister Diane, almost "blew a gasket" as he revealed to me years later. In Juvenile Court I told my version of what had happened and was acquitted. It was an accident but it left an indelible imprint on my mind. Even today, I have a dislike – and a hearty respect – for sharp knives.

One of my early attributes was a good singing voice. Someone suggested I join the choir at Stubbings Anglican Church on the Henley Road under a kindly pastor who looked as if he had jumped out of a Charles Dickens novel. His name was Rev. Nathaniel Nairn and he took to me kindly. "You're tall, Bob, carry the cross," he said, and smiled as he observed my surprised face. A farthing was the smallest coin of the realm in those days, a quarter of a penny, and we were paid three-farthings a service, and sometimes we would sing at three services on a Sunday. However my days at Stubbings were short lived. One day Mr. Hunt, a dedicated organist and choir director, caught me laughing in the choir stalls, and acidly asked me to leave: "Egby, you are an inveterate atheist."

It was at that point that I lost faith in God, the church and all that it stood for. I always believed that churches should be happy places. Does God want to see long, dreary faces in the pews every Sunday? I don't think so. I think I was a radical even in those days.

In spite of my distain over English studies, I had a yearning to write but some of my essays were so way out, one teacher branded my work as "an insult to humanity." He was a cricket enthusiast and objected to a piece suggesting that the old English game would be better played by robots. I had recently read Czech writer Karel Capek's "Rossum's Universal Robots," and was convinced that our culture would one day be dominated by machines equipped with some form of artificial intelligence. Capek was right.

AN INTEREST IN THE STARS

Strangely, my thoughts were attracted to phenomena beyond Planet Earth. Stars, planets, the solar system, comets, they all intrigued me. One day, I met Peter Dance, the fellow who had been born 10 days before me. He announced he was joining the British Astronomical Association at Burlington House in London. "They meet every month and have some fascinating speakers such as Will Hay and the young Patrick Moore," he told me. So I leapt at the chance to go along. At fifteen years of age I found the Universe, the Cosmos totally intriguing. As my life evolved, this was to be the understatement of all time. I felt a frustrated energy inside, and it drove a desire to discover. I also felt argumentative.

It happened one day at school. A male teacher started joking and asked with a smirk: "What do you young astronomers see through your telescopes?"

"Stars," I retorted instantly. "What else is there?"

"Can you see God in Heaven through your telescopes?'

"That's a silly question coming from a teacher," I snapped.

The next lesson I learned is that you do not brand anything a teacher says as "silly"- at least not if you are a student. Immediately, I regretted the statement, but the energy inside refused to lower itself. Many years later when my life was taking a different course and I was teaching and writing about the faces of the negative ego, the False Self, I would think back to this event and see it in its true light and ask, "What is stopping schools from getting into helping kids dissolve their negative egos?" The world would be such a better place, but it was many years before I learned of the power to break free from the negative ego.

But now there was talk among the staff that I should be expelled or at least suspended, but that did not happen. I apologized to the teacher and quietly resolved to get out of school as quickly as possible.

We didn't have graduation in those post-war years of 1946 and 1947. The war had drained the school of young teachers and those who had survived overseas were slow in getting back and the ones who did stay were aging. In the Easter Break exams I was at the top of my class, and break was the operative word. Dad got me a summer job charging battery accumulators at an electrical store in Maidenhead. Yes, people used to power their wireless sets on accumulators filled with sulphuric acid. I disliked the job. My hands became chapped and as Christmas was coming, my energy was feeling an urgent need to move on so I quit. An energy was growing deep inside to write, create, and even become an actor. Somehow, I sensed I was a voice lost in the wilderness of youth.

I didn't realize it then, but just before that Christmas of 1947 there was a kink occurring in the Cosmos that would change my life completely.

2

LIGHTS, CAMERAS AND ACTION

MY AQUARIAN NATURE FELT an increasing urge to do something. I tried drawing, writing and acting. I even joined the local drama group in Maidenhead. Playing Lady Godiva's husband in a one act play I had never heard about, failed to impress me. I "borrowed" money from Granny Egby and went to the movies at the Rialto and Plaza cinemas whenever I could. For a while British-born actor Boris Karloff was my hero along with Sidney Greenstreet, Lon Chaney and Bela Lugosi. I studied the screen, angles, tracking, framing and plot structure. I found I could imitate Karloff and Greenstreet, and even Peter Lorre which impressed Granny, so the way I saw it, she was getting something in return for her investment.

Maidenhead and the Thames Valley in those post-war days was home to a vast array of celebrities. Denham, Pinewood and Ealing studios were nearby and London's West End was twenty or so miles away. Richard Todd lived a mile away from us in Pinkney's Green. Ronald Howard, Leslie Howard's son lived at Cookham, Flora Robson had a cottage at Chalfont, Eva Moore who played in the movie "The Old Dark House" lived off the Henley Road. My friends and I would cycle and visit these stars to get their autographs. It was quite enlightening.

One Sunday we cycled over to Nettlebed and found Celia Johnson, the star of the 1945 classic movie "Brief Encounter" working in the garden. She gave us lemonade and her autograph, and introduced us to her husband. "Come and meet these boys, Peter. They've come for my autograph." He waved briefly and went on digging. Years later, I discovered, while sitting in a tent in the Egyptian desert that "Peter" was Peter Fleming who wrote the intriguing book, "Travels through Tartary," and was brother to famous writer, Ian Fleming of James Bond fame.

Lesson: When meeting people always maintain an enquiring mind. Of course, in those young days I had never heard of Tartary.

FINDING A HAND AT CAROL SINGING

Short of cash for the looming Christmas holidays, my friend Luke and I decided to go carol singing. In the old world, kids used to do such things. We decided to hit celebrity row, a line of top of the market cottages and mini-mansions along the Henley Road. It was a dark night and in 1947 homes were still not well illuminated, a hangover from the war years, so we carried flashlights. The first two homes were dark and dead. We discussed the possibility of calling it a night, but a little voice urged me to continue to a third home, an expansive cottage with several cars outside. Here was life!

Luke and I were into the second verse of "Good King Wenceslas" when a barrage of lights blazed and the door was flung open to reveal several grown-ups curiously peering at two cold teenagers standing on the brick steps. One man, tall, dark haired with a sharp, angular face said "Carry on. We are listening."

With all the sudden attention, we had stopped singing. So we pressed on and sang with mounting gusto. Tickled pink, the group inside started singing along with us. All of a sudden we had a community sing-along. It was all smiles and Christmas cheer.

The tall man came closer and inquired of our names. His voice was clear and polished.

"You're Michael Rennie," I managed to get out. I recalled seeing him in the British production of "Caesar and Cleopatra" with Vivien Leigh and Claude Rains, and in "The Wicked Lady" with Margaret Lockwood. I mentioned this and he laughed. "You enjoy films?"

"Yes, I've been studying film production," I managed to splutter out. I mentioned various movie techniques and somehow boldly declared my ambition to be a cameraman and writer." A little voice pushed me into saying: "I'm looking for a job in film production."

Rennie gazed at me for what seemed like a minute. "You must meet my friend - David Hand. He's making great films at Cookham." A man with a broad grin, a large forehead and a distinctive American accent shook my hand. "Come see me Monday at one - tell Sylvia you've come to see D.H."

I didn't realize it then, but there had just been a change in the Cosmos. A kink. A phenomenon. That was how I met D.H – David Dodd Hand.

"IT'S LIKE GOING TO UNIVERSITY"

D.H. was an open, energetic, broad-faced and an intensely positive man who had spent fourteen years at the famous Disney studios in California directing or supervising more than twenty successful films such as "Snow White and the Seven Dwarfs," "Bambi," "Pinocchio," "Dumbo," and "Fantasia," just to name a few.

Now in Britain, D.H. had joined movie-mogul J. Arthur Rank who wished to create an outstanding cartoon industry that rivaled Hollywood. Rank assigned Moor Hall, a 19th century manor near the very picturesque village of Cookham to be the studios and production center. Cookham flanks the historic River Thames. The house could easily have been a movie set for a Dickens or Austen novel. Tall brick chimney stacks rose above Tudor style buildings, and delightfully stained windows reflected the sunlight from the expansive gardens. A magnificent staircase swept up out of the hallway to David Hand's office.

"Best thing you can do is start on the bottom rung of the ladder," D.H. advised when I turned up at Moor Hall on Monday. "Learn from everyone you can. There's a spectrum of great talent here. It's like going to University. Be a sponge. Soak it all up." He grinned. "Production needs a messenger. Thirty-five shillings a week."

When I reached home with my first paypacket Mum and Dad had trouble getting it into their heads that at age fifteen I had a job in a movie studio working on cartoons. Mum was hesitant, as usual, and Granny Egby said: "Well, I always wanted you to become a cabinet maker. I suppose that idea has gone." Dad smiled and went back to his workshop.

The studio's Production Manager was a tall, well presented Bob Skinner who looked and sounded as if he had been reared in the Household Cavalry. He started me in production stores with colleagues Charles "Cab" Smith who lived and talked music, and Robin Tuck whose ambition was to join the Royal Marine Commandos. We provided art paper, inks, and cels - the plastic sheets upon which animated characters were painted. We also shifted drawn scenes from department to department. We also took monochrome films for pressing to Denham Laboratories, flanking the famous Denham Studios near Uxbridge. They were filming "Treasure Island" and "Adam and Evelyn " and a technician named Sid occasionally took me through the sets where a married Stewart Granger and Jean Simmons were having a much publicized affair. Gossip was rampant and folk back at Moor Hall always were keen to know the "inside track" as they called it.

We also took color material to Technicolor Laboratories, which was on the Bath Road in Harmondsworth west of London. I often hoped to meet Natalie Kalmus, the co-developer of the Technicolor process, but it never happened. Across the road in 1948 was a bunch of aging World War II Nissan huts, relics of a Royal Air Force transport base. Work was just starting on extended runways that were to evolve into Heath Row Airport, otherwise known as London Airport.

The Cookham studios were divided into two production camps - the Animaland fully animated cartoon unit under director Bert Felstead, and the Musical Paintbox unit under Henry Stringer.

The Animaland cartoons featured a cute squirrel named Ginger Nutt, so we had such as Ginger Nutt's "Forest Dragon" "Christmas Circus" "Bee Bother, and "It's a Lovely Day," all with such characters as Corny Crow, Dusty Mole, Hazel Nutt, and others. Other Animaland titles included "The Ostrich," "The House Cat," "The Platypus," "The Lion," and "The Cuckoo."

The Musical Paintbox series was semi-animated and very artistic and dwelt on British culture and history by spotlighting different parts of Britain. Titles were "The Thames," "Wales," "Somerset," "A Fantasy on Ireland," "A Yorkshire Ditty," "Sketches of Scotland," "Canterbury Road," "Devon Whey" and "A Fantasy on London Life."

A MODERN BOHEMIA

The Cookham studios resembled a modern Bohemia. It formed a balance between the technology of the day and a couple of hundred artists and technicians devoted to producing animated films. Stories were written by such talented people as Reg Parlett, Pete Griffiths, Nobby Clark. Sets were designed by Pete Banks, Jeff Martin, Perc Poynter and backgrounds by George Hawtorn, Betty Hansford, Kay Pearce and Eric Rickus.

Animators, the artists who made characters move, included Stan Pearsall, Bill Hopper, George Jackson, Frank Moysey, John Wilson, Ted Percival, Jack Stokes and Arthur Humberstone. It was Arthur who went on to become a senior animator for the classic film "Watership Down."

Another talented animator was Chick Henderson, also known as A.W. Henderson. While at Cookham, Chick wrote a tense half-hour play for radio that was broadcast by the BBC. Just about everyone at Moor Hall had their ears tuned to the radio that night. The place was brimming with talent and I readily soaked it up as D.H. had advised.

The Musical Paintbox team under Henry Stringer included such memorable personalities as John Woodward, John Worseley, Pat Griffin who later created his own animation film unit in Maidenhead, Pete Griffiths, Nicholas (Nick) Spargo, Deryck Foster, Peter Jay, Brian O'Hanlon, Waclaw (Wacky) Machan, Andre Amstutz, Ralph Wright and others. Wright, incidentally was an American import, having worked with D.H. on such Disney films as "Bambi." He later returned to Disney and worked on "The Many Adventures of Winnie the Pooh," "Sleeping Beauty" and other major productions.

MOOR HALL STUDIOS:
David Hand is pictured in a meeting with his cartoon directors. Left to right: Ralph Ayres, David Hand, Pat Griffin, Brian O'Hanlon, Henry Stringer, who directed the Musical Paintbox series, and Bert Felstead who directed the Animaland films. Photo by Studio Photographer Douglas Imray.

One of the Musical Paintbox writers was Michael Bentine, a deep thinker who only vaguely reflected the comic antics of his more famous brother, Tony Benton. Andre Amstutz went on to become a prominent illustrator for many children's books. Nick Spargo went on to work on Halas & Batchelor's groundbreaking version of "Animal Farm" eventually started his own animation company and produced the "Willow the Wisp" series for the BBC. It never ceased to amaze me that David Hand had accumulated so much artistic talent in one place, and I enjoyed and benefitted from being part of it – even a ground floor messenger and production assistant.

The Music Director for all the Moor Hall productions was Henry Reed rarely seen away from the grand piano he had in his spacious office. I often wondered how he could write the scores for so many productions simultaneously taking place, but he did.

D.H. was an energetic task master. He always gave the impression that we were on a limited budget and time was of the essence, and as it turned out, we were. Thus on many a night, lights would be seen burning in the rows of studio-offices in the gardens of Moor Hall as artists, writers and production workers struggled to meet tight deadlines.

ARTISTS ARE A CRAZY BUNCH

The initial creation of each of the "stars" – the cartoon characters, called for "Model Sheets." Each sheet contained drawings of the characters from every angle, with a multitude of expressions, and comparing the size of the character against other characters in the film. The Model Sheets were critically important for the animation team to follow.

I soon discovered artists are a crazy bunch. In their spare moments they would draw cartoons of other colleagues. Bespectacled Nick Spargo sported a sizable bushy beard that was rarely trimmed, let alone combed or brushed. Someone did a picture of him with bees, birds and moths humming around his face. A bird had a nest in the bottom of his beard. The caption said: "I'm migrating early this year."

When an artist closed his door it meant "Do Not Disturb!" Colleagues down the block would often quietly pile chairs, cupboards and cushions against the closed door, so that when the poor, overworked soul stepped out - all hell broke loose. The groans and laughter echoed through the corridors.

Social life at Moor Hall was important for releasing pent up stress. Dances, shows and lectures were frequent in the dining hall. Artists enjoyed fancy dress masquerades and created all sorts of impressive costumes and garbs. Young and totally innocent, I went as the Invisible Man. Chick Henderson tied bandages around my face, stuck a pair of heavy sunglasses on me, so that I could hardly see and almost suffocated. One of the Ink-and-Paint team dressed as the Brazilian bombshell-singer Carmen Miranda insisted on singing while she used me as a partner.

Being a messenger reaped enormous benefits for me. Many of the animators and technicians explained their work and projects. I had a yearning to draw and several artists took time out to teach me the basics, a gift I still use today in painting. One key point in cartoons: everything is based on the circle. Straight lines are a no-no.

The still-photographer at Moor Hall was Doug Imray who had an enviable darkroom, He took me through the basics of cameras, lenses and darkroom techniques, knowledge that I would use later as an award-winning news photographer in Cyprus and the Middle East.

FANCY DRESS BALL AT MOOR HALL:
This one happened at the end of 1948 -- round about New Year's Eve – the author was encouraged by Chick Henderson to go as the Invisible Man. He wrapped the face in bandages and stuck some sunglasses on the face. Egby didn't win but he is standing at the back of this group photo. Eunice Macaulay identified people in the front row: (left to right) Rhoda Leher, June Hudson, Phillipa Hibbert, Enid Hartley, Ernst Loeser, Mary Lake and Pat Williams (partial view), Joan Rogers, Bill Marshall in a sombrero. At the far left at back is Edna Jebb. Photos from Cab Smith Collection.

Moor Hall possessed a creative enthusiasm that enveloped almost everyone who worked there. I was always fascinated with the line cameras that initially tested the smoothness of the animation in black and white before scenes were committed to color production. The big rostrum camera that filmed the finished artwork in Technicolor, used negatives on nitrate: three-color separation stock. The name John Neale comes to mind. Last I heard John was still living in Maidenhead and had worked on the epic Beatles feature "Yellow Submarine." Another Moor Hall artist Jack Stokes was Animation Director for that movie.

A CATCH-22 SITUATION

I wanted to learn the trade, but bureaucracy in the shape of the union got in my way. A representative explained: "You have to be a member of the union to get into the crew, even as an apprentice. If you haven't got an apprentice-ship, you can't join the union." It was a catch-22 situation. As some kind soul explained: "It's a closed shop." Interesting! Ten years later in 1958 when I was freelance filming a ski patrol of Royal Marine Commandos on Mount Olympus in Cyprus with a 35mm Newman Sinclair camera for Movietone News, no one asked for membership of a union or anything else.

There were characters at Moor Hall rarely, if ever mentioned in film credits. One was John Milton Gurr - film editor extraordinaire. Surrounded by a fleet of Movieolas, the Cadillacs of film editing, John manipulated and synchronized the visual film with the various voice, sound effects and music tracks. There was a large contingent of very talented women who worked in Trace and Paint. Those were the people who traced the animator's drawings onto "cels" - clear celluloid sheets. Ricca McGibbon and Shirley Clemens were among the large force of special artists. The cels were then sent to the tri-color rostrum camera team, and the names Charles Pithers and Rhona Hurt come to mind. .

Another Moor Hall personality was dear Miss Freda Salberg who knew everything that ticked in Moor Hall. Her withering gaze from behind horned-rimmed glasses and ceaseless attempts to bring a bunch of crazy artists into line earned her the title of "sergeant-major." When Moor Hall live-ins had too much to drink at The King's Arms, the Bel and Dragon and watering places in Cookham, Freda would hightail it to the scene and bring them safely back to base. Next day the offending people would get harsh reprimands. But many knew her as a very kind and dedicated spirit.

Moor Hall bathed in an inventive aura. One day, Arthur Humberstone, a cool philosophical fellow, came into the stores where we kept mountainous supplies of cels and cartridge paper, and said he had a problem. They were working on "The Platypus," and needed a cell that would give the underwater impression a simple distortion without looking obvious. "Get a cell and paint it with several coatings of film cement until it distorts," I suggested. "Then do an overlay." They did and that was my contribution to "The Platypus." The effect was also used in "It's a Lovely Day." I didn't tell them that in my own private film experiments I had done the same thing to create a ghostly, eerie effect.

The personality at Moor Hall who did all the sound work was Stuart Crom-bie, a talented figure looking very American but was British to the core. He joined David Hand after working on the sound track for the Laurence Olivier film "Henry V" and provided band music for the BBC Television Test Signal in the post-war period. If you have ever seen "Henry V" you may recall the sky becoming black with arrows at the height of the battle of Agincourt. "We had to find special sounds for all those arrows," said Stu. "After many searches we recorded the swishing sounds of long whips, and did multi-layering."

Stuart had well equipped recording studios at Moor Hall and taught me various invaluable techniques for using microphones and sound effects. For instance, rhythmically tapping one's fingers on an empty wooden cigar box will provide the sounds of a galloping horse.

THE STIRLING FILMS SAGA

On January 25th 1949 Fleet Street's Daily Graphic ran a feature headline: "Six boys and one girl make a film thriller." It told of how a group of 16 and 17 year-olds were making their own film at a cost of £16. The national newspaper described it as a comedy thriller entitled "Eerie Acres."

BOYS MAKE THEIR OWN THRILLER:
This was the head in the Windsor, Slough and Eton Express on January 21st 1949. It was the first day of filming at the Clayton-East Estate. Left to right: Luke Over, Brian Cross, John Stevens, Ken Hallett, (kneeling with camera) Graham Scrivener, the author in shirtsleeves, Don Over and David Warren. The film "Eerie Acres" was shown to a packed house in the fall of 1949 and triggered a series of other films made by teenagers. Image courtesy of Baylis Media Ltd.

It started as a youth club skit written by Luke Over. I purchased a 9.5mm film Pathé camera with a standard lens for £5. Granny Egby, the source of my early life finances, funded the purchase. The film was and still is an oddity because the sprocket holes were in the middle of the film. Sounds crazy? In 9.5 mm format the sprocket holes are between each frame. The joy of this film was the picture size. Unlike the narrow gauge 8 mm or super-eight used by most amateurs, the actual picture frame was slightly less than the professional 16mm film which meant picture quality was great. We projected films onto screens ten feet across.

The story first broke in early January 1949 with the local newspaper, the Maidenhead Advertiser. We were on location. Where? None other than the spacious, aristocratic Hall Place at Burchetts Green owned by the late Sir Robert and Lady Dorothy Clayton-East, whose lives and deaths created intriguing sagas in the early 1930s. Now almost twenty years later, the new owners, the Berkshire Department of Agriculture, said we could use the exterior of the mansion for the film.

The Windsor-Slough-Eton Express sent a photographer and the posed picture showed Luke Over, Brian Cross, Jon Stevens, Ken Hallet and myself - with an exposure meter - Brian Scrivener and David Warren. Kneeling with the camera on a tripod is Graham Scrivener. It's interesting because at the rear are the giant columns and the portico surrounding the front entrance. The building is now owned by the Berkshire College of Agriculture and the regal columns and portico are long gone. A pity.

BIG TECHNIQUES ON A MINI-BUDGET

As the original producer, my job was to "fund" the project by buying the film cassettes and having them processed at Norman Greville's Photo Studios in Maidenhead. We had immense fun creating film. Several times we strapped cameraman Graham Scrivener onto the parcel rack of a bicycle and did tracking shots which came out extremely well. We built "indoor" sets on the lawn at the back of my home and used daylight. This eliminated the need for expensive lighting. It was an old trick of early movie producers in Hollywood. At one point we strapped the camera onto the end of a twelve-foot pole and took a shot looking over the rooftop onto actors on the lawn. Totally crude, it was the simplest and very effective camera boom. When one's budget is limited, creative minds are invaluable.

New people flocked to our group. Valentine Miller, Ron Edwards, Donald Over, Brynsley Pether, just to name a few, and the news coverage blossomed. We called the group Stirling Films and it made The Star, the afternoon newspaper in London, the morning paper, the Daily Graphic did a great picture feature and the BBC's Foreign News Service put out stories for listeners in Russia, Belgium and France.

I think the attraction in those days was the fact that a group of teenagers had, without any adult supervision whatsoever, created a cultural project in the post-war years when most people and communities were still struggling to get back to normal. Here were teenagers making a close to 30-minute silent movie in 1949.

THE HURTS OF THE YOUNG EGO

For me as producer-director, things started to crack up when I (and Granny Egby) could not support the weekly demands of film costs. When filming stopped, teenagers in the group offered to kick-in a couple of shillings a week, and shooting was resumed. Well, this changed the balance of energy. Making decisions became increasingly difficult, and as I later figured out: "The most effective organization in a democracy is a committee of one with power to act."

In community funding I had lost the producership. I quit. Chick Henderson, my close friend at Moor Hall Studios commented: "Ego! It hurts doesn't it, Bob. Look at it as a learning experience." Years and years later, when I wrote my first book on the perils of the False Self, the negative ego, I often thought of these days and wished I had been able to re-live them. With knowledge comes wisdom. In those days I lacked both, and I did not even realize I was learning. I was hurt. Disappointed. Insulted. Angry. Annoyed. The situation triggered a plummeting self-esteem. I felt totally helpless. I was only seventeen and had never heard of the mystical Sufis, or Gurdjieff, or Vernon Howard, of Jean Klein or a whole lot of other wise folk who had the answers.

As an exiled producer of Eerie Acres I was invited back to do the sound for the silent movie. The Sound expert at Moor Hall, Stuart Crombie, helped me by recording my narration on a 78 rpm soft acetate disk which I have to this day. Years later, while working for British Forces Broadcasting Service in Egypt, Cyprus, Aden and Germany, and later in commercial radio in British Columbia, Canada, I would often revert to a memory of Stu Crombie telling me to "talk across the mike." He stressed the importance of smiling when recording, even if no one was looking. "It carries to the listener," he said. Moor Hall left indelible impressions.

To complete the sound I then had the task of picking recorded music such as Sibelius' symphonic poem "The Swan of Tuonela" and the "Sorcerer's

Apprentice" by Paul Dukas. We even used the BBC's music for their nightly radio series "Dick Barton – Special Agent" for the chase scenes. Copyright? Never heard of it. We were teenagers in 1949 and everything was free, at least so we thought.

A PACKED 'PREMIERE" PERFORMANCE

On September 14th 1949 the 28-minute "Eerie Acres" had its premiere in the Pavillion adjoining the Stag and Hounds public house at Pinkneys Green. The place was packed. David Hand and a crew from Moor Hall turned up and applauded heartily. A surprise visitor was film producer, writer and photographer William MacQuitty accompanied by stars Pauline Bentley and Emrys Jones. Macquitty became noted in 1958 for his production of "A Night to Remember" which recreated the tragedy of RMS Titanic.

Next day at the studios D.H. said he was "impressed" with our amateur movie and added the words: "Young man, you'll go far." It was a casual prophecy with deep meaning. When I packed my bags and departed Maidenhead, the amateur film group continued with various productions and earned a humorous title: "The Movie Moguls of Maidenhead." I like to think it was the motivational spirit I received at Moor Hall.

The film club went on filming and a lot of shorts were made. The group amalgamated with another cluster of amateur moviemakers headed by an ambitious young fellow named James Franklin. Jim went on to join the BBC Television and produced and directed various episodes of "The Goodies" a crazy, mixed up, wild and woolly weekly series starring Bill Oddie, Graeme Garden and Tim Brooke-Taylor. The series started in 1970 and ran for a dozen years, and it still has a cult following. It was classic comedy of a bygone era.

THE COMING OF THE HATCHET MAN

There were many visitors to Moor Hall during the Gaumont British days. Cookham resident artist Stanley Spencer came in one day, as did actor Ronald Howard, son of Leslie Howard, Anthony Hinds of Exclusive Films, Richard Todd from Pinkney's Green, and Humphrey Lestocq. Then one day, a man named John Davis came in the front door. Production Manager Bob Skinner whispered: "Meet J. Arthur Rank's hatchet man."

A short while later, in October 1949, London newspapers printed black headlines announcing that the Rank Organization was in the financial pit. A few days later the Moor Hall crew heard the news that Gaumont British Animation would be closing as soon as current productions were finished. The entire place was closed down in early 1950. All the equipment was sold or auctioned off. The curtains were closing on a promising movie project that really did not have time to come to fruition. For me, I have memories that are priceless. David Hand ran a university and I am proud to have been a student who did "soak it all up." In my mind, he was a king.

My actual time with Moor Hall – and our amateur film group – came to an end in early November 1949. David Hand caught me at the gate one dark and wet evening after work. "You know things are ending here?" he said, peering up at the old mansion towering in the darkness behind us.

"I had heard," I said quietly. "It's been around the studios for a week or so."

"There are things happening beyond our control. They just didn't give me enough time to do what I really wanted. You've got what it takes, Bob. Create a vision. Believe in it. See it in color. Know it will happen." He patted my arm, and walked off into the night. I never saw him again. I picked up my bike at the rack and cycled home along the Switchback Road. I did not tell D.H. I already had the lay-off letter in my jacket pocket. I did not tell Mum or Dad or Granny Egby, or any of my friends at the film group. I felt incredibly sad as if I had lost something very special. Little did I know there was a chain of events formulating that would take me out of England on a journey that was beyond my imagination. There was another kink in the Cosmos and I knew nothing about it.

JOINING THE BOYS IN BLUE

My eighteenth birthday was looming and with that would come two years in the army performing compulsory National Service. As much as I have always respected the regiments and the foot soldiers, I wanted to fly higher. So one day I took the Thames Valley bus to Reading and came home that night and announced to a stunned family. "I am joining the Royal Air Force."

"When?" If Mum had had false teeth she would have swallowed them.

"Next Tuesday. November 29th. I go to Cardington."

Dad's reaction was as low key as you could get. "That's where they housed the airship, the R101," he said quietly. "Make sure you stay on the ground, Bobbie."

Another kink in the Cosmos was happening. Frankly and thinking back, I simply had no idea what was occurring in my life. A little voice popped up:

"It's the right thing to do." I did not even figure that forces I knew nothing about were sweeping me along like a great river carrying a raft. As I sat on the train at Maidenhead Station I thought of my great grandmother, Elen Egby, the Seer and her words "You will work with light." Had I blown my opportunity to work in movies? To work with light?"

I felt a presence in the railcar. It was a hand that touched my shoulder and I felt a charge of energy, rejuvenating, and wonderful energy. I wondered if it was Elen Egby or the Greek goddess. Then my negative ego, the False Self, tossed out the idea and came in with: "It's all in your imagination." I sighed heavily as the train lurched forward. Little did I know where the Cosmos was really taking me, or why.

3

RADAR, A PUB
AND AN OLD TROOPSHIP

T HEY WERE ENOUGH TO blow a teenager's mind. Huge, magnificent and historic. They reeked of an aviation age gone by. I wished Dad could have seen them. The Cardington Airship Hangars were originally built back in World War I to house Britain's attempt to break into the great airship industry.

They were the first things we saw as the bus pulled into RAF Station Cardington. They loomed over the Bedfordshire countryside like two giant, alien slugs. Each over 700 feet long, they housed the R101 airship intended for passengers and cargo bound for India. The other was the R100.

The project was short lived. On October 5th 1930, on its maiden voyage, the R101 crashed and exploded on a hillside near Beauvais, a short distance from Paris. It was, at that time, the largest machine to fly made by human beings. Forty-eight people died. In spite of a positive trans-Atlantic flight, the R100 was scrapped.

The title of the Cardington site sounded great: The Royal Airship Works. I liked that. Someone told me recently that one of the remaining hangars is used as a jumbo movie studio. But on that cloudy, dismal Tuesday in November 1949 the hangars had a hypnotizing attraction. I was awestruck. Then a male voice bellowed: "You there! You're not here to bloody gaze." That was my welcome to the Royal Air Force.

After being outfitted with uniforms, boots and a pile of other stuff, we were herded over to RAF Station Henlow. Somewhere along the line they gave me a number – 4040540 – which has stayed with me to this day. Henlow, I was told, would be our "holiday camp" for the next eight weeks. In truth it was a phenomenon called square-bashing, a system designed to get everyone to be a disciplined and fully functioning, non-thinking member of the Services. "Egby, you're not in the Air Force to think," a sergeant told me one day.

In addition to air force history, ranks and responsibilities, we were taught how to use the old .303 caliber Lee-Enfield Rifle which was first introduced into the British Forces in 1895. It was equipped with a small magazine that contained five rounds. Not much if you're being attacked. I referred to them as bullets, a reference that did not go well with Corporal Telford whose voice would have appealed to Cecil B. DeMille looking for someone to play the Almighty. I endured the discipline, including scrambling through the mud and scaling the timbers of the obstacle course. I had never been so bruised mentally and physically as I was at Henlow, and there was rejoicing when it was time to take the train to Yatesbury.

GOODBYE PHOTOGRAPHY, HELLO RADAR

Yatesbury? Surely that was the Wireless and Radar Training station in Wiltshire? Was not my ambition to be a photographer in the Air Force? The recruiting posters had proclaimed "Become a Royal Air Force photographer." The enthusiasm I had possessed at Reading when I signed on was short lived. A medical officer told me: "Egby, you have a deficiency in certain colors. That eliminates you from photography." Disappointed, I opted for becoming a radar operator. It was the last thing I wanted to do, and I think it showed in the events of 1950 through to the middle of 1953. So much for Great-Grandmother Egby's "you will work with light." Was not photography working with light?

RAF Station Patrington, east of Hull and close to the Humber estuary in Yorkshire was a GCI radar station built during World War II for Ground-Controlled Interception and operated Type 14 surveillance radar and Type 13 height finder. The Type Seven radar arrays always resembled huge rotating gates. Downstairs in a bunker-type hall was the regional Operations Center where plotters positioned and reflected all air movements in the sector on a large table-top map of the region.

Work at Patrington was frequently involved in training exercises both for the personnel at Patrington and the air crews flying day and night exercises from regional air stations. Radar personnel were billeted at RAF Sutton-on-Hull and transported every day to Patrington, sixteen miles away. The nice thing about Sutton was the easy access to downtown Hull and trains for weekend passes to visit home. Another attractive point about Sutton was a large and well-equipped darkroom with developing tanks and trays and enlargers for photographic work.

In spite of my rejection as an RAF photographer, I took to studying the ins-and-outs of photography. A number of the members of the photo club explained some of the intricacies of such things as hyperfocal distance, depth of focus as opposed to depth of field, lens manufacture and construction, film speeds and sizes, developers, acid fixing baths, enlarging, photographic papers and much, much more. I was always seen at Sutton and Patrington carrying photographic text books including the British Journal of Photography Annual 1948. I even experimented with a pinhole camera and created photos with marvelous depths of field which is one of the benefits of pinholes. Somehow I had a vision of one day becoming a photographer. I had no idea how this was to be accomplished but it was a vision that stayed with me.

THE JOYS OF BEING BY THE SEA

One day the sergeant told me I was being posted to RAF Station Easington. I was stunned. The NCO smirked, "You'll enjoy being by the sea."

The Easington station would have made a good set for one of Jim Franklin's shows "The Goodies," or one of the famous "Carry On" movies. Totally isolated on a large field filled with rabbit holes, it comprised several ancient huts flanking a 200 foot black steel tower on which was perched a disused radar unit built in the early years of the war.

Now, imagine this ugly tower perched perilously close to the edge of a 200 foot cliff being steadily eroded by an angry and hungry North Sea, whipped up by howling winds, and you have an idea of RAF Station Easington. The erosion was real. In fact my friend, Gavin Cleworth was positive the tower was already leaning towards the sea. On quiet nights while on duty at the station, we could hear earthy rumblings as chunks of cliffs slumped into the sea. It was eerie.

The most memorable night for me at Easington occurred one rainy and windy night. Every light in the place went out. A power blackout! Two of us were on duty that night, a young Jordie from the Tyne and myself.

The phone rang. It was the Paddy, the RAF police corporal in charge of the station. Calling from the village, his voice was sharp and tense. "The tower lights! Are they on or off?" Everything was off, I told him. "Jordie has a couple of hurricane lamps powered up for light around here," I said.

"There's a night exercise on. Fighters are flying low level," Paddy hissed. "Somebody has to take a couple of hurricane lights up and post them on the tower."

My body was gripped with an indescribable fear. I disliked heights intensely. "Egby, you're always craving excitement, here's your big opportunity. Up you go, mate, Okay?" He hung up.

AN ORCHESTRA FROM HELL

The steel tower was divided into ten stages or levels. The metal staircase connecting the levels was enclosed in a series of bars for protection. Each stage ended at a deck which was crossed, allowing access to the next staircase. Wrapped up in my heavy greatcoat with a poncho and scarf round my head and neck, and two hurricane lamps on the ends of a rope over my shoulders, I started the laborious climb. The ugly black painted steps glistened vaguely under the flickering lights of the lamps. The wind-driven rain stung parts of my face still exposed. I stopped frequently to brush the water off my face and scarf.

I should have told Paddy I have a weak heart and might collapse. That was not true, but it did cross my mind like a lot of other flimsy excuses. I plodded on upwards and the howling winds and driving rains intensified. For this I was born?

Then one of the hurricanes went out. I swore profusely. Swearing made me feel better. I pushed open the cabin door at the top of the tower. Relief! At least it was dry inside. I discarded my cape. No matches! What stupid twit would not have matches for this? Then I realized I should have brought them with me from the base huts.

Someone had left a radar instruction manual on a shelf. I ripped a page out and used it to relight the hurricane. Outside on the deck surrounding the radar cabin, I found more steps leading forever upwards.

I clambered up the vertical steps on the side of the cabin and tied the hurricane lights onto steel bars. My hands were numb from strapping the lamps. The constant howling winds, the pelting rain on the metal and the angry North Sea waves crashing onto the clay cliffs below sounded like an orchestra from hell. A little voice came through the cacophony: "Stay in the cabin just in case one of the lamps fails."

Three hours later I woke up on the cabin floor. It was daylight outside and the storm had long abated. I went out and watched the watery sun struggling to rise through the masses of layered grey clouds. Just then I heard a plane. A Mosquito, it was one of those peculiar British fighters made largely of wood that served so well in the war, and were still being used by many squadrons. It came in low over the North Sea, and then lifted up to ease over the cliffs. It must have been 200 feet away because I could see the face of the pilot staring back at me. A brief hand raised, then was gone. Damn, I wished I had had my camera.

"BOTTOMS UP" AT THE MARQUIS OF GRANBY

The other peculiarity about RAF Station Easington is that we were billeted in a pub, the Marquis of Granby which looked and felt as if it had been there forever. It had an aroma of old English country life. It was here we learned to play dominoes and darts and drink beer. The tavern keepers were Charlie and Pam Dixon, the nicest folk you could ever meet. They kept us toeing the line inside the pub. People were always shouting "bottoms up." At one of the local dances I met and had a crush on a local lass named Audrey. She was a wispy, pale faced creature against my lanky frame. She was curious about my future. When I admitted I didn't have a clue, she took off with Jordie.

THE OLD PUB:
In 1983 the author returned to visit the Marquis of Granby in Easington, Yorkshire and found the building had not changed since he was billeted there in the RAF in 1950-51. The Dixons had gone and so too was RAF Station Easington and the old radar tower, the site a victim of the eroding North Sea.

Life in the pub was a real joy. The Dixons and the five airmen billeted there had meals around the big wooden table and all sorts of things were discussed. It was the first time I had experienced a community sharing. No one believed I had been employed in a movie studio, and had made an amateur movie, so I didn't mention it again.

Paddy, the RAF police corporal who was about as Irish as they come, announced one day he was going home for a few days leave. He told us he planned to go into Hull, catch the train and change at Doncaster for the express to Kings Cross in London.

"Can I come along as far as London?" I asked enthusiastically. "I have a forty-eight hour pass, Friday to Monday."

"Of course you can," retorted Paddy. "It'll give me a chance to straighten out your screwed up mind." Everyone laughed.

Late Thursday afternoon my pass was suddenly cancelled. Patrington told us that a number of squadrons were staging exercises in the area and the Easington tower's lights must be operating. So much for planning a weekend at home.

I went across the street to the red telephone call box to call home. Jordie had shown me how to tap the telephone bar a number of times and make long distance calls totally free. Morals did not come into our lives in those days. Mum was her usual self, upset that I would not be there. "We're having your sister Diane's birthday party a few days early," she said. I felt sorry. I would have enjoyed helping celebrate her seventh birthday. She was a good kid and I missed her.

THE EXPRESS TRAIN AT DONCASTER

Paddy left in the early hours of the morning to journey to catch the morning train at Hull. At Doncaster, he walked over to the London express and boarded a railway carriage.

The train left Doncaster Station on time. 10.06 a.m. As it crossed the multitude of track points south of the station, the speeding train derailed. Rail cars smashed into a heavy bridge abutment. The steel girders and concrete blocks sliced through the train. The date was Friday, March 16th 1951. Fourteen people died that morning, including our Paddy.

Everyone at the Marquis of Granby was stunned. Nobody talked much. Even that night and the days that followed, there was a heavy aura over the pub. Many of the locals liked Paddy. Then one day Charlie Dixon looked at me and said quietly: "You are lucky to be alive, Bob. It's bloody lucky someone cancelled your pass."

Years later, pondering over the metaphysics of things, I might have been able to influence Paddy to pick a different one of the fourteen cars on the train. I always feel, even to this day that there was a kink in the Cosmos that diverted me from being on that Doncaster train. In life there are so many ifs, ands and buts. Nothing is certain.

"YOU'RE BEING POSTED — TO EGYPT!"

The days of summer came in 1951 and with it an invitation to join the local repertory company which was preparing for a winter performance of "Annie Get Your Gun." The show had opened in London's West End in 1947 followed by the movie in 1950 with Betty Hutton. The company felt a local production towards Christmas 1951 would be a great attraction. They cast me as Chief Sitting Bull. I learned scripts and songs and got the short end of the stick. The Royal Air Force called one day. "You're being posted to Egypt, the Suez Canal Zone."

Over the next little while I felt a growing excitement about going to the Mediterranean, Egypt and the land of the Pharaohs. The idea of leaving England, loved ones and friends bothered me and I consoled myself and them with the notion that "It won't last long. A couple of years and then I will be back." At 19 years I had no comprehension of time and space. There was another compelling driving force in my mind.

As I mentioned earlier, my father had given me an illustrated book on the Middle East, which focused on the ancient civilizations of Egypt, Greece and Babylon. History fascinated me. That, with geography, had been my favorite subject at Gordon Road School and the Middle East was always a magnet in my young mind. Little did I realize that the lands of the Pharaohs, ancient gods and spiritual beings would keep me there for thirteen years.

At this time I did not feel any inclination towards religion or theology, in fact, one day while discussing religion at Sutton-on-Hull, I got into an argument with an existentialist and a fundamental Baptist and declared: "I don't believe in any of that. I'm an atheist." It was something that simply slipped out on my tongue. In spite of my mother having me attend Sunday school and becoming a choirboy at Stubbings church, I had not studied the Bible at all. I had been Confirmed in the Anglican movement at St. Luke's church in Maidenhead but it was something done to please my mother. She enjoyed the High Anglican church at All Saints where the priests swung the smoking incense holders, but as her life progressed, she quit the church for some years, but then resumed services with the Baptists.

The declaration of being an atheist startled me, and then, for the first time in my life I started to mull over the statement I had made. Someday, sometime while in the Middle East, I had to find the truth of religion. It seemed the right place. After all, most religions started between Jerusalem, through India and China - all in Asia.

My simplistic mind did not connect any of the events in my early life with God. The appearance of a kindly and beautiful spirit when I was supposed to be dying, the predictions made by my Great-Grandmother Elen Egby, the Seer at Reading, and the various "happenings" that I took very much for granted, did not have a God-connection or even a Cosmic connection. The fact that I envisioned being in movies, did that vision get me to go carol singing with the result of a job among highly skilled film technicians? Did some power in the Universe block me from going with Paddy on that fatal train ride at Doncaster? Now, was some Universal Mind saying it is time we sent this fellow to Egypt? If someone had proposed this theory while we were waiting for the troopship to take us to the Mediterranean, I would have said, "That's rubbish. I don't believe that nonsense." But then I was young and foolish.

THE EMPRESS OF AUSTRALIA, A COOL SHIP

We boarded the "Empress of Australia" at Lytham St. Anne's near Liverpool. Even adorned in its somber coat of battleship grey, the ship with its three funnels had the character of a cruise liner. Built as the Tirpitz in Hamburg, she had, in the thirties, taken King George VI and the Queen to Canada. But immediately afterwards she had been converted to troopship requirements during the war, and was again converted after the war with improved conditions.

We were housed on one of the lower decks, in other words there were no port holes, no daylight and the air was a little heavy at times. We faced a new challenge: sleeping in rope and canvas hammocks. One quickly learned to turn over without actually moving to the edge of the hammock. It took a couple of nights to figure out how to sleep comfortably.

The high command on the ship made sure everyone was occupied and jobs were allotted cleaning decks, checking safety equipment and lifeboats, and a host of other things that someone created. Fire and lifeboat drills occurred every day. It was glaringly evident they did not like the idea of hundreds of young men, many of them still in their teenage years, doing nothing for ten days at sea.

I was wondering what task I would be assigned, when a ship's officer approached and asked me how tall I was. Six feet four inches, I told him. "That's good, because I have a job for you."

Had I replied, "Cool!" I would have been right. I spent the entire ten day voyage working in the refrigeration and food storage lockers on what seemed like the lowest deck of the ship. There was meat in all shapes and sizes hanging from hooks, and hundreds of boxes of frozen and fresh foods such as fruits and vegetables. To someone who had been through severe rationing of food during the war years, this was paradise. So the journey to Egypt was not one of sightseeing, but I did enjoy the cool of the refrigeration deck, especially in the Mediterranean when the weather became hot and humid. Of course, when we arrived in Port Said at the northern end of the Suez Canal and I was suddenly exposed to the glare of the sun, it almost blinded me.

OVERWHELMING PRESENCE OF DESERT

When I first saw the Suez Canal, it appeared like a water-road, with ships materializing and coming out of the shimmering desert. In fact, if you stand a mile or so to the east or west of the canal, the water sinks below your sight and it appears as if ships are travelling in some mysterious manner on sand. This ninety-nine mile waterway which connects the Mediterranean with the Red Sea and ultimately the Indian Ocean was opened for shipping November 17th 1869 after a grueling ten years of construction. Created by Ferdinand de Lesseps, a distinguished French lawyer and diplomat, the project relied considerably on slave labor and many lives were lost. When we arrived in the Port Said there was no indication of the turbulent history of the canal, and a large statue of de Lesseps greeted our presence.

The canal is a one-way system. There are three lakes – Timsah near the town of Ismalia and then further south, the Great and Small Bitter Lakes near a place called Kabrit. It is in the lakes that the ships bypass each other ready for the journey north or south. Nobody ever tells you anything in the services, but we soon found out we were headed for Kabrit in dusty open-air trucks that swerved haphazardly to avoid pot-holes.

We had changed to the lightweight tropical khaki garb of shirts, shorts and forage caps. These caps, which everyone agreed were ill-fitted for heads, were replaced with the Air Force blue berets shortly after we arrived in the Suez Canal Zone.

RAF Kabrit was one of five operational flying stations. The others were Abu Suier, Deversoir, Fayid and Shalufa. Kabrit was a strange radar

THE AUTHOR: In Royal Air Force uniform in the Suez Canal Zone. The year, 1951.

operation, located on the west bank of the Suez Canal between the Great and Little Bitter Lakes. The GCI array was positioned at the end of the runway, very similar to the layout at Patrington, but the Operations Centre, where controllers sat, was at Spinney Wood near Ismalia.

One thing that greeted the new arrival to the Suez Canal Zone was the overwhelming presence of the desert. You could smell it two days before the ship docked in Port Said, and as you started to live in Kabrit, you felt the dryness and the strange heavy odors that seemed to permeate everything. Dust appeared everywhere. If you sat inside or outside your billet or inside the NAAFI drinking a refreshing glass of Stella beer, within a few minutes, specks of dust mysteriously started to gather on the beer foam. There was dust everywhere, and when a dust storm blew in, we were forced to stay inside buildings until the biting, penetrating grit abated.

Arabs with ill-mannered camels often came wandering by, and a technique I quickly learned from others was not to stand within a few feet of the animals. They spit, very easily and accurately. I was convinced they and their owners had a hearty dislike for British people which soon became very obvious.

The Bitter Lake with its perfectly blue, perfectly crystal clear waters was always inviting. The Suez Canal is seawater, therefore whenever we went swimming, goggles or masks were the order of the day to avoid stinging salinity. Masks gave wonderful views of colored fish and undulating sand dunes underwater. But where there is beauty, so there are dangers. Conch shells! Buried in the sand and armed with razor sharp spikes, they were the demise of many a soldier and airman. Wading innocently through the water, I placed my right foot on what appeared like innocent sand. The spike pierced my foot by the toes. Biting my tongue to stop yelling, they treated me at the Kabrit medical center. Result: I missed parades for several days and was called "a bloody twerp" by the sergeant.

Another common malady suffered by many newcomers was "Jippy tummy" a grueling form of Egyptian diarrhea. Some wise-crackers called it "natural dieting." If you became a victim, you lost weight rapidly. Sufferers were urged to drink plenty of water to avoid the perils of dehydration, but the water itself seemed to carry fresh onslaughts of diarrhea. Jippy tummy would last a few days or even a couple of weeks. Mine lasted about four days, and since then, my immune system has been able to handle most traveling problems. I believe that ailments like Egyptian diarrhea create an antibody which stays with you, protecting you for years.

DISRAELI BOUGHT THE CANAL

It's interesting how the British became involved in the Suez Canal. It happened like this. Opened in November 1869, the Suez Canal had an immediate and widespread impact on trade between Europe and East Africa and the Far East. Ishmail Pasha, otherwise known as Ishmail the Magnificent, the Turkish Khedive of Egypt held shares in the canal's operation.

Short of money, Ishmail sold his shares to the British in 1875. Prime Minister Disraeli did a crafty deal with funding from the Rothschilds, which triggered a nasty constitutional issue in the British Parliament. The French shareholders were, however, still in the majority.

So when civil war broke out in Egypt in 1882, British forces moved into Egypt to protect its investment in the canal. This was followed six years later by the Convention of Constantinople which declared the Suez Canal a neutral zone under the protection of the British. Any Turkish influence in Egypt was ousted at the end of World War 1 with the defeat of Germany and its ally, the Ottoman Empire.

So the British stayed, cementing their residency in the Canal Zone with the Anglo-Egyptian Treaty of 1936. Signed by the ultimate playboy, King Farouk, the treaty triggered hostility from Arab nationalists. This hostility simmered until after World War II when a group known as the Wafd, a liberalist movement, scored a victory in the 1950 elections in Egypt. They promptly tore up the 1936 treaty and three years later, with Gamal Abdel Nasser at the helm, the British agreed to withdraw troops by July 1956, thus giving the land of the Pharaohs complete independence.

But this was 1951 and a whole lot of nationalists were jumping up and down expressing impatience and ultimate anger. Anti-British riots broke out throughout Egypt and all British forces were placed on immediate alert. Attempts by the British to negotiate a new treaty went up in smoke.

A HAIRY TRIP TO LAKE TIMSAH

On October 17th – a Wednesday – three of us were ordered to draw Lee Enfield rifles and perch on the roofs of two gharries (trucks) as they drove in tandem to the town of Ismailia and in particular the facilities at Lake Timsah. Stuck atop the trucks, the three of us felt extremely exposed and distinctly uncomfortable. An officer was tucked safely inside the lead vehicle.

Two days before, two soldiers in a jeep driving along the canal road had been decapitated. Arab nationalists waited for a military vehicle to appear, they then pulled a wire across the road, strapping it to trees. The wire was adjusted to head level. The soldiers were dead before the vehicle collided with the trees. This prompted the authorities to weld sharp steel bars to the front of most vehicles to avoid future decapitations. But the thoughts of attack were not far from our minds that day on our ride to Lake Timsah.

Even when someone pointed to a distinctive house with peculiar horizontal stripes and announced it had been the home of Ferdinand de Lesseps, no one seemed to be very interested. We viewed all Arabs milling around the streets as potential danger. When we arrived at Lake Timsah, the officer told the drivers to wait, disappeared inside a building, then hastily returned. "We have to return to Kabrit, so we are going to step on it." There was urgency in his voice. We wondered why.

Two days later at dawn on October 19th British troops seized all key facilities along the Suez Canal from Port Said to Port Suez. All Egyptian military and civil servants were made persona non grata and told to get out of the zone. This action triggered more riots and various buildings and homes occupied by British businesses and families were burned. It was followed on January 26th 1952 by destroyed sections of downtown Cairo noted for British, French and foreign businesses. Fires continued for about 12 hours, destroying more than 700 commercial shops and administrative offices, among them the famous and prestigious Shepheard's Hotel in Cairo. Dubbed the "Paris of Africa," it had been built for the opening of the Suez Canal so many years before. At the same time, King Farouk who had once been the sweetheart of the Egyptian people in 1936, was now seen as a "greedy, insensitive slob," said newspaper Al Ahram. He was ousted and sent into exile.

In October 1951 I was just beginning to consider Kabrit as a holiday camp posting when politics and its brother violence caught up with the unit. We were ordered to move, lock, stock and radar station. It was decided to pack up the GCI radar unit at Kabrit and amalgamate it with the GCI at RAF Station El Firdan, perched on a disused runway in the desert a few miles north of Ismalia. Again, after a hair-raising ride perched on top of a wireless truck, I arrived at the new station in one piece. De luxe travel in the Royal Air Force was a figment of the imagination, I told myself. An illusion.

MEETING AN OLD FRIEND

One of the first people I met was Peter Dance, my old friend and partner in astronomical studies from Maidenhead. We celebrated our 20th birthdays sitting in tents in the desert north of the main station, eating ham and slices of bread washed down by Stella beer. Stella's worthy of a mention here because it formed part of the service life in the Canal Zone. It was a beautiful beer but carried a punch like a steam-hammer. Quite often we would sit in the NAAFI and watch new arrivals, white skinned and dry, rush up to the bar and get a beer. Well, the new arrivals would eagerly swig the first bottle and were about to start on the second, when old crafty Stella hit them, and one by one like ten-pins, they would slide under the table, much to the laughter of the "old hands." One had to drink Stella with the utmost respect. The correct name for it was "Stella Biere Blonde" and it is still made to this day.

The days of 1952 at El Firdan seemed idyllic. Occasionally we would walk down to the main gates, two ornate swinging structures, suspended between two brick columns. That on its own would have been fine anywhere, except now there was a state of emergency and a sandbagged gun emplacement topped with a searchlight now flanked the gates.

One could not leave the station, so apart from work, going to the Astra Cinema, one had to create one's own life. Several of us got together – Burgess and Franklin were names I can recall, plus Peter Dance and some others – and decided to build a nine hole golf course. We marked it out and spent weeks clearing the area of rocks and bushes, and someone arranged for the Station truck to bring diesel oil – derve, they called it. The black stuff was spread over the "greens" and rolled into the sand to create a fairly firm base.

Grandfather Fred at Highway Garage kindly shipped his clubs out to Egypt and I was able to play for a while. But it was terribly frustrating to drive a ball straight down the fairway, to see it strike a lonely rock, and hurtle off at ninety degrees into the rough. One really had to laugh. I never won a prize and I eventually sold Granddad's clubs.

THE SPANISH INFLUENCE

Peter Dance and I also studied Spanish for a while. He studied Spanish from a Pitman's Course which demanded you try and figure out what the words in Spanish were. It was a complete immersion course. I stuck with a record course obtained from the El Firdan Education Section.

We had some idea of going out to South America and searching for explorer Colonel Percy Fawcett who became lost in Brazil's Matto Grosso area in 1925, or exploring the jungles of British Guiana after we had read W.H. Hudson's "Green Mansions," but these ideas eventually evaporated. But I did enjoy my Spanish studies. It's a very beautiful and romantic language and I adore their romantic songs and music.

Peter was developing another interest that was to become a lifelong endeavor and bring fame; Conchology or the collection and study of mollusk shells. Peter would frequently venture out into the desert flanking the Suez Canal often with me in tow carrying a small 127 film Kodak Vest Pocket camera. Peter would gently lift the branches of bushes and undergrowth and point to the great varieties of life existing underneath. It was in these shady places that he found shells, mostly small, but shells nevertheless. Whenever he found something interesting I would take pictures of the shells in their original location. I processed the films and made prints in the El Firdan darkroom. In this way, Peter started on a pursuit that he still follows to this day almost sixty years later. He is currently the author of over twenty books, mostly on shells, and frequently travels the world giving lectures and making presentations. American conchologists acknowledge he is one incredible source of information and frequently invite him to speak at their annual conventions at Sanibel Island in Florida.

SHOWTIME IN THE ASTRA

One day, Sergeant Silk who managed the Astra Cinema came up and asked me about my "theatre" experience, so I told him about Stirling films, working at G.B. Animation and the drama stuff I had done. Then I asked the obvious: "Why do you want to know."

"We've got some talent on the station and I was wondering if you would like to get involved, be an emcee, perhaps do an act and get a show together. We've got musicians as well, and even a band." He peered eagerly into my face. "The men need some entertainment, you know. We have even got a female impersonator."

A female impersonator on an all-male station? This was interesting. His name was Marc Fleming and he must have been born on the stage. He was so good at impersonating women that one was inclined to treat "her" as a woman. Marc dressed and lived the role. His feminine presence was weird but certainly added to the events. Marc was so good that some years later, I saw him billed at London's famous Windmill Theatre. Later, he was a resident performer at "The Black Cap" pub in Camden Town.

We did two shows on the big stage at the Astra Cinema. The acts seem to come out of nowhere. We had two accordionists who developed the knack of producing a Mantovani Orchestra sound, called the "cascading strings." They played such current hits as "Charmaine" with such finesse that some people thought they were playing the hit record. Another excellent act was the "Musical Four." I often wondered what had happened to these talented performers. In addition there were individual comic acts and skits, sessions by a station jazz band and a great performance when some fifty members of the RAF El Firdan brass band performed. RAF personnel from all sections helped design, build and paint scenery.

CREATIVE MOOD:
The author in a creative mood for the variety show, pictured outside a tent at RAF Station El Firdan, 1952.

I recalled the cartoon voices I had learned with Stuart Crombie at Moor Hall Studios and with some practice started imitating well known performers of the day. These included Laurence Olivier's famous Battle of Agincourt speech in the movie "Henry V." Others included comedians Robert Moreton, Tony Hancock, some of the peculiar and hilarious voices on Tommy Handley's ITMA. Another voice was Dame Edith Evans in the just released movie "The Importance of Being Ernest". I even did an imitation of Jimmy Stewart in the movie "Call Northside 777." A finishing touch for my act came from Granddad and Granny Egby who sent me a wonderful tuxedo that I proudly wore in the shows.

I introduced each of the voices by imitating BBC World Service announcer Peter King, in fact, on the second show we did, I did a corny news broadcast, which when I think about it today, I flinch at the corn. Everyone roared with laughter and applauded and the show was the talk of the Station for months afterwards.

A week after the shows ended at El Firdan, British Forces Broadcasting Service in Fayid contacted Sergeant Silk and asked if we could take some players to their studios to recreate our acts. About a dozen of us were trucked down to Fayid and I introduced the acts in my BBC voice.

Neville Powley, the dapper and energetic producer took me aside afterwards: "Have you ever thought of becoming a professional announcer?" A month later I was transferred from El Firdan to FBS Station, Fayid in the Canal Zone. My journey through life was changing and unbeknown to me there had been another kink in the Cosmos.

4

THE SOUNDS OF RADIO
AND ROMANCE

T HE GANG AT 751 Signals Unit, which had become the official name of the GCI radar station at El Firdan, gave me a great send-off party. I think they had parties as an excuse to have a few pints, but it was a warm send-off. Oh, yes, I had just been made an SAC – Senior Aircraftsman – up a notch from LAC, a Leading Aircraftsman.

A truck with a couple of lads carrying rifles took me down to Fayid. The town had grown in the months since I had last seen it from Kabrit. Apart from being general headquarters for Land and Air Forces Middle East, the escalating Egyptian hostility and a threat to nationalize the Canal had triggered an immense buildup almost overnight.

The Emergency resulted in 65,000 Army troops and 14,500 Royal Air Force personnel crammed into 1936-era facilities designed for less than 15,000. As these reinforcements arrived, 2,000 wives and children were evacuated back to the United Kingdom. Armed troops were now all over the place guarding buildings and the skies were filled with RAF planes that flitted around like swallows in a show of force. Hawker Tempests, de Havilland Mosquitoes, Gloster Meteors and English Electric Canberras all formed part of the massive military buildup in the Suez Canal Zone. I wondered what old Ferdinand de Lesseps would have thought.

My mind also pondered about what I was getting into. Broadcasting! It was one thing to impersonate a BBC announcer for a local camp entertainment, it was another to walk into a professional studio, sit behind a microphone and start talking to an invisible audience. Invisible? Yes, but you knew they were out there, or you hoped they were out there, listening. Will they teach me what buttons to push, what things to say? I had fears of being pushed into the heights of broadcasting without training, but I need not have feared anything. They had a good, well tested system.

Neville Powley introduced me to a lanky, well presented young man with an engaging smile who was also a Senior Aircraftsman. "This is Anton. He'll show you around and you'll be shadowing him for six weeks before you go on continuity shift by yourself."

His full name was Anton Rodgers and he was in Egypt serving his two-year National Service stint. Born at Wisbech, Cambridgeshire, he said he had a sister who was already an accomplished singer in the United States, and it was his plan to become an actor. "I've already done some stage work," he said easily, and reeled off credits such as "Carmen" at the Royal Opera House, Covent Garden, and the title role in Terrence Ratigan's "The Winslow Boy." He made fame sound so easy. "But I would like to work in films – as well as stage."

That evening we sat in the NAAFI drinking Stellas and sharing experiences, mine from animated cartoons and David Hand and Anton from his stage training and work.

As we sat there, I had a feeling that he was destined for the spotlight. He possessed that undeniable energy. Years later I would enjoy watching him play the French police inspector in "Dirty Rotten Scoundrels" alongside Michael Caine and Steve Martin. Through his career Anton played roles in eight movies, twenty-two television programs and series, and returned to stage productions many times.

Anton showed me the ropes of broadcasting, scheduling, the record library, scripting, announcements, what to say and what not to say. "Never swear while you are in a studio, even if you are sure the mike is off. That was one of my early goofs. I learned the hard way." He grinned. "Treat everything as if it were alive."

One program that he enjoyed was "Letters from Home." Letters came in from U.K. families asking for records to be played for their sons, daughters or husbands serving in the Canal Zone. Anton showed me how to edit them, highlighting key messages with a blue pencil. When he had enough to run for an hour, perhaps fourteen or fifteen requests lined up, we would go to the Record Library and pull the appropriate records. They were all 78 rpm disks in those days and broke easily.

Pat Livingston was the librarian. "Be careful of her, she has a tongue that resembles a nasty horsewhip," said Anton with a grin. A tough lady, but I must admit I never crossed swords with her. She was a perfectionist and very knowledgeable in music, particularly the classics.

FBS was non-commercial so a sixty-minute program ran for sixty minutes. The records of the day kept repeating themselves: Kay Starr and "Wheel of Fortune"; Frankie Laine with "High Noon,"; Rosemary Clooney and "Half As Much"; Al Martino with "Here in My Heart"; Leroy Anderson's "Blue

Tango"; Teresa Brewer's "Till I Waltz Again With You"; Johnny Ray's "Walkin' My Baby Back Home"; and Nat King Cole's "Unforgettable." They all seemed to have special meanings for the letter writers and the folks receiving the messages.

There was of course one record that was played almost every night. It was the evergreen for everyone in the Forces and no one ever complained about it being repeated. It was Jo Stafford's "You Belong to Me." It contained very meaningful lyrics: *"See the pyramids along the Nile, Watch the sunrise on a tropical isle, Just remember darlin' all the while, You belong to me..."*

The pop music ballad, which took Jo Stafford to the top of the UK charts, was written by Pee Wee King, Chilton Price, and Redd Stewart. It was the right song for the right time in Egypt. We almost went berserk playing it, but we knew thousands enjoyed listening, and the listeners were important.

INVADING THE OFFICERS' CLUB

Anton was a young daredevil and detested snobbery amid military status. One night he said: "Let's put on our togs and invade the officers club." We both wore tuxedos and walked in as if we owned the place. It was packed with brass of all shapes and sizes and several well dressed British civilians, some of whom were reporters. We ordered drinks and that was as far as we got before being recognized.

FBS engineering officer Alan Langford and Chief Broadcasting Officer Roy Morgan had Neville Powley quietly escort us out. "We'll see you first thing in the morning," snapped Powley. But it didn't happen. A short time after our ejection, a gang of Egyptians with guns invaded the compound. Two officers got killed. Everyone was on high alert after that and our transgression was seemingly forgotten. It was good that we did not stay.

Robin Macdowell showed me how to script and present a military brass band show and that was an excellent introduction to musical programs. Band shows happened every week in spite of the deteriorating political situation. Engineers Phil Harding and Alan Robson did the recording in the NAAFI hall each week. Bands from various regiments and services came week after week and played for 30 minutes while I stood at the microphone and introduced each number. Thus I was introduced to broadcasting.

My six weeks training for becoming a continuity announcer ended, and Anton gave me his blessing with an encouraging "You'll do well, Bob." But the day I made my solo broadcasting debut was impacted by an event totally unexpected.

With high enthusiasm I arrived at the FBS studios in the early morning light to start programming for the day. It was the third week in March. Phil Harding, looking grim, greeted me with the news: "Queen Mary has died. We have to play special records for the occasion. Here's what to say." He handed me a card which read: "We regret to announce the passing of Her Royal Highness, Queen Mary, widow of his late Royal Highness King George the Fifth. During this time of mourning we will be presenting special programs of music suitable for this time." Queen Mary of Teck was the mother of Edward VII who abdicated and King George VI, and grandmother of Princesses Elizabeth and Margaret.

Well, so much for my big debut in broadcasting. I spent the entire morning playing a stack of twelve inch classical records with music by Beethoven, Bach, Chopin, Debussy, Pachelbel and Schubert. Anton wandered by. "Not exactly our type is it?" he said with a mischievous grin.

"We could drop in a Vera Lynn to cheer everyone up," I muttered rebelliously.

"We'll meet again?" he said with a short laugh. "I'll see you at the executioner's block."

It was early summer of 1953 when Neville Powley came and said: "How would you like to go to FBS Cyprus."

"When?"

"Tomorrow morning. It's a bit rough. One of our people, a smoker, accidentally burned the studios down, so we are broadcasting from a farmhouse."

LAUGHTER-LOVING APHRODITE

The twin-engine Vickers Valetta took off from Fayid and headed north towards Cyprus some 370 miles away across the Mediterranean. The Island of Cyprus had always intrigued me, mainly because it carried the essence of ancient Greek culture, and I had heard from visiting airmen that there were many Greek ruins and Byzantine castles to see. In addition, they said, there were golden sandy beaches for great vacations.

As the Valetta flew over the island it appeared sun-baked with large plains and mountain peaks to the north and west. It resembled a goat hide stretched over the blue Mediterranean. It was hard to imagine that Homer in The Odyssey wrote: "...laughter-loving Aphrodite went to Cyprus, where, in Pathos she proclaimed her realm and a fragrant altar." The Goddess Aphrodite and praises of the island have been sung by poets and songsters throughout the ages ever since.

Cyprus is the most easterly of the Mediterranean islands and after Sicily and Sardinia, the third largest. It stretches about 150 miles from west to the eastern panhandle, and sixty miles from north to south. It has a ragged and often beautiful coastline of about 490 miles.

Its history is as ornate as any mosaic could be. St. Barnabus was born there but everyone who was anyone has passed through Cyprus, including Alexander the Great, St. Paul and King Richard the Lion-hearted have left their marks. It has been ruled or a better word would be possessed by Greeks, Phoenicians, Assyrians, Egyptians, Persians, Byzantines, Romans, Venetians, Genoese and Turks.

The British came onto the island following the 1878 Cyprus Convention with the declining Turkish Ottomans, in much the same way they occupied Egypt and bought their way into the Canal Zone. And like the Egyptians, Cypriots always wanted the British to go home.

Cypriots are a strange but very passionate lot. When I arrived, the island's population was about 400,000 Greek-Cypriots and 100,000 Turkish Cypriots and many had learned to live in harmony, although Greeks had an inherent distrust of their Turkish neighbors.

Every now and again the sleeping Greek Cypriots and patriotic fervor would awaken. For instance, in 1931 an angry mob burned down Government House, but when I arrived in 1953, the political scene was quiet.

STUDIOS AMONG THE OLIVES

FBS Cyprus in 1953 was hidden among olive trees in Lakatamia, a small village south-west of Nicosia. The studio was contained in an ancient, but solidly built farmhouse of clay, mud and stucco. The building possessed a distinct aroma that breathed history—if you happened to be a peasant. Smells of sheep, goats, old hay and dried out, aging timbers were everywhere. The main building, a sandstone house, was a cut above. It contained various offices with polished, wooden floors, tiled and paneled walls and wooden beams holding up a plastered ceiling.

This was the domain of the station commander who was reminiscent of a bygone age, perhaps a retired cavalry officer, who still maintained a weary horse nearby. A sword hung symbolically over the fireplace. His name was Ian Redfers Brown, a quiet, stiff-upper-lipped type. His first words of wisdom to me were: "Egby, watch the Cyprus brandy. It'll get at you!" That night I ventured into the Carleton Hotel bar in downtown Nicosia. Redfers, with friends, was still battling the brandy.

Close by the Lakatamia house was a low slung mud building which, in another age, must have served as a mule or sheep barn. It had the heavy smell of animals. This was the studio with a record library along side. The word "studio" was used loosely. After experiencing the radio efficiency of Fayid in Egypt, Lakatamia was something else. For a start, there was no control room. It was a self-serve affair. The continuity studio, the domain of the presenter or announcer was the center of FBS Cyprus. It was the size of a small bedroom – ten feet by eight – big by pygmy standards, otherwise small.

A large wooden table, scarred from the old burned out station, contained a sound level control unit. A couple of 78 rpm turntables were mounted on wooden boxes, and a large black double-sided ribbon microphone leered ominously over the top of everything. In the corner, mounted on a metal rack was a tower of electronic equipment, mainly receivers from which BBC news broadcasts from London were relayed. Engineers frequently adjusted the receivers to ensure the best quality.

There was no mechanical air conditioning. If they ever made a comedy movie, this would have been a good set. The studio door, a heavy wooden apparatus ready to breathe its last and fall apart, was on squeaky hinges. The door rarely closed because it did not fit the jamb thus air and extraneous sounds from outside readily spread inwards. The other "air conditioner" was the window, which because of the summer heat was always open. The window overlooked a field, a Greek Orthodox Church and the village of Lakatamia a couple of hundred yards away.

"What happened here?" I asked.

"The original station which was a jewel with a great concert studio burned down," said the engineers, with an apologetic shrug. "They say it was a cigarette and the curtains were tinder dry. No one took the blame so it's doubtful that the truth will ever be known."

The unavoidable open-door studio at Lakatamia provided some hilarious moments — and embarrassments — for on-air staff. First, the field outside was inhabited by several cows who had the knack of appearing at the window and mooing while the announcer was on air. Every Saturday night at six o'clock announcers would read the local announcements of events and church services for next day. That was the exact time for the church priest to toll the bells. An irate colonel once called in: "Do you people have to play those blasted bells? Sounds awful!"

Another time, a 30-inch iguana ambled in through the door. It sent the announcer scrambling out through the window. Mac the engineer drove the creature back into the woods.

Once, a priest from the church leaned on the studio windowsill and peered in and started talking Greek. He had no idea his enquiries were being broadcast over the entire island. Someone who heard it said he had lost a chicken and had we seen it.

Once while relaying the news from the General Overseas Service of the BBC, both receivers suddenly went dead. The engineers tracked down the cause: a rat had chewed through the power cable. We could smell fried rat for days.

Nature played a role too. Whenever there were heavy rains in the Troodos Mountains, the nearby Pedieos River on the Mesaoria Plain came to life. The first surges of water sent thousands of rocks and pebbles clicking and cracking against each other, sometimes for hours. It was a cacophonic rock chorus. People would call in with such remarks as "Your voice sounds awful. Are you having a bad day?"

THE DAY THE GROUND MOVED

Thursday, September 10th 1953 was a memorable day in many ways. We had gone on air at 5:55 a.m. with Billy Cotton's "Wakey Wakey" and were in the process of missing the 6:00 a.m. news relay from the BBC in London. Engineer Mac Macdonald was struggling with the receivers and I had a 78 rpm record playing. Then it happened. No announcements. It just happened. The earth moved.

Suddenly, somewhere it seemed that a huge hand was underneath the station and rocking it. The old building protested with sharp creaks, lights swung crazily, water in the red Fire buckets tipped and swayed.

"Earthquake," yelled Mac. In a flash he had disappeared.

Fearing the roof would collapse, I rushed outside. The ground continued its heaving and swaying. I clung to an old tree near the building. I felt a feeling of complete helplessness. From somewhere I had a distinct feeling, a dread that my life was about to be terminated. I wanted to do something, but failed to do anything. It was impossible. The ground kept on heaving as if herds of elephants were rampaging underneath.

Was this the end of the world? My life? Was I about to face God? Where the hell was that voice? You know, the one who always seemed to be around when I needed help. Was I supposed to believe in God? Jesus? Mohammed? Buddha? Dozens of thoughts raced through my head. Why should I bring God into this? Did I believe in God? What a time to consider this point.

Then all was quiet. The ground was still. An eerie quiet descended over the field round the radio station. I went back to the studio expecting to find chaos. The record! It was still playing Rosemary Clooney and "Come on-a My House." When it finished I casually announced: "If you were wondering what all the shaking was about, and you find out please let us know," I said and followed with a time check. No one ever briefed us on what to say in the event of a seismological event.

We soon learned that the village of Paphos in south-west Cyprus had been largely destroyed and neighboring villages seriously damaged. Fourteen people were dead and several hundred injured. There could have been more fatalities but many people had already gone to work in the fields. The earthquake lasted 29 seconds. It felt longer than that, much longer. Such were the penalties of farmhouse broadcasting.

THE TEAM AT LAKATAMIA

The staff comprised a mix of RAF and Army people: David (Dad) Davis and myself, both RAF, Irving Dee with a Groucho Marx moustache was Army, and a British civilian, Iris Russell a pleasant, good looking live-wire journalist who eventually married Shahe (Gubby) Gubenlian of Reuters in Nicosia. The engineers who kept the transmitter running were "Mac" Macdonald and Ray Joyce, a jovial sort who ran around the country in a tiny Fiat Topolino which he called "The Mouse." Why not!

The great thing about Cyprus is that I could get out and see life, as opposed to living in the restricted confines of the Suez Canal Zone. Nicosia spelled total freedom. Admittedly, Dad Davis and I were billeted in a World War II corrugated iron Nissan hut at a small Army facility on the Larnaca Road, but it was comfortable and we could get out whenever we were not on shift at the radio station. I think Dad was waiting for his wife Penny to come over from Benghazi in Libya, so while he waited, we systematically hit all the key bars including the Carleton, the Cosmopolitan, the Roxy and a place inside the old walls called John Odgers Bar.

Occasionally, I took my camera and walked through the old city of Nicosia photographing the small shops, tiny coffee shops, narrow alleys, ancient churches and people with expressive faces. I felt as if I was accomplishing something if I used my camera and without a doubt, there were many historic and interesting places to capture on film.

Cyprus was laid back. Relaxing. It was in this atmosphere that I decided to study journalism and become a reporter. It was now the summer of 1953 and

I only had fifteen more months to do when my five year term of engagement in the air force ended. Perhaps I could come back to Cyprus and really explore the place as a civilian, and perhaps a writer-photographer.

GRASPING THE ESSENCE OF JOURNALISM

There were no journalism classes available so I took to studying news story structure. I bought Time magazine and a couple of British newspapers – the Daily express and the Daily Telegraph – and selected interesting stories. On an old typewriter at the Army camp I copied news stories, studied each word, each sentence structure, and sensed what the writer was trying to say. As I copied the stories and became fully conscious of the words and the feelings, I grasped the story-telling ability of journalism.

One day, a Colonial Government report on buildings being developed in Nicosia and the expanding economy landed on my desk at Forces Broadcasting. That would make a good article, I thought, so I wrote an 800-word article and slugged it "Million Pound Development Planned for Ledra Street." I dropped it off at the Cyprus Mail, the English language newspaper and the editor Victor Bodker said he liked it. What's more, they published it and I got a byline. Wow! A thrill!

But old Redfers Browne went apoplectic! "Egby, you're a member of Her Majesty's Forces. You're not supposed to be writing for the newspapers."

I promised not to do it again. I really did not have a chance because there was another kink occurring in the Cosmos, and it happened this way.

Sometimes kinks in the Cosmos can come into one's life like a flash of lightning and you know you've been hit. Then there are the times when the kinks merge into your life without you being consciously aware of them happening, like you're sitting on lovely, sandy seashore, meditating or having a power nap, when you realize the tide has come in and you're surrounded. The way I met Iro was like that.

THE QUANTUM THING

If I had not met her that day, my life would have been vastly different. They call it something like Quantum Leaps. For instance, you need a job. Your resume is ready but you look out the window at steady rain and decide to stay at home. Tomorrow will be fine, you say as an excuse.

However, if you had gone out today, you would have got wet, taken refuge in a coffee shop, met a man who was looking for a good journalist-type writer, been given a job, and within five years made vice president of a large corporation. If you had chosen tomorrow because the weather was fine, you would return home disappointed that no one looked at your resume. Sad and dejected, you get a series of useless jobs, start drinking, frequently get fired and end up on social security.

If I had not met Iro that day, it is quite likely my life in the British Royal Air Force would have seen me sent back to England, released and wandering the streets of my home town looking for a job. As I met Iro that day, quantum kicked in and today I am still pondering over a life full of death, soul searching, fascinating people, oh, yes, and miracles. Quantum and kinks in the Cosmos are affiliated. They work hand in hand and if one is to benefit, it is important to follow your intuitive powers, and yes, even listen to the voices. In the fall of 1953 I was unaware of intuition, failed to give mysterious voices credibility and was being swept along by Cosmic Forces. And yes, I was totally unaware of those Forces too.

Another thing. In that year I did not believe in miracles and I am still a non-believer. As I found out many years later, miracles are simply energy motivated events that we fail to understand, so we conveniently attach the word "miracle" to such events. Having said that, my life has been full of them. How I met Iro was different. Perhaps an energy motivated event. Perhaps not. But it changed my life, drastically.

A LOVE BOAT FROM BEIRUT

In Cyprus the John Odgers Bar and Restaurant on Regina Street in the old city of Nicosia was famous. Resembling a spacious English pub, it was a gathering spot for journalists, entertainers, writers, diplomats, spies and terrorists, plus a strange assortment of other people. For instance, arguing on any popular topic was a retired junior counsel on the British prosecution team at the Nazi trials at Nuremberg. Another was an eighty-year old withered lady of the Russian aristocracy who smoked with a long yellow ivory cigarette holder and talked incessantly of her escape from those "cursed Reds." John Odgers was chubby, fair-skinned with blond hair, and always had his ear to the ground. Some said he worked for British Intelligence but I doubt it because he was far too open.

"There's a small group of us going to Beirut for the weekend," he announced one day. "Bob, do you want to come?"

Beirut! Lebanon! The Paris of the Middle East with French bistros, tree lined boulevards and the aroma of French baguettes. It appealed to my travel-starved mind. Conveniently, I was off-shift for the weekend. Beirut would be a great experience.

Friday afternoon we climbed on board the Italian MV Fillipo Grimani. It had once been a troopship in World War II and weighed about 7,000 tons. It had been refurbished for peacetime use and was quite comfortable with good Italian food and wines. It reached the Levant in the early hours of next day so after breakfast on board John Odgers and his couple of friends from London and myself started wandering through the port city.

Lebanon had once formed part of the Ottoman Empire but the Turks had lost in World War I because of their affinity to Germany, and the French walked in with a mandate that lasted until Lebanon gained its independence. But that quarter century of French occupation left a distinctive French culture in streets and boulevards, buildings, shops and restaurants, literature, and language. It left Beirut in a distinctive and picturesque duality – half French, half Arab. Bistros, patisseries, magasins, all had a distinctive European continental air including newspapers in Arabic and French. An English newspaper, the Daily Star had just started the year before.

A tour of the old downtown should include the Omari Mosque, the Municipality Building, the Assaf and Amir Munzir Mosques, the Arcaded Maarad Street, the Parliament Building, the Roman columns on Nejmeh Square and the historic Greek Orthodox and Greek Catholic churches opposite the Parliament. Beirut's commercial and cultural life had been enhanced in the ten years since the country attained independence from the French Mandate. The city had 80 banks, countless import-export firms, a major port and airport as well as a free exchange market. Little did I think that as we roamed the streets, wandered through shops, that I would one day be back under very much different circumstances. Sometimes it is good not to know the future.

We ended up by invading a bar that looked more American than French and I got bombed on gin and tonics. Perhaps two, perhaps three. I lost count. I don't take alcohol well. I recall staggering back to the harbor, finding the ship and sleeping in my cabin throughout the afternoon until the need for oxygen and fresh air finally made me surface. With a muggy head I climbed the narrow stairs leading to the stern and walked onto the wooden deck. There she was.

It's a picture that has stayed – no haunted me – over the years. A slim but finely shaped figure, reddish brown hair that delightfully framed her light olive countenance of finely shaped contours. Her dark brown eyes sparkled with a sense of warm delight. She must have been laughing inside.

"Are you all right?" she asked in perfect English, her voice lilting, almost singing.

"For a while I thought I was on a track to Heaven...or Hell," I muttered, my voice feeling a little hoarse. I had been smoking heavily aromatic Turkish cigarettes. I mustered a half-hearted smile.

"Take in some deep breaths," she advised simply. "You'll feel better." Her voice was soft and comforting. She was leaning on the rails watching the pink glow left by the setting sun, so I leaned beside her. I enjoyed the way she immediately suggested I relax. Her presence, her energy felt totally in synchronization with mine.

"What's your name?"

She hesitated, glanced at me as if shy. "Iro. My name is Iro. It's Greek."

"A derivative of the Hero and Leander legend," I said recalling a book I had read on Greek mythology and the gods. "Hero was a priestess of Aphrodite and a young man. Leander fell in love with her, and every night swam across the Hellespont, a dangerously narrow point in the Aegean Sea. Hero lit an oil lamp to guide him. One terrible stormy night, the winds blew out Hero's light. Leander became lost and drowned. Hero, now grief stricken, threw herself into the sea and drowned too." I looked at Iro and smiled. "That's right, isn't it?"

"You forgot to mention one thing," she said quietly. "They were in love."

"Apologies!"

"You're quick to apologize," she snapped. "What's your name?"

"Robert. Most people call me Bob. I'm in the Royal Air Force."

"Do you fly?"

"No. I'm a broadcaster but I aim to be a journalist. A writer. Perhaps write a book one day."

As the Fillipo Gramani left port and headed back to Cyprus, we walked the decks, occasionally stopping to watch the stars and the planets. "That's the constellation Orion," I said, "You can see his belt."

"Did you learn about stars in the air force?"

"No, London. One of these days I would like to go to the moon or perhaps the stars."

"Ah, you're a romanticist. Do you have a girl friend?

I shook my head. "Haven't had the time. Too busy," I said. It seemed the right thing to say. "And you? Are you married?"

Iro shook her head and gave a little laugh. "My mother thinks I'm the eternal spinster."

I gazed at her delicate face framed in dark brown hair with a reddish tinge and an almost dark golden aura emanated from her. "May I see you again?" My hand touched hers as she rested it on the ship's rail, but she did not pull away.

"How old are you?" Her dark eyes were serious.

"Twenty-one. I'll be twenty-two in February. St. Valentine's Day."

She laughed. "My God, you are a romanticist!" She paused as if building up her strength. "I'm too old for you." It was blunt, a "let's forget it" statement.

"You don't look old at all," I said stubbornly.

"Listen, you stubborn Englishman," she snapped. "I was born March 24th 1914. That makes me thirty-nine. I'm eighteen years older than you. Old enough to be your mother."

"You don't look it."

"Take off your rose-tinted spectacles," she said with a quirky smile, then observing my hurt, she added: "You're kind." There was a pause and she pulled away. "I have to go to my cabin. My sister is there."

"Perhaps we can be friends," I struggled valiantly against a seemingly impossible argument.

"Perhaps, Bob, perhaps." As she walked down the steps towards the cabins she called out in Greek "Gallee neetcha, filo mou." Translated: "Good night, my friend."

As I tried to sleep over the throbbing engines of the old ship, my mind was in turmoil. What had I let myself into? I stared at the walls, the two solitary lights in the cabin. There was a startling revelation in my life. This woman, this beautiful Greek-Cypriot lady now possessed my body, mind and if I had one, spirit. I was not sure about spirits or gods. Nothing seemed sure. Nothing seemed right. All I knew is that I wanted to be with this beautiful, intelligent woman. A part of my psyche advised: Walk away, Bob. It's the safest. You don't need an older woman in your life. What will your mother say? Dad? Well, he would probably laugh and get on with his latest project. I was still thinking when sleep overtook me.

Right after breakfast and just before we left the ship at Limassol a steward came up and thrust an envelope into my hand. Nervously I opened it, expecting a "good bye" note. On a small piece of paper was a number. Underneath was written: "If you wish to be my friend, call me." There was no signature. My heart leapt with joy, but my elation was short lived.

"You left the bloody island without permission?" cried Redfers Browne snapping out of his usual cool. "Suppose you'd been arrested, or killed in Lebanon. These Arabs are not exactly friendly."

Somehow, I managed an excuse that I went for my education, and added I would not do it again. The incident blew over.

Over the next few weeks I met Iro at her house. Her mother was an active senior but knew not a word of English. Feeling the need to learn some Greek, I did start to study the language. I impressed them both by reeling off the twenty-four letters of the Greek alphabet. I even learned a Greek poem which ended with the words "O kleftis expathoni," which translated stood for "The brigand draws his sword." Diving into Greek grammar was another task altogether. But as I studied the language many English words suddenly appeared quite sensible. For instance "kleftis" which in the poem means "brigand" also in English is the stem of "kleptomaniac" or "thief."

A HOUSE AND ANTICS IN NICOSIA

Iro and her mother Efterpi lived in one of those old sandstone homes that used to routinely decorate the Nicosia suburbs. It was spacious and cool. The floors were of stone and tile, and the home was kept spotlessly clean. The place had an interesting echo that suggested years gone by. Amid the garden's trees and bushes, which gave one a sense of privacy, were some grape vines over an old wooden trellis and an orange tree that produced the sweetest fruit. Iro's father, Theodoulos Toufexi had died five years before, in 1948.

Efterpi introduced me to Greek cooking, particularly a wonderful thick bean soup – Fasollia – which was laced with olive oil and garlic. It made the body perspire profusely about 30 minutes later. Iro introduced me to a Cypriot delicacy – which looked like micro-chickens. They were sparrows caught on the rooftop, plucked and cleaned and placed in vinegar for pickling. When ready, they had no bones and were a great delicacy. But I was never really turned on by them.

Iro's relatives were not impressed with my existence. The political climate opposing British rule was heating up and some of her relatives, a couple of uncles were definitely pro-Greek Cypriot and anti-British. Her sister's husband Andreas Araouzo was a close friend of Makarios and after independence became a cabinet minister in the new Republic. Cypriots are always extremely polite and smile even when they have a sharp dislike of a person. It takes some getting used to.

NEW STUDIOS AT STROVOLOS

Shortly before Christmas, FBS moved into brand new studios at Strovolos, a suburb of Nicosia. Well, the two continuity studios and a small concert studio were new, but the building itself had seen better days. It was an old sandstone house flanked by a couple of palm trees, a long windowed shed that became the library, and a small guardhouse, where Pavlos, an ancient Greek who looked like Akim Tamiroff in "For Whom The Bell Tolls," sat on duty. Upstairs were spacious offices. For several weeks, we continued to broadcast from Lakatamia plus doing test broadcasts from the new station site at Strovolos. Oh, yes, the station was a nice ten-minute walk from Government House and a five minute walk for the Programs Officer, a dynamic, mature woman with flaming red hair. Her name was Wendy.

One morning at the new studios, I was on shift in Continuity and reading the very routine "Test" announcements when a fair-haired, slim and quite distinguished fellow walked in and started asking questions about everything. He never did say who he was, but I did recognize him and called him "sir." This was a phenomenon I observed in life. Kings, archbishops, princes, field marshals, politicians, corporate moguls, never introduce themselves. You are expected to know. All the lower ranks always introduce themselves.

Two hours after the distinguished visitor had gone I mentioned to the Programs Officer that Sir Andrew Wright, the Governor of Cyprus had dropped by.

Wendy's flaming red hair burned like an Olympic torch. She screamed and screamed and never forgave me for not calling her from her home across the street. I did mention that I had offered Sir Robert a cup of tea and that only added to her ire. Wendy Barnes was one of those "iron" women who occasionally stalk the corridors of broadcasting. Pat Livingston was another. Both dedicated broadcasters with sharp tongues.

Although I had to work at the radio station for "Wireless for the Blind," a Christmas and New Year program where people called in and bid on a particular record, with contributions going to the Wireless for the Blind Society, I did manage to have Christmas dinner with Iro and Efterpi. I learned that Iro occasionally worked on assignment as a secretarial help. Several years before, she had had a close and promising relationship with a British employee at the NAAFI. The relationship suddenly bombed one night when the fellow's wife flew out from England unexpectedly. Iro went into a severe depression that lasted for several months.

We went for countless walks around old Nicosia, took taxi rides to see historic places, and had drinks in remote coffee shops and bistros and discussed what books we had read. I had read most of the Hemingway books while in Egypt and was now reading Thorne Smith the creator of "Topper." She laughed when I told her about the antics related in "The Night Life of the Gods." We also stopped to allow me to take photographs of historic places, and Victor Bodker at the Cyprus Mail liked to publish them. That gave me a boost but I yearned to get a real news photo.

HIGH TECH ARRIVES IN BROADCASTING

Early in 1954, the "microgroove" long play record arrived at Forces Broadcasting. On the old 78 rpm records the announcer would "set up" the record on "pre-listen" by having the playback stylus roll back and forth, so when the arm was dropped, the music started on cue.

The first long play record was brought in by Wendy Barnes as if she was carrying a gold ingot. A different playback unit had been installed with a drop-arm. There was an air of excitement as everyone gathered around. Wendy introduced the music on air as the first microgroove record played on FBS Cyprus. Then manually, she gently lowered the pick-up arm – nothing happened. The technician in the control room had omitted to open the "pot." We had to scrape Wendy off the ceiling.

The days, weeks and months of early 1954 were idyllic. When the weather was nice and warm, which was almost always, we swam in the harbor beneath Kyrenia Castle, collected beautiful shells, and chased the occasional squid.

Sometimes our bodies collided and her energy electrified my entire being. Over the weeks and months, whenever I had time off, she would take me to historic places. One she always seemed to enjoy, because we visited the place three times, was St. Hilarion, a castle perched high in the Kyrenia mountain range. From its battlements one can see northern Cyprus and on a clear day Turkey, stretching away to the north. To the south is the Mesaoria Plain, stretching towards Nicosia.

"This is where your King, Richard the Lion-Hearted brought his fiancée Berengaria of Navarre. He proposed to her in the chapel here, and later married her at Limassol." Iro shrugged and gave a pained expression. "What should have been a romantic event, turned sour. Richard the Lion-Heart was a bigamist. He had a wife in England."

"Damned Brits!" I muttered, and she laughed. But inside the smile I could feel her sadness, whether it was from the story, or a reflection of her own sadness. I slipped my arm round her shoulders. She gazed up at me and, like it was the most natural thing to do, I kissed her, and felt the energy, like electricity flooding through my body. It was the first time I had ever felt that way. I knew we were going to be more than just friends. A doorway, a gateway had opened as my Great-Grandmother Elen had said in Reading so long ago. I wondered, with a slight degree of apprehension, what adventure it would reveal in my life.

But Iro had little hope that our relationship would lead anywhere and frequently brought up the difference in ages. She had some of the darkness of Byron within her because she liked to quote him. *"When we two are parted after long years, how should I greet thee? With silence and tears."* My going away bothered her tremendously and we both knew it was looming.

TREAD SOFTLY SAID THE VOICE

Soon after, Redfers Browne said a signal had come in and I must return to my parent unit at 751 Signals Unit at El Firdan. My three-year tour in Egypt, the Canal Zone, would shortly expire and all the airmen in Draft #344 would be shipped back to England for release at the end of October.

My departure was not easy. Iro was not an optimist although I repeatedly promised I would be back as soon as I had been discharged from the air force. As a parting gift she gave me a box of Cyprus silk handkerchiefs imbued with her perfume, which was wonderful. But as the Valetta took off from Nicosia Airport, my heart felt heavy and frustrated. Regardless of my feelings for Iro, inside me burned a tremendous desire to live on Cyprus. It was the right time and place in my life. Why, I couldn't exactly say. Sure I wanted to be a news photographer, a journalist, but Cyprus was a backwater in news action, so why was my energy being drawn to the place.

Yes, I also had a powerful, restless urge to be with Iro. A powerful urge that generated an excited desire to be with the woman I had met those months ago in Beirut harbor. As I gazed out at the cloudless, perfectly blue Mediterranean sky, for the first time in my life I said quietly: "God, if you are there, I need your help." That statement stunned me. Had I said that in desperation? Why was I suffering? From being apart from Iro? Was I really in love? Is this what love feels like? The questions shot through my mind like machine gun bullets.

Suddenly she was there. The mysterious woman spoke in my mind: "If you stop thinking, you will no longer suffer. Stop thinking."

Annoyed, I wanted to ask "why?" but she anticipated my question and came back: "You will learn, Bob and you will be free."

Free? I had heard that before? Old Great-Grandmother Elen Egby in Reading. The seer. She had died eight years before, but this woman's voice was lighter. "Are you Elen?"

"The road ahead is yours. Tread softly," she said. Then she was gone.

Immediately upon my return to the radar unit I stunned everyone by putting in a request for a local release and a flight back to Cyprus. Peter Dance and my friends asked scores of questions about Cyprus and the woman I had met. In March the gharries came for the men of Draft #344 to start their journey to Britain. All my RAF friends, including Peter Dance, said their farewells.

Peter had his extensive shell collection and photos, stowed away carefully. They journeyed to Port Said and caught the S.S. Empire Windrush bound for England. A week or so later we were horrified to learn that on March 29th 1954 the Windrush had caught fire at the western end of the Mediterranean and everyone was forced to abandon ship. No lives were lost but Peter lost his collection of shells and my set of photographs. He still mentions it to this day. In fact in his 2005 book "Out of My Shell: A Diversion for Shell Lovers" Peter includes a drawing recreating one of the photos I took in the desert near El Firdan. The gutted ship eventually sank the next day while being towed to Gibraltar. Somehow I had avoided the disaster.

Squadron Leader J. F. Cowe was signing my Certificate of Service and he peered across the desk at me: "After that Windrush thing, I must say the gods must be looking after you young fellow." No lives had been lost in the Windrush fire but I recalled the words: "The road ahead is yours. Tread softly." Perhaps there was something up there, beyond our thinking, beyond our consciousness. I would have to think about it.

That summer while waiting for October, the folk at 751 Signals Unit said I could work in the office if I typed unit memos, notices and letters. This gave me an opportunity to write some short stories which were never published and every two or three days I wrote to dearest Iro in Cyprus.

In September they gave me thirty days end-of-service leave and a one-way ticket to Cyprus. As I sat on the plane I read the Squadron Leader's comments on my Service Record. "A pleasant personality. I recommend Egby for any position in civilian life which calls for loyalty, cooperation and tact. He has also had considerable broadcasting experience having been assigned to the Forces Broadcasting Service for close to 12 months, seven months of which were spent in Cyprus."

As the aircraft headed out over the perfectly blue Mediterranean I gazed back and said: "Goodbye Egypt. It's been interesting knowing you." My big regret is that I never climbed the pyramids or swam in the Blue Lagoon of Lake Timsah at Ismalia. Little did I know that in less than two years the Cosmic Forces would have me back in the Suez Canal Zone under completely different circumstances.

5

LOVE AND SPIRITS IN APHRODITE'S REALM

E URIPIDES, THE LARGELY misunderstood Greek poet, put it this way:

Love hath an Island, and I would be there;
Love hath an Island and nurtureth there
For men the Delights, the beguilers of care,
Cyprus, Love's Island and I would be there.

In normal times the island of Cyprus is considered one of the most beautiful and romantic places in the world. Iro bought me a delightful book which we both enjoyed, "A Cottage in Kyrenia" by Franklin Lushington. It gave valuable insights into life in a beautiful Cypriot harbor own. Overall on Cyprus there is an unforgettable loveliness, an aura of simplicity radiating from it. The cluster of sun baked sandy brown mountains reaching like fingers into the soft, white woolly clouds, graceful, slender fir trees draping the slopes, clear bubbling streams winding their ways through narrow gorges and gushing over rocks in seemingly mad abandonment.

Combine all of this with quaint, ages-old villages scattered along dusty tracks winding their way through the countryside, and you have some idea of the Cyprus countryside in the mid-1950s. The occasional Byzantine monastery is perched on a craggy hilltop, while in the vineyards plump blue-black grapes thrive and beyond there are patchwork quilts of fields with olive, orange and lemon trees. You may often see an elderly farmer with two oxen drawing a wooden plough tilling a field. Many villages have their Greek orthodox churches and some have tall minarets over the tops of Moslem mosques. Sometimes there is an incongruity, an indicator of a turbulent past: a Moslem minaret dominating the top of a Christian church. It was little wonder the Greek Cypriots had an inbred fear and hatred for the Turkish Cypriots. The root cause dates back to the 16th century.

It happened in 1570 and 1571 when the Turkish Ottomans invaded the island and ousted the current occupational forces, the Venetians. This is about the nicest and cleanest way one can describe the inhuman brutality and massacre of Venetians and their allies at Nicosia and Famagusta. Sir George Hill writes a vivid description in his book "The History of Cyprus." Hill reports that 76,000 people living in Nicosia were systematically slaughtered or enslaved and thousands more suffered the same fate the next year in Famagusta. Under Ottoman rule many Christian churches were erased and others, including the Cathedral of St. Sophia in Nicosia were converted to mosques, hence the minarets.

It was from this invasion that the Turks dominated Cyprus until the British took over towards the end of the 19th century. Over the years, the Greek Cypriot population evolved to about 400,000 and the Turkish Cypriot population was 100,000. This was the situation when I arrived that day in the fall of 1954 from Suez, to start a new life.

BACK BEHIND THE MIKE AGAIN

Leaving a protected existence in the armed forces is not an easy experience. I found I had to create a living, find a place to live and pay rent, and pay for food. All this had been taken care of in the Royal Air Force. Now I was alone. My relationship with Iro, while loving, was not advanced enough for marriage. While I had been away, Forces Broadcasting had made itself at home in the large, ornate stone building at Strovolos on the outskirts of Nicosia and a few hundred yards from Government House.

"You're a civilian now," said Redfers Browne. "The pay isn't much. But we are restricted, you know. If you were a UK based civilian under a War Office contract it would be different."

"How much?"

"Thirty-five pounds a month."

"When do I start?"

Next day I was back in the continuity chair. We went on the air with Billy Cotton's Band and "Wakey Wakey," followed by bright, middle of the road music and songs that included time checks and relays of the news from the General Overseas Service of the BBC.

After my shift, I went upstairs. Wendy Barnes suggested I write some feature programs thirty to sixty minutes using records interspersed with information. So I did a piece on Django Reinhardt, the European gypsy jazzman who had died the year before. Django had been a self-taught guitar player. As a teenager he lost the use of two fingers on his left hand in a caravan fire, yet he went on to become one of the most dazzling instrumentalists of the 20th century, playing with Stephane Grappelli and the Quintet of the Hot Club of France. Wendy liked it and assigned me to write other features.

I found a room near Metaxas Square, which is the Piccadilly of Nicosia for £10 a month. It was a ten minute walk to Iro's place. "You're going to starve on that salary," she announced. "Come and have dinner." Efterpi made another of her delightful fasollias. She also cooked rye bread and a slice of that was a meal in itself. As an afterthought she fried some halloumi goat cheese. I knew if I ate like this I would put on lots of weight. It was pleasant but I didn't want obvious handouts. Greek Cypriots are notoriously overwhelming when they care for a person.

BECOMING A PAID PHOTOGRAPHER

One day Iro introduced me to an American photographer, Claude Jacoby who was on assignment for the Saturday Evening Post magazine. He was going to photograph Archbishop Makarios and offered to take me along. Makarios while being head of the Greek Orthodox Church in Cyprus was a fire starter, an agitator, a political personality with high ambitions. While working at FBS I had a chance to meet a couple of officials from the Colonial Office and they were convinced Makarios was directing a campaign to get school students from the PanCyprian Gymnasium to frequently stage demonstrations. So I leapt at the opportunity to meet this man and carried Jacoby's camera equipment.

At the Archbishopric the secretary Mr. Pascalides stared at me. "Is your assistant English?"

"Nah!" said Claude nonchalantly. "He's one of us. His accent's a big off though." The photographer flashed a grin. "He's a writer too."

Inside the Archbishop's chambers, Jacoby told Makarios he would photograph him informally and asked him to continue his work. Several people came in and went, bringing papers. A young boy brought in a tray of tea and some sugared fruit. Makarios didn't take any, neither did Jacoby, but I did.

Then Jacoby mentioned to the Archbishop that he had just been in Boston and Makarios suddenly came to life. He mentioned names of people and places because he had lived there. Jacoby keyed in.

"So what is all this talk about Enosis, the Union of Cyprus with Greece? The Archbishop's countenance changed, like an actor on stage switching characters. Suddenly there was smoldering indignation in his eyes. His hands clenched the desk. Jacoby snapped the picture. Makarios lifted a hand with a finger pointing upwards. "Cyprus will be free from the Colonial yoke. We will be reunited with Greece. Mark my words. It is written." Jacoby's camera clicked again.

As we walked back to the taxi and Jacoby pushed his equipment into the trunk, he pushed me into the cab and said: "You see, when you are working with a celebrity play it smooth, nice and easy. When you're ready, say a trigger word and be ready to take the pictures. The trigger was Enosis."

THE FOUNDER AND PUBLISHER: Iacovos Iacovides, better known to many friends and colleagues as "Jacko" founded the Cyprus Mail in 1945. The author took this picture at the 40th anniversary in 1985.

Enosis! The word meant "Union" and in this case it was the Greek Cypriot call to get out from the British colonial yoke. Union with Greece. Victor Bodker, who had been a journalist in Berlin and watched the rise of Hitler, said he could not understand Enosis. "Why this island wants to come under an impoverished country like Greece, beats me."

"Why don't they shoot for independence?" I asked. "The Independent Republic of Cyprus."

Bodker huffed and stared scornfully. "Never happen! It will never happen," he retorted. "Britain will never let them go. Mark my words. These scoundrels need a thrashing." Old Victor wrote an editorial which reflected this stubborn colonial attitude. His view was greeted by other colonials, but publisher Iacovos Iacovides - known affectionately as "Jacko" knew it was time to send him back to the United Kingdom. But it did not happen for a while and Victor stayed in the editor's chair.

He called me one day. "Pop over to the Museum and get some pictures. They are working on a restoration of a statue from Salamis," he said. Salamis is the ancient city in eastern Cyprus, north of Famagusta that dates back over a thousand years BCE. It was the port visited by Paul and Barnabas. My story with pictures included an interview with one of the curators. Bodker was ecstatic and the Cyprus Mail published my work - and paid me!

Whenever I had time off from the radio station, I visited archeological digs and excavations in the Nicosia region. The work received a good play in the Cyprus Mail but my articles mailed to Britain were rejected. However,

Paul Popper, a picture agency in London took several of my pictures and sent me a check. Money was flowing! I guessed I had become a professional photographer.

APHRODITE'S WINE IN THE MOUNTAINS

One day, Paul Popper telexed with an order. A client needed photos of Kolossi Castle near Limassol, all expenses paid. I hired a taxi and took Iro along. Kolossi had been a fortress originally built in the 13th century and then rebuilt in 1454 by the controversial Hospitallers, the Knights of the Order of St. John of Jerusalem. After I had taken various photographs, we wandered hand in hand through the different passageways and paused to look through castle openings and windows. Iro watched me and finally asked: "What's wrong, Bob?"

"This place," I started to say... "This place has some strange feelings," I said. "I don't know how to describe it, but I feel there are other people here besides us. I cannot see them. I just feel a presence here."

Iro took my arm. "It's strange you should say that. I have the same impression. They do say some of these old castles are haunted." She looked into my face with her dark, flashing eyes. "Do you believe in God? Do you believe in the Afterlife?"

There was a moment of silence. "I'm working on that. I keep on getting the feeling that somebody in Heaven is beating on my door, sending me messages. But it could be my imagination. I imagine a lot of things." I shook my head doubtfully. "And you dear Iro. How would you answer your questions?"

She paused; her dark eyes suddenly became distant. "How do you say? In Greek it is Mystikismos? I think I am a mystic," she said pensively. "I have always had the yearning to be a Trappist in a monastery. They live in silence, you know. But that is not practical, so I am inclined to be a mystic," she said. "God, the Creator is everywhere, even the air we breathe." She stooped to pick a wild flower. "God is even in this flower. Do you understand?"

I gazed at the flower in her hand. "You've just broken God's neck," I observed drily.

She ignored my attempt at humor. "God is everywhere. You will understand one day."

"You are way ahead of me, dearest Iro." For a moment I turned away, and then turned back. "Iro, I really don't know what the Fates have in store for me, but things just happen as if someone is laying a path, a road before me.

One thing I know is that I would like to have you in my life." I took her hand and gazed into her eyes. "Will you marry me?"

"Ah! You are mad!" she said with a short laugh. "Don't you know I'm old enough..."

"Hell! I'm not interested if you are a goddess three thousand years old. You are right for me," I shot back.

"Oh, such brave talk! You must have Greek blood. You are wild and impetuous. A crazy man. Mad! But I am mad too. So, yes, let us get married."

Early in December 1954 at the Commissioner's Office in Nicosia we were married and at Iro's suggestion we went into the beautiful and majestic Troodos Mountains which are in the center of the island. Mount Olympus is the highest point at almost 2,000 meters or 6,500 feet. In winter it is snow-capped. A Gavrelides taxi took us up the winding, tortuous road and dropped us at the Forest Park Hotel at Platres. The manager told us that among his visitors had been King Farouk of Egypt and Daphne du Maurier, the British writer of the novel "Rebecca" had lived here for a while.

Situated in a place of astounding beauty among magnificent forests of cedars and firs with mountain peaks that seemed to be holding up the blue sky, it was a place where time stands still. We spent seven days wandering along the pine-needled trails, soaking in the aromas of the ancient cedars and sitting by dancing mountain streams gurgling over rocks. The area was still home to shepherds with flocks of peculiarly fat-tailed sheep and farmers growing fruits.

We bought some grapes and haloumi, a delightful goat cheese, and sat by a mountain spring and allowed the grapes to wash and cool in the flowing water before eating them. The taste was out of this world. Iro opened a bottle of Aphrodite, a much under-rated crisp and lively Cyprus white wine. And it was in this strange almost ethereal atmosphere that we made love and lived as if there was no tomorrow. For me it was indeed Aphrodite's Realm.

But our time, our honeymoon at Troodos was ending, and as the taxi came to collect us, the first snows of winter were falling on the high peaks. Little did I know this was an omen and I should recall the advice from a distant seer in Reading: The road ahead is yours. Tread softly."

It was from this time on that I lived in Iro's old, stately sandstone and very comfortable house among the trees off the Larnaca Road. She gave me a comfortable place for a home office where I started my collection of books and camera equipment. Her mother, Efterpi was a great cook and she kept us well fed.

THE KING OF BELLAPAIS

On quiet days a good journalist or news photographer works the beat - that is he or she visits contacts, people they know who have their ear to the ground. One such place I used to visit was the Public Information Office, or the PIO. The man heading the service was Lawrence Durrell who later penned The Alexandria Quartet and numerous other works. He had been teaching at the Nicosia High School, the PanCyprian Gymnasium and had recently quit as tension and hostilities in the classrooms became evident.

"I'm working on a Cyprus book," he told me as he gazed out of the window at people and cars passing by. "There is a part of old Cyprus with which I became enamored, but it's changing. I don't think I can watch it happen. It hurts dreadfully." Larry - everyone knew him as Larry - would publish his Cyprus experiences under the title "Bitter Lemons."

"One of these days I would like to write a book – a novel," I told him. "I sense I have a lot to learn. It's coming at me from all sides."

"Never stop learning," he said. "Stagnation is the curse of the masses."

"How do you write a best-seller?" I asked innocently, and suddenly wished I had kept my mouth closed.

"You write for grade six, the eleven and twelve year olds," he replied. "Best sellers are written for grade six which means everyone can read it." He sank his hands into the pocket of his tweedy jacket. "That's why none of my books will be true best-sellers, popular among the elite, the academics, the literary students, but not the grade sixes."

A phone buzzed and his secretary called. "Government House!"

Larry took my arm to the door. "You know where I live – Bellapais? Tomorrow night I'm having a few friends over. It'll soon be Christmas. Come and bring Iro."

Startled. "You know? We only just got married."

Durrell grinned. "I know everything!"

There must have been fifty people at the Durrell home that flanked the village of Bellapais and the half ruined monastery known as Bellapais Abbey. This is wonderfully perched high on the Kyrenia Mountain Range and on a clear day one can see clearly the coast of Turkey. It was a writer's paradise and I wished I could have lived there.

The pre-Christmas party was attended by a motley crew of Britons, Armenians, Egyptians, and Turkish Cypriots, some media, and several women of various nationalities. There were no Greek Cypriots present except Iro, which was an ominous sign. Iro felt a little uncomfortable, so we left early.

Larry's days on Cyprus would end abruptly in the summer of 1955 after he received several threats on his life. His successor at the PIO was as different to Larry as black is to white. Leslie Glass looked and sounded professional, and as I was to learn from the Americans, a "spin-doctor." He was efficiency plus. Upon reflection, these were the qualities needed for the job of running public information for colonial Cyprus.

6

THE GODS OF WAR
COME OUT TO KILL

O N SATURDAY, DECEMBER 18th 1954, we were planning to go to Kyrenia and have lunch at the famous Harbour Club, but it was not to be. News broke overnight that the United National General Assembly in far off New York was upholding the political Committee's decision "not to consider further" Greece's request that the principle of self-determination be applied to Cyprus. The vote was an overwhelming fifty in favor, none against with eight abstentions. It was political dynamite.

The Greek Cypriot newspapers bannered the news in heavy black type. One even bordered the front page in black. The all-powerful trade unions called for an island-wide strike. Everything froze, except the mob. Essential services were ordered to keep operating, but anyone defying the strike order would sooner or later face angry and violent demonstrators. By mid-morning thousands of young people, mostly students were thronging Ledra Street and Metaxas Square chanting En-o-sis! En-o-sis! En-o-sis! Many carried large white and blue Greek flags and banners that called for Union with Greece.

Remember, you're English," warned Iro as I left to take pictures. Her face was white and drawn. A number of photographers, mostly Greek Cypriots, were moving around on the outskirts. I attached myself to them. A screaming mob came down the narrow street like a monster. A British owned and operated store was the target. Sticks smashed windows followed by rocks. The owner came out screaming and protesting. When rioters beat him with sticks, he wisely sought refuge in a cold storage locker. Later he emerged bruised and angry. "I've had enough of this shit! Where are the police? I'm heading back to Blighty."

By keeping a low profile, popping into hotel doorways and alleyways, I managed to get photos and stay safe. Signs advertising British and America goods were smashed by the mob, and the Cyprus Government's Tourist Office lost over a hundred windows.

The police arrived at noon in the shape of a hard-hatted baton squad made up mainly of Turkish Cypriot police and directed by British officers. A nasty battle royal ensued. The police were untrained and not familiar with riots. The stones pelted down like heavy rain. The police withdrew and shortly afterwards returned with tear gas. The shells landed in several places at once. Youngsters started coughing and choking as the gas caused irritation to the eyes, mouth, throat, lungs, and skin. The crowds fled to side streets and alleyways. By late afternoon, the battle subsided and everyone went home.

Iro and her mother greeted me at the door. "What is that awful smell?" asked Iro sniffing my shirt. I told her about the tear gas, the smashing of shops and the Englishman.

"You need to grow a beard," she said suddenly. "It would be safer."

Some months before, I had mentioned the idea but had declined it. Iro's argument was sound. "British servicemen are generally clean shaven. A beard would distinguish that you are not one of them." So I grew a beard and when I could not stand a face full of hair, I trimmed it into a good sized goatee - recognizable but small. Little did I think then, it would stay with me for forty years.

GETTING TO KNOW THE CYPRUS MEDIA

During that winter I made friends with the Greek Cypriot Press Corps. Felix Yiaxis, who as a freelance photographer and cine-photographer, serviced Associated Press and Movietone News. There were two other photographers, Phanos Smart and a man known simply as Demetrakis – Photo Demetrakis. They were a good bunch to hang out with.

The Cyprus Mail offices and presses were in an alley off Ledra Street, the main thoroughfare in the walled city. Victor Bodker was still holding forth as editor, and Jacko was the publisher. The assistant editor Doug Grant had a peculiar sense of humor, especially when under stress. Yangos, Jacko's brother, was in charge of advertising and administration.

Downstairs was the press, an enormous flatbed which produced the daily newspaper. I always thought of it as a steam locomotive. The pressmen were mostly Greek and Armenian. They operated everything including a flock of noisy Linotypes. These one-operator printing machines for setting type date back to the 1860s. Their advent revolutionized the newspaper world. The man or woman sits and works a keyboard, much like a typewriter. The machine is adjusted for font and size and makes a lot of clicking as the type drops into lines, which gave it the name Linotype. The end result is a page of type embedded in molten metal flowing at about 550 degrees Fahrenheit. Needless to say the press room was always warm, smoky and quite noisy.

Rumors were rampant that the Greek Cypriot "Enosis" was growing. Minor altercations occurred in the streets, schools and coffee shops. The Archbishop made frequent fiery speeches and delivered stirring sermons in various churches. But it was at Paphos on the south-west corner of the island that signaled real trouble was lurking ahead.

A PRELUDE TO WAR

January 25th 1955, a 100-ton Greek caique, a white wooden sailing boat equipped for fishing appeared off the coast. Named Ayios Georghios or "Saint George" in English, it weaved its way into a dark and isolated cove near Paphos. Eight Greek Cypriots from Chlorakas village were waiting with a small boat to take off the cargo. As they worked, Cypriot police and British troops responding to a tip, surrounded the cove and arrested everyone on the shore.

The Ayios Georghios promptly fled to the safety of the open sea but was intercepted by a Royal Navy corvette, HMS Comet. But even as navy personnel boarded the caique, the cargo was dumped overboard. Navy frogmen retrieved the load of arms, ammunition and explosives—enough to start a small war. The incident and trial went by generally unnoticed by the international media. No one, it seems, took seriously the anger and discontent smoldering in Aphrodite's Realm.

A strange silence draped itself over Nicosia. The news media almost went into hibernation with nothing to do, nowhere to go, nothing to think about except sit on the porch, sip Cyprus brandy sours and eat souvlakis. We puffed endlessly on State Express cigarettes made on the island. No one seemed to be aware of the dangers of smoking in those days. Anyway, we all sensed there were other dangers lurking in the ancient bastions. The Ayios Georghios incident was a prelude to war. A symptom. The writing was on the wall.

Preparations that had lasted for months, even years, were complete. Caches stashed with pistols, revolvers, rifles, shot-guns, Brens, Stens, light machine guns, bombs, grenades, mines, dynamite, TNT, fuses, detonators and instruction books were full. The leaders were ready to deal out death, destruction, intimidation and violence. These were the actions they believed would free Cyprus from her so-called "colonial slavery."

THE FIGHT BEGINS WITH BOMB BLASTS

On the afternoon of Wednesday, March 31st 1955 the order went out to saboteurs. Telephones could not be trusted, so couriers in fast cars delivered the leader's orders to strike certain targets. The leader was an aging George Grivas, a retired Greek Army colonel, Markarios had imported from Athens. He was to be known as Dighenis the Leader. In recent months he had secretly recruited a team of freedom fighters, men such as Gregoris Afxentiou who was seen on the first night, then not seen again until surrounded on the rain-soaked Troodos Mountains.

I had worked the evening shift at the broadcasting station and decided to walk home alongside Alan Robson. As I left him at the Cosmopolitan Club, we both remarked that the night was eerily quiet. Not even a dog barked and cars on the roads seemed fewer than usual. It was eleven-forty-five when I reached home and Iro was still up. We had cups of hot cocoa together and were just thinking of going to bed, when the silence was ripped by several heavy and prolonged explosions which echoed through the buildings. Windows vibrated. Dogs started barking in chorus. Efterpi shouted from her bedroom. Iro turned white.

My first reaction: "Someone's bombing Nicosia Airport." The sounds were reminiscent of wartime bombs.

"It sounds like fuel tanks exploding," Iro cried, as she rushed to the front door and peered anxiously into the darkness.

In two minutes I was dressed and out on the sidewalk armed with camera and electronic flash. All down Larnaca Road shutters were open and faces peering out. People called to one another in tight, fearful voices. I ran up the street. Alex Eftyvoulou, a Greek Cypriot reporter working for a British weekly, was reversing out of his driveway.

"It's Wolseley Barracks," he cried. "Get in."

Alex drove his old British Morris Minor as if chased by devils, tearing round corners, seemingly on two wheels. We screeched to a stop outside the closed iron gates of the barracks. A military policeman, holding a small handgun, stopped us. "Sorry, no admittance."

What's happened?" we asked in chorus.

"Nothing!" he retorted, seemingly oblivious of the smoldering building in the background, clouds of smoke billowing into the night sky and soldiers, shouting and running about trying to organize water hoses.

"So what the hell is that burning hole in the roof?" I cried out.

"Nothing!"

Just then a military fire engine hurtled down the street and the policeman opened the gates for it to enter. We trotted alongside the blind side and got to the fire. I started accumulating great shots of the firemen when Colonel Tiger White, the Army PR snared and pushed us into a lit doorway. As he did so, a three-ton army truck packed with armed troops careened in and stopped. Armed soldiers spread out in all directions creating a security guard round the barracks. A sergeant ordered more troops to search the grounds and the barracks themselves. Someone cried out that the radio signals section at the back was badly damaged and burning.

"Tiger, who did this?"

"Wrong question!" snapped the colonel easily. "You men should really be at the broadcasting station. There's real trouble there."

"Forces Broadcasting?" I suggested.

"Good Lord, no! The Cypriot outfit. Cyprus Broadcasting at Athalassa on the Larnaca Road."

A RADIO STATION ABLAZE

Moments later we were in the Morris Minor hurtling back through Nicosia. I knew the Cyprus Broadcasting was only a couple of years old and was providing programs in Greek, Turkish and English. Several times I had been called upon by its English news director to freelance and read the evening news, so I was well aware of the building. As we soared up the hill towards the studio, we sped past the lumbering Nicosia Fire Brigade's heavy truck. Alex had no time for speed limits, or fire engines, when going to a story.

The night sky was Dante's inferno. The whole of the studio block was ablaze. Spiraling columns of black and gray smoke fingered the night sky. A large sound-proof orchestra studio, one of the finest in the Middle East, was completely gutted, leaving only a skeleton framework, smoldering beams that protested in the night sky. Civilians, Cyprus police and British troops continued to arrive and strove to prevent flames from spreading to other buildings. It soon became obvious that the main building including all the studios, control room and recording stages were gutted and useless. Still, in the face of defeat some hardy workers braved fire-filled corridors to rescue movable radio equipment and furniture and frequently came out with their clothes on fire.

The heat was so great that while we were photographing firefighters and radio station employees frantically salvaging equipment, our clothes and hair were being singed, a phenomenon we failed to notice until next day.

From talking to everyone involved including the security guards, we pieced together what had happened.

Just before 12.30 a.m. a gang of six men, all masked and carrying firearms, had taken the security night watchmen at the studio entrance by surprise. The elderly guards were bound and gagged. The invaders had set a circle of dynamite round the studios and generator rooms and detonated simultaneously. The explosion brought the roof crashing down, snapping and shorting out electrical points that triggered the devastating fire. The attackers flittered away just as quickly as they had come, leaving the two terrified watchmen tied up in the security hut.

A British military explosives expert told us next day that the explosives were professionally set. The Colonial administration revealed that the attackers had been led by a one-time Greek soldier, Gregoris Afxentiou. Police and British security forces were alerted all over the island. Two years later, I was to be on a wet, lonely mountainside when Afxentiou was surrounded in a bunker.

A MESSAGE FROM DIGHENIS

It was a long night. We were sitting in Alex's car parked in Metaxas Square discussing the night's events. The grey light of dawn was heralding another day. Suddenly a small car raced across the square and hurtled off down Ledra Street leaving a shower of strips of paper in its wake. Under his car headlights Alex read and translated the message.

> *"With God's help, with faith in our honest struggle, with the support of Hellenism, and with the support of the Cypriots, we undertake the Struggle to get rid of the English Yoke, with the slogan our fore-fathers left us: Bring back your shields or fall on them. Greeks wherever you are, Listen to Our Voice. Forward together for the Liberty of Cyprus."* It was signed: *"E.O.K.A. The Leader, Dighenis."*

"You know what the date is, Alex?"

"April 1st 1955," he said. "I sense this is no April Fool's joke."

Over breakfast I spent almost an hour explaining to Iro what had happened during the night, and she in turn translated for Efterpi, then I got into bed and slept. Early afternoon Iro woke me with the news that Colonial government installations, offices and police stations in Limassol, Larnaca and

Famagusta had been bombed, some fifty incidents in all. Luckily no one had been killed, which seemed like a miracle.

The Cyprus Mail used some of my photos under a banner headline, "Dynamiters Start Operations in Cyprus" and I immediately telexed the agency editor in London but he replied "There are rumors Winston Churchill is retiring. Airmail them to us." This was depressing. They had taken several of my archeological pictures and got them printed in several magazines, but the checks that came through were unimpressive so I had to find a new photo service.

It bothered Iro to see me this way, sitting on news pictures that should be selling to more than just the Cyprus Mail. During lulls in the news, she insisted we visit places she enjoyed. One was at Kyrenia. Famously known and loved as the Harbour Club, it was a quaint little bar and restaurant run by a charming husband and wife team who knew everybody and everything. The wife was better known as Judy Shirley, who had been a vocalist with Geraldo and his Orchestra in England and fans visiting Cyprus used to make a beeline for the Club just to see her. When we arrived, the place was full of British expatriates bemoaning the rising number of bombing incidents.

"These scoundrels should be thrashed within an inch of their lives," cried a pompous old man with the air of a retired military officer. It was a wild and woolly gathering of Britons from another age. We left.

"They don't even realize that colonies are things of the past," said Iro as we walked along the harbor road, and dived into a Greek Cypriot bistro and ordered a meze and glasses of Cyprus wine. "Look at the Mau-Mau in Kenya, riots in Singapore, and in West Africa the nationalists in the old colonies are all crying – give us our freedom. It's happening here."

"This is relatively new in Cyprus," I said.

"Not really," she came back. "Cypriot nationalists burned down Government House in 1931. It is not good here. It's going to get worse."

THE COSMOS IS LISTENING

Douglas Grant, Bodker's assistant editor who started life in Portsmouth, England, had arrived in Cyprus a few months before me, but he had daily newspaper experience from working in Britain. He enjoyed smoking a pipe, and lit or unlit, it was always dangling from his mouth. "The thing for you, Bob, is to get in touch with the big Fleet Street agencies. That's where the excitement is. That's where the money is. You have the enthusiasm and you're developing good journalistic skills."

"Most of the London papers and agencies have stringers here," I said.

Doug paused, grabbed a piece of paper and wrote the name and address of a big photo agency in London and pushed it into my hand. "Try these people. They don't have anyone here. I don't guarantee they will jump for you, but try."

My hopes soared and I airmailed a letter. Every day I stood waiting for a reply. Ten days went by before the mailman delivered a reply. I tore it open eagerly. Crash! My hopes evaporated in two seconds..."unable to use your services...we will notify you if an opportunity comes up." Eighteen months later as I was going to the Suez War, they actually called me and I had some measure of delight in saying, "Sorry, I'm all booked up."

But that was in the future. Now, I was really down. I sat in the darkroom at the Cyprus Mail and felt totally miserable. A little voice inside me kept saying: "Failure! Failure!" but another voice, not inside me, manifested itself in the darkroom walls. "The Cosmos is listening. The Cosmos is now." It was that woman's voice again. Somehow I pulled myself together, grabbed my camera and went upstairs. It was Sunday. A Cyprus Mail pressman just coming to work called out: "Bob, you have a visitor."

A man with a light khaki linen jacket, checkered shirt, and a rounded face with dark thinning hair walked in. "Dennis Oulds, staff photographer, Central Press Photos, London. I'm hoping you can help me."

Stunned, I stared at him in amazement. I didn't realize it until years later. There had been another kink in the Universe.

LEARNING FROM A FLEET STREET PRO

Dennis Oulds had just flown in from London and needed someone to show him around and make introductions on the British, Greek and Turkish Cypriot sides. "One other point, if you know of a freelance cameraman who hasn't any ties, we could certainly use him."

In this way my life changed. During the several weeks Dennis and I travelled all over the island and by sheer accident we were on the scene in Famagusta when rioting broke out. It was as if the event happened to order.

Dennis had acquired some good shots, and that taught me a lot. "Never take a picture unless you can see it in print," he once told me. He sported a Speed Graphic, a beautiful camera. I had a Rollieflex.

Back in the office Douglas Grant and I were having tea and sharing experiences with Dennis. The phone rang and Doug took the message.

"Somebody's strung a banner across the walls at Metaxas Square," he said softly. That was Douglas, pure cool.

The Venetians during their occupation had encircled Nicosia with massive walls and bastions. It was almost dark and already there was a throng of people, mainly youngsters in the square. Street lights dimly illuminated the heavy black letters on white canvas: "Go Home English. We will fight to the last man to free our beloved country from your yoke." It was signed E.O.K.A.

Opening my camera I started taking pictures. Out of nowhere a gangly teenager with a jutting jaw blocked my path. "English spy," he cried. "English spy. We should kill him now."

A REPORTER NAMED NICOS

When some wild teenager starts yelling to a crowd of potential rioters that you are a spy and should be killed, well, that shakes one's total existence. A bolt of fear streaked through my body. Doug and Dennis had disappeared and there were no other journalists in sight. Worse, I appeared to be the only Englishman in the square. My knees felt like jelly. I hoped they would help me run. The gangly teenager came back: "He's a spy. Kill him."

Just then a young Greek Cypriot with a strong angular face and carrying a notebook came swinging in and shouted at the gangly youth to shut up in Greek. I sensed he was scolding the kid for harassing me. Relieved to see this threat disappear and thankful that no one in the crowd had responded, I mustered a tight smile at the newcomer.

The fellow carrying a notebook turned out to be a reporter with Philelftheros, the Greek Cypriot newspaper. "Nicos. Call me Nicos. My family name is Sampson."

I didn't know who he was but I appreciated him being there.

"Come on, don't try your luck much longer," he said, steering me through the crowd to a nearby oasis where he treated me to a coffee.

"You got the pictures okay?"

I nodded. "Thanks very much. It's much appreciated."

"It was nothing," he added with a shrug. "Perhaps one day you can teach me how to take good photos."

He turned out to be a very likable, intelligent young man – twenty one years old. He told me he detested communists for what they had done to his father, but he never elaborated on that. Finishing his coffee he disappeared into the night.

People were standing on the terrace of the Nicosia Palace as I pushed through looking for Dennis.

"Mr. Oulds? He's gone out," said the desk man. I walked down the street and almost collided with Doug Grant who was standing in the shadows talking with Daily Mail foreign correspondent Ralph Izzard, who two years before had climbed to the 18,000 foot mark on Everest wearing gym-shoes while covering the famous Edmund Hilary expedition.

A policeman attempted to remove the banner and that drove the crowd into a frenzy. There were now several thousand people in the area. The crowd threw stones at street lamps, and one youth scaled a flagpole and hauled down the Union Jack. Cheering youths stamped on it and moments later it was burning. The crowd wanted bigger and better things.

I was itching to get a picture. "If you go down there now," cried Doug shaking his pipe, "you won't need a funeral, because there will be nothing to bury. Take your time. There will be plenty of pictures later when the security forces come in."

THE WRATH OF THE CROWD

The crowd seemed to cool down after the flag-burning and an hour later when the Security Forces arrived, it was a meager showing. A solitary Land Rover, with an officer and two military policemen. They tried to get through the crowd on Evagoras Avenue but youths defiantly blocked the path, and started jumping on the steel fender at the front.

The British trio realizing their mistake, attempted to back off, but was again blocked. The driver sounded the horn. That was fatal. A youth threw a stone at the driver. It hit him in the back and he doubled over the wheel. The officer jumped out of the vehicle and drew his pistol. The driver, in panic, stepped on the accelerator, and charged the crowd. The crowd went berserk. The three men hastily evacuated the vehicle and with guns drawn, escaped down an alley. So much for security forces intervention.

The enraged crowd flipped the vehicle over and petrol poured out from the tank. In a moment, someone threw a lighted match and woof! Flames engulfed the vehicle. I caught up with Dennis Oulds, who was down the street by the British Institute Building. Ralph Izzard was nearby, Colin Reed of the Daily Express and several other reporters were observing from a distance.

I moved back up the street and found Alex standing between the Grecian pillars of a Greek Cypriot Cinema. I changed the film in my camera and bravely decided to move closer to the burning Land Rover. It was bravery without wisdom. Being young and still a tyro, I had not learned that it was unwise to take rioters faces when perpetrating criminal acts.

My flash instantly illuminated the scene. Frenzied Greek Cypriot youths dancing around the burning British vehicle froze instantly. Upon reflection, I don't think any of them could be identified, but they were not me. They were a crowd angered by a British colonial government and they wanted to destroy anything and everything in sight. And now that included me.

Two Greek Cypriot youths immediately accosted me. Alex tried to help but wisely pulled back. A stack of boxed Coca-Cola bottles on the steps of the cinema instantly became weapons. A bottle hurtled through the night and smashed on the column behind me. Another flipped off my shoulder. Inspired by an overwhelming fear, I raced down an alley flanking the cinema and came out onto Larnaca Road. I could hear shouting and wild taunts echoing from all areas. Bottles were crashing all around as I ran through the night.

As I raced through parked cars, a youth suddenly blocked my path. In sheer terror, I smashed my camera into his face and he fell down. One of the great things about the Rollieflex is they are heavy enough to make good weapons and still go on working. I slipped by and raced down Larnaca Road. My heart throbbed violently, my lungs wanted to explode. A brick came from somewhere and hit me in the ribs. I plunged into somebody's darkened garden and raced down a driveway, and came out on another road. I did not think the mob was after me. Still I kept running. I raced round another road and came back onto Larnaca Road right outside Iro's house. I could see rioters a couple of hundred yards away. I slipped into Iro's garden and threw myself under the bushes and tried not to breathe.

When all seemed quiet I was about to move when I heard someone behind me in the garden. It was Iro. "What on earth have you done?" she hissed as she helped me into the house.

"I took a picture at the wrong time," I said.

Blood was trickling down my face, my shirt was torn in several places, my right hand was cut, my chest was hurting from bricks and bottles, and my body was a bag of nerves.

"You're lucky to be alive," Iro said, as she cleaned my wounds.

AN OLD BRITISH SYMBOL BURNS

The telephone cracked the quiet. It was Douglas. "I heard what happened. Alex says you had a rough time. You were the only one to get a picture of the

Land Rover. It's out now." He paused then added: "Can you come over. The mob is attacking the British Institute."

The British Institute was a symbol of Britain and the Empire. An imposing building, it overlooked Metaxas Square and the D'Avila bastion.

"It's on fire. The whole building is going up," Doug continued. "Can you come over?" I could well imagine the scene. The old wooden building now tinder dry with age, could easily go up in flames. While its rooms were very interesting and picturesque, the Institute possessed a large comprehensive library, numerous historical records and documents, letters and various artifacts. Many Cypriot students had used the place to study.

Iro and her mother protested as I put on clean clothes and headed up the street towards Metaxas Square. Two fire engines and numerous firemen were struggling with hoses and shooting jets of water into the building but the old building was beyond all help. British troops were now in evidence and journalists were mingling among the crowds that had now become subdued. Dennis was busy taking pictures. Ralph Izzard of the Daily Mail had artfully fooled the rioters by adopting a traditional Cypriot habit of walking up and down the street pushing an old bicycle. He had seen everything.

"This is a disgrace," he said softly in his quiet, educated voice. "This business should have been squashed by the police when it started at seven o'clock and not at midnight by the troops."

"Why did the troops wait so long?"

Izzard shook his head. "Everyone who was anybody, the colonial big-wigs, the brass hats of the military were all hobnobbing at Government House with the Governor. There was no one to give orders!" Alex came by and butted in: "They were all attending a Battle of Britain anniversary party."

Monday morning's Daily Mail in London flashed a startling headline. "I'D SACK THE GOVERNOR FOR THIS." Ralph's story was powerful and correct, but the headline had been created by a foreign desk editor. People in Britain and Cyprus were shocked. Ralph went into the shadows of the Ledra Palace Hotel where many of the correspondents stayed. We didn't see him for several days. Many people were under the impression Ralph would be sent packing to Lebanon where he lived. But any embarrassment was not over.

Six days after the British Institute fiasco, the Governor of Cyprus, Sir Robert Armitage was replaced. Whitehall assigned the job of handling the rebellious island to a tough military man, Sir John Harding. Harding, a career officer had served in both World Wars. In World War II he had seen action in North Africa and Italy, and eventually succeeded General Alexander as commander of the British Forces in the Mediterranean. He became a Field

Marshall in 1953 and was assigned military governor of Cyprus on October 3rd 1955. He had 42 years of British Army experience.

Sir John was tough and he quickly shook the Island. Short in stature, he possessed a dynamic personality. In some ways he looked and sounded like an English version of James Cagney, He bravely predicted E.O.K.A.'s days were numbered and the British media loved it. In the days that followed his arrival, he implemented a State of Emergency and backed it up by importing more troops from Britain and other points around the world.

THE GOVERNOR FLEXES HIS MUSCLES

The Governor John Harding immediately started meetings with Archbishop Makarios, and after photographing the initial meeting, Cyprus went into a relatively quiet spell. International reporters were assigned stories in other countries.

One Friday morning, Nicos Sampson came into the Cyprus Mail. "You promised to teach me how to take photos," he said and produced a small Voigtlander Vito with 35mm black and white film. I spent an hour explaining focusing, depth of field, different uses of film, and how to pose and frame news pictures. He thanked me profusely and said he would tip me whenever he found a story.

It was a Friday and I walked to Regina Street for a haircut and a beard-trim. Coming out I wandered over to the Regina Cinema where "The Bridges of Toko-Ri" starring William Holden, Grace Kelly, Fredric March and Mickey Rooney was showing. It was based on the book by James Michener. Should I go in? I enjoyed reading Michener's works. While I was thinking, Nicos came up and invited me in. So we sat together and he was enthralled with the movie, particularly the role played by Rooney as a gutsy helicopter pilot. As we walked out Sampson said: "That was exciting. I'd like to be in a war - even just covering it." Years later, those words were going to come back and haunt me.

We walked up the street. A young man on a motor bike came skidding round the corner, spotted Sampson and braked in front of us. He spluttered out garbled Greek I couldn't understand. I stared at Sampson. "What's happening?"

"Makarious! The British have arrested him and flown him out of Cyprus."

The Archbishop had gone and nobody had a picture. The date was Friday, March 9th 1956. We subsequently discovered he had been exiled to the Seychelle Islands in the Indian Ocean.

E.O.K.A. RETALIATES AND SO DOES HARDING

Well, if the colonial government had expected a leaderless country to take things quietly, they were wrong. E.O.K.A. retaliated by killing policemen, collaborators, and bombing offices and restaurants where British people frequented. The situation deteriorated daily.

Harding retaliated with a bevy of harsh measures. Bomb explosions or shootings resulted in town curfews, schools were closed if there were anti-British activities, and detention camps – some people called them concentration camps – were opened. The old fortress of Kyrenia Castle was used, and a number of detainees escaped, which created a lot of criticism from British expatriates. So, Camp K was built and opened at Kokkinotrymithia, a few miles west of Nicosia.

Under the State of Emergency regulations the carrying of unlawful weapons, bombs, dynamite and incendiary devices by Cypriots carried the death penalty. Nine such executions took place behind the grim, high walls of Nicosia Prison. There were accusations of "flimsy" and "circumstantial" evidence leading to convictions in the Special Courts where trials were often seen as speedy, often with circumstantial or flimsy evidence leading to a conviction.

Michael Karaolis accused of killing a Cyprus policeman Erodutus Poullis, and Andreas Dimitriou accused of trying to kill an Englishman, were both found guilty and sentenced to death by hanging. The British Labour Party called for a reprieve, as did U.S. Secretary of State John Foster Dulles but John Harding was adamant that both men should be hanged. In response E.O.K.A. kidnapped a Lance Corporal Gordon Hill and Corporal Ronnie Shilton and carried out reprisals. Both were executed.

Dawn was breaking over Nicosia prisons when the executions of Karaolis and Dimitriou took place. Felix Yiaxis, Phanos Smart and myself photographed a picture of total agony and despair. A little old lady attired in black clothes with a black shawl over her head that partially covered her face, stood a short distance from the prison gates.

She clutched her breast with both hands as an Army officer came out and announced the deaths of the two young men. Michael Karaolis' mother gave a short gasp. It was as if her own life had left her. It was a big picture for Central Press Photos in London, the British media and it brought tears to my eyes. For the first time in my life I started feeling the true meaning of man's inhumanity to man. The executions triggered riots in Cyprus and Athens, and curfews were declared in Nicosia and other communities.

It was May 1956 and one could feel the clouds of war and its brother death, scudding across the skies. For this I would tread softly?

7

THE RIGORS OF
NEWS PHOTOGRAPHY

I S THERE ANY GLAMOUR in being a news photographer and a reporter covering foreign assignments? At one time in my early life the idea did appeal to me, but it did not last long. The vision was slowly and helplessly dashed by various elements. My relationship, my love life with Iro, was being sorely tried too. The constantly developing news situation frequently saw me rise at the crack of dawn and not return home until late in the evening. This flung an aura of sadness on both of us.

Upon reflection, 1956 was the most hectic existence of my life. Stark, memorable lessons would cut into my life like a flock of arrows. I had only been out of the protected life of the Royal Air Force for just over a year, and here I was living in a foreign country, married to a foreign lady, working as a news reporter and photographer in a culture with a people I barely knew and to cap it all, a state of war was brewing all around.

Early in the year I took a week off and flew off to England. Mum had written a letter admitting she and Dad were divorced, the house at 36 Edith Road had been sold, and she had rented rooms. "He finally went off with one of his lady friends, Barbara from the flower nurseries. That was a scandal there," she said when I arrived in Maidenhead. If anyone could be bitter, it was Mum. I sensed that Dad had cultivated various girl friends years before. When I was a young teenager cycling round gathering autographs from local celebrities, I came home and showed her the signature of Eva Moore, the star of The Old Dark House. On the next page was the signature of Eva's daughter, actress Jill Esmond who had once been married to Laurence Olivier.

Mother had stared at the signatures and as she returned the book to me, commented: "Did you see your father there?" It turned out that Dad had performed some electronic work for Eva Moore and had made several visits to the house when Miss Esmond was there. Now, in 1956, almost ten years later, Mum was still sorting out stuff from the Edith Road house so I enquired about my autograph book. "I remember, it got wet and fell apart, so I threw it out," was all she said quietly, as if she no longer cared.

I stayed for several days and failed to mention my marriage to Iro. I don't think Mum would have understood. My sister Diane was living with Mum and my other sister, Sheila, was away working. I returned to London and spent time exchanging briefs with John Lacey, editor at Central Press Photos in Gough Square, Fleet Street and Dennis Oulds. There's nothing like sitting in a Fleet Street pub after work and drinking English beer. It felt good, but I felt an overwhelming urge to be back to Cyprus and Iro.

Working as a freelance overseas has lots of pros and cons. If you are working a news hotspot, the most profitable function is to be a freelance. Staffers for most news organizations get very few bonuses for treading the avenues of war. As a freelance I would send packages of exposed film or developed negatives of bombings, killings, political events, riots, and even feature material via overnight air freight to London Airport. A Central Press courier on a motorcycle would pick them up and speed back to Gough Square. Central Press printed and distributed photos to various publications. Our agreement was on a fifty-fifty basis which seemed fair.

My news pictures appeared all over the place including such publications as the London Illustrated News, The Sphere, Paris Match, the New York Times, and of course many British newspapers up and down the country. I think the Daily Telegraph ran the most.

WORKING THE PICTURE BEAT

When a dramatic news event occurred, the fastest way to send photos in the 1950s was by radio transmission via Cable and Wireless. I had an office at the Cyprus Mail newspaper where I set up a darkroom. The deal was that the Cyprus Mail could use any of my photos in return for my using their offices. They even paid me a nominal sum for any pictures printed, which was good.

So when I had hot news photos I would rush back to the office, squeeze into the little darkroom, and process the film. As I related earlier, I used a Rolleiflex with 120 film and 12 exposures on a film. From time to time I would experiment with cameras picked up along the way. Jacko, the publisher, had a four by five cut film Linhof Technika which produced beautifully sharp pictures for features but was relatively useless in riots. I acquired an old Palmas camera which almost got me into a lot of trouble towards the end of my Cyprus days.

A SPECIAL NEWS MAN:
Felix Yiaxis was a dedicated news and newsreel photographer. He was always on the news watch, frequently leaving his wife to run his photo shop on Onasagoras Street. When Cyprus became a Republic it named him as the Father of Cyprus Photo-Journalism. Without a doubt, he was. Always a gentleman!

Most organized photographers develop film at 68 degrees Fahrenheit. Well, Cyprus was different. The developer, Kodak D-76 was some 80 degrees on a warm day and the acid fixer (hypo) was that too. Film was developed in 90 seconds, fixed in another 60 seconds, and dried in another minute. When time was of the essence, the processed film would be dunked in a tray of methelated spirits and held under a hair-dryer. This way one could dry a film in a couple of minutes. Pure hairy but in an emergency, well anything goes.

The negative slips into an enlarger and you make a print. For radio transmission the actual image had to be five by seven inches. Developed, fast fixed and fast washed, and printed, I would rush out to a Lambretta scooter, loaned to me by Jacko, and race like a mad person through narrow streets and alleyways to the Cable and Wireless offices in the heart of the old city. One hand held the handlebar and the other held the print for rapid drying by the breeze. I often wondered what I looked like. No one ever captured me on film.

The offices of Cable and Wireless originally flanked the main Nicosia post office, the law courts and bombs and riots were always happening in the vicinity of Attaturk Square, so they moved out to a guarded transmission station in a field near Nicosia Airport. Here they had a ten foot steel wire fence and a heavy metal gate. Photographers would arrive at the gate and call for the civilian security guard who always ambled at an infuriating snail's pace across the lot.

One day, my competitor Felix Yiaxis who serviced Associated Press, was already in the line-up when I arrived at the gate. For being first he would get a ten minute edge over my photo arriving in London. He desperately called to the guard to hurry up. Something in my mind spurred me to extraordinary action. I gripped the edge of the print between my teeth, and scaled the ten foot fence, tearing my pants. I fell down onto the grass, scrambled up and raced into the office.

Felix got so mad with me. "Do you have no sense of right or wrong?" He was such a gentleman he was unable to swear or curse. Although my photo got to London first, I always felt guilty about that incident. But my climbing the fence got me valuable minutes and gave Central Press the edge in getting my photo out to London's afternoon newspapers. Whenever I mentioned this to journalism students later in my life, it always triggered a deep discussion on ethics and morality. What would you do?

THE REAL REPORTERS

Photographers were the real reporters in Cyprus. The gathering point for the foreign media was the famous Ledra Palace hotel outside the walled city. Sometimes there would be a hundred reporters from a vast variety of countries gathered in the bar, all trying to fathom out what happened during the day.

To this end many of them would corner a photographer or newsreel cameraman returning from events, buy him or her a drink, and milk the cameraman for information. They would then write the story as if they had been on the scene. Luckily, some of the reporters, particularly the old-hands, actually did come to the scene of riots, political events and killings.

Most of the good reporters in those days were veterans of other conflicts such as the Spanish Civil War, World War II, the Korean War, the Communist-French conflicts in Indo-China and Kenya's Mau Mau situation, and had learned to stay in the safety of their hotels. Some like Dennis Martin of the Daily Mirror, Ralph Izzard of the Daily Mail, Geoff Thursby of the News

Chronicle, Keith Morfett and John King of the Daily Express, George Evans of the Daily Telegraph did get out and work beside photographers and I readily helped them. Vincent Ryder of the Telegraph was there too.

FOUR RESIDENT REPORTERS:
Among the resident reporting and photographing team was (l to r) Georges Der Parthogh of the Times of Cyprus; Bob Egby (the author) of the Cyprus Mail and Central Press Photos, London; Wally Kent who serviced several London newspapers; and Demetrakis, who provided news photos for the Associated Press and Greek Cypriot newspapers.

The secret to being a good news photographer is to be relatively fit and keep a camera round your neck – but not just a camera with a lens cap on – but a camera ready for action.

Dennis Oulds used to tell me: "That camera must be part of your body. Wherever you go, you are ready to shoot that picture. If you have to think aperture, focus and anything else, you've lost it." Consequently I never left the house without a camera on my chest or shoulder. Lens caps? I threw them away. I once saw a reporter trying to take photos with a lens cap on. He learned the hard way. Forget lens caps.

When Iro and I went to the movies, or to visit one of her friends, or simply go for a walk, the camera was with me. It became part of my body. This was valuable advice and I lived with it. In fact whenever I was walking along city streets, I held the Rollei in my hand with my finger ready to press the button. Thinking back, I always had the strange idea that if any gunman was going to shoot me I'd like to die knowing I had a photo of the killer. I lived and slept with my camera. I was never ever seen without it.

My work was creating negative ripples in our married life. After the British Institute tragedy, Iro was sure that I would get killed trying to take a photo, or if not, some E.O.K.A. gunman would see me as a possible target. Cypriots who worked for the Colonial administration or British businesses and were felt to be collaborators, were shot in the back of the head either as they walked to their car or while seated at a barber's shop.

On top of this, Iro's friends and relatives expressed dislike over the fact that she had married an Englishman at a time when the country was at war with England. Her sister, Mrs. Araouzo visiting from Limassol warned Iro of severe consequences, and this upset my wife very much.

SAD NEWS ON THE HOME FRONT

When I arrived back from England, still feeling unhappy about my mother's situation, Iro had some news that shattered my thoughts even more.

"I'm pregnant!"

The way she announced it and the tone of voice clearly showed her displeasure. Instinctively, I reached for her hands but she pulled away. "I'm almost forty-two. I cannot believe it. Why should this happen to me?" She stared at my horrified face and then added: "To us."

"Do you realize I will be a really old woman of sixty when our baby is eighteen years old?" she cried, finally talking my hands and letting me put my arms around her.

In the days that followed, she became terribly moody and depressed. Somehow, I was caught between media work and Iro at home. Everything was rushed, chaotic, stressed, and unpleasant. Efterpi walked around the house talking to herself and frequently shaking her head because Iro refused to eat. I hugged the old lady but often, I too didn't have the appetite to eat.

One day, I came home from the office. Efterpi was a flurry of hands. She told me that Iro was very sick and had been taken to a clinic nearby. It was round the corner, so I raced there on foot. At the front desk, a doctor took me into a consultation room.

"I'm sorry to say Mrs. Egby has had a miscarriage, probably due to her age. She's going to be all right. She's resting. If you come back tomorrow she will be sitting up."

Stunned, I walked home through the night, my mind full of questions but there were no answers. I brought Iro home the next day, and she immediately went to bed. We sat and talked but the life seemed to have left her. She wanted to smile, but it kept on slipping away. It seemed that she was switching something off.

A week later, I spent several hours next door at the Atlantis Hotel interviewing and photographing visiting British comedians and musicians. It was dark when I reached home. The door was locked and bolted.

"Go away, Bob. It's all over. Your place is with your photographs and newspapers. That is your destiny. We both made a terrible mistake. What we had is lost – gone forever." Her voice came through the locked door. "Find yourself a place to stay, and I will have someone take your belongings over to you. Please don't bother me again."

And that is how it ended. I made several attempts to talk to her, but she was adamant. Years later when I came to study the signs of the zodiac, I realized she had been an Aries. One of the qualities of that sign is stubbornness. Once an Aries has made up its mind, nothing on earth will shake it. The other thing is that once an Aries has been hurt, they rarely if ever talk about it but it stays stacked away and hidden in the recesses of the mind and body. You can be dead and buried and the Aries will still talk as if you are alive. Stubbornness is one of their strengths or perhaps weaknesses. It all depends where one stands, and right now I knew I was locked out of Iro's life.

Some months later, a cousin of Iro's took me aside, "Iro expected you to return and discuss the situation. She expected you to go back and argue, rationalize, plead, but you simply went away."

"I had no idea of that," I responded. "She told me to go away, so I did."

"You have a lot to learn about women," smiled the cousin. "The fact you did not return and debate your relationship, upset her more than anything. She was really hurt."

That night I recalled the words of long ago, spoken by my great-grandmother Elen in Reading: "...you will hurt people, even loved ones, until you set yourself free." I mulled over those words and could not fathom an answer.

LIVING ON MURDER MILE

Doug Grant pointed to a building up the street from the Cyprus Mail. It was called the Louis Hotel and it was above the Louis Travel Agency. The manager, a salesman with the travel agency said I could have a room for £10 a month.

It was neat and tidy with washing facilities, a bed, a wardrobe and a carpet. A large window overlooked the roofs of buildings at the back. A shower and bathroom were down the hall. An aging prostitute lived in the next room but I think she was close to dying, not from overwork, but severe emphysema and still smoking. A couple of cabaret girls lived in a room at the end of the corridor. The main advantage of this room and the location of the hotel became obvious very soon after my arrival at the Louis Hotel.

I was now living on Ledra Street, soon to be known in Britain and elsewhere as the notorious "Murder Mile" because many a British soldier and some British policemen ended their lives there at the hands of E.O.K.A. gunmen.

The narrow street started at Metaxas Square and the Venetian D'Avila Bastion, and ended near Attaturk Square in the Turkish Cypriot area. The Square was the real center of the city as most of the public offices and the Commissioner's office were there. In normal times Ledra Street was a pleasant and picturesque route lined with small shops peddling jewelry, clothes, souvenirs, cameras, coffee and lots more. The place where I did my grocery shopping was Fereos, right on the corner of Ledra and Regina Streets.

THE "WATCH YOUR BACK" HABIT

One never knew when an E.O.K.A. gunman was going to shoot you in the back, so I developed a habit that took years to cure. Walking along the street, I continually watched people and vehicles behind me by observing reflections in the shop windows. The first few days of turning one's head produced pain in the neck and shoulders, but after a while the discomfort went away. Two years later when I visited London, I noticed I was walking down Regent Street doing exactly the same thing—watching people walking behind me. Doug Grant and several other British people developed the same habit.

Guns were not my business, so I never carried one. One young English reporter who got a job at the Cyprus Mail, started day one by showing everyone in the newsroom that he had a German Luger. That was 11 a.m. Mid-afternoon, someone delivered a sealed envelope to his desk. It was a death threat. That evening, he was on the night flight to London. Things happened fast in old Cyprus.

One character I really enjoyed chatting with was Thomas "Paddy" Rooney, a British police sergeant recently brought out from London. He was a typical British bobby, pleasant to see, but totally out of place in downtown Nicosia. Seeing British police on the streets made me feel quite nostalgic. One day, we stood on the corner and I noticed he was not carrying a gun of any sort. "Where's your gun, Paddy?"

"Goon?" his Irish accent stretched the word "gone," and he smiled easily. "What makes you think I would ever carry one of those dreadful things? I'm here to keep the peace, not break it. The moment you carry a gun you're one of them."

Paddy invited Doug and myself to his St. Patrick's Day "bash" coming up. I smiled as he helped an aging Cypriot woman across the street. His was a character difficult to forget. Two days later, March 14th 1956, while walking his beat on Hippocrates Street in Nicosia, a gunman shot Paddy Rooney. He died on the sidewalk in a pool of blood. He became the first of twelve British policemen to die in the Cyprus Emergency.

TOSSING GRENADES OFF THE ROOFTOPS

In the wake of killings, the Security Forces cordoned off the entire downtown area and conducted searches of shops, offices, homes and hundreds of people were physically searched. As the days passed, shopkeepers and other business people in Nicosia began to feel economic pressures. Tourists disappeared overnight and regular shoppers were leery of certain areas and stayed away. The sight of heavily armed military patrols did not encourage shopping of any sort. One never knew, even on the quietest of days, when the Security Forces would cordon off an area and conduct searches and make arrests.

GRENADE BLASTS PATROL: A Greek Cypriot student demonstration on Murder
Mile turned violent when a hand grenade, tossed from a rooftop, exploded in a Land
Rover killing one soldier and injuring several others. The attack happened right in front
of a group of reporters and photographers, including an American CBS Television
camera and sound crew. May 24th 1956.

One day I heard a lot of female voices outside the newspaper offices. Brian Wright, a seasoned British editor who had joined the Cyprus Mail rushed in: "Hundreds of girls – students – attacking cars." I seized my camera and raced out. Ledra Street was swarming with wild and seemingly crazy girls, many attired in school uniforms, chanting in chorus for "Enosis," and "Engleezi go home." Suddenly the girls started running away. A British Land Rover jammed with South Staffordshire Regiment men emerged and screeched to a halt. Soldiers, carrying rifles and stens leapt off and chased the young women into the side streets. Suddenly, there was a lull in the rioting.

Alex Eftyvoulou materialized, accompanied by a two-some from the CBS Television Network in New York. Paul Bruck was the cameraman and Frank Kearns was the reporter and sound recordist. "We're late," Paul observed. "Is it all over?"

"That's doubtful," noted Alex pulling at his beard. 'They always regroup."

We moved down the street and suddenly a mob of demonstrators carrying more Greek flags and banners emerged from a side street. Their numbers were swollen and there were male and female students now, perhaps five-hundred strong. Alex suggested, because we had cameras, we should go upstairs into an office and look down. The dentist didn't even stop working as we invaded his office. Below, another vehicle carrying troops arrived. There were seven soldiers facing the mob. A brave officer seized a Greek flag from a rioter and that triggered a renewed frenzy and the troops withdrew. The crowd moved up Ledra Street so we decided to come down to street level.

It was at that moment that another Land Rover full of South Staffords swung onto Ledra Street, slowed for a moment, then started coming towards us. The CBS crew decided to film it. Frank Kearns slipped on his headset. Paul did a panning shot as the vehicle, only a few feet away, passed him. Suddenly a dark shape, the size of a baseball but ominously black, plummeted down, thrown out of a building across the street.

"Bomb!" shouted Alex, diving into a doorway.

It exploded in the midst of the troops. In an instant their bodies were flying in all directions. Screams, shouts and confusion. Men holding lacerated arms and legs sat in the smoke. One soldier holding his head, tottered to the sidewalk where he sat down. One woman, shopping nearby, screamed and fell over in a faint. Paul stopped his camera and gazed at the scene, unable to believe the carnage. He and Frank had filmed it all, even the explosion.

Suddenly the wrecked Land Rover was on fire. Smoke and flames were everywhere. Rescuers, many of them Cypriots, helped the wounded soldiers move away. More troops arrived and took over. I had a series of photos for Central Press, and I was changing film, when another explosion occurred.

"Onasagoras Street," cried Alex, pointing to a parallel street a hundred yards away. "Pheneromeni Church area."

We all ran through the narrow side street to Onasagoras. An E.O.K.A. fighter on a rooftop had dropped a grenade on a South Stafford foot patrol. More carnage!

The blast had caught one soldier tearing at his back. Another soldier carrying a rifle under one arm, used his other arm to support the wounded man. Behind, sat a Greek Cypriot shop owner holding a bleeding leg. It told the stark tragedy of Cyprus. Next day the Daily Mirror in London ran my picture on the front page with the headline: "Murder Bid on Bank Holiday." It was May 1956.

In Britain, indignation ran high. Governor Harding decided the time had come to be ruthless and ordered the Security Forces to wipe out the killer gangs hiding in the mountains. Massive search operations were launched and included an intensive hunt for the elusive Colonel Grivas.

MURDER BID ON BANK HOLIDAY: This was the headline in Britain's Daily Mirror as it ran what it called "one of the most dramatic pictures yet received from Cyprus." A British soldier of the South Staffordshire Regiment holds up a wounded comrade, a victim of a rooftop grenade. A Greek Cypriot shopkeeper, also badly hurt, sits on the step holding a bleeding leg. May 24th 1956.

8

THE HUNT FOR GRIVAS, THE LEADER

G EORGE GRIVAS WAS A Cyprus native, born in Nicosia in May 1898 and educated in the Pancyprian Gymnasium. At eighteen, he left Cyprus and became a cadet in the Military Academy in Greece. As a lieutenant, he was engaged in the invasion of Smyrna and Thrace in Asia Minor in the Greco-Turkish War of 1918-1922. The Turks had lost the region in the post-World War I Peace Conference in Paris. But Mustapha Kemal Ataturk was building the new Republic of Turkey and his army was enthusiastic and fought valiantly, so the Greek campaign was a disaster. The incident had been Grivas's introduction to war and it left him nursing a deep hatred of the Turks.

Grivas had spent time in German-occupied Athens in World War II and was well aware of German interrogation and elimination techniques which he brought with him. Now, after a long but unexciting career in the Greek Army, Grivas, at the request of Archbishop Makarios, was back in Cyprus. He was a perfectionist in charge of a cause in which he ardently believed.

Governor Harding's tough military driving force was Brigadier M.A. H. Butler, commander of Britain's crack fighting team, the 16th Independent Parachute Brigade. A small but wiry man, he had a humorous but leathery face. I had met him several times, but tonight I was having a quiet drink in the Cosmopolitan Club when a figure slipped onto the next bar stool and prodded my shoulder.

"Don't say who I am, play it easy," he said softly. It was the Brigadier, known to his many friends as "Tubby." Why they nicknamed him that I never figured because he had a slim, wiry physique. Attired in a cream linen, open necked shirt, and light grey flannel slacks, almost touristy, he appeared as the most docile man in the world, which was far from the truth. Paratroopers are the brothers of the Royal Marine Commando.

"What are you doing here?" he asked with a grin.

"I could ask you the same question," I said with an easy laugh. We ordered drinks.

"Aren't you getting good news stuff on our operations?"

"It satisfies the writers, the correspondents, but photographers need pictures and we are not getting anything worth while," I explained. "You are getting all the good points for invading mountain villages, bringing in EOKA people and scouring the land for Grivas, but there are no pictures to back up your claims."

"What do you want?"

"We need to come with you and report and picture things as they happen."

"Bob, there's a pretty big press corps on the island these days..."

"No, I'm thinking like the media do in London," I went on. "They set up a pool - one reporter, one photographer, one newsreel cameraman, and one news agency type. They would cover everything and systematically report back to the press corps and share material."

Tubby sat quietly for a while, gazing down into his glass. Suddenly, when I was beginning to think he had not been listening, he turned and faced me head on, his eyes were bright and there was a stream of excitement in his voice. "If you put this to the civilian PR people – Leslie Glass – and explain it in the way you've just told me, I will see what I can do with my people." He touched my arm. "Young fellow, it's a good idea and I think you'll get some good material for the papers back home. But it will be tough going – and dangerous too."

HUNTING IN THE MOUNTAINS

There were four chosen who could spend a week or more with the Parachute Regiments: John Davies of British Movietone News, Vincent Ryder of the Daily Telegraph, Paul Bruck of Columbia Television and myself for Central Press Photos.

The operation, code named Lucky Alphonse, was headquartered in and around the old-stone walled Kykko Monastery in the Troodos Mountains. Dating back to the 10th century its official name is The Holy and Royal and Stavropegic Monastery of Kykkos. It is reported to be the wealthiest and best-known monastery on the island. The original building, subsequently destroyed and rebuilt, was founded by the Byzantine Emperor Alexios I Komnenos during the crusade led by Peter the Hermit about 1095. Archbishop Makarios started his spiritual journey there as a monk in 1926. Among its ikons is one said to have been painted by St. Luke.

The journey in Land Rovers and various trucks created a dust storm along the twisting country and mountainous roads. Armed paratroopers riding on top frequently choked and wrapped their faces in scarves and cloths.

The Monastery forecourt looked more like a movie set than a place of Greek Orthodox religion. Trucks with spindly radio aerials were parked all over the place, troops were moving in and out of tents, a stable had been converted into a mess, and an outhouse had been turned into a temporary working prison.

Seven E.O.K.A. fighters had just been caught in a mountain hideout and were being brought in. As we leapt from our vehicle and started taking pictures of the men, it was clear their recent lives in a mountain cave had left them dirty and disheveled and apparently hungry. Their clothes were wet and ragged, and none had shaved for about a week. One man was shoeless and now had a festering foot. It was indeed a pitiful sight to see these men, their dull, lifeless eyes reflecting defeat. Paratroopers with guns added to their misery. So within twenty minutes of our arrival, the team had pictures and newsreel coverage, and things looked promising.

We made up our camp beds in what turned out to be the Officers' Quarters, a large barn-like structure with stone tiled floor, and heavy wooden beams that supported an ages old tiled roof. Everything was cloaked with the dust and grime of centuries. Washing water was obtained from the water-bowser truck next to the cookhouse. Shaving each morning for the others presented a problem because they only had one mirror between the three. Me? Well, I had my beard.

The capture of seven E.O.K.A. fighters was insufficient reason to return to Nicosia, so we spent our days moving around the operational area, which Tubby Butler's deputy commander, Colonel Norman Tailyour of the Royal Marine Commando calculated was about 500 square miles.

Now, considering the total area of the island is 3,572 square miles, we were looking at a search area of one-seventh of the total land area. And 2,000 Para and Commando troops were doing it. Lucky Alphone was the biggest anti-terrorist drive ever carried out on Cyprus, and although the Security Forces captured various fighters, considered "small fry" as one officer put it, the entire focus was really on one man – Colonel George Grivas or Dighenis the Leader. The most hunted man on the island now had a price of £10,000 on his head.

Tubby Butler had a hunch that the E.O.K.A. chief was somewhere in the search area. "If he's inside, then it's only a matter of time before we get him," he said one evening while sitting outside the control room truck.

"What will you do when you get him?" asked John Davies.

"Bury him," Butler said with a forced smile. "Hopefully, there won't be much left of him except to put him in a hole. But in my experience it will not be a great search network like this that gets him, but some lonely traffic policeman stopping a car for not having tail lights. It's ironical."

THE DAY THEY ALMOST NABBED HIM

It was the next afternoon, that men of the 3rd Battalion almost nabbed Grivas. Sergeant Robert Scott was winding up a patrol after climbing across a mountainside of loose shale. Leading his men, he turned down into a thickly vegetated valley with a rough path that would lead back to HQ. Wearing thick-rubber soled boots the men moved quickly but maintained silence. Some fifty yards ahead, Scott spotted some boulders flanked by bushes and trees.

Suddenly a head and shoulders popped up from behind the rocks. The mustached, mature figure was wearing a gray singlet. For a second, both men were totally surprised, as if viewing an apparition that should not be there. Both reacted simultaneously. Scott fired his sten. The old man ducked and was gone. As the patrol raced forward they saw the old man disappear into the bushes. After searching the area, the men returned to the place of first contact. They found a small camp.

Several blankets, the smoldering embers of a fire, a mug of shaving water and a brush, automatic weapons, a pistol, a pair of binoculars and a tell-tale beret, a Sam Browne belt and a ragged pullover. These were quickly identified as belonging to Grivas.

How? Well, the fleeing old man had left a camera, and as Tubby Butler's people quickly developed the film, it showed Grivas surrounded by his men posing in the forest of the Troodos Mountains and wearing the clothes. It was the first solid proof that Grivas was leading E.O.K.A. Butler and his troops were justly jubilant.

"We know he's here in this area," said Tailyour. "Now we'll intensify the hunt." He prodded the map inside the control room. "He can't travel far. There are too many of us around. You should be able to get some good coverage."

Now we were torn. The Nicosia PR people and the media wanted us back to describe our experiences and get hold of the E.O.K.A. pictures and they all wanted us back soon. Vincent Ryder and I wanted to stay. Finally we agreed. We would all drive down overnight, give a press briefing the next morning, then return to Troodos. Somewhere a woman's voice was still urging me to "tread softly" and I did not understand. I really wanted to be out with the troops in the mountains searching for Grivas. The energy wanted us to go to Nicosia. I wondered why.

PROOF GRIVAS EXISTS!:
This is one of two photographs taken on a box Brownie showing that former Greek Army officer George Grivas was in Cyprus leading an E.O.K.A. group. Security Forces found the camera in a mountain camp after Grivas was briefly spotted. Grivas is seated center, surrounded by his lieutenants. Photo issued by Cyprus Public Information.

The heavily attended press briefing was chaired by the new chief spokesman for the Security Forces, Bruce Langley. The session appeared to satisfy most of the media. Langley handed out the captured photos of Grivas and his group, and also some of my photos.

DEATH IN HIGH PLACES

Afterwards we headed for baths and by early afternoon we were waiting outside the Ledra Palace for the truck. A three-ton swung in and a young captain jumped out and got us into a four-some. "They want you all back up at Kykko. It's urgent?"

"They've captured Grivas?" quizzed Paul Bruck.

The officer shook his head. "No real details yet, but I understand a number of our men have been killed by a sudden forest fire. About eighteen!"

It seemed impossible. The adrenalin started pumping. We climbed on board the truck and made ourselves comfortable. On board were six of the toughest looking Paras I had ever seen, a Vickers sub-machine gun, boxes of ammunition and right by my legs, several boxes of dynamite. The Para corporal in charge advised: "If we're ambushed on the way up, don't think twice about getting away from this truck. There could be a bit of a bang." Who said life among the Parachute Regiment was a breeze?

The headquarters around Kykko Monastery was now a busy first-aid zone, treating men with burns. Thin smoke and a smell of burning lurked everywhere. A truck came through with scarred and blackened bodies which were placed in a temporary outbuilding serving as a mortuary. Helicopters flew in and started taking the injured to a British Military Hospital.

A bearded monk attempted to make the sign of the cross and spoke in Greek. A Para snarled: "Get the f... out of here, you bloody terrorist." Monasteries were well known for harboring E.O.K.A. fighters. One is inclined to think it was organized chaos. On top of everything, the narrow road to the tragedy was cluttered with trucks coming and going.

Colonel Norman Tailyour said: "It's still very dangerous out there, the forest fire is still burning and the winds are turning. But if you wish to risk it, I'll make my Champ available. There's plenty of food in the back, plus a bottle of Cyprus brandy." He forced a tight grin.

Vincent Ryder, who had already written a story for the Nicosia press corps decided to wait out at Kykko, stating it was a picture story. As we were about to leave on the Austin Champ, Brigadier Butler came hustling up.

"There are strong indications that the forest fire was deliberately set in the lower levels of the valley. A breeze carried the flames through the tinder dry firs," he said. "We think Grivas and his men started it as a diversion to escape. Whatever way you look at it – it's murder."

This put a whole new light on the fire. "How many confirmed dead?" asked John Davies.

"Twenty-one dead," he said. "About the same injured."

Our driver started to reverse to make a turn. Just then two paratroopers armed with stens came running towards us and climbed aboard. "Guards," cried the Colonel with a slight shrug. "Just in case you come across Grivas. We think he used the fire to escape, so he's probably on some other mountain."

As we moved onto the dusty road, eight trucks loaded with Gordon Highlanders swept into the parking area - their faces grim and drawn and darkened with smoke. "They've been out since noon fighting the fires," explained one of our guards."

Night was closing in and we would have to stop somewhere. We were still a mile away from the disaster scene when it was decided to break for the night. The Paras built a fire, served tea and sandwiches. No one touched the brandy. We slept on blankets and pine needles.

THEY DIDN'T SEE IT COMING

Dawn was shaping up over the eastern peaks as we decided to move on and shortly after we could see most of the blackened countryside. The guards at a roadblock let us through. As we moved over the brow of the hill, a scene of ghastly devastation lay before us. As far as the eye could see, the hillside was bare and littered with charred stumps. Some trees were still burning, and the stench of smoke was everywhere. The road was shrouded in grey ash.

Then the road twisted and became a shoulder. The scene was terrifying. Personnel trucks, armored scout cars. Jeeps lay gutted on the track - some had spun off down the hill. All were burned black. It was here the majority of the nineteen lost their lives, simply sitting in their vehicles.

"They didn't see it coming," said the corporal accompanying us. "Our medic says the men sat in their trucks virtually unaware they were being asphyxiated before being burned to death. There was nothing they could do. The medics say they were still sitting there – dead – holding their weapons." Then he said quietly. "That bastard Grivas deserves to burn in hell."

Everyone felt sick. We took photos and news film. I pulled back and got a general view. The picture they used in London shows two figures inspecting a burned out truck. One is John Davies whose 35mm Newman Sinclair camera is parked on the road in the foreground. The valley itself was on the edge of the "killing" area where Grivas was briefly seen and almost caught earlier in the operation. Typical of the forested valleys, it was packed with thousands of tall, slender pines, all tinder-dry in the scorching Cyprus sun.

THE VALLEY OF DEATH:

A scorched landscape high in the Troodos Mountains and charred vehicles are all that remains after a raging fire engulfed British Paratroopers in the search for Grivas and his fighters. Twenty-one Britons were killed or fatally injured while sitting in their trucks and another eighteen were injured.One observer said the fire just came at them like a flash of lightning. Daily Telegraph correspondent Vincent Ryder called it "the Valley of Death." Above: Photo shows two of the burned trucks. Below: The fire scene in the Valley of Death. It was said that Grivas deliberately set the fire knowing the winds would carry the flames into the operations area, although this was never proven.

Investigations showed that the fire had burned for over a day on the valley's western flank. Suddenly, it had been caught by a freak wind. Flames roared through the pines at speeds of 30 miles an hour, burning and killing everything in its path—all within three minutes. Soldiers creating a firebreak were immediately trapped. Others were caught in two three-ton lorries as they sat asphyxiated, frozen, then burned. One soldier described the fire as a "giant blow-torch killing everything in its path."

Soldiers who survived told hair-raising stories. Major Michael Walsh of the 3rd Battalion and his batman, Private Richard Planson, were two of these. Walsh said: "I raced up the bank. I could feel the flames catching up with me. The heat was scorching. Terrible. Then I fell, and by a miracle I rolled backwards over a small spur into a clear patch."

Reg Planson, 23-years-old described the horrors: "The flames came at us like an express train. "Somebody screamed for us to get out, so I ran along the road. The flames were already jumping it. I had no alternative but to run through them. I must have been the last one to get out that way."

THE VALLEY OF THE SHADOW OF DEATH

Each and every survivor had stories to tell. Even rescuers were challenged. Medical Officer, Lieutenant Sutton racing in his vehicle to get to the injured was suddenly confronted by a huge wall of fire. Accompanied by a medical orderly, they threw themselves onto a stony patch as the fire engulfed the Land Rover, reducing it to a skeleton moments later. Although burned, Sutton and the orderly pressed on to help the injured.

Other medical officers were dropped into the still burning disaster area by helicopter. They were Lieutenant Basil Shadlow and Captain John McLaren. All along the stricken mountain road, medical orderlies were shouting for new dressings while injured men lay groaning on the wayside, waiting to be evacuated. One officer suffering burns, stood dazed in the middle of the road. He repeated the horror: "My whole company is written off."

Within five hours all the injured had been evacuated to the RAF Hospital at Akrotiri in southern Cyprus, and preparations were being made to bury the dead in a mass grave at the British Military Cemetery near Nicosia.

This was the price paid to catch Grivas. Somewhere out there in the mountains the wily E.O.K.A. leader was setting up another camp. When the final tally was made – twenty one British soldiers were dead.

At Kykko Monastery, we climbed aboard a truck to take us back to Nicosia to share the material with a waiting press corps. We each had vivid memories, so we were in a relative silence each digesting what we had seen and experienced.

Just a short distance away on a grassy hillside among a cluster of slender, graceful fir trees, a small cluster of Paratroopers were kneeling in prayer and the soft spoken voices of the weary-faced men could be heard on a gentle breeze. The lorry driver stopped for us to get out and watch. In the center of the congregation, stood a major, a Scottish padre attired in a white surplice, his head bowed and his hands clasped together. As we walked away, we could hear their voices. Then the padre's voice came over them all: "Yea, though I walk through the valley of the shadow of death..." Psalm 23 seemed so appropriate.

Yes, I had seen, smelled and touched the valley of the shadow of death, and I wondered where on earth God was in all this tragedy.

9

TERRORIST TARGET?
THE CYPRUS MAIL

S HORTLY AFTER THE TROODOS Mountain tragedy, the British Government announced that Lucky Alphonse had been more successful than critics had suggested. In finding Grivas' mountain hideout, soldiers had discovered a bundle of papers written by Grivas, including personal documents. They became known as the "Grivas Diaries."

The documents revealed the structure of E.O.K.A., the trials and errors made, the affiliation with Archbishop Makarios and various other prominent persons in Cyprus, including the husband of Iro's sister. The discovery prompted a fast re-shuffling of the E.O.K.A. organization, which brought about a quiet period on the fighting front. It also caused many less active and relatively unknown members to become non-operational and seek safer positions in sheltered lives. British Intelligence officers were now certain that only 50 to 100 Greek Cypriots were left to be fully active after the re-shuffle. Details were published under the title: "Terrorism in Cyprus" by Her Majesty's Stationery Office.

The problems were two-fold. (1)The discovery and re-shuffle had reduced the E.O.K.A. fighting force to hard-core and fanatical members. This meant that attacks would be of a higher level, more assassinations and strategic bombing attacks.

The other was this: (2) In his diaries, Grivas wrote on March 2nd 1955: "....I instructed Hermis as follows: He is to take charge of all the work in Nicosia town, including the direction of both combat and killer groups. One of the targets for the latter group will also be the CYPRUS MAIL offices. The managerial staff is to have their homes reconnoitered and their habits observed, and the killer group is to be readiness..."

This paragraph caused more than a slight stir inside the usually active newsroom. It triggered feverish but cautious discussions as to its true meaning. Most of the staff claimed the meaning could not have been plainer. I pointed out that this was the middle of 1956 and the Grivas order was well over a year old, dating back to 1955, and if anything harmful was to occur, it would have happened by now. Some of the reporters wished they were on a regular battlefront. At least you know where you are and where the enemy stands. The Grivas papers were shot down the next day during a visit to the newsroom by Nicos Sampson armed with his camera.

"Egbiss, you don't look well. Too much work?"

He always used the Greek in my name. I reached over and gave him a copy of the Grivas Diaries.

"Sure," he said quickly. "I saw it yesterday. It's nothing but lies! Lies and lies! Invented by the British to incriminate our Archbishop."

"Whitehall doesn't have the imagination to create such a document," I protested.

"So how does this worry you, Egbiss?"

"The piece mentioning the Cyprus Mail," I responded. "The part where Grivas orders the killer group to be in readiness and keeping a watch over us."

Sampson grinned mischievously. "So where are they? These killer groups? Are they standing at your door? It's nothing but lies! Lies! Lies!" He picked up his camera and left.

A TIE-IT-YOURSELF BOW TIE

Edward Bonici Mompalda managed a higher class British clothing store on Murder Mile called Spinneys. He was Maltese and engaged to a beautiful Greek Cypriot girl whom he planned to marry soon. Bonici was always pleasant to chat with and a dedicated worker. He always expressed a deep love for Cyprus. He hated violence and was always urging the restoration of tranquility to the island. Consequently, it was only to be expected he was a volunteer for the Emergency Special Police Force. This made him high on the list of E.O.K.A. targets.

I was his last customer. It happened like this. Walking past his shop window, I spotted some bow ties. I found that regular ties were getting in the way of my cameras. "I need a clip-on," I told Bonici.

"Ones you tie yourself look better and more natural," he said showing me a British made tie. In five minutes he showed me how to do it, and I bought a multi-colored model. I paid and started to leave the store. Looking back, I called out: "I'm having lunch at the Imperial. Care to join me?"

"No, thank you very much," he cried as he locked the door. "I have an appointment." With that he crossed Ledra Street and disappeared.

I was sitting down in the Imperial Hungarian Restaurant when the shots crackled and echoed through the streets. We found Bonici face down in a growing pool of blood. Dark bullet holes like black eyes stared from the back of his shirt. Felix Yiaxis had joined me as we raced along the street to the murder scene. Three Cypriots appearing uneasy came up and looked at the body. It was as if everything was happening in slow motion. Other people were arriving including Cyprus Mail editor Brian Wright and Nicos Sampson, holding his camera.

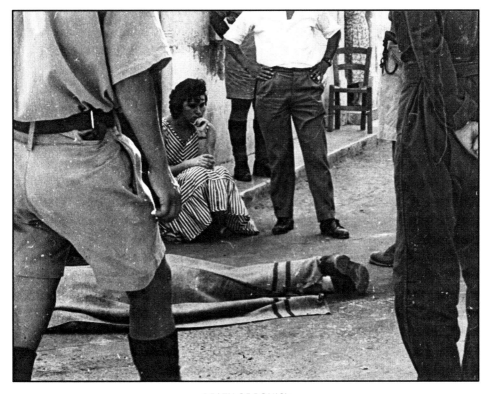

DEATH OF BONICI:
Fianceé Drosoulla Demetriadou sits besides the body of Bonici Mompalda, a salesman at the Spinney's Store on Murder Mile. This picture brought an Honorable Mention in the News Photo section of the British Press Pictures of the Year 1956.

Then a young woman arrived like a whirlwind. "That's his fiancée," whispered Felix. Wearing a pleasantly striped summer dress, Drossula Demetriadou started screaming. Someone threw a small blanket over Bonici. It partially covered his body. As we started to take pictures, the girl turned hostile. "Take pictures if you dare," she screamed, "Go awa y! Leave us." She ran up to Felix and beat him on the chest. A man took her by the arm and tried to calm her down.

Glumly, she sat on the edge of the sidewalk right near Bonici's body and held her face in her hands. I remember this so clearly. A voice said bend down and take a picture. I hesitated, then bent down and took the picture of the distraught girl sitting beside Bonici's body. The scene was framed by the legs of the policemen. I pulled back and rolled the Rollei handle.

Then Nicos started taking pictures of Bonici's face at such an angle that he caught the long trickle of blood leaving the man's mouth and winding down towards the gutter. Hell, I thought to myself, and I taught this man to take photos? I felt disgusted.

A British officer, Major Dick Stuckey arrived with several soldiers of the South Staffordshire Regiment. He shouted sharply at Sampson for taking such pictures. Sampson withdrew and stood by another Greek Cypriot reporter. "Take a general view," urged the voice. "Take everybody," it said. It was here that I took a view of everyone on that death scene and later I discovered a truth - it pays to get a general view of a murder.

At the Cyprus Mail darkroom I rush processed the film and radioed a photo of the girl seated next to her slain fiancé. The following morning it was on the front pages of most of the Fleet Street dailies. Jacko, the Cyprus Mail publisher congratulated me as his paper carried the picture too. "You're a good news photographer, Bob," he said and took me over to Antonakis Bar for a drink.

Things did not end there. A few days later my picture of the Bonici murder was reprinted in many newspapers. Bonici's girl-friend, Drosoulla Demitriadou made a statement on the Cyprus Broadcasting Service vigorously condemning Grivas, whom she called "a filthy murderer," and telling him to "Get out of our island." Then with nothing to keep her in Cyprus, she sadly boarded a plane and left for London. As London newspapers ran the Drosoula story, they reprinted my photo.

Little did I know at that time but the pictures I took that day of the murder of Bonici Mompalada were to be reprinted in yet another surprising story.

TURKS VERSUS GREEKS

In the summer of 1956 a new phrase started to make headlines: Intercommunal Strife. It came with a new degree of ugliness. In normal times, most inhabitants do not consider their ethnicity, but these were not normal times. As the E.O.K.A. campaign loomed to new heights, the Turkish Cypriots saw the writing on the wall and feared genocide. Greek Cypriots in turn feared the fiery Turkish psyche.

Aphania is a small community between Nicosia and Famagusta. The trouble started when a Turkish Cypriot policeman was shot dead by an E.O.K.A. gunman. Within an hour or so, the Turkish Cypriots of Aphania, plus supporters from other Turkish Cypriot communities, were on the warpath. Greek Cypriots were attacked and severely beaten. Greek Cypriot shops were set on fire, along with Greek homes. A large farm, loaded with grain dust, exploded into the night sky.

Nicosia taxis were forbidden to run intercity without a permit. Paul Bruck and I got a ride with Alex Eftyvoulou and Vincent Ryder joined Keith Morfett in his rented car. We arrived among a fleet of fire trucks and ambulances feverishly working among blazing buildings. In the main street Turkish Cypriot leader Dr. Fazil Kutchuk was furious. "The Greeks have gone too far this time," he cried waving his arms. "I don't think I can stop my people this time. In fact, I'm not going to try."

"But this will mean civil war," Keith Morfett put in.

"If that is what it takes, we will do that. We will annihilate the Greeks. They have been getting away with murder for far too long," said Dr. Kutchuk. "I foresee civil war and division for a long, long time."

It was a dire prediction that eventually came true and saw Cyprus divided for many years.

British troops converged on the whole area arresting demonstrators and ordering others to get back into their homes. It was 1 a.m. when I arrived back in the Cyprus Mail and Doug Grant was waiting anxiously for pictures. "If you get a move on we'll be the only paper in Cyprus to carry pictures." We were. At 3 a.m., the huge flat-bed starting churning out newspapers with dramatic pictures and my story.

Brian Wright and Alex were still around. "This will make Foley hop," said Alex with a chuckle.

Charles Foley was a former foreign editor at the Daily Express in Fleet Street and as the situation developed, established a daily newspaper called the Times of Cyprus. It quickly became the Cyprus Mail's opposition. He had recruited journalists who knew Cyprus well and could write dramatic stories. People like Georges der Parthogh and Alan Anderson.

Someone made coffee. Did we really need to stay awake? I was ready for bed. It had been a long night and it was almost dawn. But Fate had other plans.

"Listen," said Alex suddenly. We listened. It was the distinctive sounds of fire engines clanging their way through Nicosia. I can't recall who piled into

Alex's car, but it was a crowd of journalists. We raced helter-skelter after the fire trucks.

The fire trucks swung into Hermes Street, the dividing line between Greek Nicosia and Turkish Nicosia. Several shops were ablaze. In just a few hours intercommunal riots had spread to the capital city. Three stores, all owned by Greek Cypriots were ablaze. The Turks were on the warpath. This created a new and ugly dimension in the Cyprus situation. British troops searched side alleys and questioned passers-by, attempting to identify the fire starters. It was light when I finally got to bed at the Louis Hotel.

As I went to sleep I was wondering what Iro was doing...

Midday next day, I staggered into the Cyprus Mail bleary-eyed and sluggish, to be greeted by a new development. The Government's Security Committee had announced it was taking a new initiative to prevent intercommunical riots. They ordered a double barbed-wire fence be built across the entire diameter of the old Nicosia, separating the Greek from the Turks. Nicosia was to become a divided city.

CELEBRITY WRITERS AND A HINDU SEER

Not every day was grim - it just seemed like it in 1956. I found myself spending a lot of my free time with journalists based on the island, or writers coming to take a look.

One was Keith Waterhouse representing the Daily Mirror. I gave him an escorted tour through the Troodos Mountains and some of the villages. Keith went on to become a famous novelist, columnist and screenplay writer.

Another was Randolph Churchill, writing for the Observer newspaper. I met him talking to Cypriots and Security Forces on Murder Mile. He asked me where journalists spend the evening hours. I mentioned the Dolphin outside Nicosia on the Kyrenia Road. Mr. Churchill turned up that evening and Theo, the dynamic owner-manager royally entertained him. Just about anyone of the Cyprus press corps was there and Randolph let his hair down and danced with any of the ladies who wished to dance with him.

He finally turned his attention to a very nice woman reporter named Barbara who was visiting Cyprus. Champagne was the drink for most nights. It flowed like water. Randolph managed to get one of Barbara's stylish shoes. He decided to fill it with champagne, and could not understand why it required so much. Finally, the media's laughter drew his attention that something was wrong. Barbara's shoe was toeless.

CHURCHILL ON MURDER MILE:
Randolph Churchill, the son of Sir Winston Churchill talks with British troops patrolling Murder Mile in the heart of Nicosia. Mr. Churchill was reporting for a British newspaper.

One lunchtime, when everything was quiet in the office, an old withered man with a leathery brown face came into the Cyprus Mail. His frail body was wrapped in robes except for his arms and legs. His sandals had seen better days. He introduced himself as a Hindu Yogi and he looked hungry. So I shared my haloumi goat cheese sandwich, which pleased him.

He tucked part of it away in a small canvas bag, then took my hand and said in perfect English: *"You will go to the far side of the Americas and you will come back to the east and go to the desert lands. You will come back through the darkness into the light and you will know and understand the meaning of the One Self – that which is the true self within you."* Clasping his hands, he bowed and was gone.

While I was pondering this, there was a kink in the Cosmos that took my life in another direction.

A RETURN TO EGYPT

It was the first day in September 1956, John Lacey, senior picture editor at Central Press called: "Can you get across to Egypt tomorrow? Australian Prime Minister Robert Menzies is going to meet President Nasser. You'll be back in 24 hours."

Although I had been busy covering Cyprus, I had from time to time caught up on the growing dispute over the Suez Canal Zone which had been evacuated by the British.

There was a political international tug-of-war happening. In a nutshell: Britain and the United States withdrew an offer to fund the Aswan Dam on the Nile. Egypt had upset Britain and the U.S. because it officially recognized the People's Republic of China during the tense relations between China and Taiwan. Egypt came back on July 26th 1956 by nationalizing the Suez Canal. This action took the British and French stockholders by complete surprise.

Nothing is straight in politics. This got a whole lot of people upset, notably Britain, France and Israel. The Canal's owner was the Suez Canal Company, an international company based in Paris, with Britain as a major shareholder. British Prime Minister Anthony Eden publicly described the take-over as "theft." The Israelis realized that with the British forces gone from the Canal, Egyptian forces were right on their border in the Sinai Peninsula.

In August a conference of nations met in London in an attempt to find a diplomatic solution. Eighteen proposals were adopted, and these were to be presented to President Nasser of Egypt. In essence, the proposals offered Egypt representation on the Suez Canal Company board and a share in its profits. The messenger was Australian Prime Minister Robert Menzies who, because of his long involvement in politics, was held in high esteem by many nations.

A number of journalists and photographers arrived at Cairo Airport just in time to photograph the arrival of Mr. Menzies and the delegation. I had grown to dislike "arrival" photos of anybody, so I quickly made my way to the Cosmopolitan Hotel on the Talat Harb in downtown Cairo. It was ancient and stately, reminiscent of another age, but comfortable.

The journalists were still talking about the expulsion from Egypt of Sefton (Tom) Delmer, one of the Daily Express' top correspondents. Tom had been escorted out of the hotel, and he took it jubilantly, holding his fists high in the air, as the Egyptian police took him to the airport. Delmer did it in style and everyone praised him for it.

The Egyptian PR Directorate called and we were hustled over to a palace where the initial meeting took place. President Gamal Abdul Nasser was there with his representatives and Robert Menzies with his delegation.

It was fascinating being in the presence of two great international leaders. I thought back to the time when I was a Senior Aircraftsman serving in the Suez Canal Zone. It was only a brief two years before in September 1954 that the RAF had given me its blessings, and a ticket to Cyprus. What an immense tide of water had flowed under my bridge of life. I stood and sensed the dynamics of these two leaders, and instinctively knew the meeting would end in failure. The Egyptian rejection came on September 9th. Would there be war? It came sooner than most people thought possible.

TRAGEDY FROZEN IN TIME

Meanwhile the Cyprus situation developed with more killings, more violence, more riots, and more troop reinforcements were shipped in. With the troops came a number of British policemen from various towns in Britain. Remember Danny Rooney? Well, he had been one of the early arrivals. Now more were arriving.

Friday, September 28th 1956 was a day of horror. The British media head-lined what happened this day as "Murder on High Street."

Just after 10 a.m. the offices at the Cyprus Mail saw a new journalistic light. A new reporter Roy Bellm arrived and was talking with Victor Bodker. Although the aging Victor was shortly to depart for the UK, he suggested the Mail needed more local features. Finding my camera empty, I sat and reloaded while I listened to Mr. Bellm.

10.26 a.m. A sharp rattling noise outside. I initially thought one of the printers had dropped a box of lead type. Victor looked out of the window into the closed alley. He watched as the Ledra Street kiosk operator ran in with the news.

"There's a killing outside!"

I grabbed my camera and raced out to Ledra Street. Victor and Roy were ahead of me. On Murder Mile shoppers and strollers were rushing to get away. On the street I could see three prone figures! All had been shot. I immediately recognized all three as British police constables who had recently arrived in Nicosia. Each one was in civilian clothes, shirts and pants.

As I walked onto the street I started taking pictures. It was automatic. I could see one man was dead; another was on his back, waving his arms and in the throes of dying. The third man, trying to stay on his feet was looking up

Murder Mile. He had a gun drawn. Victor Bodker was coming towards me, calling out to everyone to call an ambulance. A lady named Mrs. Leyland whose husband often came into the paper, had been shopping and was walking by. That is the moment I took the picture. It was tragedy frozen in time.

Roy rushed up to the wounded man and helped him sit down on some steps. Suddenly many people gathered around to help. "Ambulances won't come," said a Greek shop manager. "They're scared. Let's get a taxi." Victor flagged one down.

"MURDER ON HIGH STREET":
This was how one Fleet Street daily headed this picture. Three British policemen, while walking along Murder Mile were shot by an E.O.K.A. gunman. Two of the policemen died, while the third, Sergeant William Ivor Webb with five bullets in his body, went on firing as the gunman ran away. The two who died were Sergeant Hugh Carter and Sergeant Cyril Thoroughgood. Nicos Sampson later wrote a story on how he conducted this killing. This photograph was included in the Encyclopedia Britannica Exhibition in 1956.

Two minutes later the wounded man and his two dead comrades were on their way to Nicosia Hospital. The first British troops arrived and started searches. Meanwhile I was developing the pictures and a few minutes later I

124

was on my Lambretta scooter, on my way to Cable and Wireless. The girl behind the counter at the cable office gasped as I handed her the picture.

The British media splashed the story and my photo. One headlined it: "Murder on High Street," another "Death at High Noon," and "EOKA Killers Slay British Bobbies."

The victims on that Friday, September 28th were Sergeant H.B. Carter, and Sergeant C.J. Thoroughgood, both deceased. The third man, Sergeant W.I. J. Webb, who received five bullets, miraculously recovered and told how he had fired after the fleeing E.O.K.A. gunman.

But all was not finished that day. That night two vehicles were ambushed in the Kyrenia mountains and a W.V.S. Mrs. Mary Holton and Private C.V. Read of the Wiltshire Regiment were killed. Also on that day, Sergeant Jepson, who five days earlier had been shot while returning from church with his wife and ten-year old daughter, died of his wounds. A black Friday that is hard to forget. September 28th 1956.

For a while it looked as if things were to be quiet. I figured I needed a rest. At the local photo shop was a young lass named Lilian and we became friends. We spent several days having picnics on the golden sand beaches at Famagusta, and like all European families – she was Hungarian – her mother came too. It was almost as if the mother was orchestrating the relationship, which failed to appeal to me at all. They were very kind and hospitable, but I simply wanted friendship, someone to converse with, not marry. It was strange that this should be happening at a time when Iro was applying for a divorce. Upon reflection, my year had been so busy with work; there was never any time for reconciliation.

10

THE GUNS OF WAR AT SUEZ

T HROUGHOUT AUTUMN OF 1956 Britain and France started deploying large contingents of aircraft and ground forces to the islands of Cyprus and Malta and the airbases at Akrotiri and Nicosia became overcrowded. E.O.K.A. became almost a cover but no one took that idea seriously. RAF bombers were stacked wing tip to wing tip at RAF Station Luqa in Malta.

The British Royal Navy deployed the aircraft carriers HMS Eagle, Albion and Bulwark, while France had their naval destroyer Jean Bart and the aircraft carriers Arromanches and La Fayette on station. In addition, British naval ships Ocean and Theseus acted as launching points for the first British helicopter-borne assault.

PASSPORT TO WAR:
This is the British War Correspondent's Licence RN 14 for R. Egby
representing Central Press Photos Ltd., of London. Dated November 6th 1956.

E.O.K.A. and many Cypriots were wondering what was happening. British and French troops were everywhere and transport vehicles were all painted with the letter "H." With the coming of the French, a team went around painting signs, "Tenez à gauche!" which were directed at the French long accustomed to driving on the right. It meant, "Keep to the Left."

The Suez War otherwise known as "Operation Musketeer" started on the last day of October, Halloween, with a bombing of strategic military targets in Egypt. The Egyptians retaliated by sinking all 40 ships present in the canal, effectively closing it to all shipping.

On the ground in Nicosia, teams of journalists and photographers were attempting to get accreditation and cover the war. After jumping up and down, I managed to get accreditation with the Royal Navy, which as it turned out, was the best of the bunch. I still have my accreditation card as a British War Correspondent.

Carrying our credentials, Geoff Thursby of the News Chronicle and myself - representing Central Press Photos - raced out to the Nicosia airfield where Brigadier Tubby Butler was supervising the assembly of the Third Battalion of the Parachute Regiment who were to be dropped at El Gamil Airfield.

Tubby, standing on the tarmac, stared at us in surprise. "You really want to come on this picnic?"

We nodded enthusiastically. "We are ready," said Geoff.

"Have you done a drop before?"

Geoff nodded but I shook my head.

The Brigadier stared at me. "One, you haven't experienced a drop, and two, you're probably too heavy. Sorry, Bob."

Disappointed, I turned away, and heard Geoff being accepted for a ride. Whether he dropped or not, I cannot recall, but he produced an excellent graphic description of the drop at Egypt's El Gamil Airfield. A total of 668 British Paratroopers were dropped on November 5th followed by 470 French Paratroopers. The Royal Marine Commando made the first British helicopter assault in the Suez War.

GOING TO WAR ON THE MANXMAN

As the drop took place, the Royal Navy war correspondents were being taken aboard HMS Manxman for the worst yet exciting sea passage I have ever experienced. The Manxman was a twin-funneled Abdiel-class fast cruiser minelayer and had seen first class service on the Malta convoys in World War II.

A very friendly Rear Admiral took us all into a large cabin and said, "There's a nasty little swell and we are going to take it at speed. You would be advised to sit on the deck and enjoy the trip to Port Said."

We soon caught on. The Manxman got up to speed, some 32 knots in what we thought was a substantial if not chaotic swell. "What'll you have?"

asked the Admiral. The crew served us drinks while we sat on the floor, clinging to the walls and the carpet. Luckily I never get seasick but it was a trip to test those with weak stomachs. Larry Burrows, the lean English photographer for Time-Life sat next to me. "I'd take a picture if I could stand," he muttered with a grin.

At Port Said we found we were to be billeted on the HMS Forth, one of Britain's submarine depot ships. Launched on Clydebank, Scotland in 1938, she had an imposing stature. In simple terms the Forth was a service and repair facility for submarines. She had come from her station at Msida Creek in Malta with over 1,100 men.

We had a couple of surprises. As accredited Royal Navy correspondents we had expectations that we would be at sea, and not have access to shore news, where all the action was. A Navy officer put our minds at rest.

"We'll be in port for the duration. You can come and go whenever you please. You are guests of Her Majesty's Royal Navy and you have honorary ranks of Lieutenant Commanders."

They had given us naval jackets and trousers before leaving Cyprus. I shook my head in pure amazement: Two years from El Firdan and Forces Broadcasting in Egypt. Now I'm an officer. It was an enjoyable experience, and more was to follow. Larry Burrows and I shared a very comfortable two bunk deck cabin on HMS Forth. The ship was tied up in Port Said from which we could conveniently observe the comings and goings on the dock and the city beyond.

We dropped our bags and headed for the shore. There was no fighting, but armored vehicles and soldiers were everywhere. We met up with a number of Army correspondents who were not too happy about their accommodation. "We're in a wrecked apartment with shell holes in the wall for ventilation. There's no power for lights and we're cooking on primus stoves. They bring water in," said one unhappy reporter. Larry Burrows and I kept a low profile on accommodation. We both concluded that if you have to go to war, go Navy.

IN THE HEART OF PORT SAID

A PR Land Rover picked us up and took us on a tour of the town. Streets were littered with rubble from blown up buildings, a team of Arabs under British supervision was picking up Egyptian bodies, stacking them on a truck and hauling them to the cemetery. We spotted several hundred Arabs raiding a bakery and carrying away loaves of bread and sacks of flour. Some sacks had broken open and Arabs were now a ghostly white trying to run away. A little boy in a dirty, cotton striped galibeer, dropped an opened bag of flour which spilled over the street. Whenever you photograph children, you get down to their level. It makes all the difference. We did and got a great picture.

SUNKEN SHIP IN THE CANAL:
It was eerie to see and photograph sunken ships in the once busy waterway. This one was taken from the bridge of a ship, most of which was under water. In the background is HMS Manxman, the ship that brought the Navy correspondents over from Cyprus.

In the bombing, two massive oil storage tanks had been hit by Israeli planes. Black smoked drifted above the town and the stink of burning oil permeated everything. There were no signs of the Egyptian Army and I heard one British reporter quip: "They're training for the Olympics." We heard there were casualties on all sides, particularly the Egyptians. At the Port Said cemetery there were bodies in the gates stacked six feet high. The odor was atrocious and the flies were something else. I shuddered at the sight, but I took photos anyway. They were banned by the military censor.

As far as the eye could see, there was the strange and unnerving sight of sunken ships littering the Suez Canal. One does not expect to see parts of the upper structures of ships peering above water. It's eerie. The Royal Navy provided a shuttle and took me out to one of the half-sunken ships. I climbed on the bridge of the dredger Paul Solente and took pictures of other sunken vessels with Port Said in the background. Later, I got a helicopter ride and took pictures of the famous Canal with its sunken ships.

One major change from my first arrival in the Canal Zone with the RAF in 1951 is that the large statue of Ferdinand de Lesseps that graced the waterway had gone. An angry mob pulled it down earlier in the year when Nasser nationalized the Canal.

I encountered a civilian Alan Bennett who, with his wife and family, had maintained a business in Port Said for 15 years. Disgusted, he was heading for home at Slough in the U.K. He said there were some thirty-five British business people quitting Port Said. When I had been in Cairo for the Robert Menzies visit, several British businessmen had been accused of spying, but the accusations appeared to be idle threats. Still, foreigners in Egypt did not feel safe.

During our travels, we met up with some French, Israeli and more British correspondents and photographers. Terry Fincher was there, along with Magnum's David (Chim) Seymour and Jean Roy of Paris Match. Jean was interested in events occurring in Cyprus and said he planned to come over soon. Regarding Paris Match, I mentioned his magazine had run a full page picture of a young twelve-year old being arrested in a Nicosia riot earlier in the year. "Hey, I'll check in with you, Bob," he said.

HELICOPTER OVER THE FRONT LINE

There had been a ceasefire some two days after the invasion started, which bothered a lot of army people. So things were relatively quiet. The Army PR people were offering photographers helicopter rides close to the front lines for aerial shots.

British Army pilot John Gary left the railway station at El Cap, some two miles north of Kantara and quickly took the helicopter up to 2,000 feet. We immediately spotted the British and French lines with troops ready and waiting. Some 400 yards to the south I made out four Egyptian tanks, two field gun emplacements plus a lot of little figures moving about. The helicopter moved east over the salt flats and swooped down over the French Foreign Legion. They waved to us. We went back to flying over the British lines.

I felt sad that the invasion had stopped several miles north of El Firdan and the town of Ismalia. I could vaguely make out the old El Firdan airstrip which had been the home of my old radar unit, 751 Signals. Beyond and in the haze, was Ismalia and Lake Timsah. The trip was uneventful, at least so we thought.

As we landed several officers and PR types raced up. "Are you all okay? The Jippies were shooting at you all the time."

Pilot John Gary commented: "Didn't hear a thing." Mechanics searched the aircraft and found only one bullet hole in the rear fuselage. We had been lucky.

A SADNESS IN THE PRESS CORPS

Next day, we took a drive down the Port Said to Ismalia Road, found some French Foreign Legion troops swimming naked in the Sweet Water Canal built by de Lesseps to provide water to construction teams. It was off bounds to British troops as a "severe health hazard," because village Egyptians were known to dump refuse in it, bathe and more. We also got pictures of a camel that had parked itself on the railway tracks and refused to budge. The camel owner was filled with terror. He feared some soldiers would shoot the animal, but nobody did.

We went as far as a road block near El Cap, took more pictures of troops behind sandbags and armored cars and started back. Most of the troops were out in the desert flanking the road. As we headed north to Port Said we heard isolated shooting. Should we go back? There was supposed to be a cease-fire. The consensus was nothing is happening.

Just then, a Land Rover passed us going south towards the front line. We recognized David Seymour of Magnum and Jean Roy of Paris Match. They waved as they hurtled by. That was the last any of the press corps saw of the two alive.

Harold Evans, a Daily Telegraph reporter and later editor of the Sunday Telegraph in an essay on Reporting in Times of Conflict wrote: "A cease-fire had been declared, but they were stopped by a British officer and warned not to go beyond his final outpost. They gave him the 'V sign' and roared on. The next order was from an Egyptian outpost: Stop. They roared on again, only this time they were machine-gunned."

CENSORS AND THE UN ARRIVES

Getting stories on the war out of Suez was a challenge. They were all heavily censored and a delay was imposed on photos and newsreel film so the pictures arrived late and lost much of their immediacy. When I think of the immediacy that is available today through satellites, it's like being in a different world.

Would the Suez War have been different if the landings, the fighting, the burning oil tanks, the sinking of ships in the canal had been made available on CNN and BBC News as they happened? Even with all the electronic apparatus available today, most people have no real idea of what happens in war. And the real politics of war remain hidden, sometimes for months, even years. Even the internet with so-called instant video fails to reveal the root causes and effects of war.

On Wednesday, January 25th 1957 two hundred Norwegian soldiers of the United Nations Police Force arrived in Port Said on a special train flying the blue and white U.N. flag. Two hours earlier it had come across no-man's-land at El Cap into the British Zone. As they left Port Said station and marched through the streets, they were mobbed by over 1,000 Egyptians. The British Army who were on stand-by, then stepped in to give the Norwegians protection. The scene was observed by over fifty correspondents and photographers.

Initially the U.N. force was greeted by the Egyptians but then the agitators took over and instigated a riot. Lieutenant-General Sir Hugh Stockwell, commanding the Anglo-French Forces, drove onto the scene and the rioters gathered round his Jeep. The General promptly jumped out and ignoring the risk, grabbed a rioter by the arm and dragged him over to the nearest British soldier. "Put this fellow under arrest," he cried and somehow this small incident seemed to quite the mob. It was a photo I enjoyed taking. The outbreaks of rioting continued spasmodically. One American journalist, Arch Parson was shaken up when he got too far into the mob.

With the arrival of the United Nations forces, who were Norwegians, everything should have been quiet, but a lot of returning Egyptians decided to get rough with the British Forces who were now expected take a back seat while the U.N. took the lead. There was confusion because some sources proclaimed that the British had to protect the United Nations troops. Anyway there were outbreaks of riots in Port Said. We said goodbye to HMS Forth and caught a plane to Cyprus. By evening I was in the Cyprus Mail, packing up material for London. I wrote several stories for the Cyprus Mail, including a picture I had taken from the bridge of one of the sunken ships in the canal.

GREAT NEWS IN PHOTOGRAPHY

A letter from John Lacey at Central Press in London contained great news. My photo of Drosoulla Demetriadou sitting beside the body of her fiancé Bonici had received an Honorable Mention in the British Press Photos of the Year 1956 – News Category. And the other picture of the three British policemen on Murder Mile was to be included in the Encyclopedia Britannica Exhibition. Wow! When these things happen one feels elated. I wanted to phone Iro and tell her, but I don't think she would have been impressed, so I resisted.

As the days passed, the authorities came up with a human cost of the Suez War. Total British dead: 16, with 96 wounded. Total French dead: 10. Israelis dead: 189. The number of Egyptians killed was never really made clear and the Egyptian Government never revealed the true numbers. Sources estimated 650 were killed by the Anglo-French operation and 1,000 killed by Israel.

As I pondered the Suez War and its victims, I wondered where God was in all this and if he was around, did he care, or was he on holiday in Spain? The God aspect just didn't make sense. Perhaps one day someone will explain God to me, I thought as I mulled over a brandy sour in Antononaki's Bar.

11

THE SEARCH FOR
"HARD CORE KILLERS"

B Y EARLY 1957 PEOPLE in Britain and editorial writers were expressing anger and frustration over the Cyprus issue. The situation was frustrating. British lives, both military and civilian, were being lost and few if any E.O.K.A. gunmen were being brought to justice. In addition Turkish Cypriots were succeeding in having a "voice" by launching retaliatory attacks on Greek Cypriots.

British troops returning from Suez bolstered Security Forces and anti-terrorism operations assumed a twenty-four hours a day, seven days a week activity. Cyprus seemed thick with troops. So much so, it was impossible to move even a few miles without travelers being stopped for identification. Still nothing happened.

Many of the top newspaper correspondents returned home or back to base, and I felt bored. You could only visit Theo's Dolphin or Antonakis or the Cosmopolitan bar so often and I didn't feel like drinking.

Winter had come early and by early January severe blizzards had dumped thick snow on the Troodos Mountains, making many roads impassable. Some mountain villages were cut-off completely and in the middle of the conflict, an RAF Valetta transport aircraft dropped food and supplies to marooned villagers. Air Force PR Don Scott-Reid suggested I might go along for pictures. He forgot to tell me the door on the Valetta was open for the aircrew to push out boxes of food supplies as the aircraft hopped over mountain ridges, tree-tops and villages. I almost froze to death, but I did get some good photos.

Biting cold winds coming from Russia and Turkey in the north drove many of the E.O.K.A. fighters to abandoned caves and to seek refuge elsewhere. This was the second winter for George Grivas and his mountain men and they were ill-prepared for the cold, heavy snow. Caves and mountain camps were admirable in the hot summer months. But now these were wet and cold and heating was a no-no because where there's fire there is smoke, and troops were everywhere.

So it was necessary for Grivas and the men to move down into the lower level villages and seek refuge in homes, churches and farms. But villages had informers and although many communities had been "cleaned of traitors" by E.O.K.A. it was still necessary to post look-outs. Villagers became anxious. If they were found to harbor terrorists, the penalties could be severe, certainly years in prison or even a death sentence.

In Nicosia Major General Douglas Kendrew, Chief of the Security Forces told his teams: "Anything unusual, anything that does not appear normal, children who appear nervous and anxious, sounds in the night especially vehicles moving, dogs barking for long periods, people standing on corners, bringing in excessive food supplies, we want to know about it."

"Cypriots aren't going to breathe without us knowing about it," he said. "Don't waste a minute. I want the hard core killers."

Kendrew's intelligence teams worked round the clock, moving through villages, talking to Cypriots who liked to talk, even about the weather. Tiny, almost seemingly insignificant information trickled in and the clean-up began.

On Tuesday, January 15th 1957, suddenly and without warning, 3,000 British troops penetrated all the roads leading into the Troodos Mountains. The troops came in at dawn and within a few minutes the entire mountain area was cordoned off. A special raiding force of men from the 2nd Parachute Regiment surrounded the villages of Sarandi, Omodhos and Kannavia.

The work of intelligence was paying off. A fire was burning in the grate of a village house. A child kept looking nervously at the fire. It was doused and underneath a stone was a secret trapdoor leading to a large room. Eureka! Inside was a large group of E.O.K.A. fighters. Similar discoveries were made in the other villages.

Grivas lost eighteen of his top lieutenants. Men like Polycarpou Yorgadjis, Argyrios Karademas, Nicos Spanos, Nicos Georghiou, Kyrakos Matsis, Haralambous Hambis and Kyriacos Kokkinos. All carried large rewards for their capture. It was indeed a black day for E.O.K.A. Information kept flowing.

Hours later, Markos Drakos, a 24 year-old gunman, third to Grivas in the organization and largely responsible for mountain ambushes, was killed. After running and taking refuge in a cave during a thunder and hail storm, he emerged to find himself face to face with a British patrol. It was a race to fire first and Drakos came in second.

THE HUNT FOR AFXENTIOU

The "Wanted" list was getting shorter. But besides Grivas the leader, there was still another important killer to be caught. Gregoris Afxentiou. He had the privilege of being the first known terrorist in the E.O.K.A. Struggle. He was identified as one of the team that dynamited the Cyprus Broadcasting Station at Nicosia on April 1st 1955, almost two years before.

Kendrew's intelligence teams increased the pressure. Afxentiou was known as a lone operator. Very few people knew where he was because he kept moving. As second-in-command to Grivas, he, like the leader, rarely stayed in one place for more than two days. He disliked and distrusted even good Cypriot supporters, and he chose hideouts that were in the highest and most difficult parts of the mountains. But the snows had driven him down into the lower levels.

It was now raining and Afxentiou had spent more than his usual number of days in Makheras Monastery, a large sprawling building perched on a Rocky plateau in the eastern Troodos. He was becoming anxious and was ready to move on when a courier arrived: "The British are coming. Tomorrow morning."

Afxentiou and the four men with him moved out, carrying blankets and supplies with them. They were Antonis Papdopoulos and Phideas Simeonides who both carried $5,000 rewards on their heads, and Andreas Styllianou and Augustinos Efstathiou. They moved down the valley into heavy brush where a temporary hideout had been constructed. Afxentiou objected to the corrugated iron roof, although it was well covered with earth and bushes and chances of discovery were rare.

It was the young Efstathiou who once ran a sandwich stall on Murder Mile who told me the story. "They found us this morning at 3:30. Earlier we saw a goat-herder further down the valley who might have seen us. We don't know, but sometime afterwards we heard the helicopters coming and we knew we didn't stand a chance. We sat in the hideout half asleep, half awake. Then a clatter of stones really woke us up. Someone was outside above us, sliding down the slope. Then we heard a shout for us to surrender and leave our weapons behind."

"Afxentiou told us to go, and we obeyed. I was surprised when he failed to follow us. I thought that perhaps he expected the soldiers to believe there were only four of us, and he could hide low and escape later. But perhaps he had already decided to stay and fight it out."

Covered with burns he had received in the hideout, Efstathiou smoked a cigarette a reporter had given him. "I'm sorry it's all over. I've been fourteen months in the mountains. I never killed anybody. I'm a patriot."

The four men from the hideout had surrendered to men from the Duke of Wellington's Regiment. Leading the patrol was a Greek-speaking liaison officer, Lieutenant John Middleton. "We knew Afxentiou was in the hideout, so we sent Efstathiou to go back and tell him to surrender because he was completely surrounded."

Efstathiou went, and immediately a sten gun opened up from inside the hideout. Middleton thought Efstathiou had been killed. A hail of bullets came from the hideout. One killed Corporal Peter Brown.

And so a siege began in earnest. The battle lasted some nine hours. More troops moved into the valley to support the Duke of Wellington's Regiment. It was now raining heavily and everything was becoming soaked, and that is when the press crew, including myself arrived.

To make matters worse, we didn't have overcoats and the path towards the hideout was thick mud. We rarely if ever wore overcoats. Geoff Thursby of the News Chronicle cursed gently as he slipped down the bank in front of me as he tried to avoid a line of bedraggled soldiers in capes carrying boxes of ammunition. It seemed ironic that the only people in the dry were Afxentiou and Efstathiou in the hideout.

"Burn and blast them out," was the order from higher up. Shortly after soldiers draped in water-proofs and carrying large cans of petrol on their shoulders arrived. The media stood above the scene on a rocky abutment and as the day progressed it became quite hairy. Not only did we have the putrid stink of exploding dynamite, the humidity of the drenching rain, but bullets occasionally zipped by treacherously close to our heads.

We were drawn between lying flat unable to see anything, or crouching or standing up and risking being shot, so we crouched, peering through the rain as sappers poured gallons of petrol down the slope, so that it swamped the hideout. Afxentiou must have smelled it because a grenade came hurtling out and exploded in protest. The Bren gunners stationed at strategic points in the valley opened fire, and bullets crackled and ricocheted off the rocks. For some time we had no idea who was shooting at who.

Someone lowered a beehive explosive charge loaded with fleschettes over the top of the hideout. Fleschettes are steel pointed objects like darts. They're used in anti-personnel explosives where attackers seek to inflict serious injuries.

"Down everybody," cried a sergeant nearby. A terrific explosion shook the air, rocks hurtled perilously close to everyone and the sound echoed eerily through the neighboring mountains.

Moments later, a volley of shots burst from the hideout. Afxentiou was still active.

"The beehive has to be directly over the hideout" said a colonel. "It has to be placed at its weakest point." This, he explained, was an extremely high risk task. "If Afentiou hears someone approaching he could easily flip a grenade backwards onto the roof."

A captain stepped forward. "I'll do it, sir." He was a tall, well built officer and wore a thin smile on his face, the sort of smile which really means, "It's a challenge." Heroes are like that.

Wasting no time, the captain picked up another Beehive explosive and tucked it under his arm. He checked his pistol, adjusted his water-proof, and then slowly worked his way down the mountainside. Everyone watching felt the tension mounting. Once, the captain's foot slipped, but he quickly regained his balance without a sound. There was nothing else for us to do but watch. A deadly tension enveloped. Even the rain seemed to stop.

The captain was now directly above the corrugated iron roof and we watched as he laid the charge. One false move meant death. He could slip off the roof right into Afxentiou's sights. Killing would be easy for the E.O.K.A. man. The Beehive was in position, and the captain gingerly started back up the slope. At the top, he looked at his watch. It had taken exactly six minutes. To us, the watchers, it seemed like hours.

We asked the colonel who the captain was. "Oh, he's Dennis. Dennis Shuttleworth, an ex-Rugby International fellow." (Note: *Dennis Shuttleworth became a Brigadier and played Rugby for England and was always active in the game until he passed away in April 2001, aged 72.*)

A DEATH IN THE MOUNTAINS

A shattering roar bellowed across the valley and echoed through the gray mountains. People in villages miles away claimed they heard it. Columns of thick smoke gushed up through the rain. Suddenly a small figure scrambled out of the hideout ruins and with hands held high cried, "I surrender! Don't shoot! I surrender!" It was little Efstathiou. Soldiers brought him up towards us. I got the picture as they scrambled up the slope.

SUVIVOR OF A TEN HOUR GUN BATTLE:
Augustinos Efstathiou is marched up the rain soaked mountainside by a member of the
Security Forces. Eftstathiou suffered burns in the second attack. He had gone back to the
hideout in an attempt to get Gregoris Afxentiou, Grivas's second in command, to surrender.
The E.O.K.A. fighter died in the hideout.

"Where's Afxentiou?" called a reporter.

"Dead!" said Efstathiou. "He killed himself."

Someone nearby said something about "a brave man." Most of us nodded. He had certainly died bravely in ten hours of tough fighting with all the odds against him. It seemed he had died bravely and well, but this was no pardon for the crimes and murders he had committed for E.O.K.A.

One would think that this was the end of the hunt, but Kendrew's intelligence officers had been following leads and they spent hours talking to all the captured men and the survivors. Somehow, someone casually mentioned a house in Nicosia. It didn't seem important. Nothing special. But in the art of intelligence gathering every fragment of information may lead to something.

But it was the mention of that seemingly unimportant house in Nicosia, and the link that intelligence picked up that would personally shatter my status as a journalist and an individual. And it happened this way.

THE HOUSE AT KRESNA STREET

Roy Bellm, working the night desk at the Cyprus Mail, handed me the communiqué from the Government's Central Newsroom.

"Security Forces with Special Branch Officers this morning raided a house in the Nicosia area. They found large quantities of arms, ammunition and explosives hidden in a hideout under the house. This find is known to be the largest discovery of E.O.K.A. arms since operations began. The explosives are in a dangerous condition and will be disposed in-situ."

It was infuriating. No address! Over the next half hour I made calls to people who should know something, but nobody was around. It was late evening. A man I had come to respect a lot was a major named "Bomber" Harris. Bomber was the coolest man I ever met. He thought of bombs and explosives as a chef would work with butter and sugar. It never disturbed him to work with a flashlight in a dusty three-foot tunnel under a house and dismantle a land mine.

"Sorry, he's out" said the woman. "Call again in the morning."

The fact he was out at 11.00 p.m. was indicative of things happening. We checked our friends at one of the Greek Cypriot newspapers and asked if they knew of British troops cordoning off an area in Nicosia.

"Kresna Street, in the Kaimakli-Kermia area," said the voice.

A few minutes later we were in Roy's car heading for the north-east area of Nicosia. It was typical suburbia. Bungalow-type houses, Americans would call then "ranch" houses, packed relatively close together for middle-class workers. We managed to find Kresna Street after about an hour of searching the maze of roads and cul-de-sacs. The area was principally Greek but close enough to Turkish Cypriots that it was unlikely to draw attention as an E.O.K.A. ammunition storage facility.

We had just found Kresna Street when a dark figure sprang up before us. We expressed relief at seeing a Turkish Cypriot constable.

We showed him our credentials and he pointed to a Security Forces truck parked outside a house. A sergeant checked our credentials again. "You're here for Number 14," he said. "Major Harris has just left and will be back at six when it's light."

We spent the night sleeping lightly on comfortable chairs in the publisher's office until five. We were back on Kresna Street shortly after six. The place was swarming with police and C.I.D. men carrying sandbags into the house. Soldiers were carrying furniture and stacking it on lorries. Several soldiers were cutting down bushes around the house.

"Oh, it's you," said Bomber Harris with mock disgust. "What do you want now?" We always figured he was living on borrowed time and promised never to use his name in news stories. He grinned. "As you're here, come on in." He led the way through the front door and turned into a bedroom. It was almost empty except for a bed frame and a framed photo of Queen Elizabeth and Prince Phillip on the wall.

"Special Branch and the Security Forces raided this place two nights ago. A couple was in bed and showed complete surprise when we broke in. He should have been. He's a Greek Cypriot policeman," said Bomber with a shrug, watching Roy making notes.

Bomber continued: "Special Branch searched the house, an outhouse, and even the attic but found absolutely nothing. "Everyone was convinced there was something in the house. My boys came over and started looking into cracks in the walls and searching for double-backs in cupboards, and tapping the floors in the kitchen for false places, but found nothing.

"Finally, just as we thought we had wrong information, one of the boys spotted a loose tile under the couple's bed. Under it was a trapdoor and below that a large hole, about six feet deep and three feet across," said Bomber. "Inside was an E.O.K.A. arsenal."

"And inside?" I asked eagerly.

"Thirty-three automatic pistols of various makes, fifty-three bombs, mostly home-made. They're still counting the ammunition, but there are over 2,000 rounds," he said. "Apart from some mines and various other pieces of terrorist equipment, there are about 800 sticks of dynamite."

"Wow! And you've moved it all out?"

"Everything except the dynamite. There's enough to wipe the whole of Krensna Steet off the map," he said. "Take a look" We stuck our heads down the hole and took a look. The air smelled heavy, warm and sour. It was the closest I had ever been to so much dynamite.

"Whew! Why can't you move it, Bomber?"

"Dangerous! It's damp! Very dangerous! Air circulation down there is nil and that's why it is getting warm. We couldn't possibly move it, so we're going to blow it up later this morning."

"And this couple, this policeman and his wife were sleeping on top of this?"

"Strange what people will do," grinned Bomber with a vigorous nod.

"So what on earth are we doing here, if it's so damned dangerous?" cried Roy suddenly.

"Just thought you would like a thrill," grinned Bomber. He was like that. "Anything else I can do for you?"

"A picture of you in the hole?" I asked.

"Not bloody likely!" he retorted. "We often take risks, but never a stupid risk. Come back when the place goes up."

Later that morning Bomber had photographers peering over a wall of sandbags about one hundred yards from the house. The entire residential area around the house had been evacuated for 300 yards. Residents stared from behind a barbed wire barricade a quarter of a mile away. Sandbags had been placed around Number 14 to minimize the effects of the blast on adjoining property. We stood eagerly awaiting the blast. Bomber came by. "Watch for falling debris about five to ten seconds after the blast," he cried and ducked away.

The count-down was on. Somewhere along the way I had discovered that the secret to taking good explosion pictures is to wait. As you hear the explosion say, "One-thousand" which takes about one second, then take the picture. If you wait longer you get a cloud of dust and smoke.

The explosion slapped our ears. First there was a sucking sensation, then terrific pressure blowing in. Pieces of wood, masonry and tiles rained down on everything around, some perilously close. Dust and smoke shrouded the remains of where the E.O.K.A. arsenal had been.

Bomber stood outside the gate looking at the hole. "Not a bad job. Not a bad job at all, considering the amount of dynamite."

THE END OF THE STORY?

Roy took me back to the Cyprus Mail, and I prepared photos to radio to London. A few days later, I took a picture of the couple as they were facing a judge in the special court in Nicosia. The London papers boomed: "Couple Slept on a Bed of Dynamite." I thought it was the end of the story. I was dead wrong.

It was a casual response of an E.O.K.A. fighter in the distant mountains that had led Security Forces to a regular three-bedroom house at 14 Kresna Street in the suburbs of Nicosia and a big E.O.K.A. arms cache.

Now, in the Cyprus Police laboratories, expert technicians were examining thirty-three automatic pistols found in the Kresna Street arsenal. Each weapon was meticulously scanned for unique identifiable characteristics that would match it to any crimes committed and also for fingerprints.

Slowly but surely the experts created a list of murders that were connected to several guns, in fact, after a few hours there was evidence that a small number of weapons had been used in killing British people, mostly in the Nicosia area. Some of them showed distinct fingerprints.

By the end of the day the authorities had enough evidence against one man. The word went out: "Arrest Nicos Sampson!"

THE HUNT FOR A KILLER GROUP LEADER

Photos of the journalist, now a hot suspect, were flashed to all security offices and units on Cyprus. Special Branch men, seconded from Scotland Yard, raided Sampson's home and the houses of relatives. Others raided newspaper offices and known haunts including Murder Mile restaurants. People who had known him were questioned. But Nicos Sampson had disappeared.

Special Branch Chief, John Burge was patient. "We'll get him sooner or later," he said confidently. "We have time on our side. Sooner or later, he'll slip and show himself, and we'll be there."

Sampson must have known this. I could imagine Nicos hiding out, patting his trusty gun. Was this a display of bravery or was he a psychopath who really did not understand the consequences of his actions? Some Britons suggested the latter. Knowing Sampson from a dozen encounters, I would say it was acting. He was a born actor. He always liked drama and he loved movies that portrayed heroism and bravery. He talked about "The Bridges at Toko Ri" for days afterwards.

Then one evening, John Burge got the tip he wanted: a lonely country house, about three miles outside Nicosia. Special Branch officers surrounded the place. Burge and an officer smashed their way through the old wooden door. The hallway was in darkness. Another door and a crack of light. Another kick and the door flew open.

Sampson was there attempting to shove the magazine into his weapon. Not wanting to shoot, Burge saw his chance. He leapt at Sampson, grappling with the Sten, and both men toppled over.

"You'll never get me, I'll kill you first," Sampson cried.

For some moments there was a scuffle. Burge's companion raised his pistol, butt first and struck Sampson's head. The man rolled over unconscious.

The officers found a young Cypriot boy cowering in fear in the corner and other officers looked after him. Sampson finally regained consciousness. "Kill me! Kill me! Please mister, I have failed. I cannot suffer it any longer."

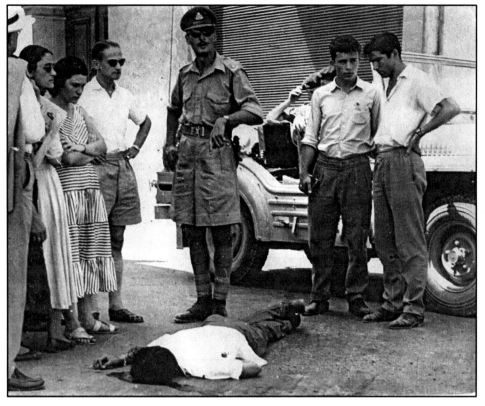

SAMPSON ON THE SCENE:
A spirit voice urged the author to take a general view of the Bonici murder scene. He did and it shows journalist and E.O.K.A. Killer Group leader Nicos Sampson holding his camera, standing to the right of the officer. Sampson, in his own newspaper, later told how he conducted the killing. Standing next to Drosoulla Demetriadou is Brian Wright, editor of the Cyprus Mail. The Army officer at center is Major Dick Stuckey of the South Staffordshire Regiment.

It was now raining and they drove back to Nicosia in open Land Rovers. Totally wet, they walked into Security HQ and were welcomed with cheering.

Late that night, Sampson told his story to John Burge which was taken down as a statement. "I was the leader of the execution group. I know you will hang me. You must understand. I am a fanatical nationalist, and I hate communists. I was the best reporter in Cyprus. The police arrested me in Famagusta once, but I was innocent. I was sent to prison for three months."

"It was then that I began working for E.O.K.A. I joined the execution squad through Karillas in August 1956. I first killed the two U.K. policemen on Ledra Street. People say I committed twenty murders."

Months later in a Nicosia Special Court, Sampson denied the statement. "No! No! No! Untrue! Every time there is a killing, they say Nic Sampson, Nic Sampson."

The evening Sampson was captured, I telexed Central Press. "The Bonici killing. General view. Sampson is standing to the right of the British Army officer, holding a camera." The Sampson arrest was a sensation. Next morning newspapers ran my general view of the Bonici murder scene. It pays for photographers to get general views. You never know who might have a story.

I thanked that little voice for the tip and later that night, I pondered; did that little voice know what was going to happen ahead of time, or was it a friendly suggestion? Was the little voice in my life a spirit? And if it was, does this mean there is a God also? I recall Rev. Nathaniel Nairn at Stubbings Church saying on Sunday, "God is spirit."

But there was another side to the capture of an E.O.K.A. killer group leader and I mulled this over too. The arrest of Nicos Sampson, the friendly reporter, the man whom I had taught to use a Voigtlander camera, the fellow I had joined in the Regina Street cinema to watch a war film, the man who helped me the night they burned down the British Institute, left me perplexed. I had experienced a number of surprises since being in Cyprus, but this was the most sinister, the most terrifying. You never know your friends.

SAMPSON ON TRIAL

In the Special Court in Nicosia, the first charge leveled against Sampson was for the murder of British police Sergeant Cyril Thoroughgood. You may recall it happened outside the Cyprus Mail. Of the three British policemen shot, two died, and one survived. That survivor, Sergeant William Webb was brought in to testify. Looking pale and fragile Webb told of how three policemen were walking down Ledra Street.

"Suddenly, I heard shooting," he said. "I half turned and saw my two friends being shot. At the same time I was shot myself. I was hit five times, and I still have one bullet in my back. I fell among broken glass. Shots were still fired at me. I drew my pistol and fired back. But they ran away."

The Prosecutor: "Who shot at you?"

The courtroom tensed.

"Who shot at me?" he repeated slowly. Suddenly he lifted his arm and pointed at Sampson. "That's the man, there. He shot me. He was a little closer than he is now."

It looked like a closed case against Sampson. The judge asked if force was used against the accused for obtaining a statement.

Burge hotly denied this, but it was insufficient. The case was dismissed. If a wave of jubilation surged through Sampson's mind, it was short lived. The Prosecutor had another charge, which under the State of Emergency carried the death penalty: possession of a firearm on the night of his arrest. Sampson's lawyers had a difficult time with this one, there were too many witnesses. It was an open and shut case. Sampson was sentenced to death.

FATE PLAYS IN FAVOR OF SAMPSON

But if we all thought Sampson would be hanged at Nicosia Prison, we were very much mistaken. Fate was on Sampson's side. It so happened that during the appeals process launched by his lawyers, the political situation in Cyprus took a change for the better. Archbishop Makarios was released from his exile in the Seychelles and went to Athens. With his arrival in the Greek capital, there were hopes that with his release, talks aimed at bringing a solution to the Cyprus problem might be concluded in talks at Zurich. Reluctant to arouse any more hostility among Greek Cypriots, Governor John Harding ordered a reprieve and commuted Sampson to serve life imprisonment.

Three days later on September 13th 1957 Sampson was taken on board an aircraft bound for London and a British prison. He served less than a year and a half before being set free under the Amnesty Terms in March 1959. In just over a year, he was to come back into my world with some startling revelations of how he saved my life.

12

LUCY AND THE DESERT KINGS

I N THOSE EARLY MONTHS of 1957 Cyprus had become less of a picture story and more of a dialogue and writing story. On the political scene there were efforts to get discussions going that would resolve the Cyprus conflict. While I was thinking about visiting the family in England - Mum and my two sisters, Sheila and Diane - a rumor came that the Chief Justice of Cyprus was "involved in something" in the other Mediterranean island of Malta. The idea intrigued me and I found myself checked in to the five-star Phoenicia Hotel in Valetta.

Malta prides itself on its beautiful historic buildings such as the Grand Masters Palace and St. John's Cathedral, and the Phoenicia parallels that beauty with a gorgeous entrance. In November 1949, Princess Elizabeth and Prince Philip stayed there. It displays many paintings, mostly by Maltese artists. Thus, it has lots of appeal for people of all ages.

John Perry, a writer with Mabel Strickland's "Times of Malta" said enquires had drawn a blank and it appeared to be a non-story. Then he added: "My wife and are going out to dinner tonight. We have a lady friend. Would you like to come and make a foursome?"

Lucy was a slim, delightfully well formed 29-year-old who had been born in Malta. Her family name was Cassar-Torregianni and the Torreggiani's ancestral links went back to the 1500s and the Florentine Renaissance sculptor Pietro Torrigiano. His work is preserved in Westminster Abbey, a gilt bronze at the tomb of King Henry VII and his queen. Other works are preserved in various parts of Europe plus two busts in the Metropolitan Museum in New York. Torrigiano had a violent temper and is said to have broken fellow student Michelangelo's nose in a quarrel.

Of course, this really had nothing to do with the way Lucy's presence impacted me. She was wonderful! Electrifying! Sexy! The curvature of her body stirred deep feelings in my mind, my heart and my body. Her smile and her flashing eyes seemed to call out to me and I desperately wanted to be with her. I said some dumb things that night. The words flowed non-stop from my mouth.

"Are you married, Bob?"

"No, I was recently divorced. A Greek Cypriot lady whom I loved a lot."

"Do you plan to get married again," asked Lucy, with an air of innocence.

"Five times!" I said. The words were out, flowing like a mountain spring gushing from a rock. I learned later when studying metaphysics that Aquarians are inclined to make rash, provocative statements. It's almost as if they are so bored with their current life, they wish to stir controversy just for the sheer hell of it. But that night in early 1957 my energy was rampart and I seemed to be testing the others.

The other two including Lucy, seemed stunned by my statement. On the way back to the Phoenicia, the couple dropped Lucy off at her apartment. "Would you like to come in for a nightcap?" asked the electrifying woman. A few minutes later I found myself in an armchair with Lucy's body draped around me, hugging and kissing. I carried her into the bedroom where we made earthy, passionate love and it was like Hemingway had written years ago – the earth moved! Well, it did.

For my seven days in Malta, Lucy and I wandered through Valetta and Sliema and watched the fascinating, colorful boats. We took a taxi to Imtarfa where Lucy had friends in the military base there. Her familiarity with them triggered waves of jealousy and a strange resentment and anger, feelings I had difficulty controlling. Those negative egotistic feelings stayed with me for many years before I found the skills which brought about the freedom to break away. Jealousy was to cost me many friendships through the years, as we shall narrate.

LUCY IS MARRIED

One day, I discovered that Lucy was married to a Royal Navy officer and had two young children, Dorothy and Martin currently with their father in England. So it was with disturbed emotions that I flew back to Cyprus on a Skyways flight. When one feels jealousy, anger and its companion, mistrust, the result is suffering. I suffered because I did not know of any way out, apart from throwing myself off a tall building, the prospect of which made me shudder. I dislike high places.

There was no logic to it. I had no idea why I was feeling this way. It was frustrating, irritating. One evening when we had been sitting in a cabin on HMS Forth at Port Said, an American reporter said, "Egby. You have an ego problem. You need to get out of it." Was this the suffering that Elen, my great grandmother, referred to when she said, "You will set yourself free." The idea perplexed me. I sensed there was something in my suffering and her prediction, but I did not know what.

ENGLAND AND A CHANGE IN DIRECTION

A month after returning to Cyprus from Malta, I found myself in England at Harrow where Lucy was staying with her life-long friend, Skyways flight attendant, Nan White. Lucy said she was getting a divorce. I met her husband, Dennis who seemed a nice chap, very intelligent, and his concern was that I should look after Lucy. I confirmed that I would.

Cyprus was dead from a news picture point of view, at least that's the way I felt. The team at Central Press, appreciating my need to earn money on which to live, suggested I get a news connection, an agency where I could sell my stories. I remembered once meeting George Pipal of Scripps-Howard/United Press and he said: "If you ever need a job, check out Leo in the London office."

I found Leo (I think his last name was Stecker) tucked away in a small Fleet Street office. "So you were an accredited war correspondent at Suez and you got a big British Press Pictures award, yeah, I recall the photo. That gal, Drosoulla, she's in England now," he said enthusiastically as he scanned my resume. "We could have used you at Suez."

Over lunch in a corner of a smoky Fleet Street pub thronged by a mob of writers, columnists and reporters, Leo said: "Amman, Jordan. The young King Hussein is having a rough time holding onto his throne. We could use a good freelance out there. I'll set up collect facilities." Next day, I was at London Airport on my way to the Hashemite Kingdom of Jordan. "I'll find a place for us to live," I told Lucy and I was gone.

The Arab Airways DC3 touched down at Amman Airport and I was glad to get off. An Arab in a galibeer had entertained some passengers and terrified others by sitting in the aisle and making tea on a small Primus stove fueled by kerosene. Nobody stopped him so I think he carried some weight.

In Amman the air was oppressive, dusty and humid. Arab Legion troops and Bedouins were everywhere. At the Amman Club Hotel in the downtown, correspondents were still discussing in stunned voices how Army nationalist officers had attempted to overthrow the 22 year-old King Hussein and the Bedouins or "Bedou" as they were known, had left their desert camps and came to town on their camels to save their monarch.

For two days the Bedou sorted out the rebels, unmercifully decapitating offenders with their swords. The situation was now quiet, tense but quite.

Colin Lawson had watched the rioting from Hussein's Palace and some keen editor had run a headline: "The King and I Face the Mob," and given Lawson a byline. I must admit that after listening to the press team in the hotel, the actions of the Bedouin in Jordan made events in Cyprus seem fairly civilized. From that point forward, I developed a deep respect for the Bedouins.

THE KING OF JORDAN

Hussein was a Bedouin. The kings of the Hashemite Kingdom of Jordan claim a direct descent from the Islamic prophet Muhammad and claims to be the oldest tribe in the Arab world. But in those days of 1957 he was a survivor and looking back I'm sure he had a guardian angel. His grandfather, King Abdullah frequently took the young Hussein to the mosque for prayers.

One day the aging King gave his grandson a medal, a keepsake to wear. Shortly after, on Friday, July 20th 1951 a Palestinian extremist, fearing that the King would work for a peace pact with neighboring Israel, assassinated Abdullah as he attended the Al-aqsa Mosque in Jerusalem

The 15 year-old prince immediately chased the gunman who stopped and fired at Hussein. The bullet glanced off the medal and Hussein's life was saved.

Hussein was destined for the throne faster than he or anyone else imagined. Abdullah's son, Hussein's father Talal was crowned King of Jordan but was forced to abdicate because of mental instability. In this way Hussein was proclaimed King of the Hashemite Kingdom on August 11th 1952 at the age of 16. One day, while shopping in downtown Amman, a merchant, discovering that I collected stamps, sold me two stamps for a few dinars. They featured King Talal, but were never issued because of the abdication, and were generally destroyed. I still have them in my collection.

Hussein was as British as they come. After basic education in Amman, he went on to attend the Victorian College in Alexandria, Egypt which had become the "safe house" for Royal children whose fathers had lost their European thrones in World War II. The College was founded in 1902 by Barings Bank, one of the most highly trusted and esteemed financial houses in Britain. (It collapsed in a mind-jarring scandal in the mid-1990s). Hussein went on to Harrow School in England and took his officer training at the Royal Military Academy at Sandhurst. He loved flying and could fly just about any aircraft.

With the situation returning to normal in Amman, the international media departed. Vincent Ryder of the Daily Telegraph took up residence at the Amman Club Hotel. Vincent was a crossword enthusiast and thoroughly enjoyed taxing his mind on doing his newspaper's daily challenge.

Every day we would walk up to the Government's Information Office. George Halaby, a tall, slim Arab whose mouth always had a cigarette dangling, was the stringer for INS, the International News Service which was soon to be acquired by United Press. He always kept his ear to the ground and George discovered a cottage on a hill overlooking the downtown that Lucy and I could rent. From the rear of the cottage there were over 200 wooden steps down to the main street, or one could call a cab which would come to the front door. We didn't need an alarm clock to awaken in the morning, the call to prayer resonated everywhere from a mosque close by.

Also nearby was the Jabal al-Qal'a, also called Amman Citadel, a national historic site at the center of downtown Amman. The L-shaped hill is one of seven jebels that comprised the original city. The area has been occupied since Neolithic times and like Jericho, between Amman and Jerusalem is among the world's oldest continuously inhabited places.

LUCY ARRIVES WITH NEWS

Lucy arrived with the news she was pregnant which was stunning. A child? The idea was thrilling. I decided not to write to Mum and my sisters in England until the baby arrived. Lucy quickly got the house in ship-shape. The cottage was surrounded by lots of green bushes and some palm trees, which kept the place fairly cool. We soon found out the shortages in Amman. No fresh milk. We became fans of KLIM, the powdered milk which failed to taste the same, but one did get used to it. If you look at KLIM, it is MILK backwards. Reading backwards is a gift I picked up at the Cyprus Mail reading the print galleys upside down. Eventually we discovered almost fresh milk packed in strange triangular bags.

As the only resident British journalist and news photographer in Amman, we were Open House for many of the journalists passing through. They brought drinks and food and all had a good time. Among them was Joe Alex Morris who was working for United Press but was destined for the Los Angeles Times. I had met him several times in Cyprus. Joe brought with him a whole crowd from the Cairo offices of Time Magazine. Geoff Thursby turned up and brought Dennis Martin of the Daily Mirror. Some evenings I felt we were living in a press room. The discussions were always vibrant and informative. Frank Kallsen of the American CBS network came too, in fact just before Christmas 1957, he asked me to operate his 16mm sound-camera on top of a building flanking Nativity Square in Bethlehem while he talked about the upcoming festive season.

One unusual United Press international correspondent who used to come to the house with Joe Morris was Russell Jones. When Russian tanks invaded Budapest, Hungary in 1956, Russell held out as the sole American reporter. Frequently under fire, he managed to smuggle out up-to-the-minute coverage. For his work he was awarded the George Polk Memorial Award from the Overseas Press Club, the Sigma Delta Chi Award for International Reporting, and the Pulitzer Prize for "excellent and sustained coverage...at great personal risk." To talk with him you would never think he was a journalistic hero. Cool and a great fellow to be with.

TAXI TO BAGHDAD

I was still getting used to who-was-who in Jordan when United Press sent me a telex. "King Saud state visit to Iraq, May 11th. Need pix." Baghdad was about 500 miles east of Amman. "We have two days to get there," said Joe Morris. "Let's get a cab."

Getting a taxi for long distances is not unusual in the Arab countries. Scheduled limousines leave every day for distant cities and the fares are relatively good, at least they were in 1957. The Baghdad limo had already left, but the taxi company mustered a driver, fluent in English. We grabbed our bags and my camera outfit. I flashed a "bye" to Lucy and within the hour we were headed north-east.

Our first town was Mafraq which is a renowned spot for housing people you don't particularly like. The Jordanians housed Jewish soldiers captured from east Jerusalem captured in the 1948 war, and the British Forces had an encampment there which was to be evacuated later that month. Then we headed east along a highway that was more of a dusty track than a motor way or autobahn. We passed the occasional truck piled high with boxes, and desert tribesmen herding their goats.

The driver knew we were close to the Iraqi border. If we had been driving ourselves we would have gone straight across. There was not a soul in sight. The driver stopped. His name was Asa. We asked him why we had stopped. He held up his finger signaling silence.

We stood outside the car. There was nothing anywhere except white sand. Then they came. Fast moving dots at first, leaving a trail of dust. We gradually distinguished who they were. Arabs - seventeen of them, in billowing robes, with headdresses - carrying long barreled rifles and all riding sleek, healthy looking camels. They gathered round and invited us to coffee. From out of nowhere a Primus stove appeared and a tall coffee pot. Demitasse cups. You could feel the power of the coffee. Invigorating.

A tall, distinguished Arab officer who spoke some English explained this was a unit of the Arab Legion. "We protect the border between our countries," he explained and asked about our visit to Iraq. While we were talking, an old American Dodge appeared from Iraqi territory and spotting the Legion, decided to make a detour south across the open desert. The officer waved his hand, barked some words and eight Legionnaires immediately mounted their camels, and raced off in pursuit. If you have never seen a racing camel, they are a magnificent sight to behold. They race in slow motion and cover immense amounts of ground. The soldiers cut off the car, but it changed directions and sped away. Then the Arabs, sitting on their camels, raised their long barreled rifles and started shooting. The bullets must have hit the car because it stopped suddenly and three men staggered out. Two had their hands in the air; the third was holding a bleeding stomach.

"Drug runners!" said the officer casually. "They never learn."

It was just like watching a scene from a movie. I had taken several pictures of the Arab Legion men gathered around the coffee pot, but they were reluctant for me to take pictures of the drug smugglers. It astounded Joe and me that soldiers perched on top of speeding camels could actually hit another moving target. The officer smiled. "As you Americans would say – No problem!"

We headed east. During the night, the driver said we should sleep. He pulled out blankets and we sat beside the car. It was not comfortable. Three hours later we were driving on again. We passed Habbaniyah which was a Royal Air Force Station which was either closed or closing. We arrived in Baghdad and booked into a hotel overlooking the Euphrates. The entire 500 mile journey had taken twenty-four hours.

AN INCIDENT IN BAGHDAD

King Saud of Saudi Arabia arrived by air, escorted by an Iraqi fighter "Guard of Honor" and was welcomed by King Faisal in his early twenties. Saud was trying to build closer relations with both Iraq and Jordan. Enthusiastic crowds mobbed the motorcade as the monarchs were driven into the city. For a couple of days it was all pageantry and splendor.

The Prime Minister of Iraq was a long-time soldier and politician Nuri es Said who was quite pro-British. Although Iraq was a close ally of Britain, King

Faisal, under pressure from his own population, was forced to give his support to Egypt in the Suez War. That was to bring fatal repercussions the following year. Somehow, as I photographed the two monarchs and Nuri es Said, I sensed that their days were numbered.

The Iraq Times on May 11th noted who was in town to cover the events; Stephen Harper of London's Daily Express. Joe Alex Morris and Robert Egby of United Press, Frank Kallsen of the Columbia Broadcasting System, Douglas Stewart of the BBC, with a crew of two cameramen, John Mechlin of Time-Life, Homer Bigart of the New York Times, Vincent Ryder of the Daily Telegraph, Ralph Izzard of the Daily Mail, Philip Potter of the Baltimore Sun and Richard Beeston of the News Chronicle.

The "Baghdad Diary" columnist added: "Joe Morris of the United Press has been on roving assignments in the Middle East since early this year covering major events. He has already been to Lebanon and Syria, Aden, Teheran, and more recently Amman. With his companion photographer Robert Egby, he made the trip from Jordan by car. Both are on their first visit to Iraq."

At one event I managed to get a great panoramic picture of the two kings flanked by their ministers and supporters in a highly decorated marquee. Magnificent silk drapes and beautiful Persian carpets provided luxury décor. The moment one stepped into the marquee you forgot you were in the middle of a hot, dry desert.

SPLENDOR OF A STATE VISIT:
In mid-May 1957 King Saud of Saudi Arabia made a State Visit
to Iraq. The two monarchs – Saud and Faisal – held court in a large marquee, decorated with
wall and ceiling fineries. There was no indication it was in the desert. The author's pictures
of the event were published in the London Illustrated News.

Later, at a banquet King Said was in his robes and King Faisal was in a business suit. I was about to learn something the hard way. The rule is: never, ever photograph royalty, especially Arab royalty while they are eating. It's a big no-no. So I took a picture.

BANQUET FOR TWO KINGS:
When Kings Saud and King Faisal held a banquet in Baghdad, it was attended by many dignitaries. A court protocol stated that photographs should not be taken of royalty while eating. The author, unwittingly, took this picture and was promptly arrested.

Within seconds I was seized and dragged off. Not roughly, but strongly guided out of the banquet room. An English-speaking Iraqi army officer reprimanded me and I apologized profusely pleading total ignorance. They were about to take me somewhere for "questioning" when an aide of Prime Minister Nuri es Said intervened and I was released and able to resume work. I later found out that Joe Morris was talking to Nuri es Said in a corner of the banquet hall, and spotted me being hauled out. It's good to have friends of influence in high places as I was finding out.

The London Illustrated News published both the panoramic picture and the picture I should not have taken of the two kings eating. It was not the end of the story. Somehow word got back to Amman and a young man I had come to know and respect in the Government offices. Zaid Rifai took me aside and said: "Word has it you were arrested in Baghdad." He grinned. "We Arabs have some peculiar habits." He was the son of Jordan's Foreign Minister, Samir Rifai who had been a political figure in the old Trans-Jordan before it became the Kingdom of Jordan. The Rifai dynasty has provided prime ministers to the kingdom. Zaid, who was in his early twenties, was destined to become prime minister, as was his son. It was Zaid who kept me posted on stories that were beneficial to both Jordan and United Press.

THE DEAD SEA SCROLLS INCIDENT

When you work as a freelance reporter or photographer, it's important to have contacts, and you need to visit them regularly and check in on what's happening. One man who had his ear to the ground all the time was Dan Brown of the USIS — that, as I understood it then was the United States Information Service. Its mission was to broaden the communication between Americans, their institutions and their counterparts abroad. It was good to check in with him on a dull news day.

"Are you following the Dead Sea Scrolls issue?" asked Dan.

While in the Royal Air Force, I had chance to read articles on the mysterious Dead Sea Scrolls and how they were discovered by Bedouin shepherds exploring in the caves at Qumran overlooking the Dead Sea. Archeologists and Bedouin tribesmen had discovered a whole fleet of caves with fragments of scrolls and remnants of some 800 manuscripts dating from 200 BCE to 68 CE. The finds made everyone very nervous, mainly the church, which exerted pressure to have the scrolls and their messages kept secret. Today much of the Dead Sea Scroll material is available on the internet, and a book detailing the peculiar things that went on concerning the scrolls was written in the 1990s by Michael Baigent called, "The Dead Sea Scrolls Deception." But this was my life in Jordan in 1957.

Dan Brown continued: "Ever since the Rockefeller people withdrew financial aid to the project there's been upheavals. The fellow who headed up the Department of Antiquities, seemingly since the biblical times - Gerald Lankester Harding - left last year amid the political turmoil. When the Suez War occurred, the scrolls were all moved for safety reasons to Amman. Earlier this year the Minister of Education nationalized them. "

"Nationalized?"

"Well close to that," said Brown. "He claimed all ancient manuscripts which were discovered in the area of the Dead Sea for the Palestinian Archeological Museum." He gave me an address and suggested I get some photos of the scrolls.

At the Department of Antiquities, I pictured two of the curators examining a section of a copper scroll. It was brown and looked almost like leather. I dispatched it to London and the U.P. picture desk seemed elated. I couldn't understand why another photographer had not asked to see them.

The story surfaced again late in December 1957 when the Jordanian Council of Ministers declared the actions of their Minister of Education to have been illegal. The scrolls were thus denationalized. Sources indicated that any new research funding from overseas would not occur if the famous scrolls were nationalized. The power of money! Still, whenever the Scrolls are mentioned on the news, my mind always goes back to my days in Amman Jordan.

AN UNUSUAL AMBASSADOR

I had just returned from Baghdad to our Amman home when I received a call from the British Embassy. Within the hour I was seated in Charles Johnston's comfortable office sipping fresh lemonade.

"Do you speak Russian?"

His question blew me away. "No, but I've always had a fascination for the Romanovs. I'd like to seriously research that era and perhaps write a novel."

"Good, you might want to chat with Mrs. Johnston – that's Natasha – she has Russian blood."

The ambassador queried my knowledge of Cyprus and E.O.K.A. Then when I mentioned I had been a war correspondent at Suez and had been to Cairo for the Menzies event: "That whole thing should never have happened. Mr. Menzies is a great fellow but totally wrong for the job, and we should have let the Israelis and the French sort it out. We have an unfortunate inclination to get ourselves into deep political trouble. Everything dates back to Disraeli." He paused. "Are you coming to Mafrak on May 31st? Our people can give you a ride if you need one?"

I mentioned I had passed through Mafrak on the way to Baghdad.

"It's the end of the Anglo-Jordanian Treaty," said Mr. Johnston. "We're handing over the RAF base to the Jordanian Air Force. Everybody will be there. My secretary will make arrangements." As I turned to go, the ambassador said: "If you're not doing anything on Sunday afternoon, bring Lucy and come over to the house. Bring a swim suit too."

A secretary, who had come in to place some material in the ambassador's tray, took me aside as I was leaving: "Mrs. Johnston's a very nice lady, just like someone you'd meet at the Women's Institute. You wouldn't think she was a Princess of high Russian nobility." Subsequently, Lucy and I found that summary exactly right. Natasha was a warm, highly interesting personality and she always made us very welcome.

A PR photographer and I travelled in a Humber Hawk to Mafrak. We were in a short convoy. The ambassador's car was behind us and a Land Rover with a bunch of armed guards was in front and another behind. "You never know in this place. They take pot shots at you from nowhere," commented the photographer.

BRITISH BASE HANDED OVER:
On May 31st 1957 the Royal Air Force base at Mafrak in Jordan was handed over to the Jordanian Air Force by British Ambassador Charles Johnston. King Hussein saluted as the Union Jack and the RAF Ensign were hauled down and replaced by Jordanian flags.

All the way, along the 60 miles between Amman and Jordan, there were Jordanian Army troops. Armed soldiers were positioned on hill tops and prominent sand dunes about every quarter of a mile, guarding the route and watching for any trouble. "The days when Kings used to travel on a camel or horse in relative freedom have long gone," Charles Johnston said later in a moment of nostalgia. "When I served in Cairo during the war, King Farouk used to wander around with just a couple of unarmed servants. Today, Kings, Princes, Prime Ministers and the rest are living under guard. You may say it's their security but they're also prisoners. It's how you think about it, of course," and he smiled whimsically.

RAF Station Mafraq was a small air base, comprising a collection of World War II Nissen huts and tents. The runways must have been the easiest to maintain in the entire British air force – they were made of hard-baked earth, thus their size and length allowed any aircraft, jet or prop-driven to land and take-off. The Station was close to the Jordanian village of Mafraq. The Ambassador's car did a circuit of the station and the village, and we followed. As I viewed the place, I recalled a memory I had in my early days at El Firdan that I would not mind being posted to RAF Mafraq. My friends looked at me with odd expressions. Mafraq was another world. Now I could see why.

The ceremony for the hand-over of the base to Jordan was attended by members of the Jordanian Army and the Air Force, and members of the British Royal Air Force. King Hussein arrived and stood on the covered dais along with Mr. Charles Johnston and various officers of both countries.

Amid speeches under a blazing desert sun, the British Union Jack and the Royal Air Force Ensign were hauled down and replaced by the flag of the Hashemite Kingdom of Jordan and the Jordanian Air Force Ensign. It was all pomp and circumstance, and it felt as if Britain was capitulating, but when one thinks about it was only right that a country should have full possession of its country. Afterwards we had tea and sweets and on the way out noted that the guards on the base were already members of the Jordanian Forces. My pictures made several British newspapers including the London Illustrated News.

ROYAL HUSSARS LEAVE AQABA

Five weeks later, I found myself and my cameras almost 200 miles south of Amman at the Red Sea port of Aqaba, which in those days was little more than an Arab fishing village. And if you stood on the beach you could see Eilat, the Israeli town on the gulf. Joe Morris, another reporter and I were here to cover the final end of British bases in Jordan. No ceremony, simply an evacuation of the British Army base after thirty years. It was July 8th 1957 and 250 British soldiers of the Tenth Royal Hussars were shuttled on small craft out to the troopship Devonshire. The last British soldier to go was Colonel

Cordy-Simpson, Commander of the Aqaba Garrison. I clicked a picture of the Colonel stepping off Jordanian soil.

On the way back along the desert road, we stopped to view the strange rock-carved buildings of Petra, the one-time home of the Nabateans. You get into Petra by riding a horse through a very narrow rocky gorge. We rented horses and I'm sure the nag was on its last legs or poorly fed. Joe Morris cracked: "Bob, with your size you should carry the beast." He was also a mine of information. He told us Lawrence of Arabia had come this way years before which made us think. Many years later when I saw "Indiana Jones and the Last Crusade" I realized Harrison Ford and Sean Connery had ridden horses through the same narrow gorge. It brought back memories.

I took pictures and later did a feature which sold to a travel magazine in the United States. We also stopped for supper at an Arab road-house. Eggs were micro, mainly because desert chickens do not have the feed to create large eggs. We shared a 12-egg omelet along with Arab bread and washed them down with a coffee that made one's hair stand on end, accompanied by a rapid pulse. It was hairy. I could not sleep for hours.

As our Dodge taxi hurtled along the desert road, we saw sections of the Hejaz desert railroad near the town of Ma'an. It brought back thoughts of Lawrence and the Bedouins who fought the Turkish Ottomans. I love the desert and wanted to spend a few minutes wandering and touching the sand, but Joe had to get back to Amman.

Thinking back to Mafraq and Aqaba and the departure of British Forces, I had the distinct feeling the British Empire was fading. When we were at the Johnston's, Nathalie asked how things went at Aqaba and I expressed the feeling.

"It's not new. It started with India. Once the Raj went, and that was ten years ago this year, the Empire went into decline," said Charles. "It is happening everywhere. Suez, Kenya, Malaya, and yes, your Cyprus. Turmoil, the desire for change, the desire for independence, is everywhere." He paused and looked at the trees at the end of the garden. "We must not be pessimistic. Britain is a survivor, but more than that, it will do greater things in different ways. They're already talking of designing high speed inter-city trains. There's a new wave coming about in Britain and Europe. The colonies are dying, so are the old ways in Britain. We must think progressively."

THE BRITISH HOUSE IN AMMAN

The "British House" as most correspondents knew it, looked like something out of an Agatha Christie oriental novel. Although designed by a fellow from Palestine almost thirty years before, it had the air of a French or Turkish caravanserai. A three story stone building was built with an attractive enclosed courtyard. Each level had a gallery around it onto which bedrooms opened. There was an imposing dome in the main hall, the sort of dome one would find in a cathedral and the dining room and offices opened off the big hall. A fairly large swimming pool was in the lower garden flanked by a bamboo hedge, lilac bushes and an abundance of flowers, resembling an English country garden. Lucy and I always enjoyed our visits to the British House. We found a eucalyptus tree and Mrs. Johnston told us they were good for colds. "Place them in a pan of boiling water and the aroma works well on head colds," she said.

Natasha was always the perfect lady, the perfect hostess and projected a modesty that most visitors loved. She was of the Royal Family of Georgia, Princess Nathalie Bagration-Moukhranskaya. Her mother, who had been Princess Tatayana of Russia, was now Abbess of the Russian Convent on the historic Mount of Olives in Jerusalem. She invited us to join her in a visit to the Convent, but other events always seemed to get in the way.

Correspondents were always welcome at the buffet lunches given by the Johnstons. At one such event, I rubbed shoulders with a young man with a fresh but mature complexion. Perhaps twenty-years old, he had pale but gently sun-tanned features. He said his name was Zaid...Zaid Rifai. George Halaby told me later he was the son of a leading Jordanian statesman, Samir al-Rifai.

Through Zaid Rifai, I started taking news pictures of events at the Royal Palace in Amman. It started shortly after we returned from Baghdad. The King liked to be photographed with visiting dignitaries, and I enjoyed the calls.

A ROYAL REBUKE?

Just before June 8th when old King Saud was about to land at Amman Airport for a seven day State Visit to mark the commencement of the Baghdad Pact, King Hussein cornered me and said in perfect English: "Mr. Egby – Robert – I understand you had an interesting lesson in protocol in Baghdad." Then he smiled. "Enjoy your stay here. Whenever you wish to take photographs call my people." I smiled politely. As I reached home I wondered: "Don't these people have anything else to talk about." I knew then that in that remark the King was telling me in his own way that in royal Arabic affairs one must toe the line. The State Visit went off fine.

Hussein was a lead-foot. While studying in England, Sandhurst cadets reported that he always liked to drive fast. Somewhere along the line he received his pilot's license and credit for this must belong to an RAF Wing Commander Jock Dalgliesh. I had the privilege of taking a photo of Dalgliesh, instructing King Hussein in the cockpit.

One day, the Dutch aircraft manufacturer, Fokker, brought into Amman one of their F-27 Friendships which had been introduced to the world a couple of years before. It was designed as a European replacement for that old warhorse, the Douglas DC-3. It had two high-wing Rolls Royce Dart engines, a pressurized cab which held some 30 people. The Palace called me to say the King was going to "take a look" at this new aircraft and I should come for a ride.

AT THE JORDANIAN ROYAL PALACE 1957:
His Royal Highness King Hussein, 23 years old, flashes a side glance towards Jordanian Elder Statesman Samir Rifai. The author, armed with still and movie cameras, works in the background.
Photo by: Studio Haig, Amman.

Probably half a dozen photographers and reporters climbed aboard and found the King in the co-pilot's seat which was a picture on its own. We never did find out who the pilot was but he took us up for a circuit, then touched down and allowed the King to operate the controls. Hussein flew the aircraft like a veteran commercial airline pilot – then he "feathered" one of the props and the plane flew some distance on one engine. Some of the media was still shaking when we got off the plane. I must say, I felt a little chilly.

"Everything all right?" asked the monarch as he stepped down.

"Absolutely!" I lied, then quipped, "I'll be fine by next month."

Hussein grinned and I realized that in spite of all the pomp and circumstance he was still a youngster, but he had an excellent mind and he needed it. He knew he was walking a tightrope.

THE DIFFICULT LIFE OF A MONARCH

There were so many stories in Jordan. The 1948 war over the establishment of Israel next door and the elimination of Palestine, had resulted in half a million refugees living in Jordanian camps and they had been there ten years, unable to move, unable to progress, unable to migrate elsewhere.

When I asked Zaid al-Rifai why not, his response was, "They are waiting to return to their homeland." Privately, I figured they were being held as political hostages. To allow them to disperse to better lives would have brought severe reactions from other Arab countries such as Egypt, Syria and Lebanon – all housing refugee camps.

The unrest that had occurred when I first arrived in Jordan had resulted in 550 Jordanians receiving severe sentences – fifteen years plus – for just declaring themselves members of a Communist party, or refusing to deny membership.

Egypt's President Nasser was talking with Syria about forming a United Arab Republic and was putting pressure on other Arab countries to join. Nasser was concerned about the Communists taking power in Syria. The two Hashemite kings – Hussein and Faisal – were put on the spot and created their own Union. The wily King Saud of Saudi Arabia refused to join although he worked to maintain good relations.

The Union had some interesting problems. It would have one king and one prime minister and Nuri es Said in Baghdad appeared likely to assume that position over Jordan's Ibrahim Hashin. There were doubts that two kings could rule one Union on a practical basis.

Hussein, in spite of his being twenty-one, was beginning to age from seemingly constant threats against his life and hearing considerable criticism over his actions in the Arabic press. One day, I was outside the palace when Charles Johnston emerged and stopped at the bottom of the steps waiting for his car.

"Do you get the feeling that the King's days are numbered?" I asked casually.

"He's told most of his inner circle that for the sake of Arab Unity he would be willing to abdicate in favor of one monarch," said the ambassador. "And that would be Faisal."

I did a story for United Press in London quoting "sources" and it created a flurry of calls from Middle East correspondents and it was confirmed.

KING SAUD IN AMMAN:
Two kings greet each other at Amman's Airport. King Hussein of Jordan and King Saud of Saudi Arabi. 1957 was a year for concern over unions in the Arab countries and the need for solidarity.

After the Fokker Friendship plane flight, the King's Chamberlain would call: "Mr. Egby, His Royal Highness has some visitors you may wish to photograph." After you hang around royalty for a while you realize that such a statement was not a request, it was an order delivered in royalese. Normally they would give me a day's notice. Once, the Chamberlain called to ask if I could come up right away. I said "Sure." Lucy hit the roof. "Why didn't you tell him we're about to sit down to Christmas dinner?" As it turned out, the visitors were representatives from the Office of the U.N. Secretary General Dag Hammarskjöld and they really did not wish to be photographed. Oh, well.

THE HOLY PLACES AND THE PRESENCE

Ever since my mother sent me to Sunday School – which did not last long – I was intrigued with Jerusalem, therefore I spent a number of visits exploring the city, meeting people and walking through the Via Dolorosa, sometimes called the Way of Suffering. One person was a Franciscan priest, Father Roc who seemed attached to the Church of the Holy Sepulchre, although I was never able to figure out in what capacity.

He gave me a variety of stories, such as: "Did you know that since the Crusades the keys of the Church of the Holy Sepulchre have been held by a Moslem family since 1887 because our churches cannot agree." He grinned. "It's safer that way."

In researching the story I discovered that five years after Saladin captured Jerusalem in 1187 he assigned responsibility for the Church to two close Muslim families. The Joudeh family was entrusted with the key to the maind door and the Nusseibeh looked after maintaining the door. Twice every day the Joudehs bring the key to the door and it is then unlocked or locked by the Nusseibehs. It started in 1192 and still occurs to this day. The keys for one of the great centers of Christianity are held by Moslems. When I mention this in lectures there's always some hot-blooded Christians who come up with such statements as "Poppycock!" and "We should do something about that."

Father Roc who must have had some good journalistic blood in his veins allowed me to film inside the Holy Sepulchre with its countless candles that almost asphyxiated me, mainly because candles burn oxygen.

The church has been built and rebuilt and patched up several times over the centuries. It was badly damaged in 1927 by an earthquake. If you do not know, it is built on the site venerated by many Christians as Golgotha, the Hill of Calvary, the scene of the crucifixion and burial place of Jesus. The Church is controlled by different Christian denominations, each having a part of it and contributing to its maintenance: They are the Catholics, Armenian, Greek Orthodox, Syrian Orthodox, Coptic and Ethiopian.

"Where are the Copts?" I asked curiously.

Father Roc smiled. "Come," he said and took me upstairs to the flat roof of the Church of the Holy Sepulchre. There we found a small open-air chapel and altar, all painted in white and seated on a white stone bench at the arched entrance was a young novice priest in black robes engrossed in reading a Penguin edition of the Holy Bible. A great picture, but a number of Christians wrote objecting to my showing Copts on the rooftop of the Holy Sepulchre. I responded: "Better that, than not at all." The reason they were exiled to the roof of the Holy Sepulchre was, at that time, a lack of money. They were unable to support the church.

THE DOME OF THE ROCK

If you visit the historic church you cannot miss another great landmark, the beautiful shrine of the Dome of the Rock. Built on a platform over the Rock of Mount Moriah more than 1300 years ago, the Dome and the shrine Al-Aqsa Mosque commemorates the Prophet Muhammad's miraculous journey to the Seven Heavens. It's also the place where King Abdullah was going when he was assassinated. His grandson Prince Hussein escaped.

I spent many days working on stories in Jerusalem. I sensed it was a special place and possessed different energies, although it was going to be some years before I actually was cognizant of them. When Father Roc allowed me to film inside the Holy Sepulchre, I felt a distinct presence there - an energy - something very different. Something beautiful. Afterwards, Father Roc took me to the Convent of the Sisters of Zion where we had a vegetarian soup and bread.

"So you felt something?" asked the Father with a faint smile. "What was it like?"

"I don't know. A presence. Perhaps a spirit."

"Did you not tell me you were a non-believer? An atheist?"

"My logical mind has trouble with all the claims made by the church, but somewhere above all that, is some force, some energy."

"Some day, some where, you will find the peace you seek," he said, his dark brown eyes gazing at his soup - then he looked up. "Do you meditate?"

"Don't think I ever will. I have too much energy. Too much to do. I heard it's a total waste of time."

The Father smiled. "When you kill your ego, my son, you will start to find peace and enjoy life."

We stood up and thanked the sisters and returned to the street. Two Greek orthodox priests were having a fist fight. I felt disgusted, but I declined in my mind to take a photograph. Soldiers came and arrested them.

"Bob, I didn't tell you this," the Father said quietly, "but religion is not the place to find peace. Look higher into the Light. Create your life in the Light. Breathe the Light. Work with the Light."

On the way back to Lucy and Amman, I recalled the words of old Father Roc. I wanted to be with him. Hear other things he had to say. I had never met a priest like him. He was different. He had used an expression I had heard as a young teenager, many years before – "Work with the light!" Great-Grandmother Elen Egby, the seer at Reading! She had used that strange phrase. Now a priest repeated those words in Jerusalem. Was it a coincidence or a manifestation of natural energy, perhaps spirits? No, why would they be interested in me? I had no answers and that was frustrating. How could I kill my ego? And what good would that do? The absence of knowledge hurt me deeply and I failed to know why.

A RUSH TO THE ITALIAN HOSPITAL

Back in Amman I found George Hallaby at the house. "Lucy's in Labor!" he said. "I've called a taxi."

Lucy tried smiling above the pains that seemed to come every few minutes. She seemed very brave as we helped her into the taxi. The driver was really scared she was going to have our baby in his car, but George speaking in Arabic, put his mind at ease. The Italian Hospital of Amman was the first hospital set up in Trans-Jordan and dates back to 1927. It is located in the heart of the old city and as the taxi suddenly stopped, the sisters came out and helped Lucy into the inner-sanctum. "We'll let you know," said a sister, firmly easing us out of the building. She didn't even ask us if we wished to stay.

The taxi took us home and as we arrived in the cottage, the phone rang. It was Lucy: "We have a baby girl!" It was that fast.

It was January 20th 1958 and we called her Roberta Jane. Suddenly the cottage seemed full with a new energy. There were new routines I had not even imagined. Feeding. Washing clothes. Waking up during the night for changing diapers. How could one small child create so much havoc?

Leaving Lucy to venture out on news assignments was one thing, but leaving Lucy and the baby for hours, sometimes half a day, struck a hard note in my conscience. I felt I needed to be around and help her. Inside, I felt a tug of war developing. My work versus my responsibility to my sudden family. To make matters worse, there had been a lull in international news and revenues from photos were getting smaller each month. A few months earlier I had started stringing for the Financial Times of London, picking up economic developments in Jordan and wiring them to the newspaper.

One story that proved shocking for the picture editors at United Press was the ceremony marking the start of oil exploration and drilling in the desert. It happened in 1958 and everyone who was anyone was there including the King. There were cars, trucks and buses surrounding the event. Even a camel had been tied up near the center of things. A number of people including the King spoke on the possibility of petrochemical developments in the country. Suddenly, and without any warning, an Arab walked up and with a sharp knife slit the camel's neck. It was immediately followed by a huge spurt of blood. Everyone applauded while the camel slowly died in the hot desert sun. George Halaby explained that the success of the venture would be enhanced by the sacrifice of a camel. It is tradition, he said. When my picture of the dying camel hit the U.P. Picture Desk in London, the fellow just getting ready to go for lunch almost had a coronary.

Incidentally, in those days, news photographers never took photos showing victims – or animals – dying in a pool of blood. Except for that camel picture, which was never published, none of my pictures - while showing victims of fighting and terrorism - ever showed blood. Why? Newspaper readers at home eating breakfast didn't want to see blood. It was only with the Vietnam war and the advent of live television that news pictures became more bloody.

A KING FOR GETTING THINGS DONE

One story that went to both UP and the Financial Times was a feature on the proposed Ghor Project, a seventy mile canal linking the Sea of Galilee and the Dead Sea on the Israeli-Jordanian border. The Ghor with its many flat terraces is fertile, but the problem preventing agricultural use was water. The Ghor Canal Project was designed to remedy the situation. Later, I heard the 1967 Arab-Israeli War halted the work in the southern area. At a news conference on the site, King Hussein spoke of the many things he was envisioning in his country. He possessed a fire, a passion for getting things done, and I think many people appreciated this.

Wherever I travelled in later years, I always kept an eye on the Desert King. Under his forty-seven year reign, things happened. During the 1960s major industries such as phosphate, cement and potash were developed and a network of highways linked major communities throughout the kingdom. When I was there, one in ten families had water, electrical power and sanitation. Today, it is almost 100%. The literacy rate of 33% in 1960 has escalated to over 85%. Reports show that Jordan scored the world's fastest annual rate of decline in infant mortality from 70 deaths per thousand in 1981 to 37 per thousand in 1991 – ten years.

King Hussein was a people person. He would always stop to ask how you're doing. He fully understood that the people of his country was the biggest asset, and he always encouraged people everywhere to achieve and be proud of their achievements, their ancestors and their growing families. I was in New Jersey when the news came over that Hussein had crossed into the lands of Spirit and his ancestors. It was February 7th 1999. I felt a deep sadness at his parting, but by then, I understood the higher life, and knew the Desert King was in a safer, more rewarding place.

In the spring of 1958 our savings were dwindling and Jordan did not possess a high rating in international news and I really wanted to get back to action and work in Cyprus. So, after much thought and discussion, Lucy and I decided on a plan of action. She and the young Roberta would return to her mother's home in Malta and stay there until I had rebuilt our savings in Cyprus and had a place for us to live. Neither of us liked the idea, but it was pure economics that governed the decision. Neither of us knew that it would be many months before we would be together again, and I would have photographed another war and been shot at in my room and on a hillside by a sinister three-engine aircraft.

13

CIVIL WAR AMONG THE CEDARS

SOME PEOPLE CALL JOURNALISM and news photography "Life in the fast lane." I often drew the impression that I had lost control of my life. I arrived back in Cyprus from Jordan and checked into a room at the Nicosia Palace Hotel overlooking Metaxas Square.

"A message for you, sir," said the front desk fellow.

The message: "Get a flight soonest to Beirut! Check into our bureau at the Palm Beach Hotel. How!" I never did find out what "How!" meant, but United Press ended most of its administration messages that way.

Lebanon, the Motherland of the Phoenicians and Land of the Cedars! Over the centuries anyone who wanted to build ships, particularly the Babylonians and the Egyptians, raided the magnificent cedar forests of the Lebanese hills and mountains.

The Viscount airliner took me from Nicosia to Beirut, the capital of Lebanon. As the plane banked, my window revealed the Corniche, the seaside promenade and beyond the picturesque harbor. My thoughts swept back to that day four a half years before when I met Iro, a delightful figure as she stood on the upper deck of Italian MV Fillipo Grimani. It seemed so long ago and now she was gone. Torn out of my life.

I encountered James Whitmore of Time-Life at Beirut Airport and along with three other journalists, we shared a crowded taxi downtown. "There are a growing number of pro-Nasser demonstrations occurring. Some really bad," Whitmore said. "Supporters of the new United Arab Republic comprising Syria and Egypt want Lebanon included. Lebanese Muslims and the powerful Druzes are really pushing for it. Washington is really concerned."

Ever since the French evacuated some fifteen years before, the country had operated on an interesting political structure. The president was always a Maronite Christian and the prime minister a Moslem. In normal times, this was a workable arrangement. But these were not normal times. A few days after I arrived, Nassib Matni - the Maronite anti-Shamun editor of At

Talagraph, a daily newspaper known for its outspoken pan-Arabism - was assassinated as he left his office. The date: May 8th 1958.

Larry Collins, the young, energetic United Press staffer at the Beirut bureau came back from visiting the U.S. Embassy and exclaimed: "The State Department is really getting hot under the collar. They have teams of analysts being flown in."

"Maybe they will send in the cavalry," commented George Pipal, an old time UP editor who had flown in from Cairo to head the Beirut Bureau. It was an incredible prophetic statement.

Lebanon had earned a beautiful and justified title: "The Paris of the Mediterranean." I recalled being here in October 1953 and walking the distinctly French tree-lined boulevards with bistros and magazine stores and pastry shops.

Now the United Press people were housed in the Palm Beach Hotel, and across the road was the Excelsior with a magnificent pool where we could swim at the end of a chaotic day. Across the way, silhouetted against the Mediterranean, was the St. Georges, one of the most glamorous and prestigious hotels in the world.

The St. Georges was Lebanon's place to be. Anyone who was anyone stayed there. Built and run for almost thirty years by its French owners it was, until 1958, the location for finding movie stars, former kings and queens and princes who had lost their regimes, business people, agitators, dissidents, writers, spies and counter spies, and the international press corps diligently searching for tips.

My problem was I did not have any contacts in Beirut and I was almost completely foreign to the Lebanese situation. Yes, like most people in the Middle East, they have an understanding of what is happening in neighborhood countries. But to be able to come and start working, one has to rely on colleagues and the team at the UP Bureau, who went out of their way to brief newcomers.

Joe Alex Morris came by and took me to lunch in a small bistro tucked away in an arcade off the beautiful Place des Canons which is lined with shops and palms and the air is filled with the sounds of electric trolleys as they frequently rattle by. He asked after Lucy and told me of a new light in his life, a lady in Cairo named Ulla. His father, a long-time and long-respected journalist Joe Alex Morris Sr., had just written a book about United Press called "A Deadline Every Minute." I made a mental note to read it.

The book's title was a well known fact and I was finding out the hard way, as many others had before me, that UP was a share-holder owned and driven news agency, and was a relentless slave-driver. Associated Press, Canadian Press and Reuters were, in those days, associations and did not have a profit motive.

"United Press editors have no idea of time," said Joe cradling a coffee. "They'll call you at 2 a.m. or they'll even call you while you're working on one news conference, to go to another." He grinned and sucked on a Turkish cigarette. "You're finding that out, eh, Bob?"

Then he said something that I found very profound, and I mulled it over in my mind many years later. "Trouble with news agency work is you never get time to digest it. You're always writing up in the clouds, never down to earth. You never get time to digest, really mull over the deeper aspects, the human aspects. We report so fast that we never get to really understand those we write about."

A ROAR OF ANGRY VOICES

As we left the bistro, there came an overwhelming sound, a roar of angry voices. People screaming, yelling, shouting in Arabic. Curious, we both ran out into the main street. Ooops! A mob of several hundred wild Moslems were on a rampage, smashing windows, setting fire to cars and anything that would burn. A Beirut store-owner leaned out and grabbed Joe's arm. "Come inside, they will kill you."

"We're reporters," Joe protested.

"Americans! Yes, so they will kill you."

I had snatched two pictures before sliding sideways through the open door. The man, obviously a Christian, led us through his haberdashery and peered out a side door. "Go down the alley. That will take you to the main way back to L' Hôtel St-Georges." He peered at Joe nervously. "That is where you stay, no?"

"Close enough," replied Joe.

As we ran down the alley and crossed the road, police and army trucks came racing through heading for the next block. A few minutes later we heard shots and an explosion. Back at the Palm Beach, Larry Collins was battling with a typewriter and George Pipal was cradling a phone. "Bob, they've just blown up a bus," said Larry. "Our cab is downstairs. He'll take you."

A few minutes later I was at the scene. A time bomb had exploded killing two people and injuring seven. A helmeted policeman in a light khaki tropical uniform, an open holster on his belt and a lethal looking baton in his hand, allowed me to look into the bus - carnage! Blood was splashed everywhere.

The bodies had all been removed and the injured were in hospital. I took a photo of the policeman standing by the bus in downtown Beirut. It appeared in the British Daily Telegraph and various other newspapers.

LEBANESE CIVIL WAR 1958:
Three United Press newsmen stand in the shelter of sandbags in Beirut. They are Joe Alex Morris Jr, the author, and Russell Jones. Joe received various awards for "integrity in journalism," while Russell was awarded the Pulitiz Prize for "International Reporting" for his coverage from Budapest of the Hungarian Revolution. Both died in 1979. This picture is the lone survivor of a Rolleiflex contact print.

The next day, the international press corps was all excited as U.N. Secretary General Dag Hammarskjoeld arrived back in Beirut from Cairo. A bomb exploded 100 yards from the United Nations temporary headquarters. That night bombs started echoing throughout Beirut and in other cities across Lebanon. Death and destruction kept us all on our toes.

The next morning Joe Morris, Russell Jones and I toured parts of the devastated city, dodging through alleyways. At one point a street was barricaded with sandbags. I gave my camera to an Arab journalist and he took our photo. As he returned the camera, a sniper's bullet ricocheted off a wall. We dived off into a safe alley.

TRIPOLI – A HOTBED OF UNREST

One morning, George Pipal said: "We want you to get up to Tripoli for a few days and see what goes on. This is a triple-assignment. We have a 16mm Bell and Howell for you to take. UP Television wants some film. We need photos as usual, and you'd better use your writing skills for news coverage."

I grinned. I was beginning to understand A Deadline Every Minute. Oh well, as long as it's rewarded, I thought. Little did I know of the demands and terrors I would be put through. George's final words: "You're staying at the Hakim Hotel. It's right on the main drag."

A couple of things they failed to tell me. Tripoli was a hotbed of unrest. It was also the hometown of the prime minister of Lebanon, Rashid Karami.

It was also the Mediterranean terminal of the Iraq Petroleum Company's pipeline from Iraq. Up until 1920 it was the Turkish Petroleum Company but as the Ottoman Empire crumbled, it was acquired by the Anglo-Iranian Oil Company, Shell Oil Company and a French oil company named Compagnie Française des Pétroles. A pipeline brings oil in from Kirkuk where it is stored in great oil storage tanks waiting for ships to transport it to refineries in Europe. It reeked of foreign domination.

The ancient city of Tripoli is located in Northern Lebanon, about 42 miles north of Beirut. It was founded by the Phoenicians in 800 BCE. The name Tripoli comes from the Greek – Tri - meaning three and Poli stands for cities. During the Persian era it became the center of the Sidon, Tyre and Arados Island confederation, where great Phoenician minds met to debate marketing strategies, hence the name Tripoli – Three Cities. The city boasts a fortress, several great mosques, Crusader monuments, along with souks and khans and the famous Mamluk Assiba Tower built in the 15th century BCE.

If this sounds a lot, let's reduce it to something simple. The old city is predominantly Moslem and the new city is predominantly Maronite Christian. Community division is not great even on a nice day, but these were not nice days. A civil war had started.

This is the summer of 1958 and the Hakim Hotel is in the Christian section, and my room overlooks the old city and the Moslems. This, I figured, would let me see things "going on." This brave attitude almost got me killed. Every night there was shooting. It started like clockwork about nine, why, I never figured out. Perhaps after dinner - more likely after prayers. Anyway, the Lebanese Army and the police, who were mainly Maronites, retaliated in the same way every night.

A HAIR-RAISING TAXI RIDE

After browsing the city for twenty-four hours, I was wondering how I could get into the Moslem sector, see what was happening, and perhaps connect with some officials. While I was browsing, a taxi driver I had used earlier in the day came into the hotel and said quietly: "You want to visit the Old City?"

To get to the Old City safely, one had to take the road out of the new city, climb a horseshoe shaped track that climbed for about half a mile, then swing into the Moslem section. The problem was the Moslem guards on the hill frequently opened fire unless they recognized your vehicle. My taxi was recognized, he said. In spite of this, bullets kicked up dust all around us.

"Better go back," I urged in a moment of sheer terror.

The driver held a red cloth out the window and the firing ceased. He grinned at my bloodless face and drove on until we reached high ground and the original old city. The driver pointed to a smartly dressed Arab.

"My name is Hassan," he announced. He was a young wiry man who seemed to be the epitome of efficiency and very different from rural Arabs. He was wearing a white keffiyeh headdress, white shirt and blue jeans and spoke perfect English, Greek, French, some Italian and of course, Arabic.

"You're a polyglot," I observed, still trying to pull myself together.

"Polyglot!" he said easily. "Many tongues. You understand some Greek."

We had Turkish coffee, or what passed for it in a small bistro in the old city. "What would you like to see, barricades or fighters?"

"People. Fighters," I told him. "They make the best pictures."

"Fighters are still out in the villages," he said as we piled into his Renault and headed on a winding dusty track that lead north out of the old town and into the hills. For a while I could see the coast road and the Iraq Petroleum Company's operations. An oil tanker was moored at one of the long loading wharves.

"We have to keep our eyes open for the Lebanese Army," said Hassan. "They are mounting roadblocks and surveillance patrols. The situation is making them a little trigger happy."

I didn't say anything, but I thought we had encountered trigger happy Moslems earlier in the morning.

AN ATTACK FROM THE AIR

We stopped under a tree on the outskirts of a small village. "Everyone is Sunni here, so we are quite safe." As he spoke, two villagers wearing keffiyehs and carrying long barreled rifles that looked like something out of the 19th century came out of a house. Hassan listened, and then told me, "Our people attacked a military patrol about a mile down through the fields. There's been shooting, but everything is quiet now. Would you like to go down there?

Several goat paths led us down through the pastures. The fields seemed bare, except for dry grass. Some gullies or wadis as they call them, which carried water after a storm, were now dry. We found one that was a miniature grand canyon. Luckily, I was wearing my suede desert boots which made hiking through this dry, dusty terrain relatively easy.

AUTHOR SURROUNDED BY MOSLEM FIGHTERS:
You would not think that a short time before this picture was taken we were out in the country being the target of a Lebanese Air Force plane. Tribesmen north of Tripoli armed with rifles gather round the author who was only armed with cameras. As a journalist and news photographer in the Middle East the author never carried a gun. Photo courtesy of an Associated Press cameraman.

We found the twelve villagers, resting in the shade of a large tree. Two had been clipped by bullets in the exchange, and were able to walk with the others. I took photos of the group and then, an Arab who looked like George Grivas of E.O.K.A. go-t everyone moving up the hill towards the village about half a mile away.

A humming, mechanical sound encroached on the quiet of the hillside. It was a chant, a deep throbbing sound that brought back memories of Luftwaffe planes over England in World War II.

Hassan swung round and peered against the bright sun. "A plane!" he cried, first in Aramaic, then in English. "If we get caught in the open, we could get hurt. Start running."

The best wadi, the miniature Grand Canyon, was at least 300 yards away. I already had the 16mm Bell and Howell in my hands and fully wound. Everybody was running, but the twelve fighters were tired, and the two injured fellows were slow.

I felt the energy running through my veins, energy inspired by fear, a sharp, deep fear. I really had no desire to die on some desolate hillside in Lebanon. I recalled seeing photographer Robert Capa's "Falling Soldier" picture from the Spanish Civil War, and I didn't want to be like that. I didn't want to die, period! The adrenaline flooded my body, mind and soul. I raced up the dusty, gravelly gradient leading to the wadi, trying desperately to look back at the plane.

Right on the edge of the gully I stopped. Now I felt safe. The others were still fifty yards away and closing in. My lungs were bursting and I tried to hold the camera steady as the plane came in, almost skipping across the grass tufts of the desert. Two of the men stopped and started firing their rifles at the oncoming plane. A brave but dangerous gesture.

I could see the plane coming in clearly. Three engines. Unusual! My mind went back to World War II and I recalled seeing pictures of a Junkers JU-52. Suddenly everything chattered and hissed. Heavy bullets thudded into the ground, kicking up dust balls behind the running Arabs. This can't be me, I thought. Why am I here? What's wrong with a nice comfortable office and a darkroom?

Bullets danced, thudded and hissed everywhere. The plane roared by. Everyone was now in the gully, and I slithered down the slope after them. Hassan scrambled up and peered over the edge. He's coming down the hill. He'll see us in the wadi. Keep down."

Even as he spoke, the plane screamed down out of the sky and flattened out but the machine guns on board were silent. The plane banked and took off for the east.

"Are you all right? "asked Hassan.

I nodded. "Was that a Junkers?"

Hassan shook his head. It was a Savoia Marchetti. Made in Italy, it has three engines and was given to the Lebanese Air Force some years back. They have half inch caliber bullets," he said, picking one up from the dirt. "They're just heavy pieces of metal. They look like thick bolts. When they hit you, they don't explode; just rip up your body. We are lucky they didn't hit anyone."

"Why didn't he fire on the second time round?"

"Perhaps his gun was overheated and jammed. Who knows? Maybe the Gods are with us today." He grinned. "You believe in Allah? God?"

"I think I should start," I said.

AN INVITATION TO BREAKFAST

Hassan dropped me off at the Hakim Hotel. "Look, Bob, if you're not doing anything tomorrow morning, let me pick you up for breakfast. There are a couple of people you might like to meet."

Hassan took me to a well kept house in the residential part of the old city. A well dressed young man with a well trimmed beard received us at the door. I noticed he had a Luger stuck into an open holster. He peered into my camera bag, and his sharp brown eyes scanned my body. Apart from my old beige linen shirt, sandy linen pants and desert boots, I could not have carried a gun. There was no place to hide it.

Two men suddenly appeared. They were just there. I immediately recognized Rashid Karami and I sensed the other young man was his 23 year-old son Omar Karami. Both carried an energy, a sense of well-being. They were a family of lawyers and statesmen. Rashid's father Abdul Hamid Karami, was architect of Lebanese independence from France. The elder Karami served as Prime Minister of Lebanon and was the Grand Mufti, supreme religious judge in Tripoli. Both Rashid and Omar were bound for the offices of prime minister. In fact Rashid had been holding the office since 1955.

"Come and have breakfast, Mr. Egby," he said, and waved to Omar to lead the way. We sat eating eggs, cheese, melon and grapes with coffee.

"I detect an English accent," he said. "Why are you working for the Americans?"

I sensed a challenge. "We English spawned America some centuries back. We have to get in and correct that."

The response tickled Rashid. "So, what do you think of Lebanon?"

"A fabulous country. So much heritage."

"And you like the political infighting, murders, violence, lies? We lost one of our best journalists recently." Karami was referring to Nassib Matni, the Maronite anti-Shaman editor of At Telegraph who was assassinated for his Pan-Arabism editorials.

"Sounds as if the French left their way of life with the Lebanese."

Karami smiled easily.

Omar interceded. "We understand you are a photographer, Mr. Egby. Please understand that anything we say today is off the record. My father normally works through a translator although his English is very good. If you wish to do a news story, all you have to do is ask."

"Why am I here then? To take your photos?" I was blunt.

"Not us, but our people. We need to get our fighters, our people into the international newspapers. We will pass the word that you are here to take photographs. There are no conditions. We appreciate your integrity – being English."

BEHIND THE LINES TRIPOLI 1958:
Rashid Karami, Prime Minister of Lebanon (right) tells the author of current warfare events during a breakfast meeting at the Karami home in Tripoli in Lebanon. Mortars frequently fell and exploded nearby but Mr. Karami hardly blinked. He held the Prime Minister's office eight times before being assassinated in June 1987. He was a scholar and a gentleman.
Photo courtesy of O. Karami.

Just then there was a howling, whistling sound, followed by two sharp explosions.

The Karami's and Hassan did not blink. "The Lebanese Army with mortars, attempting to intimidate us," commented Omar. "They do it every morning."

Rashid Karami stared through the window into the garden as if deep in thought: "Robert, violence, conflict or wars in the Lebanon are not simply

Moslems or Christians. We are all family. When Christian soldiers use their guns they are very afraid of killing someone on the other side and it is the same with the Moslems. We have many families that have inter-married. A Christian man in the Army, if he is not careful, may well kill his father-in-law or mother-in-law, or cousin who happens to be Moslem. It is the same vice-versa." He sighed heavily, and I could sense his feeling for the Lebanese people – his people.

"You will see a lot of bravado. A lot of shooting, but very few killings. It's not that they are poor shots, on the contrary. They simply do not wish to kill, but they do like to make a show," he added. "The aeroplane yesterday. How many of the twelve did they kill? None at all. The pilot did not intend to kill, simply instill fear. When the Army tanks fire into buildings, they never use high explosives. The non-explosive shell makes a neat, round hole and passes through. It may kill someone standing in the way, which is regrettable. The intent of war in the Lebanon is to intimidate."

"As you take photographs of this so-called civil war, look for these aspects," he said. "You are free to go where you will. Take care. If I can help here's my private telephone number." Omar handed me a card.

I did not realize it at the time, but that telephone number would help in bringing stability back to Lebanon. But who was I? Just a messenger in a strange conflict. I sometimes wondered who was pulling my strings and why the voices kept prodding me to do things.

A CLOSE CALL ON THE BORDER

The next day I heard from some British and American journalists that the Moslem forces had blown up the border crossing station between Lebanon and Syria. They gave me a ride. Sure enough, the station, comprising several one story buildings, was bombed and set on fire. No one was around.

Nearby on a narrow dusty track running up to the border was a burned out armored scout car. I scrambled up the track pushing my way between the scout car and the cliff face. Turning round, I took several pictures of the armored car with the customs station in the background. A general view. Nice framing, I thought.

Walking back down the narrow dusty track, I started to edge my way between the wrecked scout car and the cliff face. Suddenly a woman's soft but firm voice said, "Watch where you put your feet. Watch where you go." The warning was urgent and tense.

I stopped. Frozen. My eyes scanned the dusty track ahead. A thin, ugly wire protruded several inches out of the dust. A land mine! Gingerly, I edged past and told the others. I started to like that little voice. Later I wondered what her name was. More thoughts. Was she God? That's interesting, I thought. Is God a woman? I yearned to know her name. Later, I wondered why she had not warned me when I went up the track the first time.

Twenty years later when I was sitting in British medium Patrick Young's closed circle at the Vancouver Psychic Society, he told me I had a guardian angel assigned to look after me. I wanted to know why she had not made direct contact with me.

Patrick grinned knowingly. "You were not ready to know such things. The Cosmos, the Universe will only make information available to you when you are ready to know."

BULLETS IN THE BEDROOM

In my visits to the Old city of Tripoli and the domain of Rashid Karami, I discovered that the Moslems had an interesting method of delivering urban or "down-town" bombs. They would strap explosives onto the steel rim inside a car or truck tire, and then set the detonator. Like children playing with hoops, they would run the tire-bombs down an alley and send them bouncing and hurtling across the broad street dividing the city and into the Christian sector where they would explode. People seeing them coming would shriek and scatter, but sometimes in the darkness it was difficult to see the advancing bombs. Destruction? Yes, but I never heard of anyone getting killed by wheel-bombs.

The nightly battle between the sides normally ended about 10:30 and nights became quiet and one could get a peaceful night's sleep.

One day, it was barely dawn. The light of a new day was struggling to get over the hills east of Tripoli. My hotel room faced east and I always appreciated a beautiful dawn sky...until...

The woman's voice hissed: "Roll out of bed. Do not stand up. Roll against the far wall, under the washbasin."

I recognized the voice from before. I rolled off the bed and across the room to the far wall. Not a moment too soon. The ripping sound was more like a cannon shot going through my room than a bullet. It was loud and deadly and carried a lethal message. My heart was beating fast and furiously. My throat went suddenly very dry.

Bursts of machinegun fire sprayed the Hakim Hotel. It seemed one very long time. I wanted to scream "Stop it! Stop it!"

I phoned. Rashid Kerami told me the shooting lasted only thirty seconds. I wanted to tell him he was not on the receiving end. But he was not on the receiving end.

"They are called Hotchkiss," he said easily and explained that in World War I the Hotchkiss was the standard machine gun of the French Army. The French had occupied Lebanon from 1920 to 1946 and a substantial number had been left behind.

"One of my men, an enthusiastic fighter, observed the United Nations flag on the roof of the Hakim and tried to shoot it down. My apologies for the inconvenience. Come and have breakfast."

It was true, the United Nations Peace Force had arrived the night before and had set up their base in the Hakim Hotel and during the night had hoisted the U.N. flag atop the building. It was not a deliberate ploy to infuriate the Moslems. The UN Observers had arrived after night fell.

Upon reflection, it was the second time in two days that the voice had whispered warnings. Whether you believe or not in guardian spirits, their voices are helpful to stay alive and healthy. It left me wondering about God.

Naturally, I informed the United Press Bureau in Beirut that my room and the hotel had been shot up. A week or so later, I received a clipping from an American newspaper. Part of the text read:

United Press International correspondent Robert Egby who has watched the fighting from the Hotel Hakim, headquarters of the UN Observer teams quoted rebel leader Rashid Karami as describing the barrage as "the worst since the war started. Mr. Egby himself narrowly escaped injury when a stray bullet whizzed into his hotel room and embedded itself in a wall."

Strangely, fighting had intensified in Tripoli with the arrival of the United Nations Observers. Government batteries bombarded the Moslem rebel positions. Soldiers started to get killed. The Army brought in several tanks and started to shoot with non-explosive shells at buildings so that they started to look like pepper pots. Then on the third day, the Moslems opened up with an anti-tank weapon. A shell pierced the armor of an old, pondering tank and barreled around inside with a roaring grinding of metal on metal. One could only imagine the carnage and the instant death of the tank crew inside. Death would have been instantaneous.

A JOB WITH THE UNITED NATIONS

A very approachable member of the U.N. Observers in Tripoli was a Hindu, Colonel Ranbir Singh whose English was perfect Oxford. A learned man, from a highly esteemed family in India. I conversed with him several times. One morning I caught him coming out of a team meeting. He was frustrated and annoyed. "Mr. Karami is not responding to any of our messages. I have the feeling our correspondence is not getting through. We need to have a meeting with him."

I hesitated. "Can I help? I have good communication with the Moslem side."

The Colonel shook his head. "Out of the question."

I mentioned that as a correspondent I visit Mr. Karami regularly and would be willing to carry a sealed letter. "There's one condition, I would like to have exclusive picture rights to the meeting—if one takes place.

Ranbir Sing shook his head. "I don't think there's a chance, but I'll get back to you." By mid-afternoon I was in the taxi and delivered the letter to Rashid Karami. The prime minister went into a huddle with some of his senior advisors. "Tomorrow at noon," he said with a faint smile, "and you can take the pictures."

Next day Hassan and I rode in my taxi and two white UN vehicles flying the UN flag followed behind. It was a weird convoy. Luckily there were no other reporters around. They had all returned to Beirut where the fighting was now intense.

The meeting between Rashid Karami and Colonel Maurice Brown of New Zealand took place at the Karami residence in the old city. It was highly significant, because Mr. Karami became the only "rebel chieftain" to have authorized UN observers to inspect his territory. The other chiefs including Kemal Jumblatt of the powerful Druzes and Saeb Salem of the Beirut region had so far blocked admission to their regions. My exclusive picture of the meeting made the New York Herald Tribune, July 9th 1958. Someone said I got a mention in United Nations reports, but I never saw one.

GET A VISA FOR IRAQ

On Monday, July 14th 1958 I was rudely awakened by a hotel clerk. I rushed downstairs to the phone. Larry Collins in Beirut: "We are getting reports King Faisal of Iraq has been ousted, perhaps killed. The borders have been closed and they say everyone must have visas. Can you get one?"

Two hours later I was at the Iraqi Embassy in Beirut struggling to get a visa. By noon, I had my British passport back. It contained an Iraqi visa and the page was loaded with stamps of King Faisal. Obviously someone in the Iraqi embassy still believed in their King.

Back at the Bureau, ideas of going to Baghdad were short lived. "The country is sealed off," said George Pipal. This was frustrating. I wanted to try getting in by taxi across the desert but no one agreed to the idea. Over the next few hours a picture emerged of what had happened.

Colonel Abdal-Karim Qassim took control of the government and the country. He ordered the King, his wife Princess Hiyam, his mother, various courtiers and personal servants to come to the courtyard. The Crown Prince Abdal-Ilah accompanied them. There they were, lined up against the wall and assassinated by a member of the coup. Apparently, Faisal and his wife were not killed at once. It was reported Faisal was sent to a hospital but died en route. Princess Hiyam reached the hospital and was treated for her wounds, but incredibly no one recognized her, and she was released. Reports claimed that sympathizers assisted her and she escaped from Iraq to Saudi Arabia and then moved on for permanent residence in Egypt.

The coup gang went searching for the Prime Minister Nuri es Said, but the wily statesman and ex-soldier had been tipped off. Disguised as a woman, he was attempting to get to British friends outside Baghdad when he was caught, and promptly murdered.

Back in the Palm Beach Hotel in Beirut I felt nauseous. I recall covering the State Visit to Iraq of King Saud and I had photographed them, and got arrested, and how Nuri es Said had ordered my release. Even when in Baghdad that time I had a strange feeling that all their days would be numbered. It was a strange sensation, and it bothered me deeply. How was it possible to pick up vibrations that foretold the deaths of a young King, his family and the Prime Minister? It was unnerving mainly because I did not understand why I had this ability.

The downfall of the Hashemite rulers created ripples all through the Middle East and many foreign capitals. One day I spotted Charles Johnston, the Ambassador having a hurried conversation with the famous American columnist Joe Alsop. Lebanon was attracting a variety of top diplomatic and journalistic guns.

THE CIVIL WAR ESCALATES

Beirut was in turmoil. Tanks were roaming the city, firing non-explosive shells into rebel-held apartment and office blocks to the point they looked like pepper pots. Moslem snipers shot from windows and balconies and from inside stores. Some tossed home-made cocktails that exploded around Army sandbag emplacements.

One night we heard of a tank battle in one of the poorer quarters. Simple street lighting and flashing guns illuminated the eerie scenes. Ever since I had started professional news photography in 1954 I used the all round Tri-X film which was rated 400 ASA. This night my Rollieflex contained a relatively new high-speed Kodak film Royal-X which was rated 1600 ASA. Although the street lighting was poor, I exposed at one second at f3.5.

The pictures were grainy, someone said "like oatmeal," but they did show the tanks, soldiers hiding alongside, and flashes of gunfire. A number of journalists were standing in doorways watching the scene, until a Molotov cocktail came spinning off a rooftop and we all fled to safety, chased by fire-dragons.

The situation across the country was deteriorating daily. We heard there was a massive Moslem army massing in the Baalbek area in the Bekaa Valley. Larry Collins was eager to see it, and took me along. We failed to find anything described as "massive." However we did find about two dozen Arab fighters with rifles and got them pictured against the famous columns.

THE CAVALRY COMETH

A phenomenon that is peculiar to war is "rumor" and there were lots in the Lebanon and reporters were often the victims. We were just getting back to Beirut when we faced another rumor. "The Marines have landed."

It was not a rumor; in fact we soon discovered 5,000 U.S. Marines were coming up the sandy Khalde Beach about four miles from downtown Beirut. The invasion caught most of the bikini-clad bathers by surprise. Saeb Salem ordered his fighters down to Khalde Beach, and when they reached the place, they were totally overwhelmed by the sight and most of them simply sat down and watched. Lebanon is always a land of contrasts.

We heard that Time-Life photographers Michael Rougier and James Whitmore caught the first wave of landing. By the time we got there, Marines were all over the place and settling in with trucks and tracked vehicles. Someone prodded George Pipal: "Here comes your cavalry, George."

The Bureau chief smiled. "It had to happen."

We learned that the Maronite President Camille Chamoun, fearful of anti-government sentiment had asked the United States, Britain and France for help. The Americans, apprehensive of the newly formed Egyptian-Syrian United Arab Republic, which was leaning towards the USSR for aid and assistance, promptly dispatched the Marines as a show of force to support the pro-Western Lebanese government. Another factor was the imposition of a pro-Soviet regime in Iraq. The Middle East was a potential powder keg.

As political observers saw it, the United States' action to intervene in Lebanon, was not aimed at Beirut, it was rather a mission to send signals to Cairo and Moscow. The presence of American troops in Lebanon seemed to defuse the strange civil war. Reports of fatalities from the war suggested 2,000 to 4,000 people had lost their lives. In my three months in the Lebanese conflict, I saw perhaps a couple of dozen dead bodies. Either the shooters were poor marksmen, or they really didn't want to kill anybody, just have a war to relax tempers. The whole thing sounded very much like a French dual, a farce.

A RETURN TO CYPRUS

So I packed up and flew back to Nicosia and Jacko at the Cyprus Mail. "I have six letters for you." They were postmarked "Malta."

This really blew me away. I had written several times from Beirut and given the Cyprus Mail as a receiving address, and somehow, the office had not forwarded them. On many occasions I seriously considered that Lucy had decided that I was not to be the man in her life, and had searched elsewhere. I knew that before she met me, she had been particularly friendly with a well known and highly respected dentist in Malta. Yes, I was jealous and insecure and these were two faces of the ego that I would carry for many years, suffering and hurting. We didn't have easy and affordable country-to-country telephone service in those days, so I sat down and wrote a long letter.

I wondered when I would be free of the suffering caused by jealousy and distrust. I wanted desperately to have a one-on-one conversation with that mystical voice that kept on popping into my life. Why wasn't she around when I felt angry and unsettled? I lay on my bed in the Nicosia Palace Hotel and tried playing a harmonica I had purchased in Beirut. I managed to find the right notes for a relatively new Italian song, "Volare" or "To Fly." I automatically recalled that the five-piece dance band played it frequently at the Night Club at the Palm Beach Hotel... and that brought back memories of a very beautiful Spanish lady named "Maria."

There were several days when there was a lull in work, and we spent several evenings having dinner and dancing and conversing. We were both alone. The Spanish that I had learned with Peter Dance at RAF El Firdan made her laugh like a rippling mountain stream, and she congratulated me. "You must practice, Bob. It's important. When you come to London, I will help you with your Spanish," said Maria.

I did not reply. As I was mulling over the position that I had no plans to live for any length of time in London, I started thinking about Lucy and the baby, Roberta in far off Malta and then I thought about Iro and how we had met in Beirut harbor, a couple of blocks away. While I was mulling my thoughts, Maria was evacuated home to London. I sensed she knew.

I put the harmonica away.

14

GOODBYE TO THE EMPIRE

I
T WAS THE FALL of 1958 and it was good to be back on Cyprus and among old friends. There was still some violence being perpetrated but international reports from Athens, Zurich and London indicated that a Cyprus settlement was at hand. Sir Hugh Foot, Governor of Jamaica had been appointed by the Queen to be the Governor of Cyprus in November 1957 and there was now a marked feeling of diplomacy in the air. Also in the year before Nicos Sampson, the E.O.K.A. killer group leader who had been reprieved from a death sentence and commuted to life, was flown to England to serve his sentence.

MAIDONIANS ON LAST PATROL:
One of the last patrols in the Colony of Cyprus comprised these men from the Royal Berkshire Regiment. All were from the author's home town of Maidenhead and area. Left to right: Private George Horwood, Private Roy Brazell, L/Corporal Johnny Palethorpe, Private Sydney Williams, L/Corporal Denis Franks and Private Richard Goom. The patrol was pictured during a patrol break west of Nicosia.

The Cyprus Mail had seen changes at the editorial desk. Ken Mackenzie, a veteran writer for The Observer was the editor and David Lewis, the deputy editor. Andreas Hadjipapas was a feature-news writer, and Pericles was the night news-desk writer. Jacko gave me a job as writer-photographer with additional responsibilities of running the night-desk. That helped stabilize my life and brought a steady income. I also got back to Central Press Photos in London. I think that United Press International, while a powerful news agency, was a little more than a man with a growing family could handle.

I found a small apartment overlooking the old Venetians bastions near Metaxas Square and Lucy agreed to join me with Roberta. I was not convinced in my mind that this was the right thing to do. I was a journalist and photographer and was used to being away on assignments. The Cyprus Mail was a little more moderate than UPI however, and Lucy took that into consideration.

The apartment was semi-furnished. It had all the basics including a one-person kitchen which upset Lucy. By Christmas, Roberta was trotting around the apartment, which was three stories up. We had a balcony and Roberta found small items, such as a tube of processed cheese and tossed it down into the street. Luckily no one complained. After years of living in a hotel, it was strange but not uncomfortable living in a small apartment.

Lucy and I were married at the Commissioner's Office in Nicosia on Thursday, February 19th 1959. It was a short ceremony, and it tickled the staff to see our year-old daughter trotting around the Commissioner's desk. Ken Mackenzie and David Lewis were our witnesses and they took us out to lunch right afterwards.

It was a memorable date because in far off London the Zürich and London Accord for the constitution of Cyprus started with an agreement at Lancaster House in London. The parties were Turkey, Greece, the United Kingdom and Archbishop Makarios for Greek Cypriots and Dr. Fazil Küçük for Turkish Cypriots.

It paved the way for an independent Cyprus. A constitution was drafted and agreed together with two further Treaties of Alliance and Guarantees in Zürich on February 1960. It was announced that Cyprus would be proclaimed an independent state on August 16th, 1960. There was a new sense of peace and prosperity in the air and newspaper work assumed a low profile. However there were opportunities for unusual stories and pictures.

Donald Scott Reid the Royal Air Force regional Senior PR Director flew me to RAF Station El Adem in Libya and I did a story on how downed air force pilots are taught to survive in the desert by plucking snails from shrubs, de-shelling them and squeezing the meaty section in a cloth, such as a handkerchief and drinking the juice—a substitute for water. Strange, I thought. I'm back photographing someone finding snails – shells – in the desert. I must drop a note to Peter Dance.

As the independence of Cyprus drew near, E.O.K.A. fighters came out of the mountains, there was an amnesty on surrendering weapons and ammunition, and E.O.K.A. suspects were freed from Camp K at Kokkinotrymithia. Among them was a young Greek Cypriot, Andreas Yiacoumis, who two years before had been charged with the murder of ROAC Sergeant Reginald Hammond in Ayios Dhometios, a suburb of Nicosia. He was taking his little son for an ice cream when he was gunned down. Mr. Justice Boyle who acquitted Yiacoumis said there were lamentable gaps in the prosecution case. He was detained under the Cyprus Emergency regulations and released in 1959 when the Cyprus agreement was signed.

MAKARIOS RETURNS AND I LEARN A LESSON

MAKARIOS RETURNS IN TRIUMPH:
Surrounded by a motorcycle escort of former E.O.K.A. fighters wearing their uniforms and armbands, the Archbishop rides into Nicosia on his return from exile, March 3rd 1959. An estimated 180,000 Greek Cypriots turned out to greet him.

On Sunday March 1, 1959 the archbishop returned to a jubilant Cyprus and an unprecedented reception in Nicosia. Greek Cypriots swarmed out of the hills and villages to welcome him. Buses and cars blocked side streets of Nicosia. The Archbishop stood in an open convertible flanked by E.O.K.A. fighters attired in black uniforms and berets and riding motorcycles. Photographers had a car in front of the procession, and I used a Linhof cut film camera and got magnificent, detailed photos of the event.

The Linhof taught me a lesson a few days later when the Archbishop went to Government House to meet the Governor, Sir Hugh Foot. It happened outside on the lawn and this is what happened. For some time I had been experimenting with old Ansco monochrome film dating back to 1944. It was war surplus and I believed it was still usable as an experiment. I had loaded several of the film holders with the film and placed them on a darkroom table, next to my regular holders.

We got the call for the historic meeting. I grabbed the Linhof and the nearest film holders. I shot two photos of the Governor and the Archbishop shaking hands. They were surrounded by reporters Larry Colins of U.P., Iris Russell of Reuters, and John King of the Daily Express. Then I was struck with the realization I had 15 year-old outdated film in my camera! Damn! Damn!

As I returned to the office the voice came through. "Leave it in the developer double time," she said and I did. Relief. Apart from being a shade foggy, it was fine. I radioed a five by seven print to London and it went to the papers.

AN HISTORIC PICTURE I SHOULD HAVE MISSED: Archbishop Makarios meets Sir Hugh Foot, Governor of Colonial Cyprus at Government House. By an oversight, the author used Ansco wartime cut film outdated by fifteen years. Still, it worked. Governor and the Archbishop are seen shaking hands. They are surrounded by reporters John King, at left, Larry Colins of U.P.,and Iris Russell of Reuters.

Wow! A learning experience! I had been lucky. The lesson: never ever leave antique film around fresh, useable film.

Events now moved with startling rapidity. The most important was the first meeting of the Transitional Committee comprising Sir Hugh Foot, Archbishop Makarios and Dr. Fazil Kutchuk. It made a great picture to see the three leaders standing together on the lawn at Government House. It was a picture that many people, a few weeks before, would have declared impossible.

THE GRIVAS DEPARTURE FIASCO

There was now one major story left: the fate of the E.O.K.A. leader Colonel George Grivas. Where was the man who had eluded 30,000 British soldiers for four years? Rumors were rampant. Perhaps he had been killed and was buried in some remote corner of the Troodos Mountains. Perhaps he had secretly left Cyprus knowing his task was completed. One rumor created amusement: Grivas is staying at Government House. One credible rumor that had reporters scurrying to Limassol was he had taken refuge at his sister's house. Another: Grivas was seen entering the Greek Consulate in Nicosia. Frustrated reporters spent many hours following so-called "trusted" leads.

Since October 1958, the Head of the Security Forces was Major General Ken Darling whose one and only target was to bring in E.O.K.A.'s top leaders. But times were changing and because of political developments, the hunt went into low gear. In fact, the British Government demanded that Grivas – unshackled – leave the island until such time as the new Government of Cyprus had jurisdiction to permit him to return. Makarios agreed to this.

In secret discussions with the E.O.K.A. leadership, Grivas agreed to depart when all arms and ammunition had been handed over to the British for safekeeping until the new Republican Government was able to take charge.

Three days were allowed for this to occur and "neutral" surrender points were established. The British agreed and stood by. There was a feeling that the Security Forces had wiped out the E.O.K.A. arsenals. The arms surrender stunned everyone. Guns of all shapes and sizes, automatic weapons, grenades, mines, crates of dynamite flooded in.

It was now a matter of hours before Grivas would leave Cyprus. Correspondents and photographers clustered at strategic points including the Ledra Palace, the Public Information Office and at Government House. Tension was taut. Would any reporter be lucky enough to interview Grivas? Some skeptical journalists, figuring that the British would not allow Grivas to make a public appearance let alone a public statement on what was still a British colony, fled to Athens to await his arrival, which guaranteed an arrival. Charles Foley, former Daily Express editor and now publisher of the Times of Cyprus had the foresight to do this. No matter how Grivas would leave Cyprus, he had to turn up in Athens.

For those of us left on the island, the search and the wait became intensely frustrating. Grivas could be flown out from two points; RAF Station Nicosia or the RAF Station at Akrotiri near Limassol. As both were prohibited areas to all persons other than RAF personnel, and people with valid air tickets, keeping watch was out of the question.

Then early on the morning of Tuesday, March 17th 1959 the BBC's early morning news announced that two Greek Air Force planes had left Greece for Cyprus to collect Colonel Grivas, who was expected in Athens that afternoon.

David Lewis and Ken Makenzie had a hurried discussion on how we should cover this. David was for trailing the Archbishop. I suggested we watch the Greek Consulate. Ken thought this a good idea and telephoned the consul, Mr. Phrydas whom he knew personally. The consul told Mackenzie: "I know nothing of Colonel Grivas' departure."

The consul must have put down the telephone with Grivas in the building, because by the time I arrived at the Consulate, Mr. Phrydas and Grivas were in the same car heading for Nicosia Airport.

Furious, I dashed after them, urging my taxi-driver to go faster. I had waited four years to get the picture of Grivas. I broke into a cold sweat. I knew I had lost. The taxi screamed to a halt, almost hitting an RAF policeman at the airport gate.

"You've just missed him," said the corporal softly. I'm sure he had a smirk. "A couple of minutes earlier and you would have seen him. All dressed up in uniform too. Had an empty revolver holster on his belt."

The dry, dusty road that crossed through the RAF Station to the air terminal was deserted. Grivas had gone! Disappointed and very annoyed, I sat on the grass verge. Daily Express photographer Gerry Gerelli, who had also been in the race, sat down beside me and pulled out a pack of cigarettes. Paul Bruck of Columbia Television and Gubby Guebenlian of Reuters stood by the RAF corporal imploring him to let them in.

Even as we flicked our cigarette butts into the dust, two Greek Air Force planes roared overhead, banked around and headed west for Athens, where Grivas would be met by Greek Premier Karamanlis and a crowd of thousands.

As the aircraft disappeared into the perfectly blue sky, my thoughts skipped back to that first night, April 1st 1955 – almost four years to the day – when E.O.K.A. made its explosive entrance onto the Cyprus scene. I thought of the countless riots, searches, bombings and violence I had seen. I thought of my friends who had not lived to see this day. I thought of Nicos Sampson, the journalist who carried a notebook and Voightlander one minute and a gun the next, would soon be free. The senseless grim and bloody intercommunal battles between the Greeks and the Turkish Cypriots.

I thought of the miraculous conclusion of the Cyprus question and the return of Archbishop Makarios to lead the new country along side the Turkish Cypriot leader Dr. Fazil Kutchuk. It was the end of a strategic point in the British Empire. All this I had seen and photographed. But the man whose organization had killed 371 British Servicemen, I never saw. I had the feeling I was about to see "The End" title coming up, but in this, I was mistaken.

Presidential elections were held on December 13, 1959. Makarios defeated his rival, lawyer and Q.C. John Clerides. Clerides' son Glafkos, a former British Royal Air Force pilot who served with honors during World War II, would later become President of Cyprus. Then as the Greek and Turkish Cypriots sat down to work out the future government of Cyprus, things became quiet. There was a lull but Cyprus is never really quiet for long.

CYPRUS BECOMES A MOVIE SET

All sorts of people were giving cocktail parties for a whole variety of reasons and a number of movie people came to the Island looking for possible film locations. One was Carl Foreman who was planning "The Guns of Navarone," with David Niven and Gregory Peck, but he chose one of the islands off the Greek mainland.

Then came Otto Preminger, who was making a film of Leon Uris' novel "Exodus," with Paul Newman, Sal Mineo, Eva Marie Saint, and Sir Ralph Richardson. One day they were filming at the Commissioner's House in Nicosia, so I popped over to take a few shots for the Cyprus Mail.

Preminger had encountered a major problem. He had requested the help of British troops to play extras but higher ups had squashed the idea, so the American director decided to hire anyone who could play soldier extras. They provided British uniforms. Many British expatriates signed up along with some Greek and Turkish Cypriots.

Extras were standing around the driveway and gardens waiting for calls. I spotted two, one of whom looked very familiar. I just could not place him, but back at the office, reporters looked at my photo. "That's Yiacoumis. Andreas Yiacoumis who shot Sergeant Hammond," they told me. Everyone was stunned. A former E.O.K.A. gunman, playing a British soldier.

I radioed the picture to Central Press Photos in London and within minutes it was splashed over the afternoon newspapers, and again in the following day's morning papers. The Daily Herald came up with the long head: Cyprus 1960: Remember Sergeant Hammond? Cypriot accused of killing plays a British soldier." The picture showed Yiacoumis in a British Army uniform smoking a cigarette on the Exodus set.

Preminger was inundated with calls from British newspaper editors. He suspended filming for two days because of the calls. I visited the set the next day and the balding director was moaning: "Who would do this?"

CYPRIOT FIGHTER PLAYS BRITISH SOLDIER:
This picture created a stir with international repercussions. It shows Andreas Yiacoumis, (with cigarette) an E.O.K.A. fighter accused of killing a British Army sergeant, now ready to play a British soldier in Otto Preminger's film "Exodus" part of which was shot in Nicosia. Preminger received so many calls he suspended production for two days.

I shrugged and said: "I did. It's my job."

Preminger took my name and repeated it several times. "Why would you do this? Do you want a part in the film?"

I shook my head. As much as I had always imagined being an actor since my days at Moor Hall Studios in Cookham, I had to say no."I recognized the Cypriot as an E.O.K.A. fighter and as he was in British Army uniform it was ironical," I told the director.

"Sure you don't want a part?"

"Sir, I enjoy your movies, and I'm sorry for the disruption, but I had to do my job. Wouldn't you?"

Preminger nodded. A week later, Lucy and I were invited to attend a cocktail party. The Governor, Sir Hugh Foot held the event for the cast and crew of Exodus. Sal Mineo was there with eyes for Jill Haworth. Hugh Griffith and Lucy got on fabulously, chatting about Malta which he knew well. There must have been 200 people there. Mr. and Mrs. Preminger were chatting with Sir Hugh Foot. I snapped a picture. Preminger pointed at me: "That man is dangerous," he said, and Hugh Foot responded: "I know! I know! He photographed me in bed recently." This statement stunned the American director and Sir Hugh explained.

OTTO PREMINGER AND THE AUTHOR:
When this photo was taken some time after the Andreas Yiacoumis incident, things had cooled down and he complemented the author on a "good story." Photo courtesy of Felix Yiaxis.

A week or so earlier, Sir Hugh had been confined to bed for a couple of days, but insisted his sickness would in no way hold up progress in the forthcoming independence of Cyprus. I took a photograph of Sir Hugh in bed, propped up with pillows, surrounded by various papers. At the bedside was a seated secretary. Preminger, listening to the Governor, stared at me, then added: "You're a rebel, Mr. Egby." They all laughed and the party went on.

199

THE END OF A COLONY

It was the end of a British Colony, but the Birth of a Republic. On Tuesday, August 16th 1960 the Island of Cyprus, Aphrodite's Isle became independent, and the curtains were drawn on a part of the British Empire. We had photographed the signing ceremonies and now it was goodbye.

THE END OF COLONIAL CYPRUS:
On his last day as Governor of Cyprus, Sir Hugh Foot invited selected people to a farewell gathering at Government House. The author (left) is pictured with Sir Hugh, along with two Greek Cypriot journalists, Efthyvoulou of Associated Press and George Lanitis of the Cyprus Broadcasting Service.

I had been there when it happened. A few days earlier I had received a letter from Government House, dated August 1960. Personally signed by the Governor, it read:

My Dear Egby: My wife and I are inviting a number of our friends to Government House on the morning of the 16th of August to give us an opportunity of saying goodbye to them before we leave for Famagusta. We should be very happy if you could come to Government House that morning between 7.30 a.m. and 7.45 a.m.

The President-Elect, Vice-President-Elect and Greek Cypriot and Turkish Cypriot Ministers have expressed their wish to come to Government House at 8.a.m. that morning to say farewell to us, and after that the Commanders-in-Chief are coming from Episkopi to say fare-well. I shall then inspect a Guard provided by the 2nd Battlion, The Parachute Regiment and leave for Famagusta where my wife and I and the boys will embark and sail in H.M.S. Chichester (there will be no farewells at Famagusta).

If you would like to come to Government House to witness these comings and goings, and to give us a chance of shaking hands with you and wishing you well we shall be delighted. Yours sincerely, Hugh Foot. Governor.

There was a deep sadness my heart because this Colony, this outpost of the British Empire, this Aphrodite's Isle, had been my home. But I had been with the Cypriots for so long and understood how they felt, that they needed their own identity, their own self-determination. I wondered too, that if Iro and I had weathered the storm over these five years, whether independence would have given us a new burst of sunshine in our marriage. But the water was gone under the bridge.

The pictures I took that day got a spread in The Sphere in London and the British and European newspapers. Historic pictures, but one I shall keep for a while is one of me, the Governor Sir Hugh Foot, and fellow journalists Alex Eftyvoulou and George Lanitis.

NICOS SAMPSON TELLS ALL

Independence opened the door for a large number of E.O.K.A. fighters who had been imprisoned or gone into exile. Among them was Nicos Sampson appearing older, more mature and possibly wiser, at least so I thought. One day he cornered me: "Egbis, I am starting my own paper in Greek. Would you like to work for me?"

I really didn't know whether to laugh, scream, or run away. The offer was so ridiculous. I stood there stunned. "I don't know enough Greek."

"Then perazi," he said. "Never mind. We have great translators."

"Let me think about it," I shot back. One did not feel like saying "no" or "yes" to someone like Sampson. It was an entirely different situation, a different ball game. I never did get back to him with a reply.

The Cyprus Mail had moved from Murder Mile to a new, larger office on Vassilios Voulgaroctonos Street in the heart of Nicosia. Sampson rented a house few doors away and started his newspaper called Mahki, meaning

Knife. It was a moderate, well presented newspaper, at first. But things were brewing.

On the home front Lucy was pregnant and at the Nicosia General Hospital on October 22nd 1960 she gave birth to our first son, a blondish little kid. We named him Gregory Bickford Egby. Gregory, because I liked the name. It sounded strong, and Bickford was a name from her mother Grace's side of the family. Grace was a Bickford and her father had served with distinction in the Royal Navy in World War I. He commanded a vessel that monitored the English Channel, so they called him "Bickford of the Dover Patrol."

One evening, some months after I had finished my night shift at the Cyprus Mail, I was walking home to our apartment, when I passed the offices of Mahki. The windows were open and Nicos was sitting at a desk, a cigarette dangling from his lips, and beaming over a front page story.

"Hey, Egbis! Look!" he called out, so I went in and he thrust a copy of his newspaper into my hand. In my limited understanding of Greek I knew Sampson was telling how he performed the shocking Murder Mile shooting that killed two British police officers and seriously injured a third, Ivor Webb.

Grinning, Sampson knowing what I would do, thrust a copy into my hand. I raced back to the Cyprus Mail, where Andreas Hadjipapas did a fast translation. I telexed United Press in London, and the story caught the London dailies.

The newspapers dug up my old pictures from 1956. They used the Murder Mile police killing and a trimmed one column of Sampson, holding a camera at the Bonici killing. The Daily Mail interviewed Ivor Webb in England as he was repairing a car engine. He said the "time for vengeance is past." He told reporters: "At the time I wanted more than anything else to kill Sampson, but now my anger has gone. The time for vengeance is past. I am not a man to bear malice."

In subsequent stories in his newspaper, Sampson told how he had killed Bonici Mompalda, the Maltese fellow who managed a shop on Ledra Street. He said he shot him, and then ran to where some girls were standing. They hid the gun under their clothes and gave Sampson his Voigtlander camera, the one I had taught him to use. He returned to the crime scene and stood around taking pictures of his victim and Drosoulla Demetriadou the Greek Cypriot girl sitting beside the body. He said he talked to reporters and photographers including myself, and no one had any idea that he had killed a person. Thinking back, something, some entity must have known. Her voice told me to take a general view, and it was the photo that showed Sampson on the crime scene.

A HAUNTING REVELATION

One of the fears we had while working on Murder Mile during the Emergency was the definite possibility that a new E.O.K.A. gunman would come to town and fail to recognize a working journalist. Overseas reporters were valued by both sides in the Cyprus dispute.

So as E.O.K.A. fighters were being rounded up, there was a distinct possibility of a new gunman, even a new killer group leader coming to town. After he returned to Cyprus and was building his newspaper, Sampson took me aside and said: "Egbis, I saved your life one day. We had a new fighter in Lefkosia and we were having coffee near the Cyprus Mail. You walked by and the new fighter looked at you and wanted to follow and kill you. He was very enthusiastic, but I told him you were a good news reporter and reported everything accurately."

The revelation was stunning. A convicted killer who had once been sentenced to death, telling me he had saved my life. It struck me in so many ways. Supposing Sampson had not been with the imported gunman, I could have been shot down easily. It had happened to others. One was Angus McDonald a young journalist who came to join Charles Foley at the Times of Cyprus.

So what was I to say to Sampson? "Thanks for saving my life. Much appreciated" or "I don't believe you" or "I'm curious. Tell me more." – what exactly would you, the reader of this, say in similar circumstances?

Me? I clenched my fist and gently tapped his arm. "Nicos, you have more surprises than anyone I know."

SAMPSON'S NEW RISE AND FALL

I recalled that day in Nicosia when we had watched "The Bridges at Toko-Ri" at the Regina Cinema. As we walked out Sampson had said: "That was exciting. I'd like to be in a war. Even just covering it." I think he had dreams of being a great hero.

Fourteen years later, what Nicos had dreamed about, came true, but not in the way he had envisioned.

We were thousands of miles away when we heard the news. Nicos Sampson, backed by a team of Greek Army colonels had staged a coup and ousted Archbishop Makarios, and Sampson in turn had been made president. It was July 15th 1974. His crazy eight-day coup triggered a Turkish invasion of the Cyprus and the occupation of the northern third of the island, a state of affairs that is still in existence today. Sampson's coup led to a heavy loss of life among the Greek Cypriots, and tens of thousands were forced to flee their homes and become refugees in their own country.

The invasion triggered a war between – the Turkish invaders, Greek Cypriot fighters (they now called themselves EOKA-B), Turkish Cypriot communities, Greek Cypriot communities and the British Forces from the two bases at Dhekelia and Akrotiri. British families had to be evacuated. In all of this, Sampson was forced to resign as president.

In August 1976, after being tried and found guilty of actions against the State, Sampson was sentenced to 20 years in prison. Subsequently, he was allowed to go to France for medical treatment and returned to Cyprus in June 1990. He was released from prison a few months later and went back to publishing newspapers which enjoyed only a moderate success. His public popularity had waned, in fact, some people branded him an enemy of Cyprus. Early in 2001 Sampson was diagnosed as suffering from cancer. He crossed into Spirit on May 9th. He left a wife and two children, including a son who at that time was running the newspapers.

THE QUEEN COMES TO CYPRUS

Once independence had arrived in Aphrodite's Realm everything changed as if nothing had happened. Archbishop Makarios, now the President of the Republic arrived at the British bases and was driven in a British Land Rover by a British soldier. It must have seemed strange to some of the troops who formed the Security Forces in the Cyprus Emergency.

Then Her Majesty the Queen with Prince Phillip arrived at the British base at Akrotiri and the Cyprus leaders, Archbishop Makarios and the Dr. Fazil Kutchuk were there to greet and meet the British monarch.

In 1961 colonial Cyprus was fast receding into history and the new republic was emerging. I was working at the Cyprus Mail, but the stories were routine and predictable. The death of Ernest Hemingway in early June upset me. I enjoyed most of his writings and had studied his style.

One day I was assigned to cover the Halle Orchestra under Sir John Barbirolli playing against a background of floodlit battlements at Kyrenia Castle in northern Cyprus. Several hundred people flocked to the event, and I managed to get a great night picture of the orchestra. It was published in the Daily Telegraph and several magazines. Afterwards Lucy had fun at a reception talking to musicians from England. Me? I felt distinctly odd, because the Castle and its harbor brought back memories of my times with Iro. It was if I was being condemned not to forget.

It happened again a short while later.

There was a gathering of the Knights Templar at Kolossi Castle near Limassol. Many modern-day Templars were there adorned in their lavish, contrasting robes. It was a great pageant and again, a great photo opportunity. Afterwards, Lucy and I wandered through the castle, and again, I was haunted by memories of my love affair with Iro and they hurt. To escape the suffering I worked harder. I didn't yet know how not to suffer.

THE QUEEN VISITS CYPRUS LEADERS:
As part of the Cyprus Agreement, Britain retained the right to maintain sovereign bases on the island at Akrotiri near Limassol and Dhekelia near Larnaca. Her Majesty Queen Elizabeth and Prince Phillip visited Akrotiri. They are pictured here with the President of Cyprus, Archbishop Makarios. On the left is Vice President, Dr. Fazil Kutchuk. This photo triggered a variety of comments from irate Britons who had lost loved ones during the Cyprus Emergency. It was one of the last big stories I covered on Cyprus.

One day in early April 1961, Donald Scott Reid flew some journalists and photographers to RAF El Adem in Libya to cover some eighty Australian veterans returning to one of the greatest battlegrounds in the North Africa campaign. They were known as the "Rats of Tobruk." and it was great being with these Aussie veterans. The P & O liner Orontes made a special visit to Tobruk with the men and their families on board. It was very emotional to see these old soldiers, some with tears in their eyes as they marched through the big stone gateway to the Tobruk War Cemetery, where 559 Australians who fought and died in the six-month long siege in 1941 are buried. The Sphere in London published a full double-page of my pictures.

Covering the events was John Russell from the British Forces Broadcasting Station in Cyprus. We sat together on the plane returning to Nicosia. "Why don't you come back to FBS? We'd love to have you back in the studio," he said.

"You know, I was only thinking the other day that we should be moving on," I replied. "What should I do?"

The old British Empire was dying and somewhere another kink was sounding in the Cosmos and our lives were changing direction. Were the seers right? I was going to find out.

15

THE ETERNAL MICROPHONE

THE FIRST TIME I flew in a jet aircraft was in October 1961. A de Havilland DH-106 Comet took me from Nicosia to London's Heath Row Airport which I had not seen since 1949 when I delivered David Hand's Animaland film for processing to Technicolor. Heath Row on the other side of the Bath Road was then a collection of Nissan huts and a little runway for RAF fighter aircraft. Now it was an expanding aviation metropolis.

The London office and headquarters of British Forces Broadcasting was tucked away in an Edwardian-era building of brick and stone, some five stories, with a couple of floors on the top, elegantly designed as penthouses. I never figured out who lived there but an elaborately designed metal cage known as a "Lift" or elevator took one up and down with clanks and purrs. HQ British Forces Broadcasting seemed like hallowed ground, the holiest of holies. Named Kings Buildings on Dean Stanley Street, it stood in the shadows of the House of Commons.

The lanky Brian Bass, whose forte was classical music delivered with a mellow, almost hypnotic voice, pushed me into a studio, thrust a script into my hands, and said "You're an old timer, Bob, this will be a breeze."

The voice-test breeze was loaded with musically related words such as Charles-Camille Saint-Saëns, L'Après-midi d'un faune, Manuel de Falla, and Richard Wagner's Lohengrin and The Ride of the Valkyries. I did not think I had fared well, but Brian came into the studio: "You're fine, Bob. Welcome to the club."

And so it was I became, what they called a U.K.Based Civilian with a contract that insured a regular income. Wow! I was thrilled. During the next hour I met such figures as Ian Wolfe, Johnny Parsons, Ted King, Terry James, Jack Pickering, Alan Langford, and Roy Foulkes who had broadcast at FBS Fayid as "Guy Roberts," and Derek Agutter whose young daughter Jenny was destined to star in "The Railway Children" and march on to other notable movies.

I also met Pat Pachebat, a veteran broadcaster who had served at the station in Trieste at the end of World War II. Brian and Pat took me to lunch in New Westminster and delivered a surprise.

"We want you to be part of the team we're creating to set up a brand new broadcasting station in Aden – South Arabia," said Pat. "First, get your feet wet again in the studios at Nicosia, and then you and the family will ship out in the next couple of months."

"Aden! What's so great about Aden?" Lucy said when I returned to Cyprus. "It's a challenge," I said. "We're setting up a broadcasting station from scratch."

SAYING GOODBYE TO OLD FRIENDS

It was difficult saying goodbyes to my friends at the Cyprus Mail, particularly Jacko Iacovides, the publisher. The newspaper had acquired a new managing editor, Herman Goult who had worked on newspapers in the Malay States since World War II. His last job had been with the Straits Times in Singapore and he talked about his times there. I never heard of the Straits Times again, until I came to writing this book in 2010.

It happened while I was researching the death of my great-grandfather Henry (Harry) Egby, the poet, composer and laborer in Reading, and Google's search engine pulled up a newspaper clip from 1931. Out of all the newspapers in the world to carry Harry's death was the Straits Times. A strange coincidence that is beyond understanding, at least for me.

There was also another editor and writer at the Cyprus Mail. Peter Hellier and his wife Ronah. They hailed from Australia, and Lucy and I thoroughly enjoyed their company.

FBS Cyprus had changed since I had been there as a locally employed announcer in the mid-1950s. The station commander now was Roy Morgan, a veteran of Palestine, Kay Donnelly, Peter Buckle, Johnny Bull, Phil Harding, David Davis, John Russell, Alan Robson and Paul Kazarine, who had a delightful, nutty wife. Willis Toogood often invited us to his rambling, old house for evening drinks and nibbles. One evening, he announced he was superman and sprang nimbly off the balcony about ten feet above the ground. But as he leapt into flight, he hit a rail lurking above and crashed to the ground. He said afterwards: "My ambitions to be a movie hero are dashed."

On Willis' dining room wall was a copy of Picasso's 1903 oil painting "The Old Guitarist." There were prolonged debates on which way the painting should hang. If you ever see it, try figuring it out. Is the guitarist sitting up or lying down?

We did some interesting outside broadcasts or OBs as they are called. One was to cover the visit of the Princess Royal on the Royal Yacht Britannia to Famagusta and somehow, Ian Fenner slipped off our rooftop position, and I had to fill in until he scrambled back up, thankfully unhurt. The perils of broadcasting.

Engineers Johnny Bull, Phil Harding and I got together with the idea of producing a 30 minute drama for television. In the early 1960s television was starving for original material. Enthusiastically, we wrote a script and had fun seeking locations in the Cyprus Mountains. In fact we had a series of "Location Finding Picnics." Johnny and Dorothy brought their tribe along – some dozen kids – and Lucy and I brought our two, and Phil brought his wife. It was not for a lack of capital that spiked the project, but time. I received my posting papers – Aden!

We boarded the one funneled vessel, the Kenya Castle at Limassol. Said to be the last of the great oceanic liners, it had been built in 1951 for the Union-Castle Line. It felt comfortable and the food was excellent. On the second day we traversed the Suez Canal, which remarkably had been re-opened for maritime traffic in 1957, four years before.

It felt strange seeing these places such as Port Said, Ismalia, Lake Timsah, the Great Bitter Lake again. I had served as an airman on a radar station at El Firdan, I had accompanied my friend Peter Dance searching for shells in the desert, I had been a broadcaster at FBS Fayid, covered Australian Premier Menzies meeting President Nasser, and come back to Egypt as an accredited war correspondent in the Suez War.

There was something intriguing in the desert that kept beckoning me. This was prevalent with my work in Jordan, travelling to Baghdad with Joe Alex Morris, and accompanying the rebels in northern Lebanon. The desert appealed to me then and I was to wait a number of years before my desire to be in the desert finally dawned upon me. Now I was going to the British Colony of Aden and the Aden Protectorate, which was all desert.

The Red Sea was something else. Pure beauty. The water was clear, crystal clear and to gaze upon it from a distance, possessed the deepest blue I had ever seen. The bows of the Kenya Castle sliced through the water, leaving a fluorescent bow wave that sparkled at night like a million diamonds. A team of dolphin frequently played, diving, twisting and leaping through the bow wave and always staying just ahead of the bow. At the southern end of the Red Sea is Perim Island, once a coal-refueling station for shipping, but now a coral island inhabited by fishermen. A volcanic isle, it stands as a sentinel in the Straits of Bab-el-Mandeb which is the exit at the southern end of the Red Sea and the beginning of the Indian Ocean.

THE BARREN ROCKS OF ADEN

You cannot miss them. Tortuous mountainous, bleached by thousands of years of hot, relentless sun and totally barren. Those are the first things one sees on approaching this age-old port. The gateway to Aden is the harbor and Steamer Point, a town of little shops, bistros and offices. Its enormous backdrop is a huge mass of rocks, the subject of Andy Stewart's record, "The Barren Rocks of Aden." The landscape gives the impression that God, while creating, stopped for lunch and forgot to come back. The phenomenon that gets you right off the top is the humidity. It permeates every cell in the body. It's deadly and I never did get used to it.

There were several communities in the colony: Steamer Point, Maalla, Crater and Khormaksar which is where the RAF Station and base were situated. Crater means exactly that. It is a town built in a volcanic crater which everyone assumes – and hopes – is dead. Maalla is a broad street lined with apartment blocks four or five stories, perhaps more, mostly built to accommodate British troops and their families. Each building is exactly the same as the other. It looks as if the builders had one architectural plan and shared it.

The thing that gets you as you leave the apartment at any time of the day or night are the beggars. They swarm like flies and they flock around presenting a sea of empty hands, moving, grasping, clinging. Beggaring is part of a acknowledged profession in Aden.

The first week we arrived a Government health inspector told me that families who wish their children to become beggars, break the child's legs and enforce a crippled life. That is why one sees children on little wooden platforms, fitted with wheels pushing themselves along on the roads and sidewalks. Tourists from visiting ocean liners cannot help but feel sorry, and help to relieve their feelings by giving cash. Aden's colonial administration attempted to stop this practice, but it was like blowing in the wind. Futile. I often wonder if this barbaric practice of enforced beggarism continues.

Our furnished apartment on the Maalla main road was spacious and comfortable. You had to climb three-four-five sets of stairs to get to it. I assumed they never heard of elevators. We had a cocktail party once – I fail to think why – and some 50 people turned up, mainly British folk and all had a good time. We had no need of the oven in the kitchen but the first time we did, it triggered an exodus of cockroaches, not just a dozen but countless hundreds. They fled in mad abandonment across the floor. It took an hour to clean them up and we never did use the oven.

Almost all the families had a maid, and we were no exception. Tall and willowy, her skin was as black as ebony. Extremely polite she never seemed to mind working for £5 or $8.00 a month. She was a Somali girl from Djibouti across the water in East Africa and her outfits were colorful and stunning. One day I was sick with influenza and stayed in bed. I vaguely awoke to find her cleaning the room. She was stripped to the waist and busy dusting. Her body was delicately contoured, and feeling dizzy, I closed my eyes and went back to sleep. I often wondered was it true or an illusion.

OUR VERY FIRST CAR:
After years of traveling in taxi cabs we decided to buy a car in Aden, an Italian Fiat. It was 1963. Here young Gregory is behind the wheel with Roberta in the passenger seat. It was bigger than Ray Joyce's Fiat Topolino in Cyprus, but people could look down on us and chat through the open sun roof. Driving in Aden was hairy. For no apparent reason and with no signals, cars in Aden would suddenly stop in the middle of the road to chat or call out to other drivers.

Eventually the Maalla apartment was not to our liking, mainly because of the stairs, and the fact that Lucy was pregnant, and so we put in for a house. They gave us one at Tarshyne which was near the beach. Initially, that sounded like fun. But then we spotted a large wire net strung out on posts in the water. "What's that?" asked Lucy.

"That," said Penny, David Davis's wife, "is a shark net."

Shark net or not, it took us a little while before we went swimming. When we were comfortable swimming, some kind soul warned us about the barracudas. "They are skinny and can slip through the shark netting. They'll take a bite the size of a tennis ball out of your arm." I never got used to swimming in Aden.

Once, engineer Dennis Phillips and I took a row boat out to go fishing. We hadn't gone far when a sting ray started to surface right below the boat. You could see part of it on one side and the rest on the other side of the boat. It must have been twelve feet across. We couldn't row fast enough to get away.

Fishing was a pleasant evening's activity. Many of the Station's crew would gather on the beach, cast their bait and stick the rods into the sand. Then they would sit down a few feet away and drink beer. You knew when you had something, because the reel would start hissing and whizzing rapidly. The trick was to get to your rod before the fish took the whole thing out to sea. It was quite hilarious to see a speeding, shouting, gesticulating white man racing frantically to save his rod, only to see it jerked out of the sand and dragged out to sea and oblivion. It happened at least once a week. We all used 80lb lines in Aden because most fish happened to be that large.

BUILDING A RECORD LIBRARY

Work at the new radio station was a challenge. Dozens of records – long play and 45 rpm – had been shipped out from Britain. Some crates had baked in the sun and the vinyl disks had become warped and could not be used. They were dumped. But the majority was fine. The work of creating the library was sheer monotony. Every day, several of us sat at typewriters creating index cards for orchestras, bands, vocalists, speakers, and making, where we could, cross-references. There was an index card for every track – the singer, orchestra and the song title. If there were different songs with the same title, we had to add the composer or vocalist. The librarian was Michael Smith.

Occasionally we salvaged a damaged LP from the garbage can. One I saved from destruction was Parlophone's "The Beatles" and their album "Please, Please Me." I stacked it with my other records and over the years it became straightened out, but I cannot ever recall playing it. I would rather listen to the big orchestras rendering their versions of the Beatles. The Boston Pops Orchestra was one.

The FBS Aden team comprised Pat Pachebat who was station manager, then John Russell, David Davis, Bill Mitchell, Kathy Emmett who had worked at Cyprus Broadcasting and joined FBS, and Pat Doody who used to amuse everyone by saying that when he was to make his debut on television in Britain he would wear tinted contact lenses. One couple was Alan Parfrey and his wife Ann. They always enjoyed playing host at a bar. On the engineering side was Senior Engineer Les Allen, Mike Farnes, Colin Rugg and Dennis Phillips

Bill Mitchell loved to do his evening announcer's shift wearing a tuxedo. Bill loved model trains and his apartment was filled with track going over wooden guideways. In fact, to get into his apartment, the visitor had to step over double tracks on a 12-inch elevated viaduct just inside the door. Often Bill could be found having a drink after work in the Rock Hotel at Steamer Point. Suddenly, without fail he would look at his watch and say: "I must be going. I have to get the five-thirty five away." And off he went.

THE OLD PROFESSION CALLS

The new station at Aden went on the air on August 11th 1962. Lady Elworthy, wife of the Commander-in-Chief did the honors. And who should turn up with the RAF brass but my old friend in Air Ministry Public Relations, Don Scott Reid.

"Are you still writing and taking pictures for Central Press in London?" he said quietly.

"Not really," I said. "I don't think my contract with FBS would allow the use of my name in bylines."

"Use a nom-de-plume," he said. "There are some stories coming up which would be good for London, but here's the clincher, they'll be good for Forces Broadcasting. So it will be a double whammy."

Don was always a good talker. A few days later, Lucy and I were invited over to his place for drinks. Noel Clark, the BBC correspondent based in Aden was there. "The Daily Mail in London is looking for a good stringer," he said. "Don's been telling me about your work. I'll put in a good word for you if you like."

I nodded. It was too easy. "I would have to use a nom-de-plume. For several years I have been thinking of writing novels under the name Lasker...Frank Lasker," I told him. It was not quite the truth. In the days following my talk with Scott Reid, I had mulled over the idea of a writing name and a little voice had said, "Frank Lasker will work for you." I was not about to divulge my voices phenomenon.

I mailed off a letter to the Daily Mail, and a short while later received a green light from D. Crosby Fisher, the Daily Mail Foreign Editor. He set up cable collect facilities and outlined his requirements.

Then Scott Reid dropped by late one afternoon. "Are you free?" I nodded, I was about to go home. "Someone wants to meet you?" We drove up the hill through the government complex to a large house overlooking Steamer Point. Don steered me past the guards and the ADCs. Don always had his way.

"Hello Egby," said a familiar voice. "What are you up to now?"

It was Sir Charles Johnston from my days in Amman. Since then he had been knighted in the New Year Honors 1959 and was now a Knight Commander of the Order of St. Michael and St. George. I immediately congratulated him, and then I added: "I think you deserve it for your work in Jordan and elsewhere. The media people always think you're a go-getter."

He didn't skip a beat. "I'm surprised you haven't called before."

Once I got over my initial surprise, I mentioned something about living in a protected environment and getting a radio station on the air. Also, my contract with FBS, and my pen-name. We had tea and he asked how things were going in Cyprus. "Hugh Foot handled that particularly well," we thought. "I'm hoping we can work things out here in Aden with the tribal people of the Aden Protectorate."

Sir Charles showed me a map of South Arabia. The Colony of Aden was at the southern tip and above it two land masses, the Western Protectorate and the Eastern Protectorate, both under Britain's responsibility for protection. "There are a number of tribes in this area; some of them still feel they are in a state of war. The nationalization of the Suez Canal Company, the Suez War, the growing threat of Nasser-inspired agitators and nationalists, and the growing number of Communists in North Yemen, make it essential that we have a stronger organization in the south here," he said.

"We are dissolving the Colony of Aden and establishing a self-governing State of Aden this year," said Sir Charles. "Next year – 1963 – it will merge with the Federation of South Arabia You are looking at an area that is comparable to England and Wales put together, so it is no small area."

"Now, if you want to see what we're dealing with, you might take a trip into the Protectorate," said Sir Charles. "It will make some interesting pictures...and perhaps a news story."

A week later, I had a call from a Captain Morgan. "I hear you want to see the Eastern Protectorate. We'll be away for three days. Pick you up tomorrow morning."

INTO THE ARAB DESERT LANDS

The Aden Protectorate was a collection of twenty Arab tribal states in a desert terrain covering just over 110,000 square miles. In comparison the total United Kingdom is smaller at 94,000 square miles. Nevada, the seventh largest state in the U.S. is 110,000 square miles, just about the same size. The British annexed it in 1839 and departed in 1967.

The Protectorate was bordered on the west and south by the Red Sea and the Indian Ocean, on the east by the Sultanate of Muscat and Oman, and on the north by Saudi Arabia and the Republic of Yemen. Today the British are long gone and the old Colony of Aden is part of the Republic of Yemen.

There were no paved highways in the Protectorate, just dusty tracks for camels, trucks and the odd bus or two. The easiest and most beautiful and interesting way of travelling to the Eastern Aden Protectorate was on the seemingly endless beaches. There were three vehicles, two trucks and a Land Rover. I sat in the Land Rover zipping across the hard sand at 60 mph. Terrifying but exhilarating. The sands were golden and very broad, perhaps two or three hundred yards wide, and the white waves looked like white horses playfully galloping out of the bluest of blue sea.

The convoy stopped at remote townships to say "hello." The Captain spoke some Arabic which seemed to impress the villagers.

We came to a village where there were several large buildings, perhaps three or four storys. Some had painted white bands around the tops, one or two were covered about half way down, and one was painted completely in white, Morgan explained: "The white signifies the wealth and financial standing of the owner of the building. Can't say that would go down very well in Blighty." Everyone laughed.

A number of Arabs gathered round our vehicles and asked for cigarettes. Their dress was fascinating. Around their galibeers were heavy belts, with scabbards holding long, curved knives, perhaps twelve to eighteen inches. Each one showed an ornate silver handle. Not one man was without a large knife or dagger of some sort. You could feel they were ready to fight and kill, if attacked. The Captain explained that tribal wars were still prevalent in the 1950s, some ten years before. The British, as usual, interceded. I was glad when we moved on.

Once we came across an oasis that looked as if it had been created in the desert for a movie set. There were lush green plants, grass and tall, vibrant palm trees surrounding the pools. I took several photographs and then knelt down to touch the water.

"Be careful! It's hot!" cried Captain Morgan's driver. Sure enough it was too hot to handle. "It's a volcanic pool. Water is boiled deep underground and surfaces here," explained the Captain.

THE TANKS CAME RUMBLING IN

We spent two nights in the desert overlooking the Indian Ocean before turning back to Aden. Along the way we stopped for a break and noticed a small sandstorm heading towards us. Out of the dust emerged two Centurion tanks. Based at Falaise Camp in Little Aden, they were manned by the Royal Scots Greys, a British Regiment that started as a cavalry force back in 1678. They were now armored and always ready for action and in Aden as part of the Emergency Forces.

I interviewed Sergeant George Mitchell, an outgoing tank commander for Forces Broadcasting and took a variety of photos. The tank crews joined Captain Morgan and our group in making tea, watched by desert Arabs. It was an enjoyable break.

Note: Over the years – forty-seven in fact – I found I had lost my notes of this tank encounter. On Line, members of the British Historic Military Vehicles Forum identified the tanks and the hat badges as the Royal Scots Greys. Then I found the Royal Scots Greys Forum and members kindly helped identify Sergeant Mitchchell from pictures displayed on my website.

Then just as I was writing the desert rendezvous of forty-seven years ago, I received an email from George Mitchell's family. They had found my website with pictures, seeking information. Apparently, George had been promoted to Regimental Quartermaster Sergeant with the Greys at their HQ in Edinburgh, Scotland. His family told me he had passed away August 6th 2007. I sent a set of my "tank" photos to both his family and the Regiment as gifts, because seeing those tanks and the crews that day in the desert left a very good memory of something that happened almost half a century ago.

Later, on the way back, one of the trucks got trapped in soft sand while we were taking a lunch break. We were about 100 yards in from the sea among the dunes. Suddenly a tall, black man mysteriously appeared, an ornate cloth wrapped about his middle and thighs. He informed us he catches crayfish and sells them to people passing by. Some of the soldiers bought the crayfish, which are like lobsters, only without claws. They live in warm waters.

BRITISH TANKS IN THE ADEN DESERT:
A 42-ton British Centurion tank sweeps across the desert sands east of Aden. The author
met them by accident and did a radio interview for Forces Broadcasting and pictures for Central
Press in London. The tanks were operated by the Royal Scots Greys based at Falaise Camp,
Little Aden. Below, the tank commander is Sergeant George William Mitchell who later became
the Regimental Quartermaster Sergeant of the Greys in Edinburgh, Scotland. Apologies, we have
not been able to identify the Loader.

Then I noticed a young girl carrying a baby wrapped in soft cotton sheets. She was half the size of the fisherman. "Is that his daughter?" I inquired of the Captain.

"Oh, no," whispered the officer. "That's his wife and baby. The wife is twelve years old. I've seen them before.

The crayfisherman smiled and let me take a picture. In return, I gave him some coins. I really don't like the idea of crayfish, or lobsters.

When I got home and told Lucy about the young wife, she cried: "What barbarians!"

"No," I said. "That's how they live here."

You might think I had forgotten my employers at the radio station. Not at all. At various times on the trek, I interviewed Captain Morgan and some of the soldiers, plus Sergeant Mitchell and the Royal Scots Greys. Back in the studio I produced a piece for one of the Stations radio magazines and sent some photos to Central Press Photos.

THE VOYAGE OF THE SCORPION

One day in January 1963 a couple of Royal Air Force officers zeroed in on our Steamer Point Studios. They carried with them a logbook that dated back twenty-one years. It told the story of how 84 Squadron, RAF flying Blenheims and stationed at Bandung, Java had been overwhelmed by invading Japanese forces. The squadron lost all its aircraft and officers and men were forced to march to a beachhead where they could board evacuation ships. But when they arrived there were no ships in sight.

They found a lifeboat which they named "The Scorpion" after their squadrons' emblem, and the Commanding Officer, Wing Commander J.R. Jeudwine, Pilot Officer "Stretty" Streatfield and eleven aircrew set sail for Australia, leaving the remainder on the beach with a promise of sending help.

What happened to those thirteen men in the lifeboat forms a thrilling saga. They encountered a Japanese submarine, sharks, and survived intense sun and heat with limited supplies of water and food. They landed at a remote spot in Western Australia and were spotted by a U.S. Navy Catalina flying boat crew making a routine patrol.

The story sounded great, so Alan Parfrey and I locked ourselves away with a typewriter and created a docu-drama entitled, "The Voyage of the Scorpion." We needed nineteen voices, plus various sound effects.

THE BARREN ROCKS OF ADEN:
Three Blackburn Beverley transport aircraft belonging to the 84 Squadron, Royal Air Force fly over the town of Crater on their way back to RAF Station Khormaksar in Aden in1963. The town was built in the crater of a long extinct volcano. The aircraft were returning from taking reinforcements to the Aden Protectorate border with Yemen. Donald Scott-Reid arranged for the author to fly and take this picture. A few days later, the Squadron asked Forces Broadcasting to do a wartime dramatization of their World War II adventure.

We roped in various people in Aden whom we knew had some acting abilities and one evening, recorded the program. The date for broadcast was set and as the day drew near, we received a powerful surprise.

Don Scott Reid had called the Air Ministry in London and their people had tracked down the only living survivor of the lifeboat, Stretty Streatfield, who had retired several years beforehand and was now living near Birmingham. The ten minute interview was taped and flown out to Aden where it ran at the end of the program. That was February 1963 – twenty-one years after the "Voyage of the Scorpion" occurred. I still have a recording of that docudrama, a copy of which is in the BFBS archives in the U.K. The story teller was Pat Doody and the narrators and producers were Alan Parfrey and myself. It's a weird experience listening to old friends and colleagues almost fifty years later. Yes, Petty Officer Streatfield said they did indeed send help to the crews left behind on the Java beachhead, but there was no one there.

Incidentally, if ever you meet up with anyone from 84 Squadron, you should know that the Squadron with its Scorpion emblem is unique. Created in 1917 it has served in most of the wars and conflicts since then. As I write, the Squadron is based at RAF Akrotiri, Cyprus and here's the clincher. In all its history this squadron has never been based in the United Kingdom.

"FRANK LASKER" AND THE DAILY MAIL

As the months went by I, using the pen-name of Frank Lasker, telexed a number of stories to the Daily Mail. One involved consignments of silver coins from the Halal Shipping Company in Aden to British brokers that were snatched by the Egyptians as the ships went through the Suez Canal. Not any run-of-the-mill coins. These were the famous Maria Theresa silver thalers of 1780 minted in modern-day Vienna for Mussolini to pay tribesmen fighting in the Ethiopian war. Total value of the consignments was about half a million pounds sterling. British and Swedish representatives were taking up the matter with Egyptian officials.

But the big story occurred over the weekend of June 22nd 1963. A large group of British servicemen and women was exploring the northern regions of the newly created South Arabian Federation. In the dark they got lost and followed the wrong desert track and found themselves in Yemen and under armed attack by tribesmen.

One section turned, backed off and retreated madly back to the border where nineteen, some of them wounded, were picked up by an RAF Belvedere helicopter and flown to Aden. The twenty-five stranded members unable to escape, took refuge in a dried-up river bed in the hills about one-and-a-half miles inside Yemen. Their only protection against the tribesmen's shooting and the searing heat was under or inside their three-ton trucks. They had neither food nor water. Finally they were captured.

In Taiz, the twin-capital of Yemen, the American Charge d'Affaires opened discussions for their release. Four British service women were released immediately and told their stories. It was revealed that five British servicemen had been killed in the action. It was a tragic story that ran for several days under front page banner headlines of "Girls in Trap" and "Army Girls Seized." And Frank Lasker in Aden got bylines all through.

Later in the year, when we arrived back in England, my mother asked about this story and said: "Bobbie, it's a good thing you didn't have anything to do with that."

Then I told her about Frank Lasker.

RODERICK ARRIVES TO JOIN THE CLAN

But I think Mum really wasn't listening, she was all eyes for her latest grandson, born in the British Military Hospital at Aden on August 7th. His name was Roderick Stuart. So the Egby family was growing. Now we had three children, Roberta, Gregory and Roderick.

In November, we said goodbye to all our friends in Aden and set sail on the SS Oriana, the last of the Orient Steam Navigation Company's ocean liners. The British Empire was fading; Aden and the South Arabian Federation became part of the Yemen Republic. And the great ships that bound the Empire together were disappearing into the pages of history.

We enjoyed our holiday aboard the ship as we traversed the Red Sea, the Suez Canal, the Mediterranean, Gibraltar, and the Bay of Biscay. As we voyaged over the ten days you could not help but notice that the days were getting cooler and windier, with frequent rains. The seas were becoming rougher, and although I looked forward to seeing relatives and old friends again, I started to miss the sun and the blue seas - and the desert. The ship hit a storm in the Irish Sea on our way to Liverpool. The gales were so strong they becalmed the sea.

There's was only one thing that disturbed us and that occurred when we were sailing north through the Suez Canal. The date was November 22nd 1963 and it was evening on board. The captain's voice came over the ship's loudspeakers with the news that John F. Kennedy had been assassinated in Dallas, Texas. That night, I stood alone on an upper deck and pondered the mystery of death. It seemed so final. So gone. Then the voice came on the gentle Egyptian breeze: "One day you will learn there is no mystery in death. Right now you have an inability to understand. One day you will be free."

Free! There was the old word again. Damn it. I didn't understand that either.

16

ENGLAND AND A NEW POSTING

I T WAS STRANGE TO be in England. First, there were the high speed inter-city trains that sped along at a mind-boggling 125 mph. Lucy and I had not been on British Rail for years, and it was a totally new experience for five year-old Roberta and three year-old Gregory. They sat there, eyes popping as we hurtled south from Liverpool to London. Roderick, three months old, was blasé to everything. Escalators and taxis in London thrilled Roberta and Gregory and they talked about these for days afterwards.

Another thing. The weather forced me to go out and purchase a raincoat. I never had one since I went overseas in 1951 and it was now almost Christmas and 1964 was approaching.

We rented a very beautiful garden cottage in Cox Green, a suburb of Maidenhead. It was to be our base for the five weeks in England before we headed for the British Forces Broadcasting Station in Cologne, Germany. Lucy's children, by her marriage to Dennis Whitaker, came over and stayed for Christmas. Several of Lucy's friends came over including Nan White who used to be a flight attendant with Skyways. My sister Diane and her husband Paul and children Dylan and Fraser came, as did my other sister Sheila and husband Tony and daughter Sarah. Luckily the cottage was fairly large. Lucy cooked a large turkey with delicious stuffing. After dinner, we went out on the lawn and someone took a group photograph. It had to be fast, there was a distinct damp coldness in the air.

THE FILM CREW REACTIVATED

The old Stirling Films group, or what was left of them, came over one evening and because I had a Keystone 16mm film camera and some negative film stock leftover from Aden, we decided to make another silent comedy. It starred Luke Over, Jim Franklin (of BBC Goodies fame), Maureen Anderson, Brian Wilson, Bernard Clarke, Donald Over, and me as the "baddie." Somehow I managed to direct the project. Shooting took place at various locations. We only had three Sundays in January, so this did not leave much time for re-shooting.

The first Sunday was solid grey cloud; the second Sunday it snowed and the third Sunday gave us a thick fog. The weather added to the hilarity. For instance, the film shows heroes chasing the villain through a hedge. On one side it was cloudy, and on the other side of the hedge it was snowing. The 15 minute film ends with a train coming out of the fog and zapping the villain. This comedy thriller entitled "Roll Call" was about a Russian spy who kidnaps a British scientist and steals secret papers from him.

Jim Franklin used his expertise in editing and did a voice-over sound-track with music and entered it in the Slough Arts Festival in the 16mm amateur film category for 1965. Surprise! It took first place. The adjudicator, Brian Little of Aspect Productions, Maida Vale described the film as "well shot, well directed and well acted." The award made the newspapers in Windsor and Maidenhead.

PICKING UP OLD NEWS PICTURES

In London, just before Christmas, I dropped by Central Press Photos in Gough Square, Fleet Street, and managing editor John Lacey, Dennis Oulds, and accountant Miss Rhodda took me out to a pub for lunch.

As we walked back to the office, that woman's voice came over. She said softly but firmly: "Get copies of your photos. As many as you can." As it turned out it was excellent advice.

John Lacey, in response to my request said: "Of course, Bob. Spend some time in the picture files and help yourself to prints."

Over the next hour or so, I selected about seventy 8 x 10 inch prints with Central Press printed cutlines on the back. It was the best decision of my career as a news photographer. A couple of years later, Central Press Photos was sold to a Saudi Arabian publishing company and my negatives, numbering over one thousand, went with the sale.

The remnants of Central Press changed hands a number of times. Hulton Library acquired the old Central Press stock, and then it went to Getty Images. After years of trying to track my negatives, including help from some UK-based photographers, with no luck at all, I posted a page on my website, showing some photographs and asking for information on the whereabouts of my negatives. That page has been up for the world to see for over ten years, and still no response. I did find one picture – Makarios's triumphant return to Nicosia – on Getty, but that was it. I had a print of that – one of the 70 picked up that day at Central Press Photos. I have the feeling that somewhere in all the transactions owners simply reduced the numbers en bloc and most of my old pictures hit the garbage.

I'm glad I followed the advice of the voice and secured seventy pictures from Central Press. Luckily, I still have a few negatives of my years in the Middle East.

HELLO COLOGNE ON THE RHINE

The days passed quickly and we found ourselves in Cologne or Köln as the Germans call it. As we arrived in early 1964 the city was brimming with life. It was difficult to believe that this important city on the Rhine had been virtually annihilated during the intense Allied bomber raids. I recalled lying down on the lawn at 36 Edith Road on a summer's evening watching the hundreds of bombers heading east through the darkening evening sky. It was a different age. Now, many of the old buildings had been rebuilt to age-old plans with an uncanny accuracy. Rhine steamers were filled with beer-drinking and singing tourists and locals, and across the river there were huge buildings for Cologne's growing Expo industry.

A German engineer at FBS showed me a photograph taken in 1945 with a landscape flattened as far as the eye could see. Only one building appeared relatively intact – the famous Cologne Cathedral, better known as the Roman Catholic Hohe Domkirche St. Peter und Maria.

It seemed miraculous that this church, with its flotilla of great carvings that took well over 600 years to build, survived the bomber raids. It was the largest Gothic church in Northern Europe and perhaps, still is. It is said that the medieval builders intended a special place for the relics, the bones of the Three Wise Men, the Magi who visited Jesus.

It was one of the first places Lucy and I, along with the children, visited. Lucy had been a Catholic and was interested. As I walked down the arched nave, I sat down to rest in one of the pews and gazed at the beautiful handiwork of artisans who had long died.

"They are in Spirit, or if you like, they are with God, the Creator," said the woman's voice. "Do you feel the presence?"

"People?" I scanned the place quickly. "Sixty...perhaps seventy."

"The presence," said the voice. "Look up to the roof."

"Reflections. Little lights."

"Spirits," she said. "There are more spirits in here than you could count. They visit here like they did when they were walking the Earth. It is the energy."

"Is God here?"

"There is no place that God is not."

"I felt the presence of something in the Church of the Holy Sepulchre in Jerusalem when I was with Father Roc? Was that God?"

"One day, when you are in the West, you will know and understand God but it is nothing you ever imagined God to be, and then only the breath, the spirit of God."

I mulled that last statement in my mind. "In the West, what do you mean?" "This is about as far west as I'm going. Except Spain."

There was no reply. She had gone. My mind went back to that day at the Cyprus Mail in Nicosia when the Hindu Yogi walked in, accepted a haloumi sandwich and gave me a reading. He had said: "You will go to the far side of the Americas and you will come back to the east and the desert lands. You will come back through the darkness into the light and you will know and understand the meaning of the One Self – that which is the true self within you."

My thoughts went back to Great-Grandmother Elen in Reading and the tea leaves.

"You will have many travels and walk many paths. Unusual gates, doorways will open and take you on many adventures. You will work with the light and heal with sound, and you will help people understand God. But before that you will hurt people, even loved ones, until you set yourself free. You need to set yourself free, but not before you are in the West. It will happen in the West and in the deserts surrounded by mountains, you will find the energy of the spirits and you will come through the darkness into the light. The road ahead is yours. Tread softly."

The thoughts puzzled and annoyed me. The Yogi had mentioned the Americas. Great-Grandmother the seer had mentioned the West, but what was this business about setting myself free. That bothered me. It sounded nonsense. I smoked more cigarettes that day than ever and that bothered me immensely. I had no intention of going to America. None at all, so I focused on the task at hand, British Forces Broadcasting, Germany.

THE WORK AT MARIENBURG

The studios and broadcasting center at Marienburg, a suburb of Cologne, was like paradise when compared to farmhouse broadcasting at Lakatamia in Cyprus. For a start there was a manned central control flanked by continuity studios and a small concert/talks studio big enough to handle groups, bands and rock groups. Along the way were editing rooms and offices. There were high quality tape decks that ran at 15 inches a second which made editing a breeze. Everything was well designed and well illuminated.

STUDIOS WITH A BOMB ON MILLIONAIRES' ROW:
This mansion in the upscale Marienburg district of Cologne served as the studios for British Forces Broadcasting Service from February 1954 until it was closed in 1991. During World War II it served as a German officers facility, was destroyed, then rebuilt after the war. When finally razed to make way for new developments, workers discovered an unexploded bomb nestled under the building. It was there when the author took this picture in 1963.

The building itself was historic. Originally owned by a Jewish family who disappeared before World War II, it was taken over by the Nazis and used as an officer's recreation and retreat center. Towards the end of the war it was annihilated in the bombing of Cologne, and with the coming of peace, rebuilt to original specifications. The Germans are good at this. Denis Scuse one of the pioneers in Forces Broadcasting, found the building plus an adjoining villa in late 1952 and the station at Hamburg, known the world over as BFN – British Forces Network – relocated there in 1953. By the time we arrived in 1964 it was a thriving and much honored broadcasting center. In the realms of Forces Broadcasting, it was hallowed ground.

There's an excellent book written by my friend and former colleague Alan Grace, "This is the British Forces Network" (1996) which tells the entire, fascinating story of Forces Broadcasting in Germany. Talking of Alan, when we arrived in Cologne, he and June had just moved out of his semi-detached home on the Volkspark, and we moved in.

If you lived in Britain or Germany in the post-war years up to my time there, you'll probably remember the radio announcement: "The time in Britain is twelve noon, in Germany it's one o'clock, but home and away it's time for Two-Way Family Favorites."

A CELEBRITY'S CAR:
Bill Crozier the Cologne host of Two-Way Family Favorites sold the author his Mercedes. It was solid, classy and purred along the autobahn.

The theme or signature tune was "With a Song in My Heart" played by Andre Koste-lanetz and his orchestra, a theme that still brings tears to my eyes and to a lot of old souls. Incidentally, over the years the title of the program evolved. It started as Forces Favorites, then Family Favorites, and finally Two Way Family Favorites.

As we arrived, Jean Metcalfe after 17 years on "Two Way" in the London studios was retiring, and was replaced by Judith Chalmers. Bill Crozier sat in the Cologne studios for seven years and retired the year after we got there.

Bill sold me his old BBC Fi-cord 7.5 ips tape recorder which was great for doing short, high quality interviews. Many years later, long after I had stopped using it, I donated it to the BFBS archives maintained by Alan Grace.

Bill Crozier also sold us his car, a delightful Mercedes, the last of the Daimler-Benz models which he claimed had belonged to the mayor of Mönchengladbach. It looked like one of the cars on the TV series Hogan's Heroes. It was in beautiful condition and zipped along the autobahn at a cool 70 mph. It was like driving a tank that floated on air.

Incidentally, there was no speed limit on the German motorways at that time. We paid Bill fifty pounds sterling, and 18 months later sold it to an army officer for 55 pounds. Lucy and the children enjoyed outings in the Mercedes and we had various picnics at Bonn, the Drachenfels, and at places along the Rhine, and we found many the wineries. We always had a glass of wine with dinner in Germany.

One place we really enjoyed was the Rhenish Open Air Museum at Kommern where they were gathering ancient buildings, houses, farm houses, schools, dance halls, chapels that are hundreds of years old. Each building is taken apart piece by piece and reassembled at the park. In one house, we saw a bed less than five feet long, and a door just as tall, showing that people living in the 16th century were much smaller than the average height today. I did an interview for the radio station and photos for Central Press. I hear that the Kommern Open Air Museum now has sixty ancient buildings reassembled in a park setting.

A NIGHTLY RADIO NEWS MAGAZINE

At the studios I started my time there as a continuity announcer but with the arrival of Pat Pachebat from Aden, I was assigned the task of creating a 45-minute news-interview program called "FBS Special" to run five evenings a week – Monday through Friday. It ran for 350 editions.

Alan Grace mentions this in his book and he writes: "Bob Egby, a former accredited Suez War correspondent, set up a network of correspondents and reporters all over West Germany and West Berlin. He equipped them with tape recorders and sent them off to cover stories in their area."

He quoted me: "We trained service personnel of all ranks – anyone showing promise and enthusiasm – and they responded well and produced some fascinating interviews. We did the program live because we frequently got feeds from various locations or a good interview would arrive just as we were going on air."

Alan mentions a case where enthusiasm went berserk. German wine festivals are always very colorful and interesting. I assigned a regular member of the staff to cover the Bonn wine festival and I told him we wanted no more than five minutes of tape which I would edit down. Most of the interviews we carried on FBS Special were two to three minutes. We ran a tight but moving show. The fellow, armed with a tape recorder, arrived at the Bonn festival and made the fatal mistake of buying a glass and tasting the wine which was freely available once you had purchased the glass. The result was some 90 minutes of tape with rambling chatter, reminiscent of the Goons, and it took half a day to cut it down to a four minute piece.

THE COLOGNE CRICKETERS:
Thoughout the 1960s the Cologne Cricket Club got together
and often roped in visiting celebrities. The author photographed one such event (and did an
interview): Back row: Thurston Holland, Station Controller; Mike Smith, Librarian; Alan Parfrey,
Announcer; Wally Barnes, ex-Arsenal and Welsh International; Kenny Lynch, Singer, Song-writer,
Actor; John Hill, RAF Serviceman; and Stan Challoner, Chief Engineer. The middle row: Bill Crozier,
Presenter in Cologne of Two-Way Family Favorites. Front Row: Ian Fenner, Commentator and Jazz
Presenter (extreme left) and second from right is Vic Widdowson, Announcer and Film Presenter
and at the end, announcer Peter Fitzpatrick.

As producer and narrator I enjoyed getting out to meet contributors to the program. One FBS staffer was Alastair McDougall who operated the West Berlin studios. He acquired some good interviews with such personalities as Count Basie, Yehudi Menuhin and Maurice Chevalier, and this was at a time when the great French actor was not giving radio interviews.

Ian Fenner, a great jazz enthusiast and a brilliant commentator took me to West Berlin to cover the Armed Forces Day parade. Those were the days when Berlin was an enclave in East Germany. The studio and office were quite small and were set on the upper floor of an old German barracks complex that overlooked Spandau Prison and the yard where its most famous prisoner, Rudolph Hess, Hitler's deputy took his daily exercise. Even while working at FBS I always carried a camera and kept an eye open for possible good news photos. I leaned against the office window. Click!

Alastair hit the roof! "Do you want to get us all arrested? The prison staff monitored all surrounding buildings. We could be closed down," he cried, pushing me away from the window. It was some time before he cooled down. He did take us on a tour of the city which was very much alive compared to its counterpart, East Berlin on the other side of the then four year old wall.

We visited the 1936 Olympic Stadium, the Potsdamer Platz with its mound of grass-covered earth that constituted the remains of Hitler's bunker and the cultural and shopping area of Friedrichstrasse. Somewhere Alastair took us to a strange restaurant with a telephone on each table, the idea being that if you liked the look of some lonely soul at another table, you called that table, and hopefully started talking. Thinking back, this was the era before the 21st century phenomenon of texting.

A SUNDAY MORNING SHOW

On top of the FBS Special, Pat Pachebat suggested I do a sixty-minute middle-of-the-road music and song program on Sunday mornings. He suggested we call it "Eggers for Breakfast." One of the reasons for this was he always called me "Eggers."

Occasionally I recorded the program earlier in the week, but for the most part I did it "live." There was a good reason for this. I was able to talk about what was happening. "It's sunny this morning in the Rhineland," or I would mention a news item of something that happened overnight. This technique gives a sense of immediacy for the listener.

The base of the program was bright, bouncy or emotional evergreens. Brook Benton and "Fools Rush In," Bobby Darin's "Mack the Knife," Louis Armstrong's "Hello Dolly," Petula Clark's "Downtown," and pianist Horst Jankowski's "A Walk in the Black Forest" and Bert Kaempfert and his Orchestra's "Red Roses for a Blue Lady." In 1964 the Boston Pops Orchestra came out with their version of the Beatles "I Want to Hold Your Hand." We played that too. I thoroughly enjoyed listening to that music and I think if the presenter, the DJ enjoys it, it is reflected in his or her voice. It was a time when radio was at its finest. Little did I think that when I did the last show, that the program "Eggers for Breakfast" would haunt me for a long time to come.

A LONG TIME BROADCASTER:
Pat Pachebat started with Forces Broadcasting in Trieste after World War II. The author knew and worked with him in Cyprus, Aden and Germany. He conceived his Sunday morning show "Eggers for Breakfast." When Pat retired in the 1990s as Chief Broadcasting Officer, he settled in Montreal, Canada. He and the author skied together at Whistler-Blackcombe and kept in touch every month until his passing, suddenly on October 7th 2008.

ALONG COMES HER MAJESTY

The FBS Special in Cologne came into its own in May 1965 for the state visit of Her Majesty the Queen to the Federal Republic of Germany. It was a demanding test for colleagues out on the road covering the events live.

For eleven days Ian Fenner, Brian Bass, Alan Parfrey, Pat Pachebat and Alastair McDougall produced a string of dynamic broadcasts in a variety of cities from Munich to Hamburg. It was the first visit of a reigning British monarch to Germany since World War II and the Queen's schedule was challenging. At Koblenz, speaking in public, she reminded people that the first of the famous Rhine steamboats was built in Britain in 1816. The enthusiastic crowd broke through police barriers and the Guard of Honor had to step in.

At Bonn, she laid a bouquet of roses at Beethoven's statue. There were all sorts of events and various parades. Alan Grace describes them in his book I mentioned earlier.

Each night, reports on the state visit were sent back to the studios at FBS Cologne for broadcast in my nightly news special. Alan notes: *On the final day of the tour Bob edited twenty hours of tape recordings down to a thirty-minute review, and then went "live" to Ian Fenner in Hamburg for a commentary on the departure of the Queen and Prince Philip on the Royal Yacht Britannia. "It was," said Bob, "a hectic time. We were virtually working round the clock, and when the Queen left, we were all caffeine addicts bouncing off the ceiling."*

A team of people who really need a lot of credit for the smooth production programming at Cologne are the engineers. There was Guenther Meyer Goldenstadt, Ludwig Marx, Hans von Gersum, Dieter Gripp and Heinz Zilliken. They all spoke perfect English and were great working companions.

AN UNSETTLING TIME

While my life at Forces Broadcasting was interesting and the people I worked with were all great and fascinating characters, underneath the surface, in the inner recesses of my mind I felt that my physical body was deteriorating.

I had been a smoker since my days at El Firdan in Egypt, but since being with FBS I had been putting on weight – 19 stones or 266 pounds – mainly because of the rich foods I was eating. In Nicosia a studio chair collapsed while I was sitting on it, and folks used to rag me about that for a long time. I think the stress of no longer being a free agent, a news hound and action photographer was getting to me. I yearned for the excitement of the news, and although things were interesting in Cologne, it was not the same as my former life in the Middle East. I tried to make the nightly news and interview shows exciting but it was stressful and draining.

Several times in Aden and again in Germany I suffered from what I thought were "boils" at the base of my spine. The doctors would give me penicillin and various other anti-biotics, and sometimes the swelling was acutely painful. The Medical Officer at the Volkspark Medical Center diagnosed it as "pilonoidal sinus," and explained that it was an ingrown hair or hairs that were becoming infected.

"Have you spent a lot of time sitting in a hot, sweaty environment like a car?" he asked. I told him about the long rides I did in Jordan, such as the Baghdad journey, where the infection first started. "I'm always sitting in cars," I said. The doctor nodded and arranged for me to have surgery at RAF Hospital Wegberg near Mönchengladbach. The nurses made me stay flat on my stomach for five days. I leaned over the edge of the bed and wrote the outline of a comedy novel. The thoughts made me laugh and other patients in the ward wanted to hear about my book. They all started laughing, which as one nurse pointed out, "laughing makes one heal quickly." I recovered quickly and put the idea of a novel on the shelf.

AND ALONG CAME SHERIDAN

A short time later Lucy was in the same hospital giving birth to our third son – Sheridan Eliot, a quiet little fellow with dark brown hair. Roderick, now just fifteen months, on the other hand was outgoing. We had a whole bunch of beautiful tulips in the Volkspark garden, so young Rod enthusiastic as ever, picked them all.

Somewhere along the way we moved out of the Wegberg semi-detached house into a fully-furnished small mansion on millionaires row in Marien-burg, which was about ten minutes walk to the studios. The mansion too was semi-detached, in a way. Our side had some eleven rooms on four levels. The other side was the Belgian Officers' Club. We had a magnificent dining room with a long table. It could easily accommodate twenty people to dinner. The most we had was a dozen and they were colleagues from the studio.

One problem in the Marienburg house, one never knew where the children were. Lucy bought a wooden gateway to stop Roberta, Gregory and Roderick from going to the upper levels. Sheridan was too young to walk at this time. On the upper level, I developed a dark room for processing black and white film and I had an enlarger for making prints.

In the cellar or the basement, there were two furnaces which burned coke, a fuel derived from coal. Coke, if you've never seen it, is rough like pumice and never shiny. It can be very rough on the hands. The furnaces provided us with hot water and heat.

One furnace was for summer use and the other, well, it could have come from the boiler room of an ocean-going ship. It stood seven feet tall and four feet wide. You could actually walk inside it. I had a matching shovel. When I first used it, I strained my arm, but after a while, it sure helped develop one's muscles. Fully loaded, the winter furnace would burn for a couple of days.

Our social life in Germany seemed to move along. We enjoyed visiting John and Dorothy Bull, who were old friends from FBS Cyprus. They had twelve children and it was difficult to figure out who was who. But they were a great family. Thurston Holland, the station controller was from the BBC. I think he originated in Canada because he often mentioned Kelowna in British Columbia, but I was never sure. Visiting him was always an enlighten-ing experience. He drank only the best brandy and was a source of information on everybody and everything. He enjoyed playing cricket and promoted the team and if celebrities were in town, he got them playing too. One Sunday I recall he had Kenny Lynch, the British rock singer and composer playing along with Walley Barnes, the Wales and Arsenal footballer.

NOT ALL KINKS ARE BEAUTIFUL

One evening Thurston dropped a bombshell. "Bob, the people at HQ in London really appreciate your FBS Specials. They are rather impressed, so they would like to have you on the staff there," said Thurston. "It will be a great opportunity for you to reach wider audiences. They want a news magazine to be syndicated to all stations." He shook his head, and added: "We will be sorry to lose you."

I hesitated. "When would this happen?"

"February or March, next year."

"It sounds wonderful," I responded. "I'll have to think about it and ask a few questions. But yes, it is a great opportunity and I will be sorry to leave." As I was talking I observed that Lucy was tight lipped and not happy.

When we got home, she let it be known in no uncertain words. "I really don't want us to live in England. If you work in London, it will mean living somewhere within a fifty mile radius, Aldershot, Reading, High Wycombe...I really wouldn't like that."

We discussed the pros and cons for several days. Then I said: "We could always quit and go back to reporting and news photography in the Middle East." I missed the work there, the way of life, the Mediterranean, the desert and yes, Iro.

"The children need schooling. They have good English schools here in Germany, but not in the Middle East," she said and I knew she was right. I also knew there were good schools in England, but she didn't want to hear that.

Then Lucy came up with an idea. "Why don't we immigrate to Canada? I have three brothers in British Columbia and they would certainly help us to get settled. The schools are good and our children would have cousins to live and play with. It makes a lot of sense."

The more I thought about that, I wanted to fight it. But the echoes of past voices lurked uncannily in my mind. Great-Grandmother Elen Egby had told me something so many years before. "You need to set yourself free, but not before you are in the West. It will happen in the West. " Then there was that

Hindu Yogi who came to the Cyprus Mail and told me that I would "go to the far side of the Americas." British Columbia in Canada was on the far side of North America. Then the woman, the goddess who appears in my life every now and again, told me when we visited Cologne Cathedral: "One day, when you are in the West, you will know and understand God."

Going west, even to Canada, was one thing. The prophets were right but knowing and understanding a God I really didn't believe in was something else.

Next day I called the Canadian Embassy and was surprised at the speed with which they called us in for an interview. Within a couple of weeks we had the green light, and I reluctantly resigned from British Forces Broadcasting and had my last day February 28th 1966. There had been another kink in the Cosmos and it left me with some ugly feelings.

WESTWARD BOUND WITH DEEP THOUGHTS

We flew KLM, the Dutch Airline from Cologne to Amsterdam, and then changed flights for an aircraft bound for Edmonton, Alberta.

"As the plane taxied down the runway at Schipol International Airport, I had some really mixed feelings and they hurt. There was a reluctance to immigrate to Canada, a land I knew little about. I would have been fine working at FBS in London doing magazine work, interviewing celebrities, editing and producing a weekly news magazine.

So I was feeling angry, irritable, annoyed that I had not made a firmer stand with Lucy. In addition I had not made a strong case for continuing to work on the FBS Special in Germany. These thoughts left a cloudy, disappointed mind which felt very depressed. I simply stared out the aircraft window at the fleeting British landscape below. It was as if I was being deprived of a life I had started out in the sunshine of the Mediterranean and somehow it was being ripped out of my body and mind. Thoughts of Iro kept surfacing like dolphins slicing out of the sea, only to plunge back in again. Another thing, I could not smoke on this long journey – ten hours – ten hours without a cigarette! The flight was going to be torture.

Damn it! I should have stayed in Cyprus and made a determined effort to repair my relationship with Iro. She was always thoughtful, kind and considerate. Yes, she could flare up when things went wrong, but so could I. I could have continued working with the Cyprus Mail and been a stringer for some newspapers in London, perhaps write a book. I had the feeling that Cyprus would always be in the news one way or another. Another thing, I was leaving my relatives, my family—my mother and my two sisters Sheila and Diane. Mother was so difficult to be with for any length of time. She was angry and depressed because my father had deserted her.

When we had been in England on leave between Aden and Germany, she had forbidden us to take the children to see their grandfather, my father, living in Henley. At the time it seemed the right thing to do, but in after-thought, it was wrong and we should have bitten the bullet and overridden my mother's demands. But it was too late now, and the children would never meet their grandfather.

So the prophets had been right. We were going west. How the blazes could an old lady in her mid-eighties living at Reading, Berkshire so many years ago, make a definite statement that I would go west. Years later a Hindu Yogi in Cyprus, a man I never saw before or have seen since, tells me I would go west. And that voice in Cologne Cathedral a couple of years ago: "One day, when you are in the West, you will know and understand God." I really didn't want to know about that chubby fellow sitting on a throne in the clouds, surrounded by a bunch of singing blondes with harps.

They had talked about breaking free from suffering. What was that about? Here I am sitting on a plane and feeling utterly despondent. I wanted to jump up and shout: "I'm bloody miserable now. Get me out of this."

There were no voices now, just the hum of the aircraft engines and the chatter of kids and people on the plane. Somewhere along the road someone would explain that right now I was starting to experience what St. John of the Cross termed "The Dark Night of the Soul," a metaphor used to describe an intensely rough phase in a person's spiritual life, marked by a sense of loneliness and depression. Little did I know then that my Dark Night of the Soul was to last a long grueling ten years.

Looking back, it was that evening at Thurston Holland's place when it all started. The requirement to move to FBS in London. That was the trigger that announced another kink in the Cosmos, and everything from then on in was like a script, a scenario. As the aircraft started on the polar route to Canada, I wondered who was writing the script in my life. For a while I really wanted to write, "This is the end."

17

THE CANADIAN EXPERIENCE

I T WAS A BITTERLY cold day in late February when we arrived at Kamloops, a cattle and services center in the heart of British Columbia. The winds came howling down out of the Canadian Rockies with a brutality that made one's cheeks feel numb. Most of the journey had been through the night and we were afforded only brief glimpses in the cold moonlight of the towering snow-clad mountains as the train weaved its way through Jasper and the Yellowhead.

Lucy's family gathered in force to greet us. It seemed like a small army. Frank, the Volkswagen dealer, the patriarch of the Cassar-Torreggianis in Canada, along with his wife, Benita – everyone called her Ben – and their six children Nita, Peter, Anne, Patsy, Vicky and Kim welcomed us to their home overlooking the city. Frank quickly told us they had dropped the Cassar name. "This is Canada now, so we make things easy for people," he said.

Then there was Bill Torreggiani with wife Mae and their three children Bernadette, Paul and Grace. Lucy's other brother was Andy, the youngest of the bunch who had made a reputation for himself crashing cars, but he survived well and got married to Judy. Later he went on to build a career for himself in the Kamloops Fire Department, finishing up as Captain. He and Judy had three children, Bruce, Kevin and Alexandra.

With all the relatives around there was always something going on, barbecues, picnics, and outings. Frank and Ben built a large swimming pool in the garden which was a welcome relief in the summer heat until Frank acquired two of the largest St. Bernard dogs I had ever seen, and they plunged into the pool too. It was when they climbed out and shook themselves that people sunning themselves got all upset, as their bodies received an unexpected shower.

We arrived on the Sunday. On the Monday I called into the Kamloops Daily Sentinel, a daily newspaper within the Thomson Newspaper empire, which the year before had become a publicly traded company in Canada. The newspaper was streamlined to present the news in the most economical manner – text in all single columns. The managing editor was a wildlife buff named George Smith and his city editor was a delightful old soul from a bygone age – Meryl Matthews.

George, who had once worked for the Daily Sketch in London, scanned my resume. "When do you want to start? This afternoon?"

"Can I get a car first?"

Lucy's brother found us an odd little car that was so strange I fail to recall what make it was. French, I think. But it did get us around. For the first few weeks, things seemed to be interesting. Everything was new. The culture was different. If you went into a bar, men went through one entrance, women through another. Liquor laws smacked of Prohibition. Pubs were hidden behind walls with no windows. There were no such things as the European bistro with little tables outside. Heavens no! You must not be seen drinking in public. The only places where one could buy spirits and wines were at provincial government owned liquor stores. The whole thing appeared barbaric.

Lucy's initial opinion of Kamloops was, "It looks like a hick town but after a while it grows on one."

Soon after we arrived in Canada, Lucy's mother Grace Cassar-Torreggiani arrived to stay for a few weeks. The families enjoyed her presence. A devoted Catholic, she attended mass every day. We had some good times, picnics, barbecues and general get-togethers. Then Grace developed a problem in her eyes and the doctor recommended surgery with a few days in the Royal Inland Hospital. Grace was a dedicated smoker and when the doctor ordered her to quit, at least for the operation and the hospital stay, she retorted: "If I don't smoke it'll kill me." She was true to her word, except no one believed her including the doctor.

Grace's operation was a success and some days later Frank and Benita picked her up at the hospital and took her to their home. We were going up to see her, when a call came through. Grace had gone to the bathroom and suffered a fatal heart attack.

That plunged everyone into shock and an overwhelming sadness. As she was buried in the Hillside Cemetery on the brow of a hill overlooking the Thompson Valley, I felt an old pang of discomfort. Death was back in my life. I had seen so many deaths in the Middle East but that was another world, another time. This was in the family and it felt cold and merciless. As I watched I pondered that question: "Is this the end of the line? Is this all there is to life?" The questions hurt like spears to the heart. And the voice was silent.

BACK IN THE EDITOR'S SEAT

My stay at the Daily Sentinel lasted nine months. We moved to Vancouver on what at first seemed a lucrative offer, but in truth it was to help an old weekly, the Burnaby Courier Examiner disappear into oblivion. Then I heard that the Kamloops Advertiser, a weekly newspaper needed an editor. The Publisher, Harry Francis and his three shareholders, gave me the job so we moved back to Kamloops.

We rented several apartments until we found a delightful old-world cottage on Royal Avenue overlooking the Thompson River. The North and South Thompson rivers combined at Kamloops and flowed down to join the great Fraser River flowing through the Canyon to the Pacific.

TRUDEAUMANIA SWEEPS THE CARIBOO:
Pierre Elliott Trudeau was the charismatic hero of the Liberal socialists as he inspired Canadians to elect him as the 15th Prime Minister of Canada. This they did and he served from 20 April 1968 to 4 June 1979, and again from 3 March 1980 to 30 June 1984. The author, then managing editor of the Kamloops News, interviewed Mr. Trudeau during political rally at Quesnel, British Columbia.

The Advertiser had a staff of three. Norman Macdonald, a good solid newsman who watched me as if I were an alien from some distant planet and a sports reporter, whose name I have unfortunately forgotten. Norman's son Neil was an up and coming photographer at that time. The good thing about the Advertiser was it paid $150 a week, $50 a week better than the Sentinel. It was now 1967.

It was a joy working for that little tabloid. I adopted a Fleet Street layout, big headlines, sharp and succinct written stories. "Long stories put readers to sleep," I told the crew, including people who submitted padded stories. Circulation started to increase. Harry Francis found new offices on the corner of Main and Second, and a new printer, with an offset. The earlier press had been a flatbed which seemed to kill good photos. Now, our photos brought the newspaper to life, and I always followed the advice of the Fleet Street sages - run a good picture above the fold or crease

We made everything exciting, even if it wasn't. We covered forest fires, floods, bull sales, skiing and the British Columbia Skating Championships at the local arena. We had a great picture of multi-year champion Karen Magnussen in action splashed across the front page. We hired a Toronto journalism student named Phyllis Johnson for several summers. She was intelligent, a fast learner and a great personality.

One day I received a tip that Lafarge North America, the French cement company was going to build a large plant east of Kamloops on the banks of the South Thompson River. It was a dull day and I really had no intention of wandering around in the bush, but something said: "Go and look." There was no indication where the plant would be, so Phyllis and I hiked through the sage-covered foothills searching for any hint of a forthcoming development. Survey stakes are great giveaways.

We were just about to give up when a large black car came and stopped a short distance away. The people had a map which they placed on the hood. They stood there animated and talking, so we moved in.

Phyllis got a great interview and I took photos of James Sinclair, President and Chairman of Lafarge on location. Mr. Sinclair was a gentleman and extremely helpful. The photographs I took that day came in useful when his daughter Margaret became engaged and married Canadian Prime Minister Pierre Trudeau.

My intuition had paid off, although at that time I had no idea as to what intuition was. When Phyllis was on her final year in journalism, I suggested she might want to work overseas. Well, she got a job with CBC, the Canadian Broadcasting Corporation and shortly afterwards headed for that hotbed of news, East Africa, - Rhodesia, Kenya, Uganda - and the last time I heard, she was still living there.

The Advertiser changed its name to the Kamloops News Advertiser and moved again, this time to its own spacious building on Tranquille Road in North Kamloops. The staff was growing rapidly and the newspaper had lost that closeness that I enjoyed. Two things had happened. It expanded to three days a week – Monday, Wednesday and Friday. The other was the arrival of Mel Rothenberger, an enthusiastic reporter who was writing a book "Who Killed Johnny Ussher?" and would go on to become Managing Editor, Mayor of Kamloops and a politician, a Member of the Legislative Assembly of British Columbia in the capital Victoria. I felt the Kamloops News Advertiser should become a daily but it was not the time. It did happen several years later, but by then I had long gone.

THE STUDIOS OF ROCK RADIO

The City of Kamloops, with a population of 6,000, was changing. There was talk of amalgamating with suburban communities such as North Kamloops, Westsyde, Brocklehurst and Valleyview, which would make a community of 45,000.

The economy was changing, more from a cattle center to a service community. More businesses were coming to the city bringing new faces, new families, all requiring accommodation. One day the Rotary Club asked me to speak at a luncheon on the "Changing Face of Kamloops." I did, and afterwards, a man named John Skelly, who had recently started CHNL Radio with affiliate stations in nearby Merritt and Princeton, approached.

"Have you ever worked in radio?" he asked.

Thus, in January 1970, four years after our arrival in Canada, I was back in a radio station, this time as a News Director. Working for Forces Broadcasting in Germany, Cyprus and Aden had been a push-over. It was pure communication, pure broadcasting, and the essence of what broadcasting should be. Here at CHNL or Radio NL as it was know, I was confronted with commercial radio. Programs including news were dotted with advertising commercials, and that went against the grain, my very soul. Not only that, it was Rock. At first I detested it and longed for the old Forces Broadcasting system but as time passed, I got used to commercials. News broadcasts interrupted by commercials even today vaguely annoy me, particularly the national news on television. Commercials taint the credibility of the news but like corrupt politicians, people accept or ignore them.

Although the station focused on Rock music, it had a good crew and I got on well with most. Dan McAllister was the morning DJ and Program Manager. Jeff Borris was the afternoon DJ, Claude Richmond who also entered politics and became an MLA in Victoria was in Sales. Claude also led a crazy bunch of great musicians called the Kamloops Rube Band which performed in parades and special events. In the news we had Jim Harrison who had come from a radio station in Windsor, Ontario and Tom Hartel, who had come back a victim of battle stress from Vietnam, but he had a magnificent broadcasting voice. Someone once said of Tom: "He has the voice of God." The sports reporter was Keith Hunt.

RADIO DOCUMENTARIES GET AWARDS

I wrote editorials five days a week and during the five years I was there, produced four one-hour documentaries, two of which won RTNDA (Radio Television News Directors Awards) and one won the Media Club of British Columbia.

One of the award-winners was "Death Valley Run – Fact or Fiction." Narrated by Hap Thiessen, it told the rigors and dangers of working on Canada's railways, Canadian Pacific and Canadian National. It covered management and the unions and the challenges of riding the trains, especially in the Canadian Rockies. Faced with a landslide, the engineers of a fully loaded freight train can only hang onto their 200 ton locomotive as it plows through. They told me it takes a fully loaded freight train headed by three locomotives over a mile to stop, by then the landslide is behind them. Passenger trains, which are much lighter, can normally stop before a landslide.

The Canadian Locomotive Engineers representative gave some interesting quotes from which we found the title Death Valley Run: "I'd say that most of our people are appalled to think that we are still being killed in pursuit of our work. You put your life on the line every time you go to work. This Fraser Canyon, the whole set-up is considered to be a death valley run and it's with good reason that most of our people have named it this."

Apart from winning an RTNDA award, a copy of the program was taken and played at the Canadian Railway Engineers convention.

THE OVERLANDER HERITAGE

Another documentary that pulled in an award was "The Overlander Heritage," which told the story of Catherine Schubert who led a group of early pioneers through the Yellowhead Pass in the Rocky Mountains and came down the North Thompson River on log rafts. Somehow they survived the rigors of the journey and some settled in the interior of British Columbia. Some went to the Cariboo Gold Rush and others to New Westminster and Vancouver Island.

Where are their descendants today? It was a question I asked myself as I mulled over the story. So I started phone calls and trekked all over the west coast. Luckily we found elderly grand-children who recalled the pioneers and talked about them on tape and showed us heirlooms. It made an exciting program and happily, it won the Media Club of Canada, Vancouver Branch's award for the "Best Radio Feature or Documentary" for 1974.

RAFT RACES REFLECTED THE OVERLANDERS:
In the tradition of the Overlander pioneers who in the 1860s sailed down the North Thompson River on rafts, the modern day rafters in 1971 and again in 1972 sailed eighty miles from Clearwater to Kamloops over two days. Rafts were built on site and most crews were dressed in Victorian settlers garb. Picture above shows a general view of the rafts watched by spectators. Below a close up of one raft. The annual raft races were organized by the Kamloops JayCees and provided historic spectacle until tragedy struck and lives were lost.

The Kamloops Jaycees saluted the early Overlander pioneers by creating in 1971 an annual raft race down the North Thompson River from Clearwater to Kamloops. Participants were asked to use logs and make their own river-worthy rafts. We always had great fun covering these races.

One day, I heard that mothers were blocking a school bus because they considered the driver was "reckless." When I arrived, some eight mothers had stopped the bus and were trying to push it backwards. In addition to doing a live wireless report, I snapped some photos. Next day my picture appeared on the front page of the Vancouver Province newspaper. I received a nice remuneration check, but more was to come. I received the Canadian Press Photo of the Month award. Malcolm Turnbull, provincial editor signed me on as a stringer, which was useful. But it all seemed hokey, and I still yearned for the excitement of the Middle East.

CHILDREN START GROWING UP

The children were growing and getting involved in outside activities. The boys were playing soccer, and because Lucy had never learned to drive, I was the chosen driver. We bought our first home in Westsyde, a suburb of Kamloops close to the North Thompson River, but it was brand new and demanded a lot of work, such as landscaping. We had a V-8 station wagon and found a dried up creek bed full of round rocks. We made countless trips to bring back rocks for a wall in the garden. I built a room downstairs as a bedroom for Roberta, but we dropped plans for expansion, mainly because of a lack of money.

We never seemed to have enough money. It was a struggle to pay the monthly bills. Every week I drove Lucy to the supermarket, either Woodward's or Safeway, where she would go in and get the groceries. I stayed in the car. I disliked seeing women shoppers wearing hair curlers. I penned an editorial and all hell broke loose. The radio station's phone lines became red hot, but we did notice that many of the curlers disappeared. One woman screamed at me: "I have to look beautiful for my husband when he comes home."

In early summer of 1971 while participating in a media tour of the new Cariboo College in Kamloops, I encountered a Time-Life reporter. I mentioned Larry Burrows from my Cyprus and Suez days. "A great photographer," I said, "I learned so much from him."

The reporter looked at me quizzically. "You haven't heard? Larry and three other news photographers were killed a couple of months ago when their helicopter was shot down over Laos."

A YOUNG CANADIAN FAMILY 1971
By now we had been in Kamloops, British Columbia five years and were now living in our own home in the suburb of Westyde, a community flanking the North Thompson River. The children are: (l to r) Gregory (11), Roberta (13), Roderick (7) and Sheridan (6). With the author is his wife, Lucy

Stunned, I thought this couldn't happen to Larry. He was just six years older than me. My mind went back to those almost halcyonic days in the Middle East. His lanky form, his peculiar smile and those six cameras slung around his neck, always ready to capture a moment of life. His easy going manner belied an acute observation of what was happening around him.

News of his death did nothing to help me feel settled in Canada. Expatriates told me that the burning desire to return to the old country takes about five years to dissipate. The desire was still burning as strong as ever. Stress consumed my existence. Frequently angry, frustrated and irritable, I started eating more than I should and one day at the end of the morning news shift I felt my face was red and flushed.

Dr. Burris did his stuff. "Your blood pressure is at a dangerous level. So is your weight. Three hundred and fifty pounds," he said. "Go home and get your stuff. I'm putting you in hospital this afternoon."

Royal Inland Hospital was my home for two weeks. The nutritionist put me on a diet that made me urinate more times than I could remember, and a physiotherapist had me in the hospital gym doing sit-ups, press-ups and several other exercises – twice a day. Lucy and the children came to see me.

Gregory looked at me lying on the bed. "Are you going to die, Dad?" He was eleven years old and I was forty. Grief! Here we go with death again.

"That's not a nice thing to say, Gregory," snapped Lucy. "He's not old enough." Nobody felt like laughing. But that hospital stay changed my life, and over the next year I visited the hospital nutritionist every two weeks and lost weight. I performed sit-ups every morning in the basement. As I lost weight I found I had new energy and managed to climb the stairs much more easily. But I still smoked. I tried so many times to quit, but each time Lucy said: "Your personality changes. I don't like that. You're miserable." Smoking really bothered me, but quitting was not on the agenda, yet.

BECOMING CITIZENS OF CANADA

After much consideration we decided to become Canadian citizens. Although we were legally landed immigrants, there was a little confusion every time we got official cards for anything. The whole family had different roots. I was born in England, Lucy in Malta, Roberta in Amman, Jordan, Gregory in Nicosia, Cyprus, Roderick in Aden, now Yemen, and Sheridan in Germany.

So in 1974 we all became Canadian citizens. We could not afford studio pictures, so I put Lucy and the children against the plain dining room wall and took their pictures. Lucy then took my picture. Anyway, we received our citizenship with certificates and ID cards. We should have felt part of the country. I think Lucy and the children did, but I didn't. It was not the country's fault. It was mine.

MOVING INTO PUBLIC RELATIONS

One day, Barney Lucas, the Personnel Director at the local pulp mill cornered me and said: "Have you ever thought about getting into public relations? We have a need for a good writer and the pay is – well, better than being a journalist." So I joined Weyerhaeuser Canada Ltd., as Manager, Public Affairs for operations in British Columbia, Ontario and Quebec. In addition to the Kamloops pulp mill, Weyerhaeuser had various wood products operations, mainly sawmills in all three provinces. It was a challenge to learn a whole new industry – forestry! But as Barney promised, the pay was better than journalism. We bought a new car and moved to a new house in North Kamloops, next to Lucy's brother Andy and Judy.

The company needed a monthly newspaper that featured people, places and events within the company so we started one, an eight to ten page tabloid. I quickly discovered that English was not the only language in the company. Employees at the Princeville veneer plant in Quebec spoke mainly French. Finance Vice President Ron Nelson's wife spoke excellent French and translated the publication each month, with me listed as "rédacteur" which means editor. So we put out two editions – English and French. The problem was people would come up and start firing off questions in French and my knowledge of the language was abysmal, but I did learn quickly.

Some people, particularly journalists, call PR people "spin-doctors" in other words just robots spinning the corporate message. There were others like me, who came from a journalistic background that practiced a radical PR. Several times my openness with the media got me into hot water with middle management but the chairman, Tom Rust seemed to enjoy my style. After I had been there for about a year, media attention dropped off and senior managers suggested at meetings there was no need for PR. Tom Rust chipped in: "The media is quiet because Egby is doing his job." The critics were subdued.

TRAINING FOR A NEW PROFESSION

The parent company of the Canadian operation was Weyerhaeuser in the United States. The head office in Tacoma, Washington State asked me to come for various training events, seminars and workshops. Weyerhaeuser was rapidly developing an image as the "Tree growing company," because they planted millions of new trees each year. But the clear-cutting of hillsides and mountainsides left horrible scars, and no matter how much you took journalists out to see the teams with their back-breaking jobs planting seedlings, and conducted tours of tree farms, the indignation and anger in the public sector was difficult to handle, particularly in Washington State and Oregon.

I once radically suggested selective logging and that brought vicious rebuttals from senior operations managers as "uneconomical."

Pat Cullen, one of the senior PR managers at Tacoma, appeared to understand my predicament. "It's tough coming from a glamorous job as international correspondent," he said over lunch one day. "I feel for you. Try to forget it."

Through various visits to the Weyerhaeuser headquarters I learned the ins and outs of public affairs, how to create business plans, write news releases, and what makes the corporate mind work. I did enjoy some of the commercials they made. In one, they showed a close-up of Canadian geese flying high above a forest. Apparently, the geese were trained to fly alongside helicopters. Weyerhaeuser also built a full scale working house in a large tree. It was the ultimate tree-house, fully equipped.

One of the things I enjoyed from being in public relations was the hours. There was no need to get up at four a.m. to do early morning studio shifts or cover evening meetings somewhere. It was from eight a.m. to four p.m. and although there were exceptions, the times fitted my idea of life. I found I had more time with the family, but then there was a snag. They were not used to having me around after years of being absent. But I sensed things were changing. I did not know what, but felt it hinged on smoking. I was now smoking forty cigarettes a day.

FROM THE WOODS TO THE WORLD

Every spring Tom Rust, a chairman of the Canadian operations, toured key facilities in the three provinces and gave talks not only to employees but their families as well. This was a neat strategy. Tom also came over as an understanding patriarch. He could talk and be at home with anyone. Generally the media enjoyed interviewing him. So Tom made my job relatively easy. But little did I know that what I was doing next would trigger the start of a life-changing kink in the Cosmos.

"You're a photographer," Tom announced one day. "Could you get out there and put together a slide show we can take across the country and show the families?"

Over the next six weeks I found myself climbing aboard logging trucks and skidders, exploring the green line at sawmills, standing in a waist-deep mud rut left by skidders in an Ontario forest, and watching cedar logs coming in from Maine to be peeled and made into veneer in Quebec. I climbed through the jungle of corridors, stairs, platforms of the pulp mill, observed the mountains of wood chips, and photographed stacks of pulp bales being loaded onto ships at Vancouver docks. Wherever an employee was working I took pictures. Weyerhaeuser pulp, I discovered, was shipped to Italy where it was great for the production of glossy European magazines. When I got back home, I faced the horrendous task of sorting out over 1,000 color slides. I wrote a script and recorded it, using my best "broadcast voice."

The show was called "From the Woods to the World." It ran eighteen minutes and was shown on a Kodak Carousel projector with synchronized pulsed sound on a Wollensak tape deck. It was an instant hit everywhere we screened it - Clearwater, Kamloops and Merritt in British Columbia, Sault Ste. Marie in Ontario and Princeville, Quebec. Mr. Rust and I did the whole tour in ten days.

FEAR OF DYING STRIKES HOME

When I returned home I was exhausted, wiped out from travelling, living in hotels, setting up shows, drinking countless coffees and becoming a chain-smoker. Thankfully, I slumped down at the table with Lucy and the kids, ate a home-cooked meal, and answered a barrage of questions.

I had just lit my after-dinner cigarette, when it happened. The kink struck me, No ifs ands or buts. It just hit me with sledgehammer force. Ugly and brutal. Terror gripped my mind and body like an iron fist. Suddenly I couldn't breathe. My lungs would not work! Thoughts of dying pierced my mind like deadly arrows. I am dying!

Dazed, I found the front door and stood outside in the evening spring air. Air seemed rare. It was difficult to breathe. Hastily I threw away the cigarette into the garden. Slowly I found I could breathe just a little. It was a weird, horrible feeling. Breathing was shallow. Very shallow. Somehow I felt the need to be alone. I walked slowly towards the North Thompson River, taking it very easy. At least my feet were working somewhat. Now I was sure it had been a heart attack or something close to it.

"God, I don't want to die?" I muttered. "Help me, God. Can you hear me?"

There was no reply. As I wandered half conscious by the North Thompson River, I wondered where that woman was, the one who's voice I would hear from time to time. "Where are you lady, now that I really need you? I'm dying and you're nowhere around." I felt totally deserted in spite of the fact that my breathing was coming back and the terrible feeling of helplessness was dissipating.

On that April evening in 1974, I resolved never to smoke again and never drink coffee again. Two years later, a doctor in Vancouver told me: "You have a hiatal hernia." He explained that the condition occurs when the upper part of the stomach protrudes into your chest cavity, the esophagus, through a weakness in the diaphragm. Overweight people are particularly prone to this condition. "It makes you feel short of breath," he said. "It's irritated by nicotine in cigarettes and caffeine in coffee."

WITHDRAWAL AND ONE LAST DOCUMENTARY

In that spring and summer of 1974 the withdrawal symptoms were severe. I became extremely irritable with just about everyone, Lucy, my kids, our friends and my colleagues at work. I found it difficult to write and I hired a writer to create copy for the Weyerhaeuser monthly newspaper. After two years with the forest industry, I returned to CHNL Radio. The energy of journalism is addictive, and I missed the thrill of instant news gathering. But, and it was a big BUT, I missed the Weyerhaeuser salary. So my return to radio did not last long. It was long enough for me to produce another radio documentary, which won another Radio-Television News Directors (RTNDA) award.

Entitled "Out of the West" the 60 minute program told of the creation of Pacific Western Airlines in the northern arctic regions, and how it had built up to an expanded fleet of Boeing 737 airliners with bases in Vancouver and Calgary. I interviewed a vast array of people, including past employees.

I really wanted to talk to a pilot, and this occurred one morning at Kamloops Airport during a 45-minute flight stop. I crouched in the cockpit and interviewed a young, vibrant Captain Chris Miles. He came from a flying family. His father had spent years flying in South America and now, his son was flying throughout the mountainous territories of British Columbia, Alberta and the Yukon. I asked him: "Doesn't this flying here ever worry you?"

He shot back: "Worry? I love it. I love flying. Every day is a great experience. I wouldn't do anything else."

The program was broadcast on the CHNL network in British Columbia on July 17th 1977.

On Saturday, February 11, 1978, it had been snowing at Cranbrook, BC, Canada and the plow was out clearing the swirling drifts from the runway at the airport ready for Pacific Western Airlines Flight 314.

The Boeing 737 came in for a touch down. As the wheels made contact, the crew suddenly caught sight of the snow plow. It was directly ahead on the runway. A go-round was initiated but the thrust reversers did not stow away properly because hydraulic power was automatically cut off at lift-off. The aircraft missed the plow, overran the runway, crashed and burned. Forty-two of the forty-nine on board were killed, among them Captain Chris Miles.

CHNL News Director Jim Harrison, my successor at the radio station, called me in Vancouver that Saturday afternoon with a request to take the Chris Miles clip and use it in news broadcasts.

"Sure," I said. Thinking back to the time I did the cockpit recording, I sensed that Captain Miles must have been a flyer in a previous lifetime. He was a dedicated aviator.

BACK TO THE WORLD OF ART

With cigarettes and coffee out of my life, I needed to do something. The woman's voice came one evening. "You learned to draw at Moor Hall Studios, you will find relief in painting with oils. It will keep your hands and mind busy.

PAINTING AFTER QUITTING SMOKING:
In 1974 the author stopped smoking, and felt an overwhelming urge to "do something" with his hands. Recalling the instruction received from artists at David Hand's Moor Hall Studios, he started oil painting. In a couple of years over fifty pieces of art were created, and many of them were sold or given to relatives and friends. He fondly recalled memories of the Via Dolorosa which leads to the Church of the Holy Sepulchre in Jerusalem and this was the result. He wonders what Father Roc would have thought.

It was a good idea. I bought an easel, dozens of tube paints, several canvas boards and started painting. I was not very impressed. The figures seemed stilted. Dead. I needed to find the finer points of painting. As it happened, Lucy pointed out that Cariboo College was presenting art classes. I attended and learned to be free with the paint. I tried creating paintings of people, horses, landscapes, but found my forte in old street scenes, particularly of European places. The old world kept calling me.

The College students decided to have a show in Riverside Park in Kamloops. We stuck prices on our works. While people came and looked, no one purchased anything. Then the teacher arrived. She gasped. "Heavens! Those prices are too, too low. Nobody buys a painting for ten dollars. Add a zero! Think big. Your paintings are valuable."

So my $10 artwork became $100 and my $15 paintings became $150, and lo and behold, they started selling. The teacher smiled. "People like to spend money on art work. If you don't think it's valuable, the public will not think so either." It was a great lesson, and I wished I could recall her name. She was full of useful ideas. "Take photographs of your work before you sell them," she told us.

In the following twelve months I did about fifty paintings, and sold most of them. Luckily, I took photographs of the works before they sold. I also switched to acrylics because they dry faster than oils. But I was still manifesting impatience and that bothered me.

THE TRIALS OF AUTO INSURANCE

Shortly after "Out of the West" aired, a visiting Vancouver radio reporter told me the Insurance Corporation of British Columbia was seeking a PR manager experienced in media for their Vancouver office. So I joined them Tuesday, August 16th 1977, and no one seemed to notice my arrival. The shocking topic of the day? Elvis Presley has died.

We bought a house in Richmond, a sprawling and growing residential township south of Vancouver Airport and I got into the groove with the Corporation. When Warren Barker, news director at CKNW in New Westminster heard of my work he called it a "suicide job." I quickly discovered an element of truth in his quip.

Created by a socialist provincial government in 1973, the New Democratic Party, the original purpose was to provide universal public auto insurance in British Columbia. For years it was discovered that private insurance companies were not living up to their promises, particularly when it came to settling claims for bodily injuries.

The new corporation made auto insurance compulsory. It introduced a limited no-fault insurance and its rules were rigid, both in the market place as well as in head office on the upper floors of the Royal Center in downtown Vancouver. The general manager was Norman Bortnick,+ who raised the ire of most reporters by avoiding questions. The Manager, Public Relations was Bev Penhall and I was named Manager, Media Relations.

Bev's first words to me: "I hope you don't take pride of authorship." I soon discovered his meaning when I wrote an 800 word news release. It went over so many desks that when it came back, it looked like nothing I had ever written. "See what I mean," said Bev with a suppressed chuckle.

The PR Department saw a number of staff members. Corrine Noonan was a writer of Insurance texts and Paula Stromberg wrote an employees' newspaper. Paula was a six-foot blonde and was a highly respected belly-dancer. When she took a vacation in Cairo, Egypt she was kidnapped by two Saudi businessmen who locked her up in a hotel room closet. When they had gone out, Paula kicked the closet door out and escaped. Paula was one of the more colorful and dynamic personalities at the Corporation.

One day Norman Bortnick sent a message down from the dizzy heights calling for me to write a speech he wished to present. He liked it and surprise, surprise, he actually sent me a thank you note. That was stunning. I was just developing a liking and respect for the fellow when few days later, after making the speech, Mr. Bortnick suddenly died.

A VOICE ON THE BUS

The pressures of working in such a restricted environment rebuilt my stress along with anger and bitterness. I desperately wanted to return to England and see my family...Mum, Dad and my sisters....and my friends. They always seemed so distant, so far away.

One day in 1977 while standing on the crowded bus heading for Richmond, my mind was drifting through things I had to do at home, when a man's voice suddenly startled me. It said "Bobbie, I love you. Bobbie I love you." I spun around. It was my father's voice as clear as a bell. But he was nowhere, of course. I reached home and told Lucy about Dad's voice as we had supper.

Then the phone rang. It was my sister Diane in England. "Dad passed away a couple of hours ago," she said.

Death! Here it was again. So final. The news shook me to the foundations. My legs felt so soft I was forced to sit down on the deck of our Richmond home. Thoughts flowed through my panicky mind. "I'm next," I told myself. Life appeared so unfair. So fragile. I completely ignored the phenomena that Dad had appeared to me on the Richmond bus. I failed to see or understand the significance. Years later, I kicked myself for not recognizing the significance of the woman spirit who had sent me warnings over the years.

Dad's death created a wave of deep hurt, a sensation that I was alone, a solitary figure in the desert of life. Dr. Ranier Borkenhagen at the downtown walk-in clinic told me to "walk, jog, get out and be physical." So I did. Every night I walked the Richmond dikes, feeling the breezes and the fresh air coming off the Pacific. The body seemed to feel better but the mind was hurting. I felt captured and distraught.

The children were living their own lives. Roberta now nineteen had gone to England to look for work in Leeds. Greg was sixteen and spent most of his evenings with friends, and both Rod at fourteen and Sheridan at thirteen were doing their own thing.

THE END OF A MARRIAGE

Lucy spent her days with friends and looking after the children. She seemed exhausted when I arrived home. We no longer talked very much. I worked in the basement for several weeks and built a recreation room with a large bookcase built into the wall.

Hoping to improve things, we bought a camper unit, and headed south for the State Parks in neighboring Washington State and Oregon. The beaches at Nehalem State Park are beautiful with miles of golden dunes, long stretches of hard sand and the sea was alive with massive white-capped Pacific waves that crashed down furiously on the beaches. We all spent so much time walking and playing on the sand. One day Rod became seriously sunburned and spent the night in a lot of pain.

I tried walking along the sands, trying to sort out my troubled mind. In this beautiful, peaceful place I felt angry, frustrated and annoyed, and sensed this was not right. The beaches reminded me of Cyprus and Iro. I wondered what she was doing. The rigidity and the bureaucracy of the Insurance Corporation seemed to pull me down. Dr. Borkenhagen said: "You need to relax and stop thinking." Relax? That would only leave me to the mercy of endless, torturing thoughts.

One day at the bus stop I met a young woman. A honey blonde, her name was Myra and she taught at a business school in Vancouver. Over several days she listened patiently to my feelings. One day, we both took the day off and sat on a log overlooking Jericho Beach, and it was there that I kissed her. It felt so right. So natural, but it plunged me into a deeper disturbance.

Next day, Lucy, her voice icy and cutting, called me at the office: "Who is the girl friend? Her perfume is all over your dirty shirt."

I didn't argue, I just let things happen. I had no excuses; I just had to get away. I felt a stranger in my own home. I found a small basement apartment in Vancouver's West End. It was dingy but I settled in. After nineteen years of marriage it was all over. Lucy initiated divorce proceedings and I agreed to support the children. I met Myra and told her what had happened. She had left her husband Larry and found an old but nice apartment on Jervis Street also in the West End. On occasions I stayed the night with her. One Monday morning I returned and found my basement apartment and the house above completely gutted by fire. It was still smoldering. I moved in with Myra, but it was no joy and I felt as if a tremendous weight was on my shoulders. I visited Lucy several times, mainly to see the children, but they were out, so I did not stay. I felt deserted and angry.

LIVING WITH MYRA

Dr. Borkenhagen, a die-hard jogger, suggested I start easy jogging every day, and I did this and gradually achieved three miles in an hour with a route that took me along the sea-wall, and I started to lose weight. Occasionally Myra would come with me and talked as we jogged.. She was constantly amazed when I mentioned Iro in Cyprus being seventeen years older than me. Myra was seventeen years younger. "Age doesn't bother me," I commented, but could not understand why.

We found a two bedroom apartment in the same building, and spent time decorating and Myra set candles everywhere. They seemed to quiet my mind, which was still disturbed with my work at the Insurance Corporation. I took to writing in the evenings on an electric typewriter and produced a novel on Cyprus, while she brought me cups of tea. Writing made me feel good, but a publisher in Toronto said there was "no market for war stories at the present time." This was while the wars continued in Cambodia, Iran had American hostages, and small wars were going on at various points around the world.

The story line started in 1940. A British army officer based in Cyprus falls in love with a Greek Cypriot girl. He's shipped off to Egypt. She's pregnant and is disowned by her parents. The officer is seriously injured in the 1941 evacuation of Greece. He recovers but never communicates with his Cypriot love. Sixteen years later, it's 1957 and he's back in Cyprus as a colonel in charge of military intelligence. Among the terrorists he's hunting is a young Greek Cypriot teenager who is being trained as an assassin by an old Greek army officer. The colonel finds out the boy is his son, and the search is on for the woman he loved and the boy he helped create before the old Greek and his son can assassinate the Governor.

The manuscript sat on a Toronto literary agent's shelf for months, which added to my woes. Today it sits in a box in my garage. Perhaps one day I will do a re-write.

I suggested that Myra apply as an adjuster with the Corporation. She got the job and started work at the Kingsway Claims Center.

"IT'S TIME TO LEARN"

One day while resting after jogging, the woman's voice popped into my head. "It's time. It's time to learn the teachings of the Universe. Follow directions."

The words echoed in my mind for exactly two days. Then Myra pointed to an item in the Vancouver Sun newspaper. Dr. Lee Pulos, a psychologist and hypnosis teacher was conducting a weekend workshop at the University of British Columbia.

I felt scared and very apprehensive. Hypnosis? I had heard and read some bad things about it. What if I could not wake up? Would this man make me cluck like a chicken? My ego was deathly afraid. I almost resisted going, but some energy insisted I must.

His voice was soft and comforting and his mellow tones, which carried a quiet confidence, resonated through my mind. At first I was scared to "let go." It did not seem right, but after several "trance" sessions during the workshop I felt very relaxed. It was the first time in my entire life I had felt so relaxed. Did I dare enjoy it?

Relaxed, I was able to focus on his lectures over that weekend, and towards the end he told us that if you continued your studies in consciousness you would come "through the darkness into the light."

Those words! "Darkness into light." The Hindu Yogi had used them that day he had come to the Cyprus Mail, and so too had my Great-Grandmother in far-off Reading so many years before. These memories triggered the thought: Are our lives predetermined? Is there anything in predictions, prophecies? If so, where is this information kept? I asked Dr. Pulos.

"There is a theory that all our thoughts, records of all our actions, all cosmic information is around us and above us," he said simply. "We just need to tune in to access that information. It's called the Akashic Records."

The Akashic Records? The idea fascinated me. Then while I was getting used to the Pulos audio-tapes, I discovered that a Brazilian medium was giving a six week night-school course in Vancouver entitled "Explore Your Psychic World."

I listened intently as she took us into a light meditative trance. Then she gave each of the dozen or so students brown paper bags with the instructions: "Just place one on your open palm, and allow whatever impressions to come into your mind. Take the first impression, not the second."

When she brought us back to full conscious, she asked each one of us for our impression.

I felt stupid and a failure. "I don't know," I said lamely. "I had a vision, an impression of a white ceramic vase. It had a pink rose on it."

The medium opened the bag and inside was a white ceramic vase with an embossed pink rose. "You have psychic abilities," she said. "We call that psychometry."

Fascinated with this new word and my apparent ability, I used all my spare time conducting research at the Vancouver Public Library. I started browsing through books on metaphysics. One book led to another. I had learned speed reading at the Cyprus Mail and this helped enormously. I studied books on Yoga, Buddhism, Judaism, Hinduism, Jainism, Taoism and Zen. I attended workshops, seminars and speeches on various religions and metaphysics. Somehow I had discovered a new world.

Then one day I came across Joseph Weed's "Wisdom of the Mystic Masters" and Upton Sinclair's "Mental Radio" and discovered telepathy and mind-to-mind communication. How was this possible? My mind became ablaze with thoughts and possibilities. I had an idea of writing a psychic novel, a thriller.

MESSAGES FROM GOD

Out in the remaining farmlands of South Richmond, I met a French psychic who had been recommended as "very good."

She held my hands, closed her eyes and started talking. "You are treading a new path which will take you through teaching and healing. You will help many people and you will hurt people who love you. I see you as a minister, speaking in a church and you will talk and listen to the dead." She suddenly opened her dark brown eyes and said: "You realize, of course, there is no such thing as death. Bodies die and cease to be, but the spirit lives on in God's Universe. Spiritualists and others teach this."

"I don't believe in God," I protested.

The woman smiled. "God has been sending messengers to you all your life, but your ego refuses to see the truth. It will happen."

My next stop was at the door of long-time Spiritualist minister and medium Rev. Gloria Brough. She stared at me for a while in silence. "I'm not going to read for you," she said bluntly. "Check in with Isabel Corlett at the Vancouver Psychic Society."

Looking back, it was about this time that another kink in the Cosmos was manifesting itself in my life, although I had no idea of what was happening.

18

MEDIUMS, PSYCHICS
AND TIME TRAVEL

T HE SECOND WEEK OF February 1979 was a time to remember. On the Monday the radio announced that my old colleague international correspondent Joe Alex Morris had been killed in Tehran, Iran. It had happened on the Saturday, February 10th. Joe had been covering the riots following the stepping down of the Shah and had been hit by a stray bullet. I had so many good memories of this great reporter. I recalled how Joe used to come to our house in Amman. We were together on that long cross-desert ride to cover the State Visit of King Saud to Baghdad. There were good times and hectic times in Cyprus and the Lebanese Civil War. I learned many valuable and finer points of journalism from Joe. He was dead at 51 years of age. Now, fate had cut the string. Death really bothered me. What is there in death that makes me feel so hurt, so helpless?

On the afternoon of Wednesday, my forty-seventh birthday, I decided to take Gloria Brough's advice and check in with the Vancouver Psychic Society. It felt right, but I did not know why. I yearned for something, but right now there were no answers.

The Society was housed on Broadway close to the Cambie intersection. It occupied the second floor of an old office block owned by the City of Vancouver. The first time I climbed the stairs it seemed as if the bricks, the linoleum covered steps, the smoky lights had seen better days. But the Society had a large following. Every Tuesday night, up to eighty people would pack the large meeting room to hear psychics, mediums, healers and other metaphysical practitioners stand on the small platform, with its old wooden white speakers stand. A kitchen was offset at the back. On the side of the large meeting room were two smaller rooms, one comfortably furnished with faded Persian carpets, arm chairs and a sofa. The other had a circle of a dozen wooden chairs encircling a small wooden table for a glass bowl with water and a vase for flowers. A light stand showed a red light. This was the room for closed circle development classes.

Society founder and secretary was Isabel Corlett. An Isle of Man native, she came to Canada from London where she had sat, learned and observed with such notable Spiritualists as Maurice Barbanell, Air Chief Marshal Lord Hugh Dowding and Ursula Roberts.

Isabel was the first person I met after climbing the stairs. She was comfortably chubby, silver haired and possessed a warm energy that reminded me of Granny Egby at Highway Garage. Her aura seemed to wrap itself around me and I immediately felt I had known her for years.

Her first words to me: "Hello Bob, we were together in Glastonbury."

I stared, unable to understand.

"In a couple of past lives. You still have work to do there."

"Where's Glastonbury?"

"England. Somerset," she said easily, "but I don't need to tell you that." I felt as if I was supposed to know. She didn't mention it again, so we chatted over a cup of tea and she quizzed me on my background which lasted a good two hours. When Patrick Young walked in, he stared at me, walked on to the medium's room, and then came back and sat down opposite Isabel and myself. Isabel said: "This is Bob; he would like to join us."

Patrick said: "I have a lady in white with you and she tells me you are going to work with the light."

Suddenly, I was very aware. "Really? She says that?"

"Don't interrupt young man," retorted Patrick brusquely. "She says that everything that is written is within you and it is time for us to work together so that you can understand and make good use of it."

"How can things be inside me and I am unaware?"

"She says you still have a gutsy ego that needs tempering. She adds you need to get out of your own way. She adds: the time has come. Do you understand?

"What's her name?"

"Elen," said Patrick, "her name is Elen and you had tea with her many years ago."

"My Great-Grandmother," I said enthusiastically. Things were beginning to move and I felt very interested. But I felt a protest within. "She was always dressed in black with a black hat and black ostrich feather."

"When she works in Spirit she prefers white, the purest of all colors."

"Ask her who the woman is with the voice? She comes to me periodically? Is that my imagination?"

Patrick shook his head. "Elen says that is your guardian angel. She has been with you since before you were in your mother's womb. Elen says you saw her once when you were sick and they said you would die."

"What is her name?" I asked eagerly.

"One day, she herself will reveal her name," said Patrick. "Elen says she is an old spirit. She was an old spirit when the gods and goddesses roamed the Earth." He flashed an embarrassed smile. "I think I have told you too much."

MEDIUM PATRICK YOUNG: The author's mentor at the Vancouver Psychic Society was British medium Patrick Young, pictured with Myra's dog, Columbus.

Was this a coincidence? I always saw that apparition in my bedroom that day as a goddess. Come to think of it I have never let go of that image. It has been paramount in my life, particularly in my relationship with women. I always seem to search for the goddess within women but I never find it.

Patrick concluded: "Elen says this is now your home and we will help you to develop your metaphysical abilities. It will be a home, an oasis until it's time to move on. She adds: In a past life you were a camel driver. This is why you enjoy and find peace in the desert."

Elen was right. I had and still have a deep yearning for the desert life. I enjoyed being in Egypt and roaming the desert with shell-collector Peter Dance. While Peter searched under bushes for snails, I would sit on the sand and let my fingers caress thousands of grains of sand, and I would ponder the number of grains – billions and billions and wonder about their origin. For an hour or two, I would find peace in the desert. It happened again in Jordan when I did a story for United Press on the Dead Sea Scrolls. I visited the caves area and sat again on the sand touching and feeling its energy and I had no idea why. It just felt right.

THE MEDIUM AND THE CLOSED CIRCLE

I found a good mentor in the shape of Patrick Young, a British medium who, in his early career sat in circle with Ursula Roberts, one of Britain's foremost mediums and healers. Ursula channeled the spiritual teacher Ramadahn. She told Patrick he would work with a Native Indian Red Cloud, and he did.

Patrick also worked at the Spiritualist Association of Great Britain, and rubbed shoulders with Harry Edwards and others and attended the opening of the Arthur Findlay College at Stanstead Hall, Essex in 1966.

With Patrick and Isabel at my elbows, I found things starting to happen. One, my energy felt different and I started to sense things that normally I would have said are not there.

Patrick brought me into his Friday night Closed Circle of developing students. The first night, we did a silent meditation for thirty minutes, it seemed like hours to my untrained mind. I was used to listening to voice-guided self-hypnosis and meditation tapes by Dr. Lee Pulos. However, after several sessions at closed circle, I found the thirty minutes of silence growing on me. Every time, Patrick would ask the circle if anyone sensed anything.

"This is silly," I said.

"Don't apologize," snapped Patrick.

I plunged in. "I have a strong sense of a banana split. Someone is thinking bananas," I said. "They're hungry and feeling deprived."

"Anyone?" said Patrick.

A young Sikh woman sitting next to me said: "This is the last day of a six weeks diet and tonight I plan to go out and have a banana split."

"That's good, Bob," commented Patrick. "Just allow impressions to come. You will often think that you are making things up. Refuse to doubt and say what you are receiving." It was good advice that I pass on to students even to this day.

I was stunned and enthused. Reaching home I told Myra who sounded interested but I sensed she was not all that enthused with my new found abilities. I shared the news with my colleagues at work and none of them were impressed, in fact Bev Penhall and Corrine Noonan were quite skeptical.

Later, Patrick commented: "You've just learned a lesson. Mystics, and we are mystics, never push our gifts, our abilities. If a person asks a question, answer the question and no more. Jesus pointed this out when he advised never throw pearls before swine. He meant pearls of wisdom." He paused then added: "He didn't follow his own advice and look what happened to him." Patrick always had an infuriating light grin when he was right.

DEATH COMES VISITING AGAIN

Whenever I was not working at the Insurance Corporation, I spent my evenings at the Psychic Society, listening to speakers on Tuesday nights, attending classes and circles. Myra was busy studying for some advanced certification as an adjuster which meant higher pay for her. If I was home I would read books on psychic development. Every day I would relax and soften my mind with meditation and guided meditation as in self-hypnosis. I wondered why I had not heard of these things years ago. My life would have been vastly different. Myra and my friends noticed a difference in my attitude towards them and life.

Suddenly, death came visiting.

My sister Diane called from Ringwood, Dorset in England. "It's Mum. She's very sick. She doesn't have long to live."

The eleven-hour flight across the Atlantic seemed to take forever. At Diane and Paul's farm, my sister revealed the story. Mother, who had suffered arthritis in her back for years, had called the doctor for extra pain killers. The clinic nurse told Mum the regular doctor was away, and a visiting doctor was taking patients. "He wants to see you," she was told.

At the clinic the doctors did a thorough examination and called Ringwood. "The arthritis in her back is covering the cancer which is why she has difficulty standing up," the doctor told Diane. He estimated she had a month or less to live.

Diane lent me her midget MG and I drove from Dorset down to Cornwall and found my mother unable to stand, unable to lift her arms to greet me. The sight seared itself into my mind and it hurt. The ravages of her condition were sickening. I held her in my arms and felt her thin body against mine. I knew she was going to die and that idea hurt too. The frustrating part is that I could do very little except talk and make her endless cups of tea and give her juice. Suddenly the voice interrupted: 'Tell Mum you love her. She needs to know that."

It felt totally stupid and unnecessary. I was soon to learn that the reaction was my negative ego clinging to an old habit, an old learning that announcing love for someone was unmanly, and a sign of weakness. I pushed those feelings aside.

As I held her pain-wracked form, I looked into her pale blue eyes and said softly, "I love you Mum. You are the best."

A brief smile flickered in her eyes. "Thank you, Bobbie for that."

For a break, I went out into the night. It was raining. A white light was shining above. The rain cast an aura around a lonely street light. I peered at that light and in my frustration and anger I cried out: "God, where the bloody hell are you? What in damnation has that woman done to deserve being so bloody miserable? If she cannot be healed, get your people – your angels – to take her soon! Soon! Please!"

Silence. The night air was still, cloaked in a strange silence. Back at my mother's place I was surprised to find that she had gone to sleep on the sofa and forgotten to take her pain pills. As I looked, there was a strange green aura around her prone figure, which I could not understand. I knew this was the last time I would see her. A few days later, my sisters, Diane and Sheila had Mum moved into the Cancer Hostel at St. Austell where they took turns staying with her until she passed over. I was back in Vancouver, Canada when she died. Death had ended another era in my life and I felt an urgent need to find out about spirits, the so-called Spirit World and yes, God.

DISCOVERING THE MYSTIC MASTERS

I went back to working at the Insurance Corporation and for a few days took time off to spend with Myra. We took the ferry to Victoria and drove across Vancouver Island and walked for miles along the wide expanses of beaches at the Pacific Rim National Park and had lunch in Tofino. It seemed a blissful time being away for a few days.

Then I returned to studying metaphysics. One book that inspired me with exercises was Joseph Weed's "Wisdom of the Mystic Masters." A Rosicrucian and a seasoned broadcaster, he explained mystical development in easy and practical ways, but was insistent on one thing: Practice! It's no use doing a spiritual or metaphysical exercise for a few days, then forgetting about it for a week or a month and hoping that when you get back, you will make progress. I learned that one needs to build up psychic energy, maintain it, and cherish it like a valuable gift.

It was Joseph Weed who taught me the psychic essentials: clairvoyance, in which one sees spirits and energies, clairaudience, the hearing of sounds and voices, and clairsentience, the sensing of energies and thoughts. Yes, all thoughts are energy.

But Weed stressed the whole basis of metaphysical development is having a quiet mind. You cannot work in metaphysics with a mind cluttered with thoughts, and initially my mind was frequently clouded with mind-chatter. It was something that I knew I had to eliminate. But how?

READING THE TIME MACHINE

Psychometry or Time Clairvoyance fascinated me from the start. In essence it is seeing events in time, which is why some people call psychometry the Time Machine. It is the 101 of metaphysical studies, the gateway to the teachings of the ancient, the hidden world, and the realm of Spirits. Everything is energy. There isn't anything in the Universe that is not energy, even space contains energy. Some is visible to the human eye, but the most part is invisible.

What blows the mind is that all the energy in the Universe is recording everything that it does. You cannot find anything that does not record itself and its surroundings.

Peculiar? Absolutely. All the atoms and molecules in your body are recording your actions and your thoughts and have been doing so ever since you were in your mother's womb. No one on the physical plain knows how it is accomplished.

The Hindus call this phenomenon the Akashic Records. Akasha is a Sanskrit term meaning Sky and Ether, hence we sometimes have the Etheric Records. Bluntly, the whole thing means a Record of Life. This gives meaning to the "Book of Life" mentioned in Revelation and other books of the Bible. If you read it, you will see how a basic function of the Universe, recording its own existence, is used by the religious powers to intimidate and control people. When at the tender age of six, I played with matches and burned down our neighbor's fence. My mother scolded me and said, "Two angels are in Heaven writing down all the things you do."

The Akashic Records are available to any genuine researcher and spiritual explorer and it is done through Psychometry. As Patrick told me: "When you access the Akashic Records, you are accessing the history of the World, humankind and all its events."

One of my earliest experiences in this faculty was one Saturday morning when I was returning from Victoria to Vancouver and waiting for the seaplane. I rested my hands on an old metal stanchion, its base embedded in the harbor wall. I closed my eyes and immediately was taken back in time to that harbor in 1914. What a different and fascinating view came to me. One and two funneled steamers were in port, one a German passenger ship, along with an old merchant sailing vessel. Flanking the harbor were warehouses and a flock of little buildings. A pall of grey smoke drifted lazily across the harbor almost enclosing a small fishing boat setting sail for the Pacific. I started to hear sounds. People talking and someone playing a piano. Then the stink of fish and seaweed came to my nostrils. I stood there for a full ten minutes gazing into the past, completely engrossed by the vision.

BOB, YOU'RE ON STAGE

One rainy day, a lady came into the Psychic Society and asked Isabel if someone could do psychometry on a pendant that had belonged to her grandmother. Isabel nodded to me. We sat in Patrick's reading room. Various scenes from the grandmother's life came flooding in, including one where, as a young woman, she was thrown from a horse and had both her legs broken. One leg had healed badly and left her with a limp for life.

"Gosh!" said the woman at the end of about thirty minutes. "I remember her limping, but we never knew how she did it. Thank you so much. How much do I owe you?"

I had never been paid to do a psychometry reading, and was taken by surprise. I shook my head. "Nothing. Nothing at all." She thrust $40 into my hand and left. Isabel who had observed my reluctance to accept money, said: "That's a serious limitation you have. Better get rid of that." She was not joking and her pale eyes reflected the seriousness of her advice.

Isabel explained the Law of Give and Take. "When people give you things – food, shelter, clothes, money – it is coming from the Cosmos and you should take it and express your thanks to that person and also the Cosmos. If you refuse to accept a gift, you are blocking their Universal right to give. You gave them a gift of a reading, but stopped them from giving you a gift of money. Think about that, Bob." She said, "It comes under the Law of Karma which seeks to balance the Universe. "

One Tuesday night the scheduled speaker failed to turn up. Some forty people were waiting to be entertained. Isabel looked at me sitting in the back. "Bob, why don't you get up and tell them about psychometry?" She introduced my talk as "Reading the Book of Life," and concluded with, "You're on, Bob."

At first I wanted to disappear down the steps, but some energy moved my feet towards the dais. Images of myself making movies as a teenager flashed by, performing on stage at El Firdan and broadcasting at Fayid and Lakatamia flickered through my mind. I stood on the platform and knew fifty pairs of eyes were watching me. "Just talk on what you know and enjoy yourself. Right now, you are the expert." It was the woman again and I sensed for some reason, she was enjoying pushing me.

Suddenly I felt a bolt of energy sear up my back. My body and mind suddenly became alert and I stood beside the wooden lectern mentally focused, alert and confident. 'Hello, we are living in a time machine. We are all making history and most of us don't even realize it," I started, and I felt the sudden interest.

"Psychometry comes from two Greek words, 'psyche' meaning 'soul' and 'metros' meaning 'measure'. Metros is the stem for the 'metric' measuring system. In truth Psychometry is really a time machine for the mind. Used properly it will take you back in time, not just for something that happened this morning or last year, but through the centuries. Many good psychometrists have accurately read energies millions of years in our past," I said.

I told the audience how we conducted a psychometry workshop one Saturday and offered some mystery objects hidden in brown paper bags. On one bag in particular, one student said the bag contained "a large bone," another said it was "a bone from a very large animal," while the third reader, after a quiet period announced "It's a dinosaur bone. I'm getting Alberta, and it's about 132 million years old." He was right, and he went on to say he could see a dinosaur taking small round stones into its mouth to enable digestion.

Human beings produce many thoughts every day, and when you live in a house, your thoughts become impregnated with the walls and the furniture. This is why two houses standing next door to one another may have different dominant energies. If you go in one, it may feel heavy and negative and you get the feeling you should leave. The next house you enter will feel bright, full of light and positive energy. This is because the people who have lived there leave a dominant positive energy. Another easy example of thought-energies can be found in most churches, they are calm and peaceful. Now observe the energy in busy police stations and you will be surprised.

Your dominant thoughts in your home leave an energy form that will stay there until the house is pulled down. You may be long gone, but your thoughts, your entry into the Akashic Records stays on," I added. "Now this happens with everything you own. Rings, jewelry, watches, heirlooms, personal effects and so on."

These were some of the points I made at that first lecture I did at the Vancouver Psychic Society. "A person trained in reading the Akashic Records – that is Psychometry – can read your life story." I then went on to tell them about my experience at Victoria Harbor and image of 1914.

A BREAK INTO MEDIUMSHIP

Somehow I took a deep breath and walked up to a slim, attractive red-head in the front row. "Would you like to lend me a watch for a few moments?"

She hesitated, and then said: "My husband only bought it today and gave it to me at supper an hour ago."

"That's all right. You can hold a flower for two minutes and it will contain your life story," I said, and several people shook their heads, mostly I think, in disbelief.

I held the watch clasped in both hands and closed my eyes. The words just came.

"He gave it to you today as a birthday present," I said lamely. Then the information came through. "Ah, but it was your birthday yesterday and he was away on business."

She nodded.

"When you were a little girl at your first year in school, you were walking home in pink rubber boots. You waded through a deep muddy puddle. The thick mud sucked one boot off your foot and you had to hop home on one foot. You mother went out and retrieved the boot."

The woman laughed. "You had everything right, except for one thing. It was my Nanny."

At that first lecture I did several more mini-readings on objects for people. Then I came to an elderly lady, neatly dressed and sitting with a very pale man at her side. I had the feeling he needed warmth and wanted to hold her hand. She offered me a man's gold wedding band.

"So, the Akashic Records say you were married in England...oh, just not anywhere, but in a church at Windsor, near Windsor Castle."

She nodded and when I asked her name, she said Joan.

I continued. "You emigrated to Canada in 1950 and your husband....okay, he tells me his name is Albert...and he worked in a saw mill. He says this is his wedding ring."

She frowned. Albert's been gone for a year...he died a year ago tomorrow."

"Who is the person sitting beside you in a brown tweedy jacket, with a pale complexion? He's holding a pocket watch and says it's time to go home."

As she twisted round to the next chair, the pale face man who had been sitting there vanished. "Joan, Albert has been here all evening, sitting with you."

She burst into tears, and suddenly I realized I had broken into spirit clairvoyance. Not only that, I had heard what Albert was saying.

After everyone had gone, Isabel and a couple of others sat down. "I saw him sitting there," confirmed Isabel. "You've been inducted into the higher realms of mediumship. There's still much to learn but you are on your way. Congratulations Bob."

A year after I joined the Society I was conducting all-day Saturday Psychometry training workshops and two years later, Patrick encouraged me to lead mid-week meditation and psychic development circles. Often, we had twenty-five people attending.

It was like leading a double life, a feeling that would grow more prevalent as the years passed. When I was not working at the Insurance Corporation, I spent much of my free time studying, reading books and attending lectures. The Silva Mind Control Method workshop gave me insights into the workings of the subconscious mind, an aspect that came in very useful when I got into a career in professional hypnosis.

I felt drawn to the Buddhist temples in the Lower Mainland and learned all about consciousness. There was enjoyment in mulling over the quotations of Gautama Buddha such as "You yourself, as much as anybody in the entire universe, deserves your love and affection." Strange, I always thought I did love myself. Soon, I was in for a shock that turned my mind upside down.

AN INTRODUCTION TO HEALING

It happened one evening at the Psychic Society and I was seated in a corner reading. Shakti Gawain's classic book "Creative Visualization" had just been published and for beginners in metaphysics this was a great beginning. I had just turned the page to the chapter "Meeting Your Guide" when Isabel Corlett got up from her desk and announced: "It's time for you to learn healing."

Healing! This would be interesting. Isabel had spent time with the great healer Harry Edwards who founded the famous Spiritual Healing Sanctuary at Burrows Lea, Shere in the Surrey countryside in 1947. Harry's healing attracted thousands from all over the world, and when he crossed into spirit in 1976, his work at Shere was carried on for many years by Ray and Joan Branch. Isabel carried the philosophy and teachings of Harry Edwards and she taught the process to selected students.

The medium's room was empty, so she pulled up a wooden chair, asked me to sit down and stood behind me. "I'm going to mentally attune myself to God and ask that I be allowed to act as a healing channel." I did not tell her that I really had problems with God, but we had talked about that before. I sensed she ignored my ideas.

"Close your eyes and relax, feet flat on the floor, your hands resting loosely on your thighs."

"Do I need healing," I said, feeling it was almost a protest.

"You're a walking pile of stress," she said gently. "You need healing."

Isabel placed her hands lightly on my shoulders, her thumbs almost touching across the back of my neck. For a while, perhaps half a minute, nothing happened, then her hands became warm and the warmth intensified, and I felt a relaxing, warm energy running to all parts of my body. It was like electricity, both calming and invigorating. Isabel did not ask if I felt it, she knew. The healing lasted for about eight minutes until it faded off, then she reached round and her hand encircled my stomach. "I'm closing you off; otherwise your solar plexus chakra will pick up all sorts of unwanted energies."

She came round. "How do you feel?"

"Relaxed and wonderful," I said. Indeed it was the best I had ever felt in my life. I had learned meditation, self-hypnosis and even Dr. Herbert Benson's impressive "Relaxation Response" which demystified the Transcendental Meditation's use of mantras and the need for a teacher or guru. Spiritual healing was something else.

"In healing it is critically important not to use your own energy," Isabel explained. "It's essential you ask to be attuned to a higher power. The power of spirit healing is much greater than yours. The Universe is full of healing energy so don't start thinking to the contrary." I knew she was talking about some of my egotistical remarks I made from time to time. Those remarks had started to bother me. I knew I still had a lot to learn.

AND A GUIDE NAMED CHANG

It was Friday night and the closed circle gathered with Patrick. There was a small wooden circular table in the center of the room with a glass bowl of water. A vase of flowers stood in the corner. A red light illuminated the small room and the faces of the dozen students. After a half hour of silent meditation, Patrick quietly asked if anyone had any messages or were experiencing any sensations.

Several people received messages from Patrick and three or four gave messages for other circle members. As much as I could, I could not see or sense where they were getting the messages from, and that bothered me. I closed my eyes and immediately went into a dream state. I knew I was both dreaming and sitting in a chair. Patrick explained afterwards that that was a lucid dream.

I decided to describe the dream as it happened. "I'm walking along an old, well-rutted road. The land is arid and bare and in the distance a ridge of grey and sandy peaks pierced the dawn sky. It's hard to see clearly because the sun has not yet risen and there is a descending moon in the west. A wooden cart pulled by an ox trundles by. A driver, half asleep is slumped on the wagon. He is Chinese. I am being drawn to a large building, perhaps a temple, perhaps not. There are many colored, ornate wooden panels on the walls. I pass through an arch and a little Chinaman appears before me. He's dressed in robes and he starts talking, but I cannot hear his voice. I sense that he is gentle and a teacher. I would like to stay here," I tell the circle. "I really want to stay with him. It's a pity I cannot hear what the little man is saying."

Patrick spoke quietly. "His name is Zhang or it's better if you just say Chang. He says he was a country doctor and lived in China until he passed over in 1893." Then he chuckled and added: "Bob, you've just met your healing guide. Enjoy!"

Just then several members of the circle exclaimed: "I can see him quite clearly too. He's small and has a beautiful green aura."

And then, I saw him. And I knew he was there and not just a dream.

In the days that followed, under Isabel's watchful eye, I started to give healing to members and people who came in off the street. I found I was doing several healings a day, mostly in the evenings before or after meetings and classes. It felt good to see people, who had come in with grim, pained faces get up afterwards and leave with a smile. I could sense Chang working because a trembling green and blue light seemed to quiver around the person being healed.

One evening, I was walking home to our place in the West End and thinking of my mother. If only I had learned healing earlier I might have been able to help Mum a little more than I did.

"You did all you could, Bob," said Chang, suddenly appearing and walking beside me. "You gave her love and you spent a week with her. That's all she needed."

"You were there?"

"The night you were giving God a rough time," he replied. "I gave her that good night's sleep without the medicine. Remember the green aura around her?"

I stopped walking and looked at the shimmering figure. "I think you had better start filling me in on God. I think it's time."

Chang nodded: "Well you can begin by letting go of all the images you have of God."

"All the images?"

"All the images," he said. "We'll talk later."

19

SPIRIT, TRAINS AND MONTE CARLO

T HE ENDING OF 1981 and the beginning of 1982 was something else. Energy was on the move and moving fast. First, Myra and I, after living together for some five years decided to get married. Born and raised in the Catholic Church in Hamilton, Ontario, getting married in a Catholic Church was out of the question. We were both divorced, so we headed over to the Anglican Christ Church Cathedral on the corner of West Georgia and Burrard, and one windy Saturday in November, the 14th actually, entered Holy Matrimony. Some relatives and a good but strange mixture of friends from the Insurance Corporation and the Psychic Society turned up. Afterwards everyone, including some spirits came over to the Hotel Georgia for the reception.

For a few seconds I enjoyed listening to Patrick Young telling a senior claims manager at the Insurance Corporation that if he trained his staff in clairvoyance and spirit communication there would be a reduction in fraudulent claims. The manager stood stunned and ready for another drink.

Christmas came and went and we thought of moving. We moved into a high-rise in the West End that gave us a better view. It was the third week in January, and I had been thinking that it was time to move on. Relations between the media and the Insurance Corporation were on a more rational, acceptable basis. The politics which had plagued the firm had been eliminated with the presence of a new president, Robbie Sherrell who introduced "Fair", an insurance program that eliminated age and equalized premiums and only penalized drivers when they had an automobile accident for which they were responsible. This had a beneficial impact on everyone including the media.

One day in that third week of January, there was another kink in the Cosmos. Change was in the air. I could feel it, but didn't know what was coming. It turned up in the shape of Gordon Adair, a highly respected financial consultant.

"Have you heard of the Rapid Transit Project?" he asked, slipping into an easy chair.

I nodded. It was a well publicized proposal to build an automated rapid transit line between downtown Vancouver, through East Vancouver and Burnaby to New Westminster. Initially, it would run twelve miles. It reeked of controversy because it required a number of people to lose their homes and property, and the trains would operate automatically without drivers. It was an age when few people knew anything about automation and computers.

"And one more thing," said Gordon in his soft, nonchalant voice: "It has to be up and running for the world to see when they come to Expo 86 in Vancouver," he said. "Mike O'Connor the Project Administrator is looking for a good public relations person to become Project PR Director." He paused and watched my face. "I suggested your name, but don't get too excited. They have a list, a short list."

Wow! Ever since I used to collect train numbers at Maidenhead railway station, I'd had an attraction for trains, and this would put me right inside. I tried not to look excited. "It sounds interesting," I said. "What do I have to do?"

"Nothing," said Gordy. He picked up the phone, muttered a few words to a voice on the other end, and listened for two seconds. "This afternoon. Three o'clock at the offices at 1200 Burrard."

"Do they want my resume?"

"They already have it."

"How?"

"Don't ask too many questions," he responded with a smile.

Mike O'Connor was a young, vibrant and enthusiastic project administrator. We had coffee and chatted about jogging. He asked about England, Cyprus and Jerusalem. Then said, "I'll let you know." It was the weirdest interview I ever experienced. Afterwards I hoped I had said the right things. An element of doubt lurked in my mind. I walked back to the Corporation where I sat thinking about trains. Just before leaving to go home, a courier arrived with a letter.

It read: *"Confirming our conversation today, I am pleased to offer you the position of Public Relations Director with the Rapid Transit Project. Your daily rate would be $220.00 per day. We would like you to start on March 1st 1982."* There was information about a Personal Services Contract. The date all this happened was January 27th 1982.

That evening Myra and I went out to celebrate. "When things happen around you, they certainly happen quickly," she noted.

"It kind of takes one's breath away," I said, and as I spoke I sensed there was some laughter echoing in the Spirit World.

In that February I realized more than ever that I was living a double life. I wondered how much of my time the Rapid Transit Project would demand and whether it would curtail my activities at the Vancouver Psychic Society. But Chang put my mind at easy when he said: "Allow everything to flow. Do not fight it."

Tom Parkinson, Deputy Project Administrator who had originated in Britain and lived and breathed rail, particularly the electronics aspects, provided a box full of reading matter. One thing that puzzled me was how rapid transit would function in the heart of downtown Vancouver, which was already crowded with traffic.

"We have a tunnel," said Tom and he took me on a tour of the half-century old Canadian Pacific Railway tunnel that ran 1.3 kilometers from the rail yards in the eastern part of the city, under downtown to emerge at the waterfront at Vancouver Harbor. "It's a single track built for steam trains," he said. "We are going to convert it by deepening the tunnel bed and have stacked trains in a bi-level configuration. East bound on one track, west bound on the other. It's a real challenge."

The whole thing was a challenge and I seriously wondered if I was up to it. Politicians were not my favorite subject. I had known too many along my path and now I would be working for them.

ON THE BEACH WITH CHANG

One day I went for a long walk along Jericho Beach. The mountains on the North Shore were snowcapped and glistening in the cold sunshine. A chilly breeze made me pull my heavy parka closer. I found a place to sit quietly near a concession kiosk closed for the winter.

Suddenly, I felt a presence. It was Chang, dressed as usual in old Chinese. He never felt the cold.

"Your career is moving along. You'll enjoy the project. The energy is right for you."

"How do you see the future?" I pondered curiously.

"Energy is always moving. It has to," said the Chinese doctor. "It's like a train on the railway. We can see the train as energy, both coming from the past, as it is now, and where it will be."

"Forever?"

"No, just until there is a bend in the railway track."

"Do you see God?"

"Always." Chang paused and stared me in the eyes. "You're still having trouble." It was a statement. "How did you see God before you became an atheist?"

"At Stubbings Church when I carried the cross? Oh, I had my doubts then. I had trouble accepting Michelangelo's The Creation of Man, or the concept that God is a chubby old man cloaked in golden robes and surrounded by winged angels playing harps," I said. "I could never accept that concept."

"First of all you need to forget such concepts," he said. "Men invented those concepts when humanity's intelligence was limited. Until recently most humans could not conceive of a superior force as anything but human. It is a natural product of the human ego. Most mystics reject the idea of a human as God. Jesus the teacher conceived naming God 'my father' or "our father." This intensified the anthropological aspect of a god-man, but it was convenient and appropriate for the audiences in the times of Jesus." He paused, and then added: "Jesus blew the whole Father title away when he said God is Spirit."

"God is Spirit. That makes sense," I nodded. "So how should we see God?"

Chang smiled gently. "How about everywhere?"

"Everywhere?"

"Be aware. Awareness is everything," said Chang. 'Be aware of life around you. The tree over there is 120 years old, and it grew from a seed hardly seen by the naked eye. You can talk about biology, but what is the force that inspires, triggers that growth? Take the grass. A grass seed might lay dormant for many years and then suddenly it springs to life."

"Because of water?"

"Water, yes. But what is the life force in the grass? In the summer take a look at the Clematis plant growing on a stake. If you place another stake a few inches away, it will send out a tentacle that will wrap itself around the second stake and grow from there. How does it know the second stake is there?"

"Plants are intuitive?"

"And more. Plants are conscious of their life. They know they have to reproduce."

"How? There is a force, a special energy?"

Chang nodded. "Plants, flowers, trees, bushes, and all wildlife are imbued with the life force and they understand life and the need to reproduce. When you did a story for your radio station on the salmon running up the river to the creeks off the Shuswap Lake, and you felt sorry for those beaten, bloody fish struggling against awful odds to ensure survival, did you not wonder what drives those salmon to do that?

"Intuition?"

"Let's call it the Force. When you were employed in the forest industry, did you ever listen to the trees? "

I shook my head and felt very unaware.

"The next time you teach Psychometry, take your students out and have them place their hands on the trunks of trees, and those trees will tell their life stories...the years of drought, forest fires, events happening around them."

"Those are the Akashic Records," I put in trying to appear a midge intelligent.

"And Akasha is what?"

"Life."

"And life is?"

I felt lost. "A Force?"

"Life is energized by the Force and God is?"

"God is Spirit."

Chang smiled. "Spirit is everywhere. There is no place that the Spirit of God does not exist. Take a breath. Do it now."

Obediently, I focused on my breath.

"Where is God?"

"In the air? Oxygen? Hydrogen?" I answered.

"All that," said Chang enthusiastically. "And that air goes to every cell in your body carrying and replenishing the Spirit of God."

"Everything is a reflection of God? Is that what you are saying?"

"Absolutely."

"So the Bible is wrong?"

"You're judging and that gets you into potholes," said Chang."The Bible is a book written by a collection of writers with the purpose of teaching. The metaphysical aspects are generally correct which shows that whoever wrote the Bible had a basic knowledge of those arts."

"They claim that God wrote the bible. Is this correct?"

Chang shrugged patiently. "Allow me to explain. When you sit in silence to write a talk or a book and then a thought, something you've never considered, but it's true, and it simply springs out of nowhere, to what or whom do you attribute it?"

"Imagination," I replied and that moment knew it was wrong.

"Perhaps," said Chang. "But how about a Cosmic Consciousness, a Universal Mind, an Infinite Intelligence? When you write you are pensive which means you are in a light altered state, which also means you are receptive to information, ideas and thoughts in the Cosmos. It is at this precise moment the Universal Mind slips through with an idea, a thought for you."

"Do you mean to tell me that somewhere, up above the clouds, there is a mind, a Cosmic brain that says – Here's an opportunity to slip something in?"

Chang's face appeared hurt. "You still have an old world awareness which is like something the camels left." His spirit form pulled closer. "Recall in Matthew (10:29) Jesus is quoted: 'Are not two sparrows sold for a penny? Yet not one of them will fall to the ground outside your Father's knowledge.' This indicates that the Universal Mind is controlling the entire universe, and even now, knows what we are doing."

"That's impossible!" I said with a critical laugh. I really wanted to say, "Bull shit!" but Chang was a scholar and a gentle person.

"That's your limitation speaking," observed the Chinaman softly. "You really have to do something about your limitations, your ego, your False Self."

"False Self? What's false about me?"

"One day soon you will answer your own question," said Chang starting to move away. "That's your next aspect of study. I leave you with Love and Light."

Chang did not leave in a flash or a burst of light, he simply was no longer there, and he left me with a lot of thoughts, heavy, ponderous thoughts - thoughts that challenged my old ways of thinking. I stopped thinking and focused on my breathing. I felt the air slip easily into my lungs and I said softly: "Holy Spirit, hello. I've been searching for you for so long."

I felt tears welling in my eyes. My False Self pushed in unceremoniously and said: "Now you're being soft."

I decided that somehow I would do something about that condition. But I still was not sure. Why is believing in something, so difficult?

RAPIDLY SETTLING IN

There was not much time to think about the image of God given to me by Chang. I needed to settle in to the Public Relations office in the Bentall Center in downtown Vancouver.

My department possessed a great department secretary, alert and efficient, named Sandra Brennan who knew everything and everybody. Already, Sandra had a wonderful working knowledge of the Rapid Transit Project. I never figured out why she did not have my job, but I was glad to be there. The job sounded hectic and almost like fun.

Larry Miller, the General Manager of B.C. Transit, the corporation fathering the Project, assigned a great writer, Lon Wood to the Project. Lon had been working with the Victoria Times on Vancouver Island, and with him came Norman Gidney, another great writer based at headquarters office of B.C. Transit in Victoria. Norman was a whizz at getting Project publications out and also helped with news releases, as did Lon. Diane Gendron was a great help in setting up special events.

As the project got under way and we developed a PR presence, we were joined by a team of talented people. Trudy Stevens, Diane Hughes, Kyla Bell and Karen Kelm. They learned quickly and were great at answering questions and helping visitors to understand the operations of rapid transit.

At one in-house party Karen, Diane and Kyla formed a trio of songstresses and someone called them the "Limettes." The word comes from the LIM the Linear Induction Motors used to drive the trains. The Limettes were fabulous, so much so they were invited to travel to Ontario and entertain the people at UTDC, the train manufacturers at Kingston, Ontario. I felt I had a great team. After SkyTrain, Karen often appeared in musical theatre, vaudeville, big band and folk song events. Her CD is called "Here to Stay" and I have a copy in my collection.

A PREVIEW PROJECT NAMED PREBUILD

Our first challenge was something called the "Prebuild" project which comprised 1,100 meters of track on an elevated guideway and a two-car demonstration train which had been built by UTDC, or the Urban Transportation Development Corporation of Ontario. By the time I reached the Project, the guideway had been built and the two-car train was shipped to Vancouver. When it arrived everybody who was anybody gathered to see, cheer or criticize. The Premier, Bill Bennett hustled over with a flotilla of ministers and bureaucrats in tow.

One was John Arnett, brother of Peter Arnett the controversial war correspondent of international TV fame. John had been Press Secretary to the Premier and was now PR Director at B.C. Transit's head office. Another person involved in PR was David Brown, a strange but imposing figure who moved mysteriously between the Premier's office and the Rapid Transit Project. Thus the Project was very political from the outset and attracted frequent criticism by the media and socialist elements in both Vancouver and Toronto.

We established a display station at the west end of the Prebuild track where the Main Street Station now stands. The two-car prototype operated well from June to November 1983 giving demonstration rides to more than 300,000 people. A survey showed that eighty per cent of visitors gave conditional or unconditional support to the rapid transit concept. It was designed to take 100,000 commuters a day from the cars on city streets.

During the fall, winter and spring of 1982-83 we created a Media Plan, and headed out to various schools, community centers and to interested groups to explain the plans. There would be fifteen stations in Phase One linking communities between Waterfront in downtown Vancouver, through East Vancouver, Burnaby to New Westminster. The Project involved a tremendous operation. Over sixty major construction contracts were let.

Letting contracts worth millions of dollars is one thing, scheduling them is another. They all have to interlock like a timed jigsaw puzzle. As I explained to various enquiries, there's not much point in having some 110-ton beams delivered, if the columns for the elevated guideway are not in place. This was a simple explanation of a complex scheduling system, which was headed by Bob Tribe.

Incidentally, the contract being let for the supply of guideway beams, valued at over $50 million, was awarded to Supercrete. UTDC in Ontario, set up a subsidiary prime contractor Metro Canada Limited (MCL) to construct the guideway.

Now, these forces, UTDC and Metro Canada, B.C. Transit in Victoria, the Premier's Public Relations staff, and the Rapid Transit Project PR Director, which was me, all were getting their voices heard, and it's little wonder the news media was frequently confused and this was reflected in their reporting. There were too many bosses on the project from the Premier down.

Both Mike O'Connor and Tom Parkinson were very supportive of my office, but occasionally their support was tested. One day, when I admonished a visitor participating in a station tour for safety reasons, I plunged into serious trouble. Mistakenly, I thought the well dressed man was from UTDC in Ontario. He was in fact the Speaker of the House in British Columbia. Mike O'Connor told me afterwards: "Egby, I've saved your soul." I knew I had to do something about my ego. It was getting in the way.

JOGGING IN FRANCE

In mid-1983 with construction of the rapid transit system underway, Myra and I decided to take a two week vacation in England where we visited my sisters, Diane and Sheila, and then went on a round-Europe rail vacation. We had purchased a Eurail Pass in Canada. We visited the new automated Metro rapid transit system in Lille that had just opened in April. That system provided some interesting color transparencies for showing, back in Vancouver. Lille was also memorable for the fact we got lost while jogging in the early morning light, and were saved by the considerate French police.

Lifestyles had changed drastically since I had lived in Cologne seventeen years before and it struck me how much had occurred when I went jogging early one morning in Paris. We stayed in a neat hotel tucked away in a cul-de-sac. I started my jog and came up to the famous Champs-Élysées. As I spun round the corner I almost knocked him over – a cop! Not just an ordinary French gendarme but a figure that looked menacingly, like something out of Star Wars. He was clad in a huge dull black bullet-proof outfit from neck to heavy black boots. His head was hidden inside a glossy-black helmet and in his black gloved hands snuggled a lethal automatic rifle. I could see his wide alert eyes staring from a slot on the helmet. His whole appearance was eerie.

"Hi!" I cried. It was a startled greeting. I followed it up with a "Bon Jour." My heart was beating like Gene Krupa's drums. Then I sensed he was unperturbed because he said in good English. "Hi Yank!" I didn't tell him I was a Canadian, but I mustered a smile and sped off towards the Eiffel Tower. The hotel manager told me that the policeman I had met was part of the night force and was replaced by standard police at sunrise. But this was 1983 and it showed how much Europe had changed in so few years. I wondered how long it would be before we saw such police on Vancouver streets.

Using the Eurail Pass, we slept most nights on the trains and toured various cities during the day before finishing up for a couple of days in the Principality of Monaco and the Monte Carlo Casinos. Lucky Myra reaped in the money on the slot machines, and I promptly lost it. It was not my time, I guess.

THE LURE OF THE MEDITERRANEAN

Next morning I went jogging by myself along the Boulevard Louis II which flanks the Mediterranean. Somewhere along the route, I stopped to admire the deep rich blue of the sea, almost motionless in the sun breaking slowly over the horizon. The beauty triggered memories of another part of the Mediterranean.

I moved down the steps to the beach and walked along the sand close to the water. The sea beckoned to me. I could smell it. There was a force, a presence that pulled me. I crouched down and ran my fingers through the cool, calm water, allowing it to trickle gently over my palm and flow back. I remembered Cyprus and Iro and the times we had spent together on the beach by Kyrenia Castle and the beaches to the west. We were in love and relished the Mediterranean background. Swimming revitalized both of us and we always felt exhilarated afterwards. I raised my moist fingers to my lips and promised myself that I would return to Cyprus, the island of my first love during the next year. It would happen but not in the way I imagined.

We took the TGV, the Train à Grande Vitesse from Marseilles to Paris. The ultra high speed train covered the 880 miles in seven and a half hours. This is the way to travel, I thought, as the train hurtled through the French countryside like a hedge-hopping aircraft.

Back on Earth at the Rapid Transit Project I ran into a new media concern: none of the fifteen stations would have restrooms. Tom Parkinson, whose knowledge of stations in North America, Britain and Europe, came up with news that the trend is to build stations without latrines. Reason? They attract crime and unhealthy elements. In addition, restrooms are costly to maintain requiring attendants to be on duty at all stations over eighteen hours a day. It was pointed out that restrooms are also available at various points along the route. The issue remained for some months before it finally died down.

RUNNING A TRAIN THROUGH A STORE WINDOW

At the summer Prebuild operation, in addition to the operating train, we also had as part of our exhibition at Main Street, something known as a "Mock-up. This was the shell of a rapid transit car completely finished, but without a chassis, wheels, motors etc. It was light enough to be moved to various locations and the Premier's Office wanted maximum exposure on the Project.

The Mock-up was shown for sixteen days at the Pacific National Exhibition Fair in East Vancouver. Again it drew record crowds and visitors had to be controlled as the lines moved through the vehicle. Afterwards, we moved the Mock-up into the Bentall Center, the massive office buildings with stores at street level. It was no easy task. One Sunday morning, glaziers removed the huge front windows on one of the stores, and a crane was used to shunt the Mock-up through the window into the store. A complete exhibition was built around the vehicle and this attracted thousands of people, particularly at lunch time.

We had our embarrassing moments. It happened during a construction photo shoot near the Main Street station. The Honorable Jack Davis, former Federal Minister and now a Member of the Legislative Assembly and chairman of the Rapid Transit '86 Committee, decided to use a portable toilet on the construction site. We were horror-stricken as a crane picked up the unit and started to move it with the chairman inside. There were shouts and a waving of arms and the crane operator let the unit down gently. Jack Davis was a little shaken but eventually smiled. "That's one different way to get publicity," he commented. He was one of the best politicians I ever met.

PRACTICING PSYCHIC EXERCISES

While working on the Rapid Transit Project, I found I could practice psychic development exercises. Whenever walking alone between stations being constructed or walking to the advertising agency, I practiced a simple but effective exercise. This is an excellent technique for developing psychic energy including clairvoyance and clairsentience and can be performed as one walks along the sidewalk of a busy street. You can also do it while sitting in a restaurant or waiting room.

You glance briefly at a stranger's face, and mentally take a snapshot picture. Then you "hold" that person's image in your mind imposing that snapshot on some neutral background, such as the sidewalk, a blank wall or plain carpet. As you do this, a variety of images and feelings related to that person will come to you. After thirty seconds, the images fade, so you pick another face.

Practice as many times as you can and you will find that simply by looking at anyone at any time, you will start to receive thoughts and feelings of that person. If you wish to stop, circle a palm clockwise over the solar plexus and say, "I close myself off." It's a very powerful exercise and my development benefitted enormously. But that's how I occupied my mind while walking the rapid transit route.

VALIDATE, VALIDATE, SAID PATRICK

Patrick's Closed Circle was a mine of metaphysical information, a psychic treasury. I started to give messages for other members of the group, and as any developing medium will reveal, it's easy to fall into the clap-trap lovey-dovey message rut. Example: "I have a little old lady in a straw hat, who says she's your grandmother, and she's sending you healing and she wants you to know you're still her special person."

If it happened in Circle, Patrick would come through the red light of the circle with a sharp, critical tongue. "Validate! Validate! Validate!" he hissed. "That sort of message is totally useless. Do you know how many little old ladies there are in Spirit wearing straw hats and sending healing and love? That's totally unacceptable. Totally useless."

His fair skinned face with sharp eyes scanned the circle. "This is urgent," he cried, almost grinning with childish delight. "Get your spirit guides to press spirits coming through for details of a unique connection. They should reveal information known only between the spirit coming through and the person having the reading."

Patrick gave an example of validation. "Grandma Mary who lived on Pickwick Lane is here. You lived with her for two years when your Mum was sick. She says you liked sardine sandwiches cut diagonally. She says Granddad is with her and wants to know when you're going to throw away his old meerschaum pipe. You see that's the sort of stuff people want to hear. Personal, practical and powerful."

At that time the only working spirit guide I had was Chang. He heard Patrick's instruction and I feared because he was a healer, he would work only in that modality. But he came through.

A young woman, who always seemed to be tense and rarely received any messages, sat looking at me in the red glow of the circle. She sensed I was going to say something. "Joan, your sister Benji – I hope I have that right – is here. She crossed over two years ago. She says you forgot to have your blood pressure pills this morning and the cat is still out in the yard waiting to get in, and you've left the bathroom faucet on." The group cracked up and Joan ran off home. She reported that the bathroom tap was on but no damage was done and the cat was now asleep in the garage.

In a closed circle, messages come much easier than when you are standing on a platform and fifty pairs of eyes are watching you expectantly. But with practice, validation does become easier and if you have a good guide, give him or her a gentle reminder from time to time.

UNDERSTANDING THE MYSTERY OF DEATH

It was through the teachings of Patrick Young that I started to comprehend mediumship – communicating with spirits – and the Spirit World, and through this the phenomenon of Death started to become clear.

After working in the Middle East for so many years where death seemed to be an everyday occurrence, it was a relief to hear from both Patrick and Chang that there is no such thing as death.

"Death is that phenomenon that occurs when the body shuts down from its Earthly reign and the Spirit leaves to return home," Patrick told us. "It is simply a process much like birth, only death is the process in reverse."

"If you sit and watch a person die, you may notice a shimmering energy lift gently out of the body, it pauses and hovers for a few seconds, and then it seems to fade away, almost in an upward motion. It is spirit changing vibrations onto a higher Etheric net. That changing of vibrations gave ancient observers the notion that one's spirit goes up to Heaven."

"So Heaven is not up there," I said. The remark sounded trite and unnecessary.

"Heaven is the Spirit World. The Yogis refer to it as the Astral World," said Patrick. "Others refer to it as Olympus, the Elysian Fields, Arcadia, Valhalla, Nirvana, and my Indian guide, Red Cloud refers to it as the happy hunting grounds. Every culture has different definitions but they all amount to the same thing."

"When you are ready, Bob," whispered Chang, "I will give you a tour of the Astral World." That news was gratifying and I thanked him.

A SNAG IN THE SPIRIT WORLD

"There's one thing you should all know," said Patrick to the circle one Friday night. "Occasionally some spirits fail to make a safe transition to the Spirit World."

Members in the circle became quietly tense and expectant including me. How could such a thing happen? The idea renewed my still lurking fear of death. Chang whispered: "Stop thinking and listen."

Patrick explained that the World Health Organization statistics indicate on average about 141,000 people die in the world every day. The vast majority make a safe transition into the Spirit World.

"Occasionally there is a snag," he said. "It hinges largely on the emotional condition of the person in the days and hours before they die and also their long-held beliefs. There are many reasons for not making a safe and complete transition.

"One, they do not believe in God, Heaven or an afterlife, and that the Earth is their only salvation. Another is the law of attraction: they desperately desire to stay with loved ones here on Earth.

"Soldiers in battle sometimes fail to believe they are dead and simply sit around waiting for orders on the battlefield and this can go on for many years, sometimes centuries." Patrick added that this is a common occurrence at American Civil War battlefields, such as Gettysburg.

Some would-be suicides start the process of dying and suddenly panic, he went on. "No, I don't want to die," they cry and attempt to cling to life, but it is too late. In their astral body, their conscious spirit attempts to hold onto the physical. There is a snag in transition.

"Listen and I will give you instructions on how to handle an earthbound spirit," he said, "because sooner or later you will inevitably come across this phenomenon."

The operative word was "sooner," and when I think about the ensuing events in my life, I often wondered afterwards if Patrick had been primed to instruct us on earthbounds.

20

A RENDEZVOUS AND A HEALING

EVER SINCE MY HANDS had caressed the blue waters of the Mediterranean at Monte Carlo, I had envisioned myself being back in Cyprus and talking with Iro. Her image had haunted me and the next year, 1984, I took time off. The Cyprus Airways jet landed at Larnaca, and it was with some tense excitement that I looked forward to seeing her again. A taxi took me to Nicosia and I checked into the Cleopatra Hotel close to where she lived.

Jacko, the publisher of the Cyprus Mail, came over soon after my arrival and gave me a hug. We sat down at a bar table in the shade by the large pool. I had not seen him for twenty years, but he looked the same as I remembered him. Chubby, smiling and always openly honest. He never held back on news.

"Iro?" said Iacovos quietly. "Iro passed away. Five years ago. She took her own life."

The news was stunning. I felt a heavy sickness swelling inside. Iro, that slim and attractive copper-tanned Greek Cypriot lady I had met on a steamship in Beirut harbor so many years ago. Our romance had flourished like a beautiful red rose coming out of the mist. I was coming out of the Royal Air Force and heading for a life in journalism and news photography, and she, approaching middle age was battling loneliness in a society that was not developed to recognize single women approaching forty. But Iro had been my first love and it seemed the right thing to do. I recalled that day at the Commissioner's Office when he married us, just a few months before Cyprus became a war zone - Greek Cypriots shouting for Enosis and fighting the British colonial administration.

I did not know where to look. I stared at the pool, the blue sky, the palm trees, then back at Jacko. Tears welled in my eyes. My vision had been shattered.

"Iro had a relationship with a stockbroker and she lost everything. Five years ago. She took an overdose of drugs," said Jacko. "I ran into her in Fereos's and she looked sad and said she was sick." Jacko and Iro had been in the same class at school.

"She's buried at the cemetery. Up the hill, on the Larnaca Road."

Stunned and totally disillusioned, I spent the evening wandering through the dark streets of the city. I could not believe it had happened, and more, it had happened five years before. I wondered why no one had told me.

Then a rational mind asked: What could you have done about it? Over the years I had longed to see her, talk to her, feel her presence and try and figure out where we had gone wrong. We had possessed such a beautiful relationship, a strange love affair, but nevertheless something beautiful and memorable. In the hotel that night, it was a long time before sleep brought some relief.

A VISIT TO AN OLD CEMETERY

The next afternoon I wandered through the dusty old cemetery, its mass of white headstones basking in the autumn sunshine. Iro had been buried with her mother and father. The cemetery appears strangely crowded, simply because there is a shortage of space.

A SPIRIT RESCUE OF SOMEONE SPECIAL:
It was in this quiet but crowded Nicosia Cemetery that the author found the earthbound spirit of Iro, and was inducted into the practice of rescuing spirits. "It was one of the most emotional moments of my life," says the author.

It was such a quiet place. The October sun shafting through the trees and painting light beams on the white gravestones. Then something strange happened.

As I stood by her grave, I felt a powerful energy suddenly envelop me - an ugly, heavy, negative shroud, a cocoon that wanted to pull me down. A sudden wave of acute depression grasped and wrenched at my body and mind. I felt a powerful desire to die. I was drenched in an overwhelming desire to kill myself.

An urgent call pierced the depression. "It's not you! It's not you!" Chang, my healing guide suddenly echoed in my head. His words were urgent, demanding and welcome.

"She's here! You're feeling her pain and suffering. You're feeling the last experiences of her earthly life. She is - as you say - earth-bound!"

Earthbound! I had only recently heard of spirits not making the transition to the Other Side. I recalled Patrick Young's voice back in far off Vancouver.

"When people don't want to die, they feel so attached to the physical world, they refuse to go over. They refuse to look up into the light. They reject all encouragement by spirit guides and loved ones in Spirit to look up. They get depressed and cold and they focus on looking down," said Patrick, "That keeps them earthbound."

Just imagine what it would be like to get caught in a dream-like state where you can see and hear loved ones but they cannot hear you. And worse, loved ones cannot touch you or even acknowledge you are there. It is terrifying.

The unfortunate earth-bound spirit is caught in a nightmare existence between the two worlds. An overwhelming frustration escalates and turns to anger. He or she becomes intensely cold. That is why if you have an earthbound spirit around the house, the cold will be noticeable in one or more rooms.

"Iro failed to cross over?" I called to Chang, as I battled the heaviness and a growing nausea.

"No, she didn't want to die. She enjoyed living, as you know," said the old Chinese doctor. "In a moment of weakness she started the suicide and then attempted to stop it, but it was too late. She has ended up neither in the home of the Spirit World, nor in the physical world."

I could feel Chang's healing hands piercing the depression.

"You are here to help her," he continued. "You recall Patrick's instructions?"

Panic! I tried to think back. Listening to a medium's words in class is one thing; actually doing a spirit rescue is another.

"We'll help you, Bob," said Chang reassuringly.

Guided by Chang, I first offered a prayer to Holy Spirit, asking for guidance, strength and protection. His voice urged me: "No judging now, no criticism. That's earth-ways. Be spiritual and loving."

Taking a deep breath to ease a thumping heart, I addressed Iro, my old love from so long ago. It was totally strange. I could feel her incredibly heavy presence, so frustrated, so unhappy.

"Dearest Iro, I am here because I love you - always have - and there are others in Spirit who love you and want to help you. I am feeling your hurts, sharing your pain but it's time to go, and it's all right to go."

There is a special place, a loving place and all you have to do is look up...look up and you will see a beautiful, pure light." Her presence intensified. Suddenly she was clinging to me, like a frightened child. She had found someone who could talk to her, understand her plight, someone she once loved, and now she didn't want to let go.

"Stress the fact that once in Heaven, she can always return to visit loved ones here in harmony and love," Chang prompted me.

I talked to her, repeating what Chang had said. I suggested to her that when she became settled with loved ones in Heaven, she could - on a better day, a better time - return to talk. Then I continued to urge her to look up into the special light, that beautiful cosmic energy above her head.

"Look up, dearest Iro. Look up! You will find your mother Efterpi and your father, and other loved ones all waiting to greet you." I could sense her mother standing close by the grave.

I have no idea how the words came. I sensed that Chang was working with my energy, but all the words that came from my mouth seemed right. "There will be others, kind, beautiful helpers who will help you to understand the situation that occurred here on the Earth Plain. They do not judge you; they only wish to help you. They love you. I love you. Always have."

After several minutes of talking, building her confidence, I felt she was ready to look up into the light. "You have the power to release yourself from this earth by holding up your head and looking into the beautiful light that is above you," I said slowly. "It is a beautiful, warm and loving light. Look up, dear Iro. Look up, and go towards the light."

Prompted by Chang, I repeated these words several times. For some time, I sensed her continuing resistance to go. She feared the unknown.

"Build up her self-confidence and her energy will lighten," advised Chang. Some fifteen minutes after I had started - it seemed like an hour - I sensed a change in the energy. "She's coming up. She's looking up," whispered Chang, "You can feel it. Feel it and learn, my friend." The invisible blanket of heaviness, cold and nausea, floated strangely upward like a rising cloud. The depression was easing and moving away.

The moment Iro looked up into that beautiful orb of Cosmic energy, the lifting started. It was powerful. Firm, loving hands of Spirit helpers reached down from the Astral World to take her up. Suddenly that ugly, heavy, clammy cold was gone. The welcoming warmth of the Mediterranean sun enveloped me.

Chang did not have to tell me: "She's with us now, Bob. She's safe. She's back home! Welcome to the healing faculty of spirit rescue."

A VASE OF YELLOW AND WHITE FLOWERS

Now the old cemetery became quiet and the sun's rays filtered through the trees and caressed the white grave stones. Shaken and exhausted by my sudden and unexpected introduction into spirit rescue, I wandered slowly round the Greek Cypriot cemetery, almost in a daze.

I sat on a monument for some minutes, then visited several other graves of old friends, including that of Robin Parker, an ex-paratrooper whose great desire was to be a sculptor of Greek Cypriot gods, but chose instead to be a proof reader at the Cyprus Mail. On most days while working, he would easily consume an entire bottle of one star Cyprus brandy but he never, ever failed to work and never appeared intoxicated.

I returned to Iro's grave. She was no longer there. The air was clear. At a Cypriot flower shop outside the cemetery, I asked the old lady in charge to create a vase of yellow and white flowers. Then I went back and placed them on Iro's grave. I concluded my rendezvous with a prayer for her safe care in the Spirit World.

A QUIET TIME IN A MONASTERY

In the days that followed I looked for a place of peace and found it in an ancient monastery on a small mountain overlooking the town of Larnaca and the Mediterranean. A taxi took me up the winding, dusty road to Stavrovouni which was manned at that time by an abbot and some dozen monks. Greek Orthodox, the monks only spoke if you asked a question. They rose at 2.30

STAVROVOUNI MONASTERY:
the Mountain of the Cross is where the
author spent several days following the
Spirit Rescue of his beloved Iro.

a.m. every day and participated in a sunrise service. They toiled in their hillside gardens and were devout vegetarians.

It is said that Emperor Constantine's mother, St. Helena created the place and left a part of the Cross here which she had found in Jerusalem. Today, it is embedded in a silver cross. And strangely, women are only allowed into the monastery on Sundays, to attend regular services. Stavrovouni in Greek means "Mountain of the Cross."

I stayed there for almost a week, sleeping in a cell, which was also a store for watermelons. Each night the abbot brought me a small flask of Commandaria, the sweet Cyprus wine said to have originated with the Knights of St. John and the Knights Templar.

And every night as I was going to sleep on the hard cot, I could hear soft lute music and a woman's voice in the distance. But when I asked the monks about it, they shrugged and walked away shaking their heads.

Three weeks later back in Vancouver the incident involving Iro had healed and subsided, and I really didn't want to tell people that my former wife had taken her own life. I just let it go.

Two weeks later while sitting in the Friday night closed circle, Patrick Young said suddenly: "Bob, may I come to you? There is a slim, dark-tanned lady here, and she has a message for you. It's very simple and she says you will understand: Her message is: 'Thank you for the flowers."

That night I went home stunned and elated: (1) Iro was doing well on the Other Side, and (2) I had received another, very meaningful assurance of continuous life on the other side of death. A validation! I did not sleep for some time. A thought kept flowing through my mind: "Wherever you are, dear Iro. Thanks."

THE EPITOME OF A KINK IN THE COSMOS

Then another thought sparkled in my mind. In the process of rescuing Iro, I had addressed Holy Spirit! God! The Universal Mind! The Creator! Somehow, it had just happened. Even in taking messages from spirits at readings and in public meetings, I had continued to deny that there was a God, but at the right time, when faced with an extraordinary situation, I had cut to the chase and addressed Holy Spirit. For some reason it felt right. Very right.

Looking back on the event of that day I realized that the whole thing, being inspired by touching the water at Monte Carlo in 1983, I was being set up by the Cosmic Forces. It might appear devious to some, but it is always for the common good. In the following year I had not mentioned going to Cyprus in the autumn, but a couple of weeks before I departed Vancouver for Cyprus, Patrick had given us an intensive and practical instruction of spirit rescue so that when I arrived in Cyprus, I would be a functional spirit rescuer. Somebody, somewhere in the Cosmos, decided it was right for me to rescue Iro, and more importantly, talk to God, the Creator, Infinite Intelligence. That, dear friends, is the epitome of a kink in the Cosmos, a sequence of events.

MORE SPIRIT RESCUES

Following the Cyprus incident, it was as if a door had suddenly been opened. Over the ensuing weeks and years I became involved in dozens of spirit rescues. Some simple, some complicated.

A three-year old boy told his mother: "A man sits at the end of my bed and sings me to sleep every night." While talking to the mother, a man in spirit appeared behind her. She identified it as her father, and the boy's grandfather. "He died last year of cancer," she said. "He didn't want to go. He had so many plans. He enjoyed singing."

While her husband and the boy went to visit neighbors, we sat in the basement workshop - the father loved his basement workshop - and with the help of Infinite Intelligence and Chang, I got the man to see the light and go up. I said everything out loud for the boy's mother to hear.

Afterwards, she exclaimed: "It's peculiar. The place is now much warmer." Earthbound spirits can stay around for years. Time appears to have no meaning. Once, while in Patrick Young's circle, I felt the close presence of a young woman, almost sitting on my lap.

"She says her name is Janet and she was murdered," I told the group. She gave details. The way she talked she was in the 1920s and thought it was still that era, yet in reality she had been earthbound for sixty years. Again, we helped her to go into the loving white light. Isabel Corlett identified her as a Janet Smith, a victim of a well publicized mystery.

While spirit rescue is beautiful, healing and caring work, it does have its hazards. A young family complained they were losing pacifiers at the rate of several a day, and this had been happening for weeks. "The place is haunted," said the mother.

While visiting the house, I spotted a young girl in spirit peeping round the kitchen door. Five years old. A flowery dress, white socks and black shoes adorned her small body. A large sun-hat kept materializing on her blonde hair then disappearing. She kept peeking at me slyly.

Her name was Annie and she tried to explain the illness that had taken her whole family away. They were farmers and lived a short distance up the hill. She thought the year was 1919. I recalled reading about the disastrous Spanish flu, a pandemic that claimed half a million lives in the United States and 50 million lives world-wide.

The little girl said her mother always gave her pacifiers. I asked her to go into the light, and she went easily. Twenty-four hours later, I realized I had made a mistake. I should have asked: "Are you by yourself or are there others?" The next day, the family in the house called me. "There's trouble. There are spirits all over the place, and they feel angry." Unable to go because I had pulled a muscle while jogging, I asked a Spiritualist minister living nearby to help out. He did, and the next day called me back: "They were mad with you because you took their daughter away. They are all right now; the whole family is on the Other Side."

The lesson I learned: always ask questions. Never let anything in spirit communications become routine. Also, always work with your guides. Over the years, various spirit rescues have come my way.

A CAFÉ RENDEZVOUS IN SEATTLE

Some time after the Cyprus rescue with Iro, I was sitting alone in a coffee shop in Seattle, Washington State, when I suddenly felt a presence. Her voice was clear. It was Iro in spirit.

Over the next little while she shared a fascinating amount of information of what happens to a spirit that has become earthbound. "To be earthbound is a terrifying phenomenon," she said. It's like being lost in a dream. People you have known don't respond. Close relatives - my sister for instance - had no idea I was in front of her, talking to her, desperately seeking her attention.

"It's worse than a nightmare because it's endless. I recall my anger growing and becoming pure rage - and everything felt cold, bitterly cold. There's a real problem when an earthbound is in this state – they attract other earthbounds with similar negative energies," she said. "But the worst part is that people you know and love, fail to respond to your calls for help."

Iro paused and I could feel her hands touching mine. "So when I heard your voice and knew you could feel my presence, it was like a ray of beautiful light. I had never wanted so much to hear from someone I knew – then it was you."

"Since I have been in the Higher World, many earthbounds have shared similar experiences with me. They all seem to have had similar heartbreaking experiences."

Iro continued: "When I reached the Higher World, I felt bruised and hurt and terribly disoriented. My experiences in your world from the death of my physical body until the time I arrived in the Light, created my own personal hell," she said. "After my initial greeting where I met my mother and father and relatives and friends who had crossed over, I was assigned a wonderful, loving entity, a teacher named Talbot. He worked with me and showed me how to let the natural healing work. One learns how to radiate love, not for any reason because it's right or wrong, but simply because it's the natural thing to do. You radiate love not to please anyone, but because it puts you into the mainstream of Being. If you are quoting me put a capital on Being." She grinned.

"You're still bossy," I nodded. Iro was a difficult woman to forget. "In the Higher World one sees Earth not through the eyes of ego or possessiveness, but through an understanding of what other spirits in physical clothing are going through," she said. "We learn to send them love, unconditional love. We do not judge. That's an affliction of physical life. I wish I had known such teachings while I was on your side. You must write a book, Bob."

VOLUNTEERS WHO WORK WITH SPIRITS

"Spirit rescue, as you call it, is very important," said Iro. "There are many spirits caught between our two worlds and they all have the common desire - they weren't ready to come over. It's not just suicides, or people suffering fatal catastrophic diseases, but those whose lives are terminated by war, famine, disasters, and such situations.

"On this side there are special guides, counselors, teachers, doctors, nurses who volunteer to work with spirits who have had trouble with transition. I am one such counselor," she added. A warm sensation shimmered over my hands. "Caught between the two worlds, one loses track of time. For instance, I had no idea it was five of your earth years before you helped me.

"There are many spirits who have been caught between the two worlds for many years. We are still receiving spirits from World War One, the Napoleonic Wars, American Civil War, and even earlier. Time has no meaning when you are in spirit.

"Urge your people to develop and train spirit rescuers. It is hard work but the insights one gets and the feeling of healing and satisfaction are great, as you well know, Bob."

"Our old friend Iacovos, the newspaper publisher, was here and has gone on. He was so happy to be reunited with his wife, Effie. They are still so busy." She laughed lightly and it brought back memories of a time long ago, when we reclined in the shade of the Venetian fortress at Kyrenia Harbor, swam and chased baby octopuses in the sparklingly clear Mediterranean, and picked and ate oranges in the garden at Nicosia.

For a moment, I thought Iro had gone, but she was still there, thinking. "You remember the Nicosia house I was building, the one with the picturesque turret, when we parted our ways?"

I nodded. "I took a photo of it. It's now a young children's school." "Well, in the Higher World we have the power to create our own dwellings. I have recreated it and it now overlooks the water. I always wanted a home overlooking the water," she said softly. "When you have finished your work on Earth, you will come and visit."

"Absolutely," I replied. "I'll be beating on your door. Do you still have those alluring deserts – what do you call them – Turkish Delight?"

"Loukoumi!" Iro snapped. "You've forgotten your Greek!" A moment later she was gone.

21

FROM RAILS INTO MEDITATION

B ACK AT THE VANCOUVER Rapid Transit offices, the Board of Directors had invited twelve firms to come up with a name for the new rapid transit system. Several came up with "Spirit" and while this was not entirely appropriate for the rapid transit system as a whole, Premier Bill Bennett caught on and decided it would be appropriate to recognize communities in the Lower Mainland. Thus, we had the "Spirit of New West Minister," "Spirit of Coquitlam" and so on.

Except for the Dunsmuir Tunnel under the City of Vancouver, the trains would be zipping along elevated concrete guideways, giving an impression of almost flying through the sky. So the name "SkyTrain" was adopted, and it seemed to make sense.

Throughout 1985 the stations started to take shape. The downtown stations at Burrard and Granville were deep underground while the others were either elevated or at ground level.

While SkyTrain was being built, the old Canadian Pacific railyards had been cleared and construction was going full speed ahead for Expo 86, when the world would come to Vancouver and British Columbia. Exhibition centers for various countries and business were taking shape. The most noticeable and it is still there, is the geodesic dome in the shape of a golf ball from the design of R. Buckminster Fuller. A glistening mirrored orb, it housed the Expo Center and later became the Science Center. It is served by the Main Street station.

One aspect of SkyTrain that needs to be mentioned is that the line saw the first application of the Linear Induction Motor or LIM as it was known on a rapid transit system. It has no moving parts. No gears or transmissions and operates independently of wheels and axles. There is some detailed information on how the original twelve mile project blossomed into a massive network serving Greater Vancouver on Wikipedia.

MOVIES ON THE NEW SYSTEM

During my time on the Project, we produced two films and JEM Productions did the shooting. A whole pile of people from the Premier's Office, down to my office, did the scripting which is probably why it never made the Academy Awards. Called "Going to Town" it tells the stories of various people boarding a train and arriving downtown. When they arrive in their workplaces, you see who they are. One was an NFL player, another a musician, another a secretary and so on. It ran twenty-nine minutes and was released at the launching of SkyTrain in December 1985.

A MOMENT TO REMEMBER IN ITALY

The second film happened almost by accident. I recalled the BBC Television News Film Unit's 1952 production which showed a Southern Railway train leaving London and arriving in Brighton four minutes later. The train raced along the tracks with dizzying and exciting speed. (Last time I looked it was on Youtube.com) I recalled this old movie, told Jem Productions and they filmed from the front of Skytrain running non-stop twelve miles to New Westminster. It came over with the train racing at dizzying speeds.

So now, what to do with it? We had lots and lots of out-takes from the making of "Going to Town" and David Brown suggested these be used as a salute to the work force that built the original SkyTrain Project. It was very worker-oriented with a ten minute running time.

A short time later, the transit authorities in Bologna, Italy were having a national conference and asked for a representative to attend and speak on SkyTrain. Mike O'Connor designated me and added: "Take the little movie." I did. There were 500 people packed in the hall. The organizers provided instant interpreters for the delegates who were all wearing headsets. Then we showed the movie which has no voice track, simply music. The title: "Thanks for a Better City."

At the end, all these Italian transit officials jumped up and gave a standing applause that seemed to go on for ever. As we went to lunch with the convention chairman, I asked why the tremendous show of applause.

He grinned knowingly. "Why? Most of them are Communists and they approve of Canadians making a movie thanking the workers." It was a moment to remember.

When I got to the Leonardo da Vinci Airport in Rome for the trip home, there was a strike of ground personnel. Nothing could be loaded. A British Airways captain came over the PA system. "I'm taking my kite out in ten minutes. If you want a ride, walk out onto the apron and climb aboard." We did, each carrying our own bags, and flew to London with a couple of beers. There was no food. So much for workers. They make life interesting.

I wrote a 22-page illustrated book for B.C. Transit at a time when SkyTrain was acting as a catalyst for development. If one looks at general views of communities along the original line taken prior to 1983 and looks at the same views, the communities are almost unrecognizable. I spent many an hour with reporters explaining the advantages of rapid transit systems in communities, but many failed to recognize the enormous potential until commercial development swept through the communities in the wake of SkyTrain.

THE SOCIAL CREDIT RAIL SHOW

Expo 86 came and went. Premier Bill Bennett and the Social Credit Government excelled in the opening SkyTrain. It was pure show business. Three grand openings, in one morning. The Opening Train, decorated with flags and ribbons, took Mr. Bennett and a cluster of VIPs along the track. There were openings and speeches at Waterfront in downtown Vancouver, Metrotown in Burnaby and at New Westminster. That was in December 1985.

RIDING THE RAILS ON SKYTRAIN:
The Minister Responsible for SkyTrain was the Hon. Grace McCarthy who took great delight in talking to many of the SkyTrain riders. Here, Mrs. McCarthy talks to a student, while the author stands smiling in the background. The Minister always created interesting waves that kept the PR people busy.

Then in the summer of 1986, Queen Elizabeth and Prince Philip came and rode on SkyTrain and we – the staff – could not get near them. Chairman Stuart Hodgson, a "friend of Buckingham Palace" escorted the Royal visitors along with the usual political elements.

THE INFORMATION TEAM AT SKYTRAIN:
As the start of SkyTrain drew closer, Sandra Brennan hired more information attendants.
Pictured here at Stadium Station in July 1985 are Diane Hughes, Sandra Brennan, Sharon Underhill and Bobbi Lochansky.

During Expo, when the world came to visit Vancouver, we had a great rapid transit exhibition at Stadium Station which attracted thousands of people to watch the "Going to Town" movie, along with scores of great construction pictures taken by Perspectives Five photographer Colin Jewall and myself. Sandra Brennan picked some hard-working, dedicated Information Attendants including Sharon Underhill, Bobbi Lochansky, Scott Stinson, Brady McNamara and Julia Downs.

Looking back, it was a strange phenomenon that drew together a team of publicists to promote a phenomenal rapid transit system which has bludgeoned today into a metropolitan wide system for helping the Lower Mainland communities develop and prosper. This team included Ray Dykes who was the head PR at BC Place Stadium, George Madden who was the Senior PR for Expo 86, Jane Duncan a marketing specialist with the Regional District transportation branch, and one fine Aussie journalist named Bob Williamson, who was always there with ideas and writing assistance in good and bad times. The Vancouver media and others called our PR group "The

Mega-Flacks." Whatever, we all worked together to put on the best show imaginable – Expo 86. It was sad to see all these talented folks disappear into their own lives as Expo closed and went back to clearing up the paper-clogged offices and other relics that had accumulated.

SKYTRAIN — MY FIRST BOOK

Even as SkyTrain was under construction, so too was the private sector developing places along the corridor. The old docks overlooking the Fraser River at New Westminster were converted almost overnight, it seemed, to flocks of stylish townhouses and apartment blocks within easy walking distance of the SkyTrain station. Similar developments took place around Burnaby's Metrotown Station which included a mega-shopping center. East Vancouver and downtown saw major development projects and at the downtown Waterfront terminal there was a cluster of mega-developments. Canada Place was built between SkyTrain and the Burrard Inlet. It became the home of the Vancouver Convention Centre, the Pan Pacific Hotel and Vancouver's World Trade Centre. It is also a major Cruise Ship Terminal.

All of these things were predicted as the first SkyTrain project took shape. As SkyTrain served Expo 86 and went on to a growing ridership, and the economy flourished in the corridor, using my cameras I rode and hiked up and down the corridor taking color slides of economic developments. From those I produced an audio-visual show on growth around SkyTrain. I also wrote my first book for B.C. Transit, entitled "On Track, the SkyTrain Story," a 24-page publication. These projects brought letters of commendations from Minister, the Hon, Grace McCarthy and APTA, the American Passenger Transport Association.

"On Track" was available on Amazon.com for a number of years before going out of print.

RAPID TRANSIT CREATES A BETTER ECONOMY:
Up intil the middle 1980s New Westminster docks were largely deserted warehouses and wharfs. With the advent of SkyTrain the entire scene changed almost overnight as apartment blocks, homes, hotels and a market sprang up. And this was just the first phase of SkyTrain completed in 1985. The author took these photographs while preparing an audio-visual show for B.C. Transit.

As I write this chapter, SkyTrain has developed even more than we ever imagined back in the early 1980s. Built for the Expo 86 World's Fair, it has since become the world's longest automated light rapid transit system utilizing double tracks and serving the Greater Vancouver metropolitan region. The system uses the same family of linear induction motor-driven trains as the Scarborough RT line in Toronto, the Putra LRT in Kuala Lumpur, Malaysia, and the JFK AirTrain in New York. It is a tribute to those early pioneers who ardently believed in the system and what it could do for British Columbia – Mike O'Connor, Tom Parkinson, Larry Miller, Bob Tribe, Hon. Grace McCarthy, Hon. Jack Davis and the team that worked round the clock to get that initial SkyTrain Service up and running in 1986.

A CHALLENGE FOR A SEER

One day, when the Board of B.C. Transit was gathered to hear and decide on financial advisers and auditors for the Corporation, a vice president, Bob Lingwood came into my office on the executive floor at the B.C. Transit head office in South Vancouver and said: "You're the psychic seer. Who are they going to select?"

I had the list of about nine company names and so I pulled out my pendulum, and it gave me the answer. "Not one but two," I said. "B.C. Transit will contract two companies." I named them.

Lingwood shook his head. "I don't know how you do it," he said as he left my office. "It boggles the mind." I was right.

How did I get from the Project Office in downtown Vancouver to the corporate offices in south Vancouver?

Well, with Skytrain operating with its own management and staff, the original construction project was disbanded and Chairman Stuart Hodgson appointed me as "Media Counsel to the Chairman" which was fine for the time being. Trouble was, the work load did not ease up.

In the fall of 1986 the Social Credit politicians were seeking a re-election with a new leader, Bill Vander Zalm and they wanted all the help they could get, so I was given the task of writing elements of speeches for politicians and others.

One was for the visit of Ralph Nader, the consumer affairs advocate speaking to business people in Vancouver; another was for Jean Chretien who was running for the leadership of the Federal Liberal Party in 1990. Chretien ultimately became Canada's 20th Prime Minister. How I got these writing assignments, I never did find out. It was one of the mysteries of B.C.

Transit. I sometimes wondered who I was working for, which was a little disconcerting. But there was always something happening and I think Chairman Stu Hodgson had a lot to do with it.

A FADING MARRIAGE

Was I married? Some days it felt I was and other days I had trouble remembering. Myra had become involved in her work as an adjuster at the Insurance Corporation of British Columbia and was now studying to become a bodily injury adjuster that required one to study extensively and be conversant with a giant book called "Gray's Anatomy: The Anatomical Basis of Clinical Practice." It had well over 1,500 pictures of parts of the human body and was described as "the most anatomical atlas available." For the layman to browse its pages is mind-boggling and I often wondered how Myra had the mental dexterity to spend countless hours over the book. She accomplished a promotion to B.I. Adjuster which took her into a new area of auto insurance.

Now as the urgency of my work at B.C. Transit was reduced, I found time to visit England and my sisters Sheila and Diane. At that time both had become certified hypnoanalysts, a profession that intrigued and appealed to me, mainly because I had already studied various forms of meditation and altered states of consciousness.

Diane drove me to see Stonehenge on Salisbury Plain and afterwards we had lunch at a vegetarian restaurant in Salisbury. "That was fascinating," I said, "to see those old stones. I could feel the energies of the druids and the Celts."

"You need to go to Glastonbury," Diane said suddenly. "Something tells me you need to go."

"That's strange you say that. When I first visited the Vancouver Psychic Society in February 1979 – seven years ago – the first words Isabell Corlett said to me were – 'Hello Bob, we were together in Glastonbury.' Then she added – 'In a couple of past lives. You still have work to do there.' I shrugged. I had no idea what she was talking about."

Diane was enthused. "It's time you remembered. We'll go there tomorrow, and I'll tell you about it on the way."

22

THE GLASTONBURY CONNECTION

A S SOON AS WE walked along Mary Magdalene Street and turned into the main gate of the Abbey, two things happened. I found an absolute peace in my mind and body. It was almost like a trance. Still and silent. The second phenomenon was that I knew I had been here before, not in this lifetime, but in times long ago. But I digress. Let's start at the beginning.

Glastonbury, the Isle of Avalon and its famous Tor, a grass covered hill built by the ancient Druids, is tucked away amid the gentle rolling hills of Somerset in England's West Country. It attracts pilgrims from all over the world. To many, it is a holy shrine. Some call it the "New Jerusalem." Others see it as a mystical and psychic vortex. Numerous books have claimed it is the last resting place of the saints. For many years, Glastonbury's status was an embarrassment to its owners, the Church of England.

Glastonbury is a giant mosaic of numerous legends—several extremely controversial as I discovered. At its peak, Glastonbury had 2,000 people, 500 of them monks. It was powerful among the abbeys and monasteries of England. In 1539 King Henry VIII ordered Glastonbury totally destroyed under the general Dissolution of the Abbeys. Its great stones were hauled away to be used for buildings, walls and roads.

Glastonbury is known for its ancient leylines, invisible power lines stretching across England pass through Glastonbury. It's also known for its Zodiac, a peculiar land formation spanning 12 miles. And here's the catch: It can only be seen and appreciated from thousands of feet up. Question: Why does it exist? Was it a space signal?

Glastonbury is also the last resting place of King Arthur. His remains were found there in 1191, and reburied with ceremony under the eye of an English monarch.

Arthurian legends abound at Glastonbury, and many books have been written on Arthur. In 1662 Joseph of Arimathea's tomb was found and promptly hidden again for fear of Puritanical reactions. In recent years, the descriptions and measurements provided by the monks in spirit to Bligh

Bond have been subjected to mathematical scrutiny. The dimensions of Joseph's original church and chapels–all circular–contain cosmic power.

AN ABSOLUTE PEACE OF MIND:
The author stands at The Galilee, the entrance into the remains of the ancient Glastonbury Abbey in Somerset, England where an eternal aura of peace prevails.

For instance, the diameter of a circle positioned within a square of Joseph's compound is 79.20 feet. Change feet to miles – 7920 – and you have the diameter of the Earth. There are many cosmic numbers associated with Glastonbury, such as all measurements, whether in Celt, Roman, Jewish and English, all reduce to nine, a most powerful number in numerology.

HOW THE LEGENDS STARTED

The legends of Glastonbury are undying and appealing. They center around Joseph of Arimathea, a rich merchant who donated his prepared tomb for the crucified body of Jesus. He has a brief mention in the New Testament, but Jewish texts indicate he owned a fleet of ships that traded into "the Isles" – present day, Britain, and in particular Cornwall and Somerset. Ancient Cornish mines provided valuable tin and the Somerset mines provided lead for the Roman army weapon builders. Tin and lead from England and copper from Cyprus were used to make bronze.

It is said that Joseph was an uncle of Jesus and took the boy with him on voyages to Cornwall and Somerset. Readers of the Bible will recall there is an eighteen year absence in Jesus' life between twelve and thirty. If you think that one of the greatest spiritual teachers for humanity did not travel, it's best to think again.

WATER FROM THE HISTORIC WELL:
The Glastonbury Well is steeped in Christian tradition. It is said that Joseph of Arimathea hid the Chalice here, hence the name – Chalice Well. The spring produces 25,000 gallons of water a day, year round, and never fails. The water runs through old healing baths and also a fount where one can drink or touch the water. Here the author's sister, Diane Egby-Edwards, a frequent visitor to Glastonbury feels the energy of the water.

Glastonbury was an ancient Celtic and Druid center, and as many visitors have discovered, it is a psychic vortex, similar to Stonehenge in Wiltshire, Sedona in Arizona, Mount Ararat in Turkey, Macchu Picchu in Peru and other points around the world. The vortexes generate powerful positive energy and most sensitives can feel it easily. I once saw a long-haired young man stand on the Tor at Glastonbury, and his hair flowed straight up as he was caught in the vortex. The Celts built the famous Tor at Glastonbury.

Was it this Cosmic power that drew Jesus to Glastonbury? Whatever it was, it is said Jesus built a small temple, a chapel, a place for worship out of wattle, which is the weaving of branches and twigs to form a construction. Legend has it that Jesus prayed and meditated here as he conversed with the druids. It was a special place.

A BOAT CAST ADRIFT

After the crucifixion, the followers of Jesus were hunted down, persecuted and murdered by the Sanhedrin, the Jewish Council. St. Stephen was the first at Jerusalem. Even though Joseph of Arimathea was a Sanhedrin councilor, he was arrested and with a group of close friends beloved by Jesus, placed in a boat without oars, cast adrift and left to the mercy of the elements.

Who was in the boat with Joseph? Well, George Jowett, in his classic book "The Drama of the Lost Disciples," refers to Cardinal Caesar Baronius, Curator of the Vatican Library in his Ecclesiastical Annals (Circa 1600 A.D.) Baronius named them as: St. Mary, wife of Cleopas; St. Matha; St. Lazarus; St. Eutropius; St. Salome; St. Clean; St. Saturnius; St. Mary Magdalene; Marcella, the Bethany sisters maid; St. Maximin; St. Martial; St. Trophimus; St. Sidonius (Restitutus) and Joseph of Arimathea.

Jowett notes that many other sources insist there was another member of Joseph's party in the boat, not recorded in the Cardinal's Mistral report. It was Mary, the mother of Jesus. According to sources, St. John appointed Joseph of Arimathea "paranymphos" to the mother of Jesus because John was a hunted man and not in a position to care for Mary. As paranymphos, it was Joseph's responsibility to look after the mother of Jesus; therefore she was in the boat too.

The boat, with its occupants, was found by druids in the Marseilles area of southern France, and given escort to England, where Joseph and his group made their way to the safety of Glastonbury. It should be mentioned that Glastonbury was situated in the extensive marshes, generally impenetrable by Roman soldiers. The area was drained and reclaimed by monks centuries later.

It was here that Joseph set up a refuge and evangelical center. He trained and sent missionaries to various parts of Britain and Europe, where they taught the mystical teachings of Jesus. Bishop Ussher, (1581-1656) the controversial Irish clergyman in "Britannicarum Ecclesiarum Antiquitates" wrote: "The British National Church was founded A.D. 36, 160 years before heathen Rome confessed Christianity."

A SPECIAL PLACE FOR MEDITATION

It was on the site of the original wattle chapel created by the boy Jesus that Joseph constructed a church, and the present church on that site dates back to Norman times. Incidentally, Henry the Eighth, whose war with Rome resulted in the Dissolution of the Monasteries, reduced the Glastonbury center to ruins, but somehow, perhaps by a kink in the Cosmos, the Chapel of

St. Joseph, now better known as Our Lady's Chapel was preserved almost intact. Every time I visit Glastonbury I head to the Chapel and meditate there.

THE HEART OF GLASTONBURY ABBEY:
Pictured above is St. Mary's Chapel, sometimes called "Joseph's Chapel." It is the traditional place where Jesus, accompanied by his uncle Joseph of Arimathea built a small wattle church in honor of his Mother. Pictured below in the lower level of the Chapel is the altar where pilgrims may meditate, pray or simply let go.

During my ten years at B.C. Transit in Vancouver, I made several visits to Glastonbury. I used my talents as a photographer to take color slides that tell the story of the Abbey. But Glastonbury isn't just about Jesus and the Celtic/druidic connection, there's much more decorating the tableau.

For instance, St. Patrick came from Ireland to finish his days there, and is buried at Glastonbury. A number of ancient kings and saints are also interred there. St. Joseph's tomb was discovered there, including his sarcophagus in 1928.

In 1907 the Church of England bought the place and hired a specialist in medieval architecture, Frederick Bligh Bond to excavate the ruins buried under centuries of earth. Bond consulted a psychic specializing in automatic writing. John Bartlett and various monks in spirit came through. They said they were "Watchers from the Other Side" and in several sessions revealed images of the old abbey and where the remains were under the earth. Bond found them as the spirits dictated and in 1922 published a book "The Gates of Remembrance" detailing his work. Totally embarrassed, the Church of England promptly fired him and covered up his discoveries until after World War II.

THE STRANGE CASE OF THE GLASTONBURY ZODIAC

In 1935 an artist named Katherine Maltwood flew over Glastonbury and discovered a fascinating phenomenon. A twelve mile radius around Glastonbury comprising hills, water-courses, woods, old tracks and lanes and ancient stones laid out a complete form of the zodiac. It can only be seen from the air. It raised the intriguing question, who in history would want to see a zodiac from thousands of feet above the Earth. Katherine called it the Temple of the Stars. It is well described with pictures in Mary Caine's book "The Glastonbury Zodiac: Key to the Mysteries of Britain."

Now, how is this for a coincidence? One day around 1990 I was having lunch with some friends from B.C. Transit in an old Tudor-style restaurant at Royal Oak near Victoria on Vancouver Island. While we were reviewing the menu, I suddenly felt the presence again, and a woman's voice murmured, "Ask about Katherine Maltwood."

Baffled that this should happen, I finally stopped the lady serving at table and asked her, "What does the name Katherine Maltwood mean to this place?"

The server stopped and smiled. "Oh, Katherine Maltwood came here from England just before World War II. This was her home and gallery until she died in 1961. You can see some of her work in the next room." And so it was. When one tunes into the Cosmos, wonders never cease.

TREKKING THROUGH ANCIENT MINES

But to get back to narration. Here I was in Glastonbury on a self-imposed photo and research assignment. The pictures of Glastonbury Abbey were fine, but I felt the urge to explore places where it was reported by tradition that Jesus visited.

In a cold November, I trekked through the remains of the tin mines scattered along the Cornish Coast. The buildings, relics of a bygone age looked stark, dark and miserable. There is a coastal hiking trail which provides some spectacular views of the mines and the sea. At one time, eighty foot waves were beating on the rocks, and I got drenched as I hiked the path a couple of hundred feet above. The moors are dotted with holes leading to the ancient mines. Some are roped off with warnings; others are not even marked, so one has to be careful.

I meditated on a rock overlooking the ruins of an old mine where its shafts went under the Atlantic Ocean. I could well imagine the miners working with the Atlantic storms beating overhead. But in my meditation I sensed the presence of the ancients. Was it psychometry that brought back a vision of several one-masted sailing vessels cruising off-shore? I could also hear voices, many voices and the sounds of metal digging and rocks falling.

I spent almost a week hiking the Cornish Coast through to Land's End. In Penzance I found "Market Jew Street" and wondered its origin. I walked the shore to St. Michael's Mount and there discovered the power of an important leyline.

Leylines are invisible power grids that cross the land. The Great Dragon Line at St. Michael's comes out of the Atlantic, crosses England cutting through Glastonbury, Bury St. Edmunds before disappearing into the North Sea. It is said ancient people used leylines to travel from one place to another. People were more sensitive in those days than today.

The ancients built spiritual sanctuaries along leylines, and when the Christians came they replaced the sanctuaries with churches and cathedrals, many of them named "St. Michael" on the lines.

You can feel the energy of the Great Dragon Line simply by standing on it, but if you have a pendulum or a pair of dowsing L-rods, they will spin like helicopter blades.

I reached Falmouth on my photo trek. It was here in 1939 on that sandy beach that I cut my ankle, and contracted the dreaded septicemia, which, according to the doctor, was going to kill me. So, here I am fifty years later, alive and on a quest.

But I felt distinctly tired. The damp air was seeping into my bones, and it left me with a distinct desire to catch the train and head back to the comforts of my sister's home in Bournemouth, but something urged me to stay the night at a bed-and-breakfast in Falmouth.

Over tea along with welcomed crumpets and cream, the little lady running the place listened to my mission. "I'm trying to get a feeling, a psychic sense that Jesus was here almost two thousand years ago."

"Are you getting a good response?"

"Yes, I feel the energy. It glows in my body like a warm light. It's very different from anything I have experienced before." Then I told her of my early work as a journalist in Jerusalem and Bethlehem and various locations in Palestine and Jordan. "It was the same there, a warm, comfortable energy even in the Church of the Holy Sepulchre in Jerusalem. The problem was in those days I didn't really believe in Jesus, God or the Afterlife."

"There is something special here," she said with a knowing smile. "You must go to St. Just in Roseland. You can take the ferry and walk to the village. There's a church there. You'll feel the warm light."

The woman told me that the centuries-old church is the focal point of a picture-postcard panorama tucked away in an equally picturesque Cornish coastal village. The tides flow into the bay in a rhythmic surge twice a day and lap at the foot of the busy graveyard flanking the old church. It's not a poor church by any stretch of the imagination. Pilgrims flock in droves to this little backwater in Cornwall.

People yearn to be buried here because of its legends, she said. The church – St. Just in Roseland – is Celtic in origin and dates back long before St. Augustine arrived to "bring Christianity" to the English Isles.

By some strange coincidence she opened a drawer and there was a copy of the church's brochure, a beautiful four-color print with several pictures. Some words contained in a box attracted my attention.

There is a legend which claims that Christ came to St. Just. The story goes that Joseph of Arimathea was a tin merchant and that when he came on business to the Fal, he brought the boy Jesus with him. During his visit, Jesus came into St. Just Pool and landed at St. Just, which it is said, was a sacred place even then and that Jesus talked to the religious leaders there. It is a persistent legend and one that crops up in several places along the Cornish coast. All that can be said is that it could have happened and that it warms the heart to have such a story associated with this lovely place.

Those were the words that next day made me take the ferry to St. Mawes but after walking some distance, the backpack seemed to become heavy and I again felt tired and was reluctant to venture further. "It's probably just another church basking in legend," I muttered.

I sat on an old wooden gate that must have dated back to Oliver Cromwell while I mulled the question: "Should I go on? Was the woman right about the energy at St. Just?"

Just then a boy came by, pushing a bicycle up the hill. He raised his arm and pointed to the road ahead. "Crikey! Look at that rainbow! Ain't she a beauty!" It was a cockney accent and completely out of place in Cornwall.

A wondrous sight indeed. A rainbow in all its glory created a perfect arc across the sky, so I walked on beside the boy and the bicycle, inspired. The rainbow, I felt, was a sign and I gazed at it for perhaps half a minute. When I turned round the cyclist had disappeared. Strange, I thought.

A RENDEZVOUS IN ROSELAND

For a start, the name Roseland has nothing to do with roses. The locals say the word probably derives from the old Cornish word "ros" or "roos" which means promontory. The Roseland was different two thousand years ago. Almost an island, ships could travel up the estuaries, drop anchor at St. Just and replenish their onboard water supplies from the well that still exists today.

St. Just Church was clearly of Celtic origin. The present church was consecrated in 1261, and during renovations a few years ago, a Roman coin of Emperor Constantine (ca. 274-337) was found.

The energy at St. Just is something special. A tropical-like air permeates everything. Palm trees grow here year round amidst an array of tropical plants in the churchyard, that flourish even in the British winter. Like Glastonbury, St. Just, because of the legend, was an attractive place for Christians to be buried and so the graveyard is full.

After browsing through the church I concluded there was little difference between this and other ancient churches. A little disappointed, I finally sat down on the flint wall by a Celtic stone cross. I felt a beautiful and relaxing peace.

"So, are you convinced?" It was a voice somewhere behind me, yet very close. I spun round. No one there. Then I realized it was my psychic senses working. "So, are you convinced?" The voice somewhat heavy and mature was persistent. It was male.

"Convinced about what?" I asked, a little annoyed that the peace was being disturbed. "That the boy Jesus was here?"

"Isn't that what you are searching for; evidence? "

"I'm putting a slide show and lecture together on the Legends of Glastonbury."

"Is that your excuse?"

Irritated, I said: "I would like to use my psychic abilities to prove that the boy Jesus and his uncle Joseph of Arimathea were here."

"Will anyone believe you? Humans are notorious unbelievers when it comes to such abilities. Many people, reading the Bible, doubt the validity of Jesus with the woman at the well."

I felt a growing impatience. "What are you trying to tell me?"

"Nothing," said the voice with a rolling laugh. "There are more important things to consider than what Jesus did or did not do." There was a prolonged silent pause. "Is your understanding of Spirit – of the Creator – any more enhanced by knowing that Jesus built a wattle church at Glastonbury, or that he came here and spoke to the Celtic elders?"

Somehow I wanted to respond philosophically but it did not materialize. The voice went on.

"When you worked in Jerusalem and filmed inside the Holy Sepulchre or walked along the Via Dolorosa where Jesus walked, did you feel spiritually enhanced?"

"It was a good and unique energy. There's a different energy in Jerusalem. Even though I was a skeptic, it gave me a warm and comfortable feeling. Many of the thousands who thronged the streets felt it." Suddenly, a thought struck me. "How do you know what I did in Jerusalem?"

"A warm, comfortable feeling?" echoed the voice, ignoring my question. "Is that all that matters? Did it enhance you spiritually?" After a brief pause, the voice continued. "You will go home and do the lectures and slides and share the warm, comfortable feeling with others. But you yourself need to study – you need to understand the teachings of Jesus. They are truly mystical and they are contained in the Sermon on the Mount."

"Hey, I'm not exactly a Christian. I follow mystical teachings. I'm really a Spiritualist"

"Excellent. Jesus wasn't a Christian either," said the voice, close to laughing. "He was a Jewish rabbi, a teacher. The Sermon on the Mount is a collection of the deep and ancient teachings he learned during his travels among the mystical elders. Study them and you will know your path. You will understand your Quest."

"Quest?"

"In a quest, the seeker looks for enlightenment, to be at one with himself or herself. To be at one with the Consciousness of the Universe – Cosmic Consciousness, the Universal Mind. Go home and study the teachings. Perform the slide shows. Allow people to be intrigued. But always remember the teachings, and one day you can share them with others. Write it like a teaching manual, no complicated philosophies, something that will help the Quester educate himself or herself. I will leave you now, but I will be back. Rest assured."

I wanted to hear more from this soft knowing voice that had suddenly gate-crashed its way into my life. "What's your name?"

"You may call me Paul. But names are of no importance, as you will see. But that will do for now."

I sensed he was about to leave. "Wait! I have an important question."

"Yes?"

"What does God look like?"

There was a distinct sigh that echoed across the churchyard. "You can't see God! What are you? Blind?"

"Wow! Have you got some learning to do," said the voice.

"All right," I put in, "what do you look like? Your voice sounds old."

Paul laughed. "Nothing in Spirit is what it seems. That's another lesson for today."

Frustrated, I cried: "I only asked a simple question. What do you look like?"

"Recall the rainbow? Well, I was the boy with the bicycle." Laughter echoed round the stone walls of the ancient church before it faded away. Then the voice came back and cried from a distance "I almost forgot- Father Roc sends his blessings."

Back in Vancouver I assembled some 150 color slides and put together a two hour show that covered most of the strange events that occurred at Glastonbury and in the west of England. Over a period of ten years I gave some fifteen shows entitled "The Incredible Legends of Glastonbury." And every time the show went on, in addition to people coming, the spirits came. One night, a bunch of monks who had served at Glastonbury in the 15th century came and one declared that Isabel Corlett, my sister Diane and I had all lived and worked at the Abbey.

This is why, whenever I return to Glastonbury, I feel totally at home.

23

BREAKING FREE AND A NEW LIFE

I T WAS 1988 AND a number of things had happened. The winds of change were blowing and I felt the urge and the need to move on. Myra and I decided to go our separate ways. She bought a neat little house in Port Moody and I found a duplex in Squamish, a village between Vancouver and Whistler. I needed exercise and had learned to ski downhill on the slopes of Blackcomb-Whistler. It was there that I found a British family who were to be my close friends. Norman and Gloria Ellott had a property management business handling the expansive chateaux and log cabins that flank the mountains at Whistler. They liked skiing and introduced me to hiking and in summer we went hiking on the spectacular trails at Garibaldi Park in the Coastal Range Mountains.

RAINBOWS END IN SQUAMISH: When the author acquired the small duplex on Perth Drive in Squamish it was named "Rainbows End," but he cannot remember why. A neat little place where meditation and development circles were held.

For some time Chang and Paul, the spirit teacher I had met at St. Just in Roseland, had been urging me to follow the higher mystical teachings. Patrick Young had several times over the years urged me to "get out of your own way," and I knew that it focused on my persistent negative ego that attracted suffering in my life.

I had been meditating and working as a psychic and medium for a number of years but still had some negative habits that destroyed relationships and hurt loved ones, friends and colleagues. Patrick Young had often told the closed circle members, "If you want to be a good medium, you have to get yourself out of the way." When someone asked him to explain that, he laughed: "You need to kill the Ego. It's your False Self. Depending on its force, it will taint your work as a medium - messages will be tainted with your inclinations, limitations and biases." Then he added: "So too will your personal lives. It is important for a person to find their True Self."

SKIING ON TOP OF THE WORLD:
In the 1980s the author took up skiing at Whistler-Blackcomb in British Columbia and had many outings on the slopes with friends Norman and Gloria Ellott. Pictured here are Norman and the author, seemingly at the top of the world.

UNDERSTANDING THE ANCIENTS

In desperation I started reading all the books that started to come my way. I discovered that the teachings I was seeking originated with the Aryans who mysteriously moved into India some 10,000 years ago. Some sources say they were the survivors of Atlantis. Whatever their origin, they knew the difference between the Negative Self – the False Self and the True Self. Over the centuries, the teachings were generally forgotten, but a thread was kept and confined to the mystery schools.

One group of Aryan mystics moved to Persia and became known as the Sufis, the wool gatherers. Eventually they became the mystics of Islam and their philosophies were developed and perfected.

At the end of the 19th century, a Russian, George Gurdjieff spent fifteen years studying the Sufis, and afterwards, with a journalist Peter Ouspensky established a school in Paris. From there the teachings spread and were carried by modern teachers including Vernon Howard, Jean Klein and Eckhart Tolle.

RESIST JUDGING

I worked hard to study and even more important, to understand the teachings. One element that all the teachers expound is this: Resist judging. One exercise I found and later used to teach in my classes was this: Refrain from judging. Decide not to judge, cast an opinion, criticize anyone including yourself for one hour. Once completed, observe how you feel. You may be pleasant surprised.

Vernon Howard said that it is essential to seek the truth in the right way, and this starts with having a right frame of mind – and an open mind, ready or even desperate for change. I was now desperate for change.

I had done many things in my life, worked among some great animators in cartoon films, served in the Royal Air Force and became a broadcaster. I had learned from some of the great journalists of the age, and had become a journalist myself – an international correspondent. I had won a prestigious award for British news pictures, reaped four awards for radio documentaries in Canada, been a managing editor of a Canadian newspaper, represented Weyerhaeuser Canada and the Insurance Corporation in media relations and been public relations director for the building of Skytrain, North America's first completely automated rapid transit system. In addition I had become a metaphysical practitioner, a psychic medium and a teacher.

UNABLE TO SAY "I'M SORRY"

But, I still had a problem. There was a hole, a gaping hole. It was a serious deficiency that kept coming up, from the depths of my being. I did not like, let alone love myself. I frequently said things that hurt people and I had difficulties in living with the women in my life. It was always Work versus Them. Iro, Lucy, Myra always had to take second place in my busy life and it created a bitterness and a guilt in my mind that this occurred.

THE CHILDREN WERE GROWING UP:
It is truly amazing how quickly one's children grow up. Here they are, clockwise from the top. Gregory, Roberta, Sheridan and Roderick. Truly, a great credit to their Mother, Lucy, who was always home for them.

My ego prevented me from loving myself and being able to say "I'm sorry" to loved ones – including my children – and many friends who came and went in my life. I was desperate for change. The suffering was not out there, but deep within me. There was nothing in my environment that could or should have caused suffering, far from it. The suffering was within, smoldering like an ugly fire. Great-grandmother Elen Egby had warned me when I was a young teenager, "You will hurt people, even loved ones, until you set yourself free." Those words along with Patrick's - get out of your own way - echoed frequently through my tormented mind.

I could feel Chang and Paul around me. They didn't point their fingers. They didn't say "straighten up," or "Get yourself out of it." They simply used their energies to neatly put opportunities on my path. Colleen, a student in my classes at the Psychic Society said: "Mystic Stuart Wilde is speaking tonight. I was going to go alone, but something made me think of you. Would you like to come?"

Then there was fear. It raised its ugly head. Change? What could I change into? I felt distinctly uncomfortable with that idea. Later I would learn that this idea of discomfort was manifested by my ego as a defense mechanism. I realized too that in these thoughts, I was judging myself. The judging had to stop, but how?

THE TWO SELVES WITHIN US

Gurdjieff claimed that a person lives with two selves – Self #1 which is known as the False Self and Self # 2 which is the True Self. One has to tackle and understand the False Self first.

The human subconscious mind is a recorder. It records everything that a person experiences from the time of birth through to adulthood. It observes and memorizes everything emotional in the environment and creates what is known as the Mechanical or Conditioned Mind.

One way to help understand the Conditioned Mind is to take Broadway as an example. A great actor plays a role in which the character is portrayed as angry, irritable, bored and gripped by heartache and jealousy. The actor plays the part every day because that is the way the script demands. But life is not such a fixed drama. We allow our subconscious mind to create a character using learned and mechanical responses.

Our Conditioned Mind may well project dozens, even scores of different faces during the course of a day, and the person showing these faces may well believe that these are his or her true faces.

Faces of the False Self can include: *envy, helplessness, posturing, jealousy, anger, arrogance, deceit, discontent, despair, embarrassment, deviousness, anguish, lying, worry, fear, panic, criticism, bitterness, revenge, resentment, retaliation, tension, boredom, foolishness, confusion, flattery, conceit, insecurity, shock, ignorance, possession, obsession, self-condemnation, terror and hatred.*

The False Self is a fabrication of the Subconscious Mind. It does not exist, but by believing it does exist, one has to live with it along a trail of suffering.

I discovered if you observe yourself without judgment, you can actually watch the False Self displaying the various faces of the Ego. For instance, somebody comes by and in a moment of anger calls you a nasty name. What do you do? Well, let us follow the possible reactions.

First of all you might display shock, then embarrassment, next is anger followed by resentment and then comes revenge followed by retaliation. The last face may be insecurity or a simmering residual bitterness.

If you observe yourself very closely you may find various other faces manifesting, and they all flash by quickly. The False Self is a quick-change artist; it changes faster than you can imagine which clearly demonstrates that it is not true but false.

A person dominated by Self #1 does not live or enjoy life. He or she is hounded by the many faces of the Ego-Self and this is what was meant by the term "suffering" used by the great teachers including Buddha, Jesus, Mohammed, Socrates, and Lao Tzu. Release from such personal suffering was also called salvation.

Some people when they come across the teachings respond with, "That's the way I am. I can't change." That is a lame excuse promoted by the False Self. The big mistake so many people make however, including government, the judiciary, many mental health practitioners and therapists is that believing Self #1 can be changed or reformed by mechanical or conditioned thinking.

Many anger management classes work to suppress the symptoms of the False Self, but sooner or later, often sooner, the symptoms - the old faces of the False Self - return with a vengeance. Many people have discovered it is totally useless to try and suppress the negative ego. Self #1 will defend itself and make an array of impressive promises it cannot keep. It is like asking a habitually fast driver, who keeps breaking the speed limit, to police himself.

There is only one sure-fire way of dealing with the False Self or as philosopher Paul Brunton so aptly described it; the ego must be crucified.

English artist and mystic William Blake wrote: *"If the doors of perception were cleansed everything would appear to man as it is, infinite. For man has closed himself up, till he sees all things thru' chinks of his cavern."* Sooner or later, these false illusions will crumble with the manifestation of the True Self. Illusions have no place in the realm of the True Self, the Higher Self.

THE REALM OF THE TRUE SELF

According to the sacred books, when you bring the True Self into your full awareness, it will bring salvation from suffering.

The True Self is also known as the Inner Self, the Higher Self or the Super-consciousness. It is the spirit force, the higher intelligence within us that works and operates without any conscious effort. It is the silent operator. It is within us always. It is the life force, the power that operates the central nervous system, the brain and other parts of the body and, for the most part, we rarely think about it. It is only when there is a malfunction – a deficiency or absence of positive energy – and negativity invades us, that we experience the message in the form of pain or disabilities.

It is also the love force that is reflected in every cell in our bodies. This is the most important reason that we should love ourselves unconditionally.

The True Self has all the qualities we admire in lovable people. These qualities include unconditional love, compassion, truth, happiness, strength and dedication. The True Self is the very essence of your Spirit – the essential you. It is entirely free of all negative emotions such as panic and despair. It has tremendous capacity for seeing everything clearly.

In the realm of the True Self, everything is crystal clear. You were born the True Self. The Spirit is the True Self. It is never lost, never suffers from materialism but for many people, the True Self is dominated and over-shadowed by the False Self, the Mechanical Mind. If you can imagine the True Self imprisoned by the bars of a cage, that cage is the False Self. It allows little if any warmth or love to radiate through the bars. The False Self is dominant.

St Paul knew all about the False Self when he wrote in 1 Corinthians 13: "When I was a child, I spoke as a child, I understood as a child, I thought as a child: but when I became a man, I put away childish things. For now we see through a glass darkly."

A person who is dominated by the False Self really believes they cannot change. Their ego-centered mind fears change, and in this way condemns the person to a life in a cage, or looking through the glass darkly, the negative ego.

BREAKING FREE

The great teachers, the great philosophers say that when one shines the light of awareness on the False Self, the negative ego cringes and starts to dissolve. Negative elements always avoid the light. They cannot stand awareness. Criminals and people working in negative energy, cringe when the light shines on them.

How do we shine the light of awareness on the False Self? It's a very effective, age-old technique called Impartial Self Observation.

This is another name for Awareness. Like the investigative light of journalists shining the light on criminals, the Light of Awareness is the mortal enemy of Self #1, the Ego-Self. Remember this truth: The False Self cannot be controlled or suppressed, but by shining the Light of Awareness, the faces of the ego will start to dissolve. The good news is that anyone can do this and break free. It is a secret that should have been shared with millions of people many centuries ago.

Impartial Self Observation is the entrance, the pathway, the Gateway to a new sense of Self, the True Self.

So my task was to study all the faces of my False Self through Impartial Self Observation. I started on each one, such as jealousy, and discovered as it cringed and started to fade away, so did other faces of the False Self dissolve. One big one was possession and another was foolishness. As they dissolved, I found myself free of the scourges that had haunted me since childhood.

This freedom does not happen overnight, it simply comes upon one as a dawn, a gradual enlightenment. I found I was no longer reacting to triggers the way I used to. This seemed to bother people – relatives and colleagues – around me who reacted by saying: "You've changed. You are not the Bob Egby we used to know." I get this even today when I link up with old colleagues from my Royal Air Force days or Forces Broadcasting times.

One old friend proclaimed: "What happened to that boastful, bashful Bob Egby. You don't get angry or bombastic any amore. It's much more easy to talk with you. You listen to people and allow others to express their opinions with judging."

The success of Impartial Self Observation depends on being non-judgmental. It is vitally important to remember that Self Observation should always be conducted without comment, criticism, judgment, or an expression of opinion or feelings. Otherwise it will be the old False Self intruding, and your outlook will be biased and ineffective. It would be like a shoplifter working for Security in the store that he or she is robbing.

Many teachers have various techniques for observing one's self. The best one I found and later taught at many workshops was this.

THE EXERCISE: BEING AN IMPARTIAL OBSERVER

Imagine, just imagine that there is a video camera watching you from a few feet away and you are filming yourself. Relax and spend a few minutes watching yourself, how you are sitting, how your body rests, how you are feeling, and do this without judgment or comment. Simply watch yourself. Get used to observing yourself. Practice this several times.

When someone says something that annoys you, switch on your video camera and observe how you are reacting. Watch your body, listen to your reaction, observe the deeper feelings in your mind, all without judgment. Once you have success, do not throw a party, feel jubilant or tell others. Simply observe your jubilation.

One phenomenon that you will notice is that when you perform Impartial Self Observation you can only do it in the Here and Now. It is not something you can do in the past or the future. It ensures your consciousness is performing in the present, the Here and Now.

Living in the Here and Now is the perfect mode of living. If you pause to listen to people conversing,

you wll be aware they are still living in a world of yesterday, expressing regrets, hurts, doubts, anger, bitterness and lost chances. Others may be living in the future by worrying about their health, their age, pensions, future relationships and a multitude of other things. Few people choose to live in the Now.

I discovered the best way to live in the Here and Now is to focus on your body as it breathes, moves, functions and reacts. You can do this as you walk, sit at table, drive a vehicle, etc. One great exercise for losing weight or keeping yourself trim is to observe yourself – impartially – while you are eating a meal. Observe the food on your plate, the way you pick it up, how you place it in your mouth, how it tastes as you chew it, and finally swallow it. Do this, and you will notice that your appetite will tell you "I'm full. Stop eating." Finally, observe how you feel when your appetite speaks. You can apply this observation of yourself with most of the things you do in life. Observe your feelings, your speaking and your reactions. All this is done in the Here and Now. One very apparent benefit is that your energy is no longer drained by useless living in the past or future.

There is a full description of these processes and the exercises involved given in my book "Cracking the Glass Darkly," which is available at many bookshops and at Amazon.com.

Do not rush this development. Like anything worth while it takes time to mature, like wine, but once you find the many faces of the False Self failing to reappear, you will feel free.

Once I felt confident that much of my False Self had disappeared into oblivion, I decided to share the teachings with others. I was living in Squamish, British Columbia at the time and the local Adult Education people asked me to conduct an evening course on Advanced Awareness. Twenty-five people signed up and all purchased Vernon Howard's book "The Mystic Path to Cosmic Power." There are fifteen chapters in the book and we covered it all in two-hour classes spread over sixteen weeks. The class attracted attention from Adult Education people because as I mentioned, we started with twenty-five students and on the final night, we still had twenty-four. Most night classes diminish, but this one ran the course and I received many letters of thanks, which were inspiring.

ELEN'S PREDICTION COMES TRUE

On the night I concluded the course in Squamish, a student came up and commented: "I can see you are relaxed, and you are working in the light of awareness and you have broken free of your suffering. That must be a great accomplishment."

I thanked her and on the way home recalled my Great-grandmother Elen Egby in Reading so many years before saying, "You will work with the light" and "set yourself free." I smiled softly as I recalled her voice. Then as I opened the door in my little house with the gentle light coming in from the street lamp outside I saw a figure, a spirit in my armchair by the fire. For a moment I thought it was Iro but in a flash I knew it was Elen. She materialized totally in white and her big hat with ostrich feathers was also in pure white.

"Bobbie...things are moving along for you," she said. "You are virtually free of your old self but you will still be tested. It's time to teach wherever you go. Help people release their suffering. Study the human mind and work to be gentle with the women who are close to you. You should also consider the ministry, that will open new doors for you."

Consider the ministry? Why would I want to enter the church? While I promoted the teachings of Jesus, I was not a supporter of the Christian Church.

"Elen, I love you," I started to say and then realized she had disappeared.

A NOTE FROM SISTER DIANE

I was still mulling over great-grandmother's words about being tested when I spotted a letter on the floor. It was from my sister Diane in Bournemouth, announcing she had just successfully completed a Course in Hypnoanalysis with Neil French of the International Institute of Hypnoanlysis in Bournemouth. "It's an excellent course, you should take it," she wrote.

A year later, I successfully completed the three-year course and became an accredited hypnoanalyst, which is much like a hypnotherapist, only specializing in regression, abreacting and healing. The course introduced me to the historic works of Freud, Jung and Adler, and the modern modalities of Neuro-linguistic Programming and the techniques of Richard Bandler, as well as the great psychiatrist and hypnotherapist Milton Erickson. I joined the National Guild of Hypnotists in the United States and through an additional workshop, became an "Advanced" hypnosis practitioner.

THE AUTHOR WITH SISTERS SHEILA AND DIANE:
After completing training in hypno-analysis, the author spent two months in England finishing with a practicum. Here, the trio is pictured outside a pub where they had lunch. At this point, they were all accredited hypno-analysts and accredited members of the International Association of Hypno-analysts.

I opened an office in downtown Squamish and had a flood of people seeking to quit smoking, lose weight and seeking to heal all sorts of emotional problems. People booked for psychic readings and I noticed sessions were more with spirits of loved ones rather than being just psychic. Finally, I took my leave of B.C. Transit, after being with them for ten years and became self-employed. They were a great bunch to be with.

SHERIDAN IN TROUBLE

My youngest son Sheridan had graduated from the High School in Richmond and his inclination was to study and creat art. He loved drawing and painting. He attended the Emily Carr College of Art in downtown Vancouver and studied everything intently. The students had small cubicles in an adjoining building that looked like a barn, and when Sheridan was not in class, he worked in the cubicle, using cadmium paints. It was a time – 1990 – when cadmium was declared toxic but the ban came too late. For some weeks Sheridan's painting turned an ugly black and white. Color was out of his life.

One day I got a call that Sheridan was in his second floor apartment off Broadway and had barricaded himself in. Someone had called the police and an ambulance. By the time I got there, Sheridan had tried to escape and using a rope danging outside his window, he had slid down to the back alley. The police had caught him. "He's been taken to Emergency," a cop told me.

At the hospital the doctor told me Sheridan was halucinating. "He sees everyone, including doctors and nurses as FBI or CIA agents out to kill him," he said, adding he was going to inject a sedative.

"Let me see him. I'm a certified hypnotherapist, I can relax him."

While the doctor and nurses looked on, I managed to get my son's attention and get him into a trance state and told him "You're safe now. Go to sleep and sleep deeply." He did.

Some days later, Sheridan was transferred to the hospital on the University of British Columbia campus, where he stayed for three months. Doctors were reluctant of diagnosing his affliction as schizophrenia or stating that the origin of his halucinations rested with inhaling toxic gases from cadmium paints. I felt the cadmium was the root cause, but no one wanted to listen.

When he continued with a counsellor and was given medicine designed to curb any possible recurrence of his ailment, it soon became apprarent to everyone in the family that he was not his old self. A new sensitivity to people's remarks, particularly gentle criticism, curtailed any chance of regular work. Now, almost twenty years later, he is getting back into painting and being creative.

ISABEL GOES TO THE SUMMERLAND

Work as a hypnotherapist in Squamish was brisk and I had a stream of clients from the region, mainly people who wished to quit smoking. Every week I drove into Vancouver to conduct the development class at the Psychic Center. I sensed Isabel Corlett, our founder was not well and one day I had a call from Tom Passey: "They took Isabel to Vancouver General last night. She made her transition into the Summerland this morning." Summerland is a name given to the Spirit World by Spiritualist Andrew Jackson Davis.

The news plunged me into a sense of deep loss. She had been my close friend, teacher and confidant for ten years and it was tough to get over the fact that I would not see her again. How wrong I was. She's around me even today as I write this.

Now, being my own employer, I could take time to travel and do workshops. Tom Passey, one of Canada's great dowsers and I linked up to do workshops on metaphysical development. We gave workshops in Prince George, Salmon Arm, Kelowna, Victoria on Vancouver Island, islands in the Gulf – Pender Island, Saltspring and Hornby. We also travelled into the United States and did many workshops in Bellingham, Seattle and on Whidbey Island. Many a weekend was spent traveling and doing workshops, and in the process I learned valuable dowsing skills from a master. Tom had been President of the Canadian Society of Questers, which is another name for dowsers.

He was truly a wizard and could make unusual things happen. At a two-day psychic workshop on Pender Island, students complained of a long drought and asked Tom if he could make it rain. Tom nodded and promptly conducted a Cosmic decree. His favorite quote on this was from the Bible and the Book of Job: "You will also decree a thing, and it will be established for you; And light will shine on your ways."

Next day, the island was drenched in heavy rain and the students and most of the islanders were impressed. Five days later, back in Vancouver Tom received a frantic call: "Can you stop the rain?" He apologized. "I can bring water in the shape of rain, but I can't stop it." Two days later, the rain stopped anyway. But it was the talk of the island for several years.

Tom taught me about earth, energy and geopathic zones and told of how people, totally unaware of living on a geopathic zone, could suffer sickness and death from something they knew nothing about. In my book "INSIGHTS: The Healing Paths of the Radical Spiritualist" I tell of victims who ran afoul of geopathic zones. It is so sad that the authorities in the United States and

Canada doggedly fail to recognize dangers from negative earth energies. In Europe things are more progressive.

Just when everything was running smoothly in my life, there was another kink in the Cosmos that was to change my entire direction. I met a woman.

24

A LITTLE CABIN
ACROSS THE BORDER

ER NAME WAS LIZ, short for Elizabeth and she ran a notable marine business in Squamish. I met her one dark night when the old Squamish Highway was "out." Those were the days when the road was narrow and quite often the victim of mud and rockslides that severed communication between Whistler-Squamish and Vancouver. On this particular night, a small ferry was operating between Horseshoe Bay and Britannia Beach. We were both headed for Squamish and she offered to give me a lift.

Liz was a good looking fiery Scorpio and while people born under the sign have great business acumen, relationships can be fiery and sometimes stormy. However, we seemed to get on like a house on fire. We enjoyed each other's friends, watched the same television shows (Jeopardy and Star Trek), walked the banks of the Squamish River, and played a card game called Crib.

One day, in her sky-blue Lincoln Town Car, she invited me to her "cabin at the Cove." We drove south across the Canada-U.S. border to Whidbey Island through Oak Harbor and Coupeville, to Admiral's Cove.

It seems to be a habit with quite a lot of people, they refer to country residences as "cottage" or a "little place" or a "little hideout," or "a cabin," when it turns out to be anything but small, in fact it is something quite the opposite. Liz's place at Admiral's Cove was expansive – you could have a hundred people in for a cocktail party with room to spare. It overlooked the beautiful Puget Sound, parts of which were featured in the movie "Sleepless in Seattle." Every day the cool summer breezes would sweep off the Olympic Wilderness and flutter across the blue-green waters. We could set our clocks as the high-speed Clipper zapped along the seascape on ferry runs between Seattle and Victoria on Vancouver Island.

We enjoyed the Skagit Valley Tulip Festival every spring. It seemed as if the Creator had pulled out a box of pastels and painted the landscape with a vast array of spectacular colors. "It takes my breath away to see such color," exclaimed Liz ecstatically. .

While at "The Cove" as she called it, I did some acrylic paintings on canvas but upon reflection years later, the works reflected a stress. I was failing my new career as a hypnotherapist by spending long weekends at Admiral's Cove from mid-day Friday until mid-day Monday. I found I was missing business, hence the stress. I clipped short the weekends by driving up and down myself, but I missed the companionship of driving together. On top of this Liz had made some good friends and spent more and more time with them. In spite of my Impartial Self Observation training, I sensed my False Self returning in the form of jealousy. Jealousy is one of the most difficult faces to dissolve.

The relationship ended in an exchange of sharp words. We got together occasionally at Squamish to play cards, but the original affair was dashed on the rocks. In addition to losing Liz, I also lost some good friends at Admiral's Cove. Ever since I had been at Weyerhaeuser I enjoyed being in the United States.

STEPPING STONES

I closed the Squamish office, sold my cottage and moved to North Vancouver. It was a bigger market and closer to some old friends. I acquired a small office in a Naturopathic clinic on Marine Drive where business was brisk for a while. I worked alongside some great people, Ryan Carnahan a massage therapist, Craig Webb an acupuncturist, and upstairs was a team of naturopathic physicians. Classes in psychic development were held at the clinic but they never seemed to click. Something was missing. I felt the need to move on. Someone once told me, "You must have been a camel driver in a past life." There must have been an element of truth there.

In addition to trains, I love ships. I always enjoyed news photo assignments onboard Royal Navy ships in the Mediterranean, the journey on the Kenya Castle to Aden through the Red Sea and even the voyage across to the Suez War on the HMS Manxman.

So I studied the American cruise ship industry and became a certified Cruise Counselor with CLIA (Cruise Lines International Association) and spent time cruising and visiting ships at Miami, and I actually started selling cruises, but when the British Columbia Government found out, they said I would have to join a registered agency. So, bureaucracy killed a possible career in the cruise industry.

The Vancouver Psychic Society, which had rented a city-owned facility on Broadway, was asked to vacate because the city needed office facilities, so it moved to a temporary facility. With Isabel Corlett gone to the Spirit World, it seemed the Society's days were numbered. Patrick Young had left the Society some time before.

Things were closing around me and I had a feeling that my days in British Columbia were numbered. But where could I go? West was the Pacific Ocean, north was the Canadian Yukon and the Arctic, south was the United States and Canadians were always telling me I couldn't go there because I didn't have a Green Card and they were difficult, if not impossible to get.

FINDING GOD ON A BEACH

One day I drove down to Whidbey Island and started to walk along the sandy beaches south of Admiral's Cove. It was a cold uninviting day. There was snow high up in the mountains across Puget Sound and a chill breeze swept across the water. A large weather-bleached log provided a wind break so I sat behind it and meditated.

Instantly, I knew someone was watching me.

"Ah, so," said the soft but deep voice. "Do you wish to see me? Or is my voice enough?"

"Your voice could put me to sleep," I noted.

"That's your job. You're the hypnosis fellow," came back the comment. It was followed by a short laugh, and I knew it was Paul.

"Have you found God yet?"

I shook my head. Chang once talked to me on Jericho Beach and it made considerable sense. His argument was logical. But..."

"Where does your mind tell you he is?"

"I'm still inclined to think of God as an old man, chubby, with long wispy hair, seated on a throne and surrounded by young women all playing harps and expressing adoration for the old man." I paused, and then added. "It was inherited from Mum taking me to Sunday school for a couple of months."

"That's anthropomorphic," Paul said quickly. "Why is it that human beings insist on making their God after their own bodies and minds? That's the epitome of the egocentric mind."

I felt argumentative. "The Bible says God created man in his own image."

"The scribes who penned the book left out some critical words," muttered Paul. "It should have read God created humans in the image of Spirit. There's a world of difference. You understand?"

I nodded. "You changed man and substituted humans."

There was a short sigh. "You're off target, Robert. You're talking about humanity. Can we talk about God? What is God?"

"God is Spirit. Jesus said that."

"Right! So where is Spirit?"

I shook my head vigorously. "I have no idea."

"Why don't you try opening your eyes, fellow?" he snapped, almost impatiently. "Get up and walk to that patch of grass." He watched, and then commanded me to kneel down and observe the grass.

"What do you see?"

"Blades of grass. They're green."

"No!" he cried mockingly. "Look closer? Are they alive?"

Even as I looked, a faint yellowish aura appeared around every blade. "They're alive," I said. "But I know that."

"Yes, they are alive. What makes them alive?"

"Hell! I'm not a biochemist," I muttered.

"Grass is the most important of all food sources on your planet. There are close to ten thousand species. Whole civilizations rely on grass to feed livestock, use in construction, and produce bread, liquor and sugar. Its roots are like threads, they extend into the soil, soaking up water and searching for nutrients. They are alive. Right?"

I nodded, wondering where this was going.

"What makes them alive?"

"Spirit?" I asked. "Spirit is in the grass?"

I felt a hand on my head. "Spirit is the motivating force of the Universe and beyond," said Paul, with a long sigh. "There is nothing that isn't Spirit."

A narrow path wound its way off the beach and up through some woods. Paul asked me to stop by a tree, a cottonwood I think.

"This tree started as a very minute seed, almost difficult to see, and yet there it stands in maturity reaching up to the sky," he said peering at me.

"God?" I felt I was now on his wavelength.

"Of course." He said triumphantly. "Now, you're short of breath from climbing the path. Are you conscious of the air that is flooding your lungs and body and keeping you alive?"

"God!"

"Bravo! And if the oxygen in the air that you breathe goes to every muscle, every bone, every gland, every organ, every cell in your body, God is there too. Right?"

It was raining lightly now and I could make out his astral form leaning against the cottonwood tree.

"Remember your Greek. Psyche stems from ancient Greek and means to breathe. It also means spirit and soul, depending on who you talk to," he spoke quickly, and I had a feeling he was about to depart. "That is why it is critically important for you to love everything, including your body."

"My body? I don't particularly like…" I started to stay.

"Particularly your body. Just because you've got it for a few years, doesn't mean you should abuse it. Get into the harmony of the Universe." He disappeared, but came back briefly. "Isabel and Iro told me to say hello." He paused then added: "You're old friend Iacovos from Cyprus came by. He told me to say hello." Then everything was quiet except for the breeze rustling through the trees and the rain dampening my head.

I held out my hand and a drop of water fell into my palm. It glistened and a bluish aura formed an orb around it. I stared at it for several moments and finally said: "God, after a lifetime of looking, I think I've found you."

My tongue touched the glistening orb and suddenly a spark of energy, powerful and overwhelming, shot through my body. It was totally new. Totally invigorating. Totally rejuvenating. My mind was peaceful, yet alert. The world and the Universe appeared crystal clear. I felt loved. It was no longer a word, but an immersion into something powerful, almost unexplainable, almost indescribable. It was warm, harmonious and infinite.

A breeze sprang up, but I had no idea where it was coming from. It rustled through the trees but the leaves did not move. Nothing moved, but the breeze was there. I could hear it and feel it. Patrick once mentioned something about the Shabd, the audible Life Stream. I made a mental note to ask Spirit for an explanation.

HELLO, I'M SHARON

One evening while browsing a chat room for seniors on the web I met a lady named Sharon. She had a great voice on the telephone and her emails were bouncy. She said she was getting out of a marriage and wanted to come to Vancouver to take one of my workshops. Her home was in Hightstown, New Jersey, a town on the turnpike and a bedroom community for New York City and Princeton.

I met her from a flight at Seattle and we drove up to North Vancouver. Over the next few days everything clicked. We were on the same energy and it felt good. We took walks by water, took a ride round Stanley Park and watched the sun go down from Jericho Beach. We very much desired to be with each other, but she had an aging mother in Edison, New Jersey. Sharon could not leave New Jersey, so I decided that I would move there. We celebrated by having dinner on the Seven Seas Floating Restaurant at Lonsdale Quay and we watched the evening close in over the mountains.

I recalled the Hindu yogi, who had come to the Cyprus Mail newspaper in far off Cyprus over thirty-five years before and said I would go to the west and then turn back to the east. Even with all my metaphysical studies, I still could not comprehend how these seers do it. What was happening seemed to be another kink in the Cosmos and I wondered who was pulling the strings.

This wonder became even more acute when I arrived in Hightstown in New Jersey and discovered that Sharon, my new love, had been laid off and was looking for new employment. She found something that appealed to her. The job? Secretary to a lawyer, specializing in immigration. This would pave the way for my getting the so called "Green Card" a permit to reside and work in the United States. I wondered what energy had opened the doors.

MARRIAGE AND THE SPIRITUALIST CHURCH

On February 14th 1998 we were married in Princeton by a minister from the Unitarian Church. Sharon's children, Jennifer and Clayton, both young adults, took us for a celebration lunch and afterwards we headed down to the Atlantic Shore to celebrate the marriage. On the outskirts of East Windsor and Hightstown, we rented a spacious ranch house on a street where Clara Barton, the founder of the American Red Cross once taught school.

We had a large room for spiritual development circles, a small room for hypnosis therapy and a spacious room for administration. We both had computer stations, and I learned HTML and built a website to promote my hypnotherapy and metaphysical business.

In Squamish, I had used my old broadcasting voice to create some audiotapes for clients. Each one was targeted to achieve a particular purpose. Titles included "Relax and Let Go," "Stopping Smoking," "Building Self Esteem," "Better Sleeping Habits," and there were ones for spiritual and psychic development such as "Enhance Your Psychic Abilities," "Meditations for Meeting Your Spirit Guides," "The Power of Self Healing," "Creating Prosperity," "Discovering the Journey to Loving Yourself," and others. Now in the United States, CDs were all the fashion, so we converted most to that format, and created some new ones including sleep-learning programs for losing weight and stopping smoking.

Then one day, Sharon came up with an idea.

"There's a Spiritualist Church in Westville," she said one evening. "Why don't we go?"

"Where did you get that idea from?"

"Don't know. It just came," she said with a laugh. She always laughed a lot and I liked that.

Spirits, I thought. I had done several talks at the Church of the International Spiritualist Alliance in New Westminster, British Columbia and got on very well with everyone, in fact Tom Passey and I did a couple of Saturday workshops for them. I wondered what the American Spiritualists would be like.

I collided with the pastor, the Rev. Lillian Joyce at the door and she welcomed us with open arms. She introduced us and I have never been made more welcome. It was uncanny. I sensed I saw my spirit guides Paul and Chang lurking at the back of the church, chuckling. I wondered what they were up to. I was to find out on our second visit.

A MARRIAGE IN PRINCETON, NO LESS: Sharon and the author were married by a Unitarian Church Minister in the heart of Princeton, the same place where Einstein had walked many years before. Sharon's daughter, Jennifer and son-in-law Graham were witnesses and kindly took them out to lunch afterwards. The date was also the author's sixty-sixth birthday.

The Westville Church was hosting the National Convention of NSAC – the National Spiritualist Association of Churches, which has its base at the famous Lily Dale village in upstate New York.

Lillian Joyce introduced me to the Rev. Barbara Thurman from San Francisco, California. Barbara was the NSAC President. Perhaps she was being genuinely informative or perhaps with a touch of provocation, but Lillian told the NSAC President: "Robert is a specialist in hypnosis and past lives therapy."

Mrs. Thurman stared at me, trying to maintain a frigid face, but somewhere I noted a grin. "We don't teach reincarnation," she snapped. "It's a very controversial subject."

"Controversy has followed me all the days of my life," I put in with a well intended shrug. "I was a journalist and broadcaster for a lot of years."

"So we hear," said the President. "We can use you, but first of all you need to study Spiritualism. It's quite different from being psychic." She said "psychic" with a tone of distain. I wanted to tell her that everyone has psychic and intuitive abilities but not everyone can be a medium, communicating with spirits. But I resisted the urge. Somewhere along the way I realized I had picked up feelings of diplomacy.

A THREE YEAR STUDY

That week I enrolled as a student in the NSAC seminary, the Morris Pratt Institute responsible for conducting an extensive three year home-study course in Modern Spiritualism. The MPI has its origin in the 1890s and is housed in Wauwatosa, a Milwaukee suburb in Wisconsin.

The material started pouring in and I started my studies with gusto. It seemed the right thing to do. In my own studies of various religious movements, I was already well aware of the doctrines and dogmas of other churches and religious movements which were featured in the introductory lessons.

I enjoyed learning about the young Fox sisters and their "rappings" at Hydesville in upstate New York and while many people had welcomed the fact they could communicate with spirits, there were those, particularly in the mainline churches, who were violently opposed. The extensive course covered the basis of Spirit communications, all focusing on the existence of an Afterlife.

In essence, Spiritualism is the Science, Philosophy and Religion of continuous life, based upon the demonstrated fact of communication by means of mediumship, with those who live in the Spirit World.

I found that Spiritualism teaches personal responsibility, a spark of divinity dwells in everyone, and that death is not a cessation of life, but merely a change of condition. It is the spirit that lives on. The founders of Spiritualism must have read the Sermon on the Mount because the teachings of Spiritualism reflect the mystical teachings of Jesus. And Like Jesus, Spiritualism advocates and promotes spiritual healing.

Something I enjoyed learning that Spiritualism removes all fear of death, which had been one of my acute fears while walking down Murder Mile in Cyprus or running up a Lebanese hillside, while an aircraft shot bullets all around me. I always had the feeling that the goddess, my guardian angel, that Being who seems to hang around me, was protecting me...but I was never totally sure.

Somewhere in all of this my Green Card arrived and I sensed I was in the United States to stay.

WRITING ESSAYS WITH SPIRIT

There were thirty lessons in the entire course and each lesson required a five-page essay on the subject or affiliated learnings. Whenever I sat down at the computer to write an essay, I felt Paul's presence and the words just flowed through my mind like a mountain stream. We (I have to say we) normally wrote an entire five page essay in less than half an hour and there were twenty-nine of them.

To make things more interesting, Barbara Thurman was designated my mentor and checker of my work. She frequently expressed surprise at the speed with which I submitted my work. She received a lesson and essay from me every ten days, which was my goal.

I completed the three-year course in exactly one year. There were three sections: Mediumship, Healing and Ministry and I scored 99% pass in each section. That was in 1999.

Throughout the course and afterwards, I did platform work at the Church of Eternal Life in Westville, giving talks on enlightenment and presenting messages from loved ones in the Spirit World. I found that the standard of messages was trite and mediums either did not have many communication skills with their own spirit guides, or they were not hearing or seeing the deeper information coming over.

Paul spurred me to write articles on validation in messages. It echoed what Patrick had taught us in Vancouver. Validation means an element of unique truth in messages. For instance, the medium must ask his or her spirit guide to communicate with the loved one intending to come through with a unique message. Unique information is known only between the spirit sending the message and the person receiving the message in the pew.

For instance the medium would say: "I have your husband Ron with me. He says since he crossed into Spirit, you've moved onto his side of the bed, but you won't tell the family because they will make fun of you. And one other thing, he loves it when you look at his bedside photo and say 'Goodnight, Love.' This actually happened to me.

Another unique message came for a young woman: "I have your mother with me and she says she always cleaned up after you and she says she still does it from the Other Side. You've left the hose on in the back garden and the basement is starting to flood." The young woman shrieked and dashed home. Next week she confirmed it at church.

While I certainly like the community of the Spiritualist Churches, there were things that I found which acted as blocks in Spirit communication. One was; the medium is required to stand on the dais to address the congregation and give messages. This, I found, ranked of ego, and I believed that all mediums and psychics should dissolve their false selves.

Much better for the message bearer to get down to people-level and be one of them. Unless he was addressing massive crowds, Jesus always spoke among the people, as did teachers in ancient Greece and Rome. If I had my way, podiums and rostrums would be tossed out of churches along with other symbols of religious pomposity and intimidation.

SPIRITUALIST PUBLIC RELATIONS

Barbara Thurman called one evening while I was doing the course. She often called to chat on various things going on, and I sensed she used me as an ear to sound off on people, places and events that bothered her. This particular evening she called with a mission: "We need a new Superintendent of Public Relations. What do you say?"

"I don't like the word superintendent. It reminds me of school, public works and the boss of the neighborhood swimming pool," I responded.

"Like everything else in Spiritualism, it is a hang-over from the past," she said. "We can change it. What would you suggest as a title?"

"Director or manager would be fine," I said.

"Send me a resume," she said, "and I'll put it before the Board next week."

A month later I was appointed Director of Public Information for NSAC, and my first job was to create a monthly newsletter called "News from NSAC." My old journalistic juices were flowing again. Sharon Snowman, the NSAC Secretary in Lily Dale, put out memos to the 144 member congregations including ten state associations and eleven camps. There were also four affiliated congregations of the National Spiritualist Churches of Canada in Ontario and Quebec.

In addition to email subscribers, circulation was supplemented in printed form and distributed by the NSAC office to churches and camps. Within a few weeks we had several hundred subscribers, not simply from members, but also interested people across the United States and Canada and Spiritualist organizations in the United Kingdom, Europe and Australia and New Zealand.

If it was news about Spiritualism, we printed it; even controversial material. When John Edward broke loose on the Sci-Fi Channel with his gallery readings, we carried that and when the odd regular reader responded with, "He's not a true Spiritualist medium," we carried the comments. I sensed John Edward did more for bringing Spiritualism into the open than any other medium ever did. Why? Because on television millions saw and watched his work and messages from Spirit became an accepted fact.

Mrs. Thurman said that with my background in hypnoanalysis, I really did not need to take the two-week Pastoral Skills program organized by the Morris Pratt Institute, a normally required participation by students desiring to be ordained. All I needed to do was to apply to the Board of Directors. Well, deep in my mind I had some reservations. While I was a Spiritualist at heart – and training – I really did not wish to be ordained with NSAC. It did not seem right. My reservations were based on higher learnings and the image of God, Infinite Intelligence, so for the time being I postponed making a decision on this.

A HOUSE IN WESTVILLE

During this period Sharon and I purchased a house in Westville, which is a small community across the Delaware River from Philadelphia. We had a large twenty-two by thirteen foot front room and it was here we held weekly development circles with at least a dozen regulars attending. We invited members of the public to come and "sit in" to receive messages. In this way six or seven good mediums developed quickly.

A RUSTIC HOUSE IN WESTVILLE:
Surrounded by trees, this seemingly small home was expansive, and possessed a meditation facility for some twenty-five people. The author conducted Sunday services with piano accompaniment by Sharon

I felt I had to go my own way in being ordained, so I searched around for spiritual organizations that would help, but most of them had regulations and dogmas worse than the Spiritualist Church. One in Washington, DC wanted a "donation" of $100 a year in return for ordination.

Then I found the Universal Life Church in California which would ordain me as a Spiritualist minister. They follow up their ordinations with positive and in depth education programs based on different theological teachings. Rev. Amy Long, a dynamic soul created the academic programs there and that appealed to me. Barbara Thurman told me that the ordination would have no standing in NSAC but I knew that. I also wanted to go one step further. I felt I had the qualifications to start a ministry of my own so that I could share the ancient teachings of the masters in the ways I had been taught. Rev. Douglas Hickman of Universal Ministries interviewed me on the telephone and agreed to cover us with a charter. The name we chose was Silver Birch Ministries.

In addition to our weekly classes, we initiated a monthly service on Sunday afternoons that included spiritual talks and discussions, singing of hymns and spirit messages. We purchased fifteen of the new Spiritualist Hymnals from NSAC. We also had Silver Birch Ministries registered with the county in New Jersey.

Then one night while sitting in a Princeton restaurant with Sharon, I told her of the French psychic in South Richmond, British Columbia who had predicted my doing this. She had said in part: "You are treading a new path which will take you through teaching and healing. I see you as a minister, speaking in a church and you will talk and listen to the dead." I could never figure out how the seers see so far into the future, and I still cannot.

NICOS SAMPSON BOWS OUT

It was Thursday, May 10th 2001, and the morning news on the radio announced the death in Nicosia, Cyprus the day before, of Nicos Sampson. They simply said he was a politician, newspaper publisher and former President of Cyprus and had died of cancer. They added he was responsible for the division of the Island Republic in 1974. They never mentioned anything else.

Sharon asked how I felt about his death and I simply responded with the fact that another character from the mosaic of my life had gone into Spirit. Death didn't seem so final when viewed through the Spiritualist philosophy.

"Did you hate him for all the killings?"

"No," I replied. "Who am I to judge? I don't approve of killing by anyone. It's better to resist judging. How should I see Sampson? Was he a murderer or was he a patriot, fighting for his country? It all depends on where you stand. So which side is right? If you seek to judge someone, you are forced to take sides. There is an old adage used by the ancient masters: We are not judged for our sins but by our sins. Ask yourself if judging benefits society?"

Sharon shrugged. "It's easy to fall into the judging trap... and meaningless. But it does give the person judging, a sense of power or perhaps security."

"Illusions," I said. "It's easier not to judge. Simply observe the world and enjoy."

In pondering over his passing, I simply noted that another character from the mosaic of my life had been claimed by death. But by now, I had a different view on death. As the Spiritualists say, death is merely a change of condition. And now, I understood that.

Barbara Thurman had reservations about the way Spiritualism was moving or – in fact – not moving. "We are stagnant," she confided one evening. "The old guard is stifling us. We cannot introduce anything new. We need a college of Spiritualism for higher learning and the membership has been discussing it for ten years, and every year it's shelved."

Barbara was a leader, a woman of action, and believers in the old ways had influence and were successfully blocking her. I sensed it was what undermined her confidence, created disappointment and contributed to her death. In 2002 she called one evening and she started chatting about a variety of things. I interrupted: "You're trying to tell me something about your health."

She paused. "I had it earlier and now it's back. Cancer!" she said slowly. "I'm going to give up the presidency and work on my health."

"I'll send you some healing CDs that may help," I told her, trying to sound positive but when I saw Chang standing by me shaking his head, I knew it was just a matter of time. I felt incredibly saddened by her illness. It was almost as if I was losing a close fellow traveler in Spiritualism. In those few years, we had shared many philosophical thoughts together. It was then that I decided to close "News from NSAC" and resign as Director of Public Information. I had put out forty-four editions of the newsletter.

While all of this was going on, Sharon and I attended the Westville Church. Sharon got on the Board of Directors and pushed for an elevator to service the street and two floors. Sharon continued her work in Princeton and drove there every day, but she found that shopping was getting more and more difficult. Her weight and the growing presence of arthritis in her legs made it difficult to walk. At Christmas and special times when she really wanted to get out and buy presents, I would drive her to a store that offered electric wheel chairs, and she would spend a couple of hours cruising up and down the aisles. I felt so sad watching her.

EXPANDING THE MINISTRY

It was then that Sharon and I decided to expand the Ministry to perform weddings, funerals, house and office blessings, funerals for pets and also house clearings. Sharon, an accomplished pianist and organist since childhood, would play music at the weddings. Rev. Amy Long provided some valuable material for wedding services, and I used my journalistic skills to create original and meaningful texts. Amy's book "The Ultimate Wedding and Ceremony Workbook for the Planning-Impaired," was a great help in those early days of the Ministry.

Little did I know that my services for conducting funerals would be in demand so soon. Early in 2003 Sharon suffered a cold and to me it sounded like a recurrence of a problem she had earlier. In the year before, I had taken her to the Underwood Memorial Hospital in Woodbury because she couldn't shake off a throat and chest condition. The doctors quickly diagnosed pneumonia and gave her medicine which cleared it up within a few days. This one felt the same way, except Sharon did not wish to go the hospital. I went to bed, leaving her watching television on the couch.

Sharon woke me at 3.00 a.m. "I cannot breathe. I feel awful."

I phoned 9-1-1 and within two or three minutes, a policeman came with oxygen and gave it to her as she lay on the bed. An ambulance arrived shortly after and the orderlies carried her out to the vehicle.

Feverishly throwing on some clothes, I drove to the Woodbury hospital. I sat in the emergency waiting room alone, feeling numb and totally useless. I talked to God and prayed for help. I saw my old buddy Chang a short distance away and that was consoling but he did not look happy. Then something happened. Sharon appeared in front of me. I knew it was her spirit and she must be unconscious or in a coma.

"Sharon, get back in there. Now!" I called out. I wanted to shout, scream. I failed to understand why she was out of her body.

The image disappeared.

Nervously, I paced up and down. Some minutes later a young doctor with a serious face emerged from behind the emergency room drapes and shook his head. "I'm sorry Mr. Egby. We were unable to save her. She died in the ambulance on the way here and the attendants revived her. We tried to keep her going, but it was impossible."

Stunned, I moved into the ER room. My Sharon was lying on a table. She hated to be flat on her back. I held her hand. It was still warm. I stood there caressing her arm, unable to believe that her life, her spirit had gone. I kissed her slowly on her cheeks. It felt so smooth and warm. Why? Why? Why? I felt angry – angry with the doctors and angry with God. I wanted to scream but I bit my tongue instead.

Death had come back into my life, but this time it was different. Death in Cyprus and Egypt had seemed so final, but here, well, I was a Spiritualist and I knew her spirit was out there somewhere. There is no such thing as death, only a change in condition, they said.

I felt Chang's presence close by. "She's made a safe transition. We have her. She sends her love." The date was January 7th 2003. We had been married five years all but five weeks.

GOD BE WITH YOU UNTIL WE MEET...

My mind went back two days to the small afternoon Spiritualist meditation and healing circle we held at the house. Sharon had played the piano and she announced: "In closing, I would like to play one of my favorite hymns – God be with you till we meet again." Ironically, thirty-six hours later, she was gone.

The next twenty-four hours were hectic. I called her children, Jennifer and Clayton. I think Clayton went over and broke the news to Sharon's mother in Edison, New Jersey. The doctor's report said Sharon had died of arteriosclerosis in the coronary artery. A day or so later, she was cremated and her ashes were later buried with her mother, who passed away a few months later. Sharon's mother-in-law could never understand why Sharon had died before her.

When there is a death in the family the worst thing is the shock, the next is the space, the gap that the departed person has left. Wherever I went in the house, I expected to see her.

We had both recognized the need for a good Spiritualist newsletter that reported beyond the borders of NSAC and covered Spiritualism nationally and globally and this was in production in the days before Sharon's passing. Entitled "Parapsychic Journal" it was a monthly, and the first edition went out on January 17th 2003.

In the spring, the Westville Spiritualist Church organized a memorial service for Sharon. The place was packed and the Rev. Lillian Joyce and I conducted the service.

In the weeks following her passing, I made myself busy. There was no use weeping although it came easily to me. I conducted a two day psychic development workshop for the South Jersey Paranormal Research group and that helped to stabilize me. Also, Sharon with her piano and organ talents had been commissioned to play at a wedding at a South Jersey winery.

During her last year, Sharon had been unable to work because of her weight and the condition of her legs. I managed to get a spare time job driving limousines in Trenton to supplement my income as a therapist, medium and teacher. The clients I drove were mainly sales people from the key pharmaceutical companies and their talk drove me off the idea of ever taking manufactured drugs. The limousine company was owned by Tony and Louise Pocetti.

I MEET BETTY LOU

One day, I was asked to drop off a parcel at the Pocetti's home. It was there that I met Mrs. Pocetti's mother. Her name was Betty Lou and she was standing in the garden plucking weeds from a flowerbed. I mentioned to Louise that there was a man in spirit standing on the lawn and he was carrying a soup bowl and a tennis racket. Louise told her mother.

"That's my husband Ed who passed away in 1999," she said. "He loved soup and always enjoyed tennis." She promptly asked for a full reading which I did at her home in Pemberton, near Mount Holly.

A woman named Marie came through. Betty Lou found she could not relate to a Marie in spite of my insisting it was for her. Finally, she gasped. "Oh, that's my mother. I never referred to her as Marie." She laughed.

During our conversation, Betty Lou mentioned she played in churches and had done so since a teenager. When Betty Lou and her daughter turned up at the memorial service at the Westville Church, I asked Betty Lou if she would play at an upcoming wedding I had scheduled at the Renault Winery, which is the longest operating winery in the country.

"It's at Egg Harbor City," I said and she agreed to help.

We carted the keyboard and the support equipment to the wedding venue, which was a white carousel on a spacious lawn overlooking a small lake. It was quite a walk with the equipment. While we were doing this Sharon materialized and told both of us separately: "I could never have done this."

The wedding went off extremely well and we were both paid earlier. However, after the service, the bridegroom came out of the reception and ran over to Betty Lou in the parking lot and gave her a tip for a "job well done."

ANOTHER DEPARTURE TO THE OTHER SIDE

As our officiant services became known through advertising in local newspapers and on the website, Betty Lou helped with the music and came into my life.

In far off California, Barbara Thurman came out of a seven week treatment in a San Francisco hospital. She sounded enthusiastic and wanted to do things.

Not too far away a couple of live-wire Spiritualist ministers, Lisa and Tom Butler, were heading up the American Association of Electronic Voice Phenomena by organizing the first National Conference in Reno, Nevada. Barbara Thurman was invited to do her famous spoon-bending workshop, and I was invited to do a psychic energy presentation. I asked Betty Lou to come along.

When we reached Reno, Barbara looked pale and sick. Her aura was pale and thin and she was sitting in a wheel chair. I gave her a long hug and she thanked me. We both attended each other's workshops and she left on the Sunday morning being driven by a friend back to San Francisco. It was the first week in June. I knew I would never see her again, but she did call me on the phone several times.

The last time she said: "I'm going home soon. I'm going to make sure that all those Spiritualists who have crossed over start working with Spiritualists still in the physical. Modern Spiritualism needs a shake-up. There are too many people occupying the pews and not enough getting out and telling people about our religion and the Afterlife. I'm going to work in the Spirit World to get Spiritualists to come back to the churches, groups and circles, not with simple lovey messages. We need to stoke the fires of Spiritualism and belief in the Afterlife."

Barbara Thurman, a fighter to the end, crossed into Spirit on June 24th 2003. So I lost another good friend in my life.

On July 4th Tom and Lisa Butler armed with a recording device in their experiment room with a picture of Barbara Thurman, attempted to make contact but a man came through saying "Barbara Thurman's happy...is busy." A few nights later, on July 7th Lisa Butler started the recording by saying: "We have gotten an EVP that says Barbara Thurman is happy and is busy." It was immediately followed by a loud whisper, "I'm right here." Lisa said afterwards: "I instantly recognized the whisper as Barbara! What a tireless worker she still is! What a wonderful confirmation she has given us."

THE DEEPER TEACHINGS

It was in Westville that I delved deeper into the teachings of the True Self. Spirits led me to read more books and encouraged me to give workshops on metaphsyics and also the ideal self. I protested once that they gave me too many books to study. They replied: "If you place a book under your pillow and sleep on it for several nights, the teachings will come to you." You may debate the workings of this, but I think the way it works is one's higher self seeks the author of the book, whether he or she is in the physical or in spirit, and relays the information from that person's higher consciousness. Whatever you may think, it does work.

At workshops, I found that students had great difficulty understanding the difference between thinking and awareness. Everyone thinks, mostly with memories of the past or visions of events occurring in the future. Even future happenings are based and judged on learnings or memories of the past.

Awareness is impartial observation of one's existence, Now. Awareness is a phenomenon of the present. It can only occur Now and complete awareness is Now, without judgment, comment or opinion. The moment you judge yourself you are back with the old False Self and its cache of memories. The joy of awareness is that it produces a clear mind, sanity and peace. It is at this point that all suffering disappears. You cannot suffer when you are in the Here and Now. Why? Because all pain becomes evident in the past.

Most sports demand present living. If you are skiing down an icy slope you need to be focused in the Here and Now. It is the same with playing tennis, ice hockey, and mountain climbing. If you are scaling a perilous cliff-face and you start thinking about what you're doing for supper tonight, you may not make it home.

You can practice living in the Here and Now even as you read this. Mentally observe your eyes reading the text, be conscious of how you are sitting, how you are reacting to what I have just written. Be conscious of what you are thinking. Follow the thoughts. As you practice living in the Here and Now you may well find any chronic or temporary aches in your body, ceasing to exist. They are likely to return if you return to your old self.

PROBLEM WITH OPINIONS

Another activity that sometimes confuses students and brings about suffering is expressing of opinions. We live in a highly opinionated society. Just listen to any of the news channels where reporting is reduced to relaying people's opinions. The quester, seeking peace and a greater understanding of Self, does not identify with opinions. Practice awareness of opinions and you may well be surprised that they are all based on memories, perhaps many years in the past. This is not about choices, such as selecting a meal or what time to have an appointment; it concerns opinions about yourself, your achievements, your relations with other people in your life, and opinions on subjects on which you have little or no knowledge.

Realize that opinions stem largely from the realm of the False Self, which is not your friend. It distorts memories to suit its needs. It distorts facts according to its personal desires. When one eliminates the False Self, even crucifies it, you gain a freedom that is beyond your imagination.

The False Self is the master of limitations. If you are planning a project in the future, perhaps building a home, studying for a degree, planning a family or a relationship, or perhaps going on a hiking trip to some foreign country, your False Self, relying on all sorts of memories from the past, will raise limitations in your path.

The False Self has no concept of the future. It dwells in the realm of memories and it distorts memories according to its whims and fancies. Be aware of your limitations and they will gradually fade away. Once your mind is free of the rigors of the False Self, it will be free to help you with any plans for the future.

In addition, once the False Self is out of your life, you will find your practices in metaphysics, psychic and mediumship will improve because they are not tainted with limiting thoughts and memories. This is why, whenever I conduct a psychic/mediumship development class, I always encourage students to kill the False Self. It also allows one to advance spiritually. If you consider this, you will find the False Self may well block your spiritual development.

If you have a strong belief that your church, your religion is right for you, the False Self will hold you to that belief. Even when something revealing occurs and the Truth is made apparent in some other philosophy, the False Self will block the Truth.

Once you are aware of the True Self and allow it to shine its light within and without, you will wonder why you waited so long to find it. And as you live with the True Self your consciousness will expand to understanding the Cosmos and the Creator, the Force behind the Universe.

REVEALING THE TRUE SELF

Shams-i-Tabrizi the whirling Sufi and teacher once said: "Keep God in remembrance until the self is forgotten." That according to philosopher Paul Brunton is the whole Yoga path in one short, simple sentence. It is the quest for the True Self, that part of you that is a direct reflection of God, the Force,

Universal Consciousness, the Creator or whatever you might choose to think of Infinite Intelligence.

The True Self is that part of you that reflects and embodies the spirit of absolute and unconditional love. Like a love bird imprisoned in a gilded cage, the True Self struggles to be free of the False Self, the negative ego that holds and manifests an illusory power in most human beings.

It is one and the same as Richard Bucke's Cosmic Consciousness. Once you have defeated the False Self through dissolution, you are free. Freedom may come with a blinding flash as it did with St. Paul on the way to Damascus, or it may come gradually, almost like the tide coming in, inching its way up the beach, inching its way into your life. One day, you wake up and know you have broken free.

MEDITATING EVERY DAY

Betty Lou and I meditate every day. As soon as I am in trance, I go to my Sanctuary of the Mind, which is a beautiful garden of tall trees, flowers and lush green lawns. There is a creek running through the lower level and an old rustic bridge. It is here that I occasionally meet loved ones and friends in spirit.

Right near the entrance is a little cove in the trees where a round white wicker table and chairs is positioned. If my guides wish to talk to me they normally appear as I come in. I don't know why, they just do. Chang is always there, as is Paul and we get into hilarious exchanges but always finish up on a serious level. Occasionally Isabel Corlett, my friend and tutor from the Vancouver Psychic Society, sits at the table. One day, almost nine months after she had crossed over, I found Barbara Thurman there chatting with the others.

One day Paul started: "Bob you cannot afford the Westville house. There are important things for you to do."

I stared at him.

"You have the teachings, you have the ability to write, you need to create books—books that show people how to break free from their suffering, how they can believe in the Afterlife and how they can love themselves unconditionally. This is so important."

Isabel backed him up. "You are now working with the Light, the Light of Awareness. You have come through the darkness into the light and it's time to help others create images and hope in people's lives. It's open to you now. But you must move...pack your boxes."

"Where should I go?"

"It will be made clear to you."

"You spirit teachers, you are all so damned vague," I started to say.

A short burst of laughter ran through the circle.

"At least everyone here is alive," said Barbara Thurman.

I left wondering how I could write books and get them published. I had three novels, written thirty years ago that were still sitting on shelves gathering dust. I was not optimistic, particularly when I looked in the basement at the Westville house and saw the 150 cardboard packing cases that were full of Sharon's bits and pieces.

Another thing. Isabel had used the phrase, "working with the Light." Father Roc had used that phrase in far off Jerusalem, and Great-grandmother Elen Egby and the Hindu Yogi had said, "Come through the darkness into the Light."

25

ESCAPE TO THE NORTH COUNTRY

ORKING WITH THE LIGHT - the Light of Awareness. The more I thought about this change of life, the stronger my realization of my True Self became. As the faces of the False Self diminished, I did indeed feel free. I started to sleep better and if and when I did wake up, I did not suffer from mind chatter, but simply slipped off to sleep again. Freedom allowed me to bring up thoughts when I needed to work with something. I felt more confidence manifesting in my Being and I was loving myself unconditionally, which was a prime teaching in my workshops and classes. My physical body felt better and I was able to exercise better.

I felt the urge to write but there were still too many things happening in New Jersey. I had just finished clearing the Westville house, moved my books and boxes into Betty Lou's garage, and continued hypnotherapy in a small office adjoining her house. I also did spirit readings and held workshops. Too many things were happening to allow me to write.

In addition, I found New Jersey State too busy for focused and relaxed thinking. Too many people in a hurry, particularly drivers who have the highest auto insurance premiums in the country, and many frequently display stress and are rude.

Spirit had urged me to write books and I agreed, I needed to find time, but at this moment I had no idea how this could be achieved.

But there was a kink generating in the Cosmos and it happened like this.

Betty Lou's friends Kathy and Mickey owned a small hay farm in a remote part of upstate New York and we received an invitation to visit. Great idea, I thought, we can drive across the border to Canada and visit my old friend and colleague from British Forces Broadcasting days, Pat Pachebat who had retired and settled in Montreal in the province of Quebec. It would be a good break.

Upstate New York is just the opposite of New York City. It has miles and miles of open countryside with undulating hills populated by carpets of forests, a number of gorgeous lakes with crystal clear water, and beef and dairy farms in the lowlands. There is a flotilla of little communities named after world capitals and cities like Copenhagen, Canton, Rome, Mexico, Alexandria, Belfast, Berlin, Paris, Liverpool and so on. It can be quite confusing, almost hilarious, to explain to someone in England that you took a drive through Copenhagen in less than a minute and a short while later found yourself in the little town of Denmark.

The most noticeable benefit in northern New York State is the air. It flows off Lake Ontario and is intoxicatingly fresh. Betty Lou, who in New Jersey relied on various medications for asthma, found there was no need for them in upstate New York. In the summer, the lake shores and the riversides of the St. Lawrence become crowded with tourists, fisher-people and boaters.

Businesses flourish in the summer, but when September comes, many pack their bags and leave for Florida to return the following April. During the winter you can muffle up and walk down the middle of a country highway and the only vehicle you need to avoid is the snowplow. These monsters resemble something from a sci-fi movie. They span the highway with three sets of blades. One snowy night I caught sight of one coming up behind us and almost had a coronary.

ATTRACTIVE HOMES IN THE NORTH

We had an interesting week visiting Kathy and Mickey in a tiny community called Edwards. That night, the air was so quiet it was difficult for us to get to sleep, but when we got used to the quiet it was marvelous. We did visit Pat Pachebat in Montreal and spent two days reminiscing on the old days at Forces Broadcasting in Cologne, Aden and Cyprus and the scores of people, many of them characters, with whom we worked. Pat kept himself fit in his retirement by doing PR for a Montreal-based German company, playing tennis and walking briskly around the city.

While visiting Kathy and Mickey, we picked up a real estate newspaper and found that the whole area possessed very attractive properties at great prices. When we returned to New Jersey, we got in touch with a North Country realtor, Pete Ledoux and within a few weeks we were the owners of a very large three bedroom mobile home, tucked away in a cul-de-sac in Cape Vincent's picturesque Millens Bay. It was a five minute walk to the St. Lawrence Seaway where we could watch ships from around the world heading into or out of the Great Lakes. It was January 2006.

The original plan was to spend a week in Millens Bay and three weeks in New Jersey, but the desire to be back in upstate New York became so powerful that we wanted to spend more time there, even in the snow and the frosts of winter, which are not as bad as some Floridians claim.

But then something awful happened. One morning I spotted something I didn't wish to see. Redness in my urine. Blood. I found a urologist in Dr. Mark Fallick MD in Voorhees, New Jersey and he performed an endoscopic examination. The idea is terrifying at first but one does get used to it. A video camera is inserted through the penis into the bladder. He promptly diagnosed a small tumor. A couple of weeks later, I entered Virtua Hospital for day-surgery and the offending tumor was clipped off and withdrawn. It was done under general anesthetic but they kept me in over-night. The problem is the catheter for urinating one has to wear for a week. It drove me crazy and after four or five days I pulled it out and resumed normal urination. I had to visit the urologist's clinic for six weekly injections of chemotherapy into my bladder.

"You used to smoke," Dr. Fallick remarked one day.

"Forty a day," I told him. "I quit a long time ago – thirty-one years in fact."

He shook his head. "There's always the off-chance. You're lucky you came in quickly."

CHANG EXPLAINS THE PROBLEM

We moved to Millens Bay shortly after and found a urologist in Ogdensburg, Dr. Lars Thompson with whom I could have regular checks every three months. As I write this book my inspections are every six months."

During this time I zeroed in on Chang with the question: "Why me, after so many years? Why me, after I have helped so many people quit smoking through hypnosis, several thousand in fact?"

"There was a seed, a tiny thing called a carcinogen, which had lain dormant in the body from your smoking days," explained Chang. "You experienced a lot of stress in the last two or three years through work and it became activated. It turned cancerous. It is important for you to relax and love yourself unconditionally. Get into the mind-set of loving yourself unconditionally."

Chang urged me to meditate every day and to write books that will help those who wished to be helped. "The Spirit side will always help you," he said.

Betty Lou and I meditate for twenty minutes to half an hour every day, sometimes with music, sometimes with mantras, drums, rattles, singing bowls and the metronome. The ideal method for meditation is absolute silence. It is particularly challenging for a person who is used to having a lot of noisy activity in their life, to suddenly turn it off and seek the silence, but it can be accomplished by using music and sounds and graduating slowly into the silence. I will mention the value of silence shortly.

Chang had one invaluable truth: "Learn to love yourself unconditionally and you will flow with the Cosmos."

A MANTRA FOR LOVING UNCONDITIONALLY

If you have practiced the teachings in Chapter 22, you will have discovered the power of Impartial Self Observation which shines the light of Awareness on the many faces of the False Self and normally dissolves them, or as Paul Brunton put it "crucifies" them. In addition you will be practicing living in the Here and Now and realize that this state of consciousness is the only true reality. There is no other time than right now, and as the Yogis say: "If you are not enjoying yourself right now, when are you going to enjoy yourself?"

The same applies to love. If you are not loving yourself unconditionally right now, when are you going to love yourself?

Loving yourself unconditionally is not the easiest of challenges, but as the power of the False Self diminishes and eventually disappears, the memories of the Past no longer create a barrier, but there may be some habitual limitations remaining.

Some things I learned over the years, I share with you.

Every morning as you stand in front of the bathroom mirror, look yourself right in the eyes and say out loud: "I'm fantastic, I'm marvelous, I love myself." Say it three times, and you will notice your energy runs high throughout the day.

Before you leave home, tell your plants and flowers that you love them. Tell them how great they are looking today. In addition, tell your partner that you love him or her. Note how great it feels to spread love.

After I read Japanese scientist Masaru Emoto's book "The Hidden Messages in Water" I developed the habit of talking to water. Filling a drinking glass with water, I look at it and tell it out loud or silently: "My love surrounds and strengthens you." Then I drink the water that is energized with love. Why? Because the body is – give or take – seventy-five per cent water, and when the water in the glass is channeled to all the cells in my body, it carries the love message and what better way to ensure that your body is loved.

One therapy that we learned and practice is EFT or Emotional Freedom Therapy, a process that involves tapping on meridian points on the body, similar to those used in acupuncture. Such tapping can release energy blockages that cause negative emotions. Founded by Gary Craig, if used properly it becomes a powerful energy healing technique. My sister Diane Egby-Edwards and her partner Alan Davidson, both therapists in Bourne-mouth, England, use it as a healing modality.

One of the key phrases used in energy tapping is "...I deeply and completely accept myself." If you pause for a few moments and consider this phrase you will realize it carries a powerful statement for self improvement. Here is one mantra that I use when I'm short of energy.

"Every day in every way I deeply and completely accept myself." It's more convincing if one does it in connection with energy tapping, but if you cannot, simply chant it to yourself during a meditation. In essence it is telling you that it is all right to love yourself.

If you find you have difficulty living in the present, you can use energy tapping to eliminate any limitations by saying: "Although I find it difficult to live in the Here and Now, I deeply and completely accept myself." Do this several times and observe what happens.

Another: "Although I find it difficult to love myself unconditionally, I deeply and completely accept myself."

This one is excellent if you find you have difficulty forgiving yourself. "Although I find it difficult to forgive myself, I deeply and completely accept myself." Next to Love, Forgiveness is the most powerful force in the Universe.

It really does not matter which route you use to attain your freedom. It might be Impartial Self Observation with the non-judging technique that eliminates the False Self and its memory banks of negative memories and faces, or it can be through energy tapping using the EFT or similar modalities. It is to always have an objective, a goal, a target that equates to freedom. With the False Self gone you will find you stop hurting people, especially the ones you love deeply, and in this way you find freedom.

I cannot emphasize enough the importance of living in the Here and Now, the present, because it enables unconditional love to manifest in the mind and body. When you live in the present, the Now, one no longer judges past performances but simply focuses on the current situation.

I realized I had hurt some very nice and beautiful women along the path, but now I had broken through. I felt free. Is this what Great-Grandmother Elen meant so many years ago when she said: "...you will hurt people, even loved ones, until you set yourself free?"

COSMIC CONCIOUSNESS

Once you have gotten your False Self out of the way, a form of Cosmic Consciousness will come over you. Do not fear it, simply accept it. All it does is open a door to greater understanding of yourself and the Universe.

When you love yourself unconditionally and live, work and play in the Here and Now, you will find the quiet, and as the mystical St. Paul declared, you will find the peace of the God the Spirit that passes all understanding. Do not make the mistake of imagining it. That could be the old False Self still lurking with memories. Simply allow the peace to be in your life. Allow yourself to be surprised by the peace. Resist the old desire to think about the quiet, the peace, the silence. Like when the student is ready the teacher appears. It's the same with the peace of God the Spirit. When the quester is ready, he or she will find themselves in the quiet.

Initially, the realization may last a few seconds, but once you have experienced it, it will inevitably happen again, lasting longer, and then one day, it will last forever.

This does not mean your life on Planet Earth ceases, far from it. You will still love, work and play but your career, your relationships, your activities, your body and mind will all feel different. You will still argue, debate and occasionally get pissed off, but your powers of Awareness will instantly trigger a laugh and you will see the light through any problem that occurs. But as always, you will work within the light.

BETTY LOU AND IMAGERY

Remember what the Teacher Jesus said: "Whatsoever you ask in prayer, believe you have received it and it shall be yours." (Mark 11:24) Prayer is another word for Visioning. The human mind if used properly is a powerful creator of visions.

Betty Lou wanted to be near the water. "I want to wake up in the morning and see the water, and I want to see it as the sun goes down." We both visualized a place and a short time later, the Cosmos started working. We were in Clayton. I went into a gift and jewelry store and I pointed out, "It must be nice to stand in your shop and see the water while you work."

"Oh," replied the woman, "My home overlooks the water too, so I have it both ways."

Betty Lou asked her where she lived. It was on Three Mile Point Road, overlooking Chaumont Bay, an inlet off Lake Ontario.

"We would sure like to find a place like that," said Betty Lou.

"Oh, there's a property down the road," she said.

Next morning, our realtor, Pete Ledoux, picked us up and took us to a cottage overlooking Chaumont Bay. It was wonderful. Betty Lou put in a bid for the place and word came back at lunchtime: "You've got it."

Over the next year, Betty Lou organized an extension and the BayZen Center came into being; a place big enough for workshops, classes, meditation and spiritual circles. It was also big enough for a therapy/reading room, a much needed bedroom overlooking the water, and a garage and store room.

The whole thing was visualized and it became real.

In all of these things, we took time out to learn Sound Healing with Dr. John Beaulieu and became certified sound healers. We learned that sounds can impact and heal misaligned energy in the body at the physical, mental and spiritual level. It is an effective and proven modality that uses vibrational sounds to help reduce stress, alter consciousness and create a deep sense of peace. To this end, we accumulated tuning forks, tingshas, gongs, rainsticks, didgeridoos and Native Indian flutes. We also use and teach toning, that is, using the voice to accomplish sound healing.

When you visualize something or pray for something and "believe you have received it" you trigger a kink in the Cosmos. We did just that in the north country of New York State.

WELCOME TO THE UNITED STATES

It was now 2009 and my Green Card would expire in a couple of years. I had been living in the United States for twelve years and I felt I should become a citizen. The United States had been good to me. So I went on-line and filled in the forms, printed and mailed them in, along with a check. One day, a letter came and asked me to attend an interview in Syracuse, New York. I swotted up on every possible question they could ask me and the immigration fellow who interviewed me, I think his name was Rick, did an excellent job, and invited me to come back to the Federal Courthouse and be sworn in as a citizen on November 5th. This particular date in history holds a memory. It was on this date in 1956 when Brigadier Tubby Butler rejected my request to go into the Suez War with the Parachute Regiment. It's strange how dates stay in the memory. This was going to be another strange day.

Dressed in my Sunday best, I turned up at the Courthouse to hear the Security Guard say: "Oh, the swearing in ceremony took place Monday, two days ago."

My world almost collapsed. The goddess's voice came through: "Stay calm. Walk over to the Immigration Office." I felt like running, but I did indeed walk.

A CITIZEN OF THE UNITED STATES:
On November 5th 2009 the author became a citizen of the United States of America.
It was a small, unique and memorable ceremony and Betty Lou took the picture.

Rick was there. He apologized and suggested the Buffalo Office should have notified me of the change. He then disappeared into the office and came out ten minutes later. "I have spoken to the people in Buffalo. You can come back on December 17th for a Courthouse swearing in or I can do it now."

Betty Lou murmured: "It might be snowing then."

The Immigration Office did it there and then and Betty Lou took a picture.

HEALING, THE GREATEST GIFT

The healing of any person is the greatest gift one can bestow because it involves unconditional love and helps a sick person on the road to recovery. In my book "INSIGHTS: The Healing Paths of the Radical Spiritualist" I touch on a variety of healing modalities ranging from hands-on healing, self-hypnosis, meditation and imagery, dowsing for negative energy, healing through past lives, and spirit rescue.

It is here in upstate New York that I found the peace to write and share the teachings I have acquired and learned. But is it the end of the road? I don't know. We are giving classes, giving workshops and lectures, visiting churches who invite us, conducting weddings and spiritual services for those who request them, but always, we are learning. We study constantly and test the teachings all the time. Betty Lou and I have our differences but we are aligned in energies and both have our own non-conflicting images of God.

WEDDINGS IN A CASTLE :
Every year many couples are drawn to the North Country and such places as Boldt Castle and Singer Castle on the St. Lawrence River. As an ordained Spiritualist minister the author conducts services uniting people in Holy Matrimony. "It's one of the most satisfying aspects of my life, watching people in love starting their married life together," he says. The staff at both castles are the most perfect hosts. Photo by Betty Lou Kishler.

When I started on this life trek so many years ago I had cold thoughts about God, the Universe and humanity. But once I managed to dissolve the False Self, the shrouds that hid the world and the Cosmos fell away. Once the negative ego no longer controlled my outlook, I was able to study the inner teachings of the Sufi mystics, Lao Tzu, Copernicus, the Chinese mystics, Krishnamurti, Buddha, Plato and Socrates, Gurdjieff and Ouspensky, Jean Klein, Vernon Howard and Paul Brunton's incredible Notebooks.

The greatest block to spiritual development is having a belief. It becomes a cage - a prison. It will prevent you from exploring the great philosophies. You find that difficult to believe? You can test this statement. Pick up a book written by a Catholic academic and note the sources he or she quotes, and for the most part all will be Catholic. Most Catholic authors are threatened by or fear threats of excommunication if they step outside the dictated teachings of the Church. Hence, Catholic writings cannot help but reflect literary incest. This happens in most religious writings. Belief keeps authors entrenched, even imprisoned in the ruts of belief.

My idea of God changed over the years. In my years in the Royal Air Force, when I claimed I was an atheist, I often wondered how it was possible for someone not to believe in something. It did not make sense. Religions maintain belief systems and by their very natures, keep people imprisoned. For instance, if Jesus were to walk the Earth again, most Christians would not recognize him because their belief systems are so distorted with the idol created by the Church. Father Roc in Jerusalem told me in 1958 that, "Religion is not the place to find peace. Look higher into the Light. Create your life in the Light." He knew then that I would sooner or later find peace in the Light.

HOW WE SEE THE CREATOR

Today, people ask, how do you see God, the Creator? Well, it all depends on how you mean "see." Is God hidden? If he is then he is "occult" which means hidden. Some religions object to the word "occult" although that is what it means exactly – hidden!

Some people still think of the anthropomorphic God, an entity in human form resembling a kindly man surrounded by harp-playing golden-haired angels. Jesus used the term "Father" to refer to God when lecturing to simple tribal people. That was a great idea, a stroke of genius for that time and place. But to maintain the image today is nothing more than a whim of the False Self. The False Self claims, "Humans are important, therefore God made us in his image."

Jesus the Teacher put it this way: "God is Spirit." No ifs, ands or buts. And the rest of the sentence says: "...and his worshipers must worship in spirit and in truth." (John 4:24) In other words, human beings carry the Spirit of God in physical bodies.

THE PRESENCE OF THE CREATOR

There are those who say that God, the Creator is omnipotent, omniscient and omnipresent but the critics say in this case, God is also responsible for all the evil in the world. The philosopher would point out that evil in the world is created by humankind and its False Self.

The mystical pilgrim, the spiritually minded student, sees God in everything. The two words, "God is" sums it up completely. Any additional words modify God.

It is a pity that many humans walking the planet, fail to see God in the world around them and within. Take an acorn from an oak tree, plant it, water it and care for it, and in a few years it will be a major tree in your life. What was the force that generated that tree? Not the biological process but the force that triggered the biological process. What is the force that resides in each of us and keeps the body and mind moving, living, eating, working, thinking, procreating, and loving? And where does that Life Force go when the body returns to the Earth?

Deep within is that Spirit that is being constantly reinforced by God, the Universal Spirit, the Universal Consciousness. It is the spirit that exists in all life around us and within.

My Spirit friends say there is a field of consciousness existing in the Universe that contains all our thoughts. It is continually being energized both by creative thinkers on various worlds, as well as by the Universal Mind. This is why several people scattered in different parts of the world can all come up with an identical invention or an identical cure for a disease at virtually the same time. It is why a microbe in a French laboratory can mutate into a survival mode and moments later a similar microbe in a Japanese laboratory does exactly the same thing, for no apparent reason. Everything we think creates an energy force. Everything we think becomes part of the Universal Mind, that is why if you are going to be a contributor, think positively, love yourself unconditionally and live in the Here and Now.

UNIVERSITY? DAVID HAND WAS RIGHT

Somehow, somewhere, along the road of life, I changed. I met Kings – Hussein, Saud and Faisal, I met killers such as Nicos Sampson, Archbishop Makarios and other fighters, all with a cause. I met and worked with such film greats as David Hand and Stuart Crombie at Moor Hall, which D.H. compared to a University – and it was. I really "soaked it up." I met authors like Larry Durrell and learned to drink ouzo, journalists like Joe Alex Morris and Larry Collins who taught me how to sniff out a story, Vincent Ryder of the Daily Telegraph who taught me style in writing, Iacovos (Jacko) Iacovides of the Cyprus Mail, photographers such as Dennis Oulds, Tubby Abrahams and the extraordinary Larry Burrows.

There were international diplomats such as Sir Charles Johnston whose work in Jordan and Aden should have brought more than a knighthood. I encountered a flock of great broadcasters along the way, including Bill Crozier, Pat Pachebat, Peter Buckle, Kay Donnelly, John Russell and Alan Grace. I remember Leslie Knight, a survivor of the King David bombing in Jerusalem, and radio engineers such as Johnny Bull and Colin Rugg. I rubbed shoulders with great rapid transit engineers, planners and writers such as Mike O'Connor, Tom Parkinson, Stuart Hodgson, Bob Lingwood, Diane Gendron-Cooney and Lon Wood. Then there were the metaphysical teachers, Spiritualists and mediums such as Patrick Young, Isabel Corlett, Lee Pulos and Barbara Thurman and a whole lot of beautiful people, all on their own quests, their own spiritual paths.

Writing an autobiography creates emotions as memories are relived. Some writings triggered laughter, some thoughts, often of years ago, brought tears. But I feel I learned something from each person, and in their own way they contributed to the person I am today.

A VISIT TO A LONG-TIME FRIEND:
We took time off to visit England and drove to Carlisle, an ancient and historic town between the Lake District and Scotland. It's where my friend of so many years, conchologist and author S. Peter Dance lives with his wife, Una. His house is where U.S. President Woodrow Wilson's mother lived in her childhood and Mr. Wilson visited the place several times, hence its historic connections.

I recall that elegant, beautifully aging lady, that special seer who lived on Zinzan Street in Reading, England. Elen Egby gave me a cup of tea so many years ago and told me I would hurt the women I encountered and loved as I walked the path. She was right. They were Iro, Lucy, Myra, Liz, and Sharon - all special and indeed lovable women, who deserved more than a reincarnated camel driver in their lives.

I often wonder what would have happened, had I not gone to Beirut that weekend in 1953 and met Iro. Supposing I had told that jovial barkeeper John Odgers, "no thanks," and gone about my life. I would have returned to the United Kingdom with my shell-collecting friend Peter Dance and others from 751 Signals Unit, and created a different life for myself somewhere in the West Country. Perhaps I would have found Glastonbury. Perhaps it would not have come into my life at all. One can only speculate with, "What if...?"

As my writing guide Paul just butted in: "What if? We would have found you anyway."

And yes, my life would also have been very different without the spirits - God's Messengers - I like to call them. I appreciate with eternal gratitude the help of Chang, that little Chinese healing guide, Paul the writer and speech prompter, the spirits of Isabel and Barbara who keep me in trim when I'm on the platform giving messages from loved ones in the Spirit World.

26

THE LURE OF THE DESERT

T HEN THERE IS OF course the lady in white, the "Goddess" who keeps on popping up in my life since the first time when I was just a kid suffering from a then-fatal Septicemia. It was the same voice that stopped me from stepping on a land-mine in Lebanon, urged me to take a general view photo of a murder that included the gunman, and she frequently stands afar, watching us. My spirit guides are mute on who she is, even her name. She seems to be paying more attention as we are drawn to New Mexico which is the land of incredible deserts, beautiful mountain ranges, and incredible colors that lured Georgia O'Keefe to live and paint there. It's also the place when humanity entered the nuclear age on July 16th 1945. The first atomic bomb device was exploded at the White Sands. It's also a place beloved by writers, healers, psychics, movie producers and spies.

I cannot recall when I first wanted to visit the deserts and mountains of New Mexico. When we first arrived in Canada in 1966 I had a small transistor radio purchased in Germany. At night that little unit picked up a radio station broadcasting from Albuquerque, and I listened to the news from New Mexico, and never dreamed of going there. But now, forty-four years later something was calling me.

When I first started mulling over the maps and booklets on Albuquerque and New Mexico, for some strange reason I was drawn to a place called Socorro. The community has been around for some 400 years and it sits in the Rio Grande Valley, about 75 miles south of Albuquerque. A small city at 4,600 feet, it is surrounded by a number of extinct volcanoes.

When it comes to big bangs however, Socorro has had its share. A short 35 miles away to the south-east at a place called Trinity, the scientists with the Manhattan Project on July 16th 1945 detonated the first atomic bomb test. It ushered in a new era for the planet.

The test bomb was transported to the White Sands Missile Range, in a 200 ton steel container with walls 14 inches thick. It was called Jumbo and a chunk of it survived the blast and can be found in the Socorro Plaza. If you are sensitive and you place your hands on the relic and perform psychometry, you will receive powerful vibrations. My partner Betty Lou felt the vibrations through her body. I sensed two blasts, one initial small one, followed moments later by a tremendous blast. The relic of that day is still alive with memories – the Akashic Records.

Was this why I was drawn here? I didn't think so. One place I had hoped to see was the ruins of the old Kelly Mine, but I was really reluctant to drive another 30 miles on some questionable roads to see ruins that the guide books claimed "not much to see."

I described in detail what happened that day in my book, "INSIGHTS:The Healing Paths of the Radical Spiritualist." It demonstrates how Cosmic Forces can get things done their way. A series of incidents occurred that took us to the Kelly Mine. A Tourist agent in Socorro intrigued us with the town of Magdalena, and as we were driving around the town, my GPS told us we were on the Kelly Road. Reluctantly, I drove up a ragged, rut-filled, dusty road.

Reaching the brow of a hill, we found a very old church with a sign, "St. John the Baptist, Kelly N.M." It stood alone on a plateau like a sentinel, surrounded by steel fence. We parked the car and wandered around. The church is a gallant relic of the old community of Kelly, long since gone to dust. Still, services are held here once a year, we discovered. There was no sight of the illusive old mine.

Disappointed I stared at the heavily rutted track going up the mountain. It was probably too rough for any all-terrain vehicle, let alone our rental car. "I'm not going any further," I told Betty Lou and she agreed we had had enough. Returning to the car, I was about to start the engine, when a young man on a bicycle appeared almost out of nowhere. He parked his bike against the church fence and unstrapped his helmet. "The Kelly Mine? You're almost there. A quarter of a mile up the track." He said he lived "nearby" and had come from West Virginia some three years before.

"Could we hike up," I asked cautiously.

"Sure. It's just up the track. No problem." He seemed enthusiastic for us to go on. Well, that quarter mile was the longest we had ever climbed. We noted the problems. That quarter mile is at an elevation well over 8,000 feet, so the oxygen is not as plentiful as at sea level. The track ran a steady incline over rough rocks. The sun beamed mercilessly out of a perfectly blue sky, that would have made George O'Keefe tremble in ecstasy. The sun was burning at 80-degrees. Add to this the fact we had no water, and we are both in our mid-seventies, and you have a weird situation.

I kept telling myself, "Egby, you are nuts! Why are you torturing your body like this?" Twice, our lungs felt seriously short of oxygen and we had to stagger over and rest under the shade of a red cedar. Finally, we reached the sign that proclaimed "Kelly Mine."

I told Betty Lou, "I'll just get some photos of the sign and we'll head back down. This is plain stupid. We should not have come." A battered sign declared that visitors must acquire a pass in Magdalena if they wished to visit the mine. Ha! Now they tell us! I took some photos of the sign and the distant buildings by telephoto lens and was ready to turn back, totally unimpressed when something happened.

SPIRIT VOICES FROM A GHOST MINE

Voices! Not physical voices. Spirit voices. They came in softly at first, and then their enthusiasm grew. "...hear us...he can hear us," one man's voice said, several times. "He thinks we're ghosts...that's what the others said...I think we should take cover..."

"Spirits!" I told Betty Lou. "There are spirits here." Suddenly, my body discovered the energy to walk through the gate into the mine work area. The old mine buildings and machinery stood brave but desolate in the New Mexican sunshine. It seemed strange to think that in another age - spanning fifty years - that a whole community had lived here, mining lead, zinc, silver, copper, gold and later smithsonite. Production totaled over $30 million. There were hotels, saloons, stores, brothels, stables and offices.

I asked the clamoring entities to be quiet while I found a concrete wall on which to sit while I recovered from the climb. Earth-bounds are spirits that have left their physical bodies upon so-called death and become blocked; you might call it snagged in transition of a full passing into the spirit world. For a variety of reasons some spirits, vacating dying physical bodies, are reluctant to cross over into the sanctity of the Spirit World. Reasons include an acute desire to stay in the known physical world, wanting to stay with loved ones still living in the physical, a strong disbelief in the afterlife, or a powerful skepticism about the existence of Heaven and even God.

"Who is in charge?"

An entity, who had once been a shift manager, came forward. He called himself "Tom" and when I responded with "Thomas" he corrected me and insisted he was named "Tom." He had a vague Welsh accent.

"How many of you are there?"

"Eight," he responded promptly. Betty Lou, working with a pendulum, had already dowsed the number.

I wanted to know how long they had been here.

"Ah, we've been here ever since the mine closed a few years back. We worked the mine and lived locally after she closed. Then most of us got sick and that's when funny things happened. Some of us said we were dead, others claimed we were dreaming. I don't know really. Are we dead? I don't feel dead, just sort of funny. I get terribly depressed at times and I like to find a quiet place down in the mine."

The group had obviously lost track of time. Tom's observation that the "mine closed a few years back" was in reality almost eighty years before. Earth-bounds are notorious for losing track of time, and can spend decades and even centuries wandering around repeating similar questions to visitors, particular rock hunters. Their favorite was: "We are waiting for the mine to reopen. Any idea when this will be?" No one ever answered because no one ever heard them.

Tom stared at me. "Truth is we are dead. Is this all there is?"

I told them about the Spirit World, Summerland, and Heaven as some call it, and said they should all be there, not wandering around the ruins of the Kelly Mine looking for work. "There are loved ones, sweethearts, friends, who have gone on and are still waiting for you. They are ready to help."

Most of my communication was telepathic, which is the communication medium of spirits, but when I started talking about loved ones and sweethearts, the scene changed, as if someone had flicked a switch. Warm, vibrant energy, more powerful than the sun, came surging in. "We've just been joined by whole lot of angels," I said, noting the arrival of spirit helpers who said they brought miners' loved ones with them.

To Betty Lou I said: "The miners can't see spirits from the spirit world because they are depressed and looking down."

"There's a woman in spirit here." And so there was. It was a gathering of spirits, all ready to help with the miners.

The problem with earth-bounds is they become victims of depression, and the challenge is getting them to look up, raise their vibration. After years of isolation, many mechanically look down, tuning into the earth. If only they would look up, workers from the spirit world would be able to assist them in crossing over without having to rely on spirit rescuers, like me, in the physical.

"Are you all ready to join your loved ones?" I asked Tom, but he hesitated. "They're all discussing what's happening. Wait while I talk to them." Suddenly there was a quiet in the ranks. "It's time" he said slowly. "It's time to leave."

I noted my spirit guides Paul and Chang were close by. In a prayer of protection to Holy Spirit, I asked for guidance, strength and protection and to open the way, the light, for these miners to make their last journey home.

Then addressing the eight, I described the Summerland, the Spirit World and how it is a place where they can be free again, be with loved ones and friends, and advance in their spiritual lives. "It's time to let go of the Earth, lift your heads and gaze up into the beautiful white light, shining above you." I mentally repeated these words several times and finally felt an upward movement – a vibration change – within the group. "The light is the gateway to your home," I told them. "Go with the angels and loved ones. They will guide you all home." The heaviness that had existed around the miners started to clear. A few moments later, we knew that all eight had crossed over successfully.

My spirit guide Paul called out, "All clear. Good job. Glad you came?"

Then I realized I had been set up again. Ever since I picked up the New Mexico printed matter months before while sitting in upstate New York, and started reading about Socorro, Magdalena and the Kelly Mine, it was all predestined. I had been reluctant to come at all stages. Even our friends in Albuquerque had queried us going. I kept wanting to turn back, but it never happened. Even when we reached the Church of St. John the Baptist on the old Kelly Road, I had wanted to turn back.

I recalled a time years before when I was trekking to a holy place called St. Just in Roseland in Cornwall, England. I had experienced the same reluctance to go on, until a boy on a bicycle appeared out of nowhere and urged me to go on, pointing to a rainbow in the sky. I wrote about it in, "The Quest of the Radical Spiritualist." Coincidence?

"That young man at the church...on the Kelly Road...did you have any-thing to do with that?" I growled at Paul.

A peal of laughter seemed to roll around the Kelly Mine site. "Robert, I'll never tell," cried Paul. "Cosmic secrets." Mystics have a saying: "There are no such things as coincidences, only occurrences of energy we fail to understand."

As we walked down the rough track to the old St. John the Baptist Church, we stopped to look at the ruins, shells of buildings with 16-inch rock walls that had once been part of the mining community of Kelly, New Mexico. The place still holds energies of bygone days. The Akashic Records are still strong. If you are quiet you may well hear the horses panting and coughing as they drag the ore-carts down the dusty track to Magdalena and the rail head. You can still hear the mine whistles, men walking home after shifts underground, women chatting, and children laughing.

In the eternal Akashic Records, the old Kelly Mine is still alive, still work-ing, still vibrating in time. We helped eight earth-bounds that hot October 17th, 2009, but I do have a strong feeling, there are more spirits still earth-bound lurking amid the ruins at 8,000 feet, still waiting for assistance to get home to the Other Side. As I was leaving, she was there. The spirit in white. The Goddess. Simply looking.

Again, when we visited the D.H. Lawrence Ranch north of Taos, New Mexico in the Sangre de Cristobal Mountains, she was there. I caught glimpses of her out of the corner of my eye. The Ranch is a place where time stands still.

LADY CHATTERLEY'S LOVER

I first encountered the work of the controversial English author D.H. Lawrence while serving in the Royal Air Force at El Firdan, a dusty ten minute hike from the Suez Canal in Egypt. It was 1952. Someone thrust into my hands a book entitled "Lady Chatterley's Lover," an intriguing and thrilling read for a young soul. It was little wonder, in those days, that the book was banned and subjected to law suits. Today, almost 60 years later, the subject of the lady and the gardener is like a well-worn cliché, but the eloquence of the writing, the passion, the vivid colors, live on. I always wondered about Lawrence, where he lived, loved, created and passionately observed the world from a lofty perch, nestled among the tall, aging cedars of Lobo Mountain in New Mexico.

A RUSTIC CABIN IN THE MOUNTAINS: It was here on a small ranch, a few miles north of Taos, New Mexico that the prolific British author D.H. Lawrence wrote various works in the early 1920s. He is said to have worked at the rustic table in the porch. His wife Frieda lived here, and Lady Brett, an artist and typist of Lawrence's manuscripts lived in a cabin next door.

One can find the D.H. Lawrence Ranch about 26 miles northwest of Taos near the community of San Cristobal, some twenty miles along route NM522. A faded, pockmarked sign, the victim of passing graffitists, points to a six-mile drive up a dusty, rutted, gravelly road that winds tortuously and never-endingly upwards. At the 8,600 foot mark, where the air is fresh but oxygen seems in rare supply, one finds the ranch, three log buildings, now owned by the University of New Mexico.

It's as rustic as it comes, and Lawrence and his wife Frieda, would probably find it much the same as it was when they lived here for two years in the mid-1920s.

A kindly voice from under a pick-up truck cried: "You'll find the Memorial up the hill." A narrow, modern concrete path, broken by some steps, winds through the cedars. It ends at a small, stuccoed hut, with a slanting roof. Posts and chains mark the grave site of Lawrence's wife of 16 years. It features a large wooden cross and a stone marker just to the left of the Memorial building. On the stone marker, an elegant, smiling, aging woman peers from a photograph in an oval frame.

The twelve by fifteen foot white Memorial building is almost clinical inside. Made to appear as a small chapel, the walls and rails are various shades of gold, with clean grey tiles on the floor. The focal point is a concrete altar, inset with the initials DHL surrounded by sunflowers. More sunflowers sit in two vases flanking the Memorial Stone.

A GRAVE SITUATION

While living in Vence, south east France, Lawrence became very sick. He planned to return to his beloved New Mexico where the air was kind to his tuberculosis, but death intervened. He died on March 2nd 1930 and was buried in that French community. Five years later, in 1935, at his widow's request, Lawrence's body was exhumed and cremated. His ashes were brought to the ranch by Frieda's Italian lover, and later her husband, Angelo Ravagli with the intention they would be buried at the ranch.

Apparently, Lawrence's ardent admirers and followers, mainly women, objected to the ashes being buried at a remote ranch. In the face of strong opposition, while the concrete was being mixed for the marker stone, Frieda poured the remains of the author into the mix, where they remain solidly embalmed to this day. Whether this actually happened or not, is one of the mysteries surrounding Lawrence in Taos.

Visitors to the Memorial building can see, framed on the wall, copies of the official cremation certificate and a certificate by the British Consul in Nice that the urn contained the author's ashes. A guest register inside the Memorial Shrine records visitors from many parts of the world. After Lawrence's death, Frieda married her lover Angelo. When she died in Taos in 1956, she bequeathed the ranch to the University of New Mexico.

How Lawrence and his wife Frieda came to live at the ranch in May 1924 is fascinating. They had been a homeless, wandering couple traveling the world since World War One. Lawrence, born David Herbert Lawrence in 1885, son of a coal mining family in Eastwood, Nottinghamshire, met and fell in love with Frieda, the wife of his university professor. They married in 1914 and because of his visionary and modernistic writings, which shattered

Victorian-Edwardian society, and her connections with Germany, the couple fled England and adopted a life of writing and wandering.

Mabel Dodge Sterne (later Mabel Dodge Luhan), a wealthy arts patron in Taos, had read and was deeply impressed by some of Lawrence's writings. She invited the couple to stay. Eventually, she proposed to give the nine acre ranch, then called the Kiowa Ranch, to Lawrence, but he refused. However, Frieda of noble German stock (a relative of Baron von Richthofen) accepted and the deed was made in her name. It was the only property the couple ever owned.

Literary sources say that the Lawrences acquired the ranch in exchange for the manuscript of his now famous novel, Sons and Lovers. It was said that Mabel gave them the ranch to keep them "local" but to get out of the way because of the tempestuous interactions that kept cropping up between Mabel and her jealous Native Indian lover, Tony Luhan, Frieda, Lawrence and a woman called Lady Brett, a British artist. Lawrence was nick-named "Lorenzo" and Mabel Dodge Luhan later wrote a book "Lorenzo in Taos," which includes enlightening letters between Lawrence, Frieda, Lady Brett, and Mabel. It gives tremendous insights into the minds of these people.

While at the ranch, Lawrence would sit out on the wooden porch surrounded by a garden and stately trees. He wrote his novel "St. Mawr" and commenced writing "The Plumed Serpent" there. Various writers and artists, including Aldous Huxley visited the Lawrences. Life was not always quiet at the ranch. Frieda, in a book published after Lawrence's death, mentioned frequent quarrels between Mabel, her new husband Luhan, and Freida and Lady Brett and Lawrence himself. This tense atmosphere seemed to provoke Lawrence to write or perhaps, escape.

After the Lawrences left for Europe in 1925, one of the visitors invited to the ranch by Mabel Dodge Luhan was painter Georgia O'Keeffe. She stayed several weeks there and spent time relaxing on a bench, gazing up through the branches of what was to be known as "The Lawrence Tree." One day she created a painting of the tree, which still stands there, as strong and as stately as when Lawrence sat in its shade and wrote his novels and O'Keefe painted there. Nearby is a stand with a copy of Georgia's painting.

Visitors can roam round the buildings and through the garden, touch the Lawrence Tree, and take in the meadows and the rolling distant blue hills and breathe the fresh, invigorating air, and as we did, watch the first dark storm clouds of Autumn rolling their way majestically across a perfectly bluer than blue sky.

When Lawrence crossed into Spirit, E.M. Foster in an obituary, described him as, "The greatest imaginative novelist of our generation." Besides being an author, Lawrence was also an artist. Nine of the Lawrence oils have been on display in the La Fonda Hotel in Taos since shortly after his death.

If one sits quietly by Lawence's log cabin, and allows the mountain air, delicately perfumed by the cedars, to tantalize the nostrils, you may hear the wind softly whistling through the pines and creating a meditative background, broken only by high spirit voices still interacting in another dimension. The Lawrence Ranch, eighty years since the author and Frieda lived there, is a place standing still, basking in the dusts of time.

A VOICE FROM THE PAST

The Mabel Dodge Luhan house in Taos is still there. It's now a well run hotel basking in the shadows of Mabel and her many famous visitors like Aldous Huxley, Georgia O'Keefe, Jean Toomer and Carl Jung.

In October 2010, Betty Lou and I stayed there and out of curiosity, visited the Hotel La Fonda in downtown Taos to see their special gallery of so-called "Forbidden Paintings."

The original collection consists of nine oil paintings. They're all that remains from an exhibition of thirteen paintings that were on show in London in 1929 and were confiscated by the Metropolitan Police. The paintings were banned and declared obscene. In danger of being burned, Lawrence agreed to ship the paintings out of England. The ban is still in force today.

In today's sexually active culture, the paintings have not much appeal, except that they were painted by D.H. Lawrence, the author who wrote a string of literary masterpieces and is now recognized as one of the great British writers of the 20th Century.

Eight of the nine paintings at the La Fonda Gallery show various nudes, mostly in close-up, but one actually features a landscape of colored trees with two nudes in the foreground. It is the only one that has a landscape.

As I looked at the painting, a voice came on my left side. "I didn't paint it, you know," came the distinctly English voice. He caught me by surprise and I did not know what to say, so he continued. "Frieda was upset by my other body paintings and wanted to create something of her own. She likes to paint. Still does over here. But she didn't want to sign it. I added finishing touches which upset the poor woman." It was followed by a muffled laugh.

"Lorrie, stop it," said a woman's voice. "Have some respect."

I shook my head trying to listen psychically. "What drew you to come to New Mexico – Taos?"

"Energy! Energy! It's different here. Like a magnificent volcano erupting with a cosmic energy. Don't you feel it? It's an earth energy – a vortex. Look for it and you will find it."

"Where?" I said, but he had faded away.

For the rest of our stay in New Mexico we were alert to spirit manifestations. While walking through the ancient cottonwood trees surrounding the Mabel Dodge Luhan House, Betty Lou photographed the trunk of one of the gnarled trees. For a while, we were sure there was the face of D.H. Lawrence inset in the bark but it seemed to dissipate.

SPIRITS GALORE AT PECOS

Just 25 miles east of Santa Fe is the Pecos National Historical Park. The main unit of the park preserves the ruins of Pecos Pueblo which is thought to have been established in the 14th century. The pueblo was an important Native Indian center because it stood on the edge of the Plains and also the Pecos River. It was occupied for over 400 years until the 19th century, when the last of its residents abandoned it and moved to Jemez.

The Spaniards had a mission here which lasted some 200 years. Today there are the remains of Mission Nuestra Señora de los Ángeles de Porciúncula de los Pecos, a Spanish mission near the pueblo, built in the early 17th century.

Why did we come here? Well, that's a story on its own. Down the road apace from the Pecos National Historic Park is the Forked Lightning Ranch which was bought in 1941 by E.E. "Buddy" Fogelson, a Dallas oil man and rancher. In 1949 Buddy married British actress Greer Garson and the ranch became a center for gracious living and entertaining.

Now, ever since I saw her movie, "Mrs. Miniver" at the old Rialto Cinema in Maidenhead so long ago, I was one of her fans. I saw the movie at least three or four times, and when I heard her home was east of Santa Fe, I told Betty Lou I would like to go there. Buddy died in 1987 and in January 1991, Mrs. Fogelson. Greer Garson sold the Forked Lightning to the Conservation Fund which donated it to the National Park Service to become part of Pecos National Historical Park. Greer crossed into Spirit in April 1996.

We took the tour of the old Greer Garson home and the place is beautiful. Her typewriter is still there in her office, but I think her spirit no longer roams the ranch. The spirit of the actress who was one of America's top ten box office draws in 1942, 1943, 1944, and 1945 has moved on. So we explored the old Pecos Pueblo. Little did we know we were walking into a Spirit Jamboree.

The Park has reconstructed the two Kivas at the Pueblo. Kivas are rooms built in the ground and lined with stone. A roof is supported by a heavy pole. A small hole in the roof permits entrance by a wooden ladder. Kivas are sacred places and in pueblos that are homes for Native Indians, the kivas are kept private. But in places like Pecos, the kivas are open to the public.

A SPIRITUAL PLACE AT PECOS:
At the remains of the old Pecos Kiva, spirit activity was pronounced when Betty Lou descended the ladder on Sunday October 10th 2010 and took these two photographs. The next day, when the author descended, there was some activity, but not the pronounced activity of the day before.

One kiva is near the church and the other is on the far side of the pueblo. Betty Lou and I climbed the pathway to the other kiva. I decided to sit on a park bench in the shade of a tree and perform a meditation. As I sat down I noticed several spirit forms gathered around the kiva. "There are spirits around," I called out, and I watched her go down the ladder. At 250 pounds, I was leery if the ladder would hold me.

Betty Lou took several photos inside the kiva, and when we examined them later, we found, much to our astonishment, one of the pictures was full or orbs - spirit forms. Even in her other photographs, there were orbs. Next day, we returned to the kiva and I went down into the sacred place. I could sense the spirits but could not see then. I took several photos but there were not very many orbs still there. I had the feeling that the spirits had been there on a special occasion – for what I know not. We visited the other kiva by the ruins of the old Spanish church but there was hardly any spirit activity, perhaps because in Earth life, Indians were not fond of the Catholic Church. Why would they be in Spirit?

IN THE ENCHANTED CIRCLE

If you go to Taos, the travel books will suggest you take the Enchanted Circle, a scenic route that circles through the communities of Questa, Red River, Eagle Nest and Angel Fire, before coming back to Taos. It encircles part of the Sangre de Cristobal Mountains including the Wheeler Peak, which at over 13,000 feet is the highest point in New Mexico. There was something drawing me to this Circle.

The Enchanted Circle is an 84-mile route, and it was at Angel Fire we ran into spirits. The Vietnam Veterans Memorial stands in the only State Park in the United States dedicated exclusively to Vietnam veterans. A Huey helicopter, rebuilt after having received 135 bullet holes, guards the entrance. In the memorial building we found, a fascinating chapel, an amphitheater, plus a research center with profiles and pictures of the many men and women who lost their lives in Vietnam, plus a movie room showing the HBO documentary "Dear America: Letters Home from Vietnam."

The memorial was created by Victor (Doc) Westphall and his wife Jessie after their son David was killed in Vietnam in 1968. David is buried at the National Cemetery in Santa Fe, but his parents are buried on the Memorial Site they created at Angel Fire. This special place is visited by many people every day and the chapel never closes.

As I walked out of the chapel towards the burial plot of the Westphalls, I was suddenly surrounded by a heavy, anxious, depressed energy and my eyes were filled with tears.

"Earthbounds!" I said to Betty Lou. "There must be earthbounds here. It's just like the energy at the Kelly Mine, but worse."

Suddenly a voice in Spirit came through. "Not so. No earthbounds. You need to understand, Robert," said my Spirit Guide Chang. "It's different."

Then another voice emerged:

"This is Doc speaking. When people come here, they pray. They are reminded of the war, they are reminded of loved ones they lost, and the wounds still hurt. Each one leaves that heavy energy here. It is like an old cloak. Sadness weighs heavily. They naturally impart it and we accept it."

I could feel Doc Westphall's energy coming closer.

"There is a special group of veterans here known as the Spirit Guard," he said. "Every so often, their work is to come and release the heavy energy here into the Universe, the Cosmos. If it was allowed to accumulate, the intense energy would engulf all who enter here and make their visit unbearable. A visit here should be uplifting. We want visitors to appreciate and remember their visit to this Shrine."

From this, I learned that not all negative energy banks signify the presence of earthbound spirits. It was strange, but I was to be given a demonstration of how veterans leave their hurts and emotions at the memorial.

A LUNCH IN PECOS

Three days later we were sitting on the deck of a restaurant in the tiny town of Pecos, New Mexico, 108 miles away from Angel Fire. Three mature men were sitting at the next table reminiscing of times gone by.

One, for no apparent reason started talking about the Vietnam Veterans Memorial State Park at Angel Fire and he said: "When I go there and pray for thirty minutes, I leave completely refreshed."

Spirit works in strange but understandable ways. Why should we pick that restaurant for lunch, and sit outside on the deck. We almost sat inside. But something told me to "Sit outside." We did, and I believe we were placed to hear an echo, a reinforcement of what Doc Westphall was talking about.

AN EARTH ENERGY—A VORTEX

After visiting New Mexico three times, I am convinced there is a unique and special energy existing in the mountains of New Mexico. It is an energy field that manifests from Pecos and Santa Fe in the south through Jemez Springs, Los Alamos, Abiquiu where Georgia O'Keefe lived and painted, through

Chimayo and El Santuario, the incredible healing church that some call the "Lourdes of America," and it extends through Taos and the famous Taos Pueblo, which is said to be over a thousand years old and is well preserved, Angel Fire and the Vietnam Veterans Memorial Park, and through the Enchanted Circle.

WELCOME TO O'KEEFE COUNTRY:
This is the scene at the Ghost Ranch near Abiquiu, New Mexico where American artist Georgia O'Keefe spent some fifty years wandering through the deserts and the colorful mountains creating incredible works of art.

The area is home to hundreds of artists and craft makers and their studios line the narrow streets. In Santa Fe, the capital of the State, with a population of close to 75,000, there are said to be 4,000 New Age practitioners ranging through massage therapists, Reiki, acupuncture, reflexologist practitioners along with psychics, mediums, seers and spiritual folk and dealers in crystals and precious stones. In addition, there are Christian and Buddhist monasteries. There is a new breed taking shape here, the movie makers. Ever since Dennis Hopper, Peter Fonda and Terry Southern made the cult classic "Easy Rider" in Taos in 1969, movie making has been on the upswing. Greer Garson even donated the funds for the Santa Fe Studios. Wikipedia has listed over one hundred "Films Shot in New Mexico."

It is little wonder D. H. Lawrence and Frieda loved this area so much, in fact the ranch where the Lawrences lived is within the Enchanted Circle.

The spirit of the great author said it well: "Energy! Energy! It's different here. Like a magnificent volcano erupting with a cosmic energy. Don't you feel it? It's an earth energy – a vortex. Look for it and you will find it."

So, we are looking for it. Life and the search for Cosmic energies goes on. We are heading back to find out. I sense that Great-Grandmother Elen Egby, the Seer of Reading would approve.

TAILPIECE

Oh, yes, the woman in white stood watching me conduct the spirit rescue at the Kelly Mine near Magdalena, and again while we were visiting the old D.H. Lawrence Ranch near Taos. I call her "Goddess," but I think she's a guardian angel, I'm not quite sure. I feel that she has been "the voice" that keeps popping up at critical or interesting moments. One of these days I will find out, but I suppose the revelation is not supposed to happen yet.

MEDITATING IN THE FREEDOM OF THE LIGHT:
The author meditates in Betty Lou's garden in New Jersey before heading out to speak in the Westville Spiritualist Church. The subject: "Being Free and Living and Working in the Light." Great-grandmother was so right. Photo by Ken Kishler.

They tell me the spirits, the astral guides, the angels, the messengers of God, are all around us just waiting to make contact. It is so unfortunate that millions of people walking Planet Earth live their lives without ever making contact. They are there, helping us to tread softly when there is danger or when opportunity offers itself.

Me? I don't think I would have survived on this chunk of rock without them. So I share my love with them and everyone who has been in my life and shared their knowledge and wisdom.

Tread softly, meditate, live in the Here and Now and love in Peace.

Robert Egby
Chaumont, New York
January 2011

AUTHOR'S NOTES
AND BIBLIOGRAPHY

STRANGE OCCURENCES
IN THE WRITING OF THIS BOOK

Early in my metaphysical life, medium Patrick Young told us: "There are no such things as coincidences and miracles; they are only energies we fail to understand.

Several incidents occurred during the writing of this book. During the writing of the Jordan section, I decided it would be great for my memory if I read British Ambassador Charles Johnston's book "The Other Side of Jordan." He had treated both Lucy and I very well. I found the book listed on Amazon's "Used" Section. Copies were offered by various merchants. I sent for one, and discovered, much to my disappointment, it was a book about California. I tried another. Same thing. The California book kept coming up.

Then I discovered that Sir Charles' book and the California book had been given the same ISBN number – the International Standard Book Number – by an international publisher in 1972. Each one of the merchants said they possessed the California.

Desperate, I emailed a bookseller in Ireland. He examined his copy and confirmed it was the one written by Charles Johnston. Imagine my surprise when it arrived and I opened it to find it was a first edition presentation copy and incredibly signed by Sir Charles himself.

Mabel Dodge Luhan was a larger than life celebrity hostess who patronized the arts and attracted artists, writers, philosophers, radical speakers and others to her spacious home in Taos, New Mexico, particularly in the twenties and thirties. She was an author and collected four husbands.

Among the authors she attracted was the controversial British author D.H. Lawrence and his wife Frieda, who was a relative of Manfred von Richthoven, otherwise known as the Red Baron. When Lawrence died in 1931, Mabel wrote a book containing all the letters that she and Lawrence had exchanged between each other. The Book was called "Lorenzo in Taos." Lorenzo was Mabel's name for Lawrence. It was published in January 1932.

I searched for a copy, but most of them were "collector's" items and quite pricey. Finally, I found a used copy, said to be in "fair" condition. The book arrived and was a first edition. Inside was a page of scrawled writing; "Santa Fe, NM. You have met some of the puppets that strut across these pages. You saw Lawrence in the Bank and this gives you the real, latter-day Lawrence for your south-western shelf...and it's Valentine's own day."

There is no signature, but it clearly resembles Mabel's distinctive and predictable writing. The other point: the note on the book is dated 2/14/32. The day I was born in far off Maidenhead.

During the writing of my activities in Aden, I discovered tucked away some black and white negatives of British tanks operating in the desert east of Aden. The story behind these negatives is this. In 1962/63 I was working as a journalist and broadcaster in Aden and while on a three day reconnaissance in the East Aden Protectorate with a British Army patrol, encountered two British Army tanks and their crews. They were close to the shores of the Indian Ocean.

Over the years my notes on this meeting became lost, and I wanted to use the photographs in this book. I built a special webpage with the photographs displayed, and then I started checking round the internet. The people at the Historic Military Vehicle Forum identified the tanks – Centurions – and suggested the berets worn by the soldiers were of the Royal Scots Greys. The Greys were very helpful. They identified the tank commander as Sgt. George Mitchell. No one could identify his Loader. I discovered the tanks were based at Falaise Camp in Little Aden. In appreciation, I sent the Greys a set of the photographs and gave them rights to use them within the Regiment. So, I thought everything was finished.

A couple of weeks later in early December 2010, an email came out of the blue. Sergeant George Mitchell's grandson had found the webpage showing her grandfather in his Centurion tank. George's daughter Catherine and her husband Gordon said they would love to know the odds of this. "But exactly thirty-two years ago, the Regimental Quartermaster Sergeant George William Mitchell commanding the tank, walked his eldest daughter down the aisle of an Edinburgh church and straight into my arms," wrote Gordon Forrest. "Sadly, George died on 6th August 2007 and we still miss him and the stories about Aden and his other postings." Apparently George had lost most of his photographs from that time, so we sent the George's family copies of the photos taken in the Aden desert almost 50 years ago.

Another coincidence. For over ten years, I have had several of my top news photos from the Cyprus Emergency on my website, hoping that someone would know what happened to the negatives after Central Press Photos was sold. One of the photos shows a general view of an E.O.K.A. killing, a young man named Bonici. The picture shows a British Army officer on the scene. Apart from being on display for ten years, the photo is fifty-five years old.

In late November 2010, while I was rewriting the chapter on how that photo came about, I received an email from a lady named Liz. She informed me that she found the photo on the web. The British Army officer was her father, Major Dick Stuckey of the South Staffordshire Regiment. Liz says she was a little girl living in Cyprus when the picture was taken. Her Dad, who retired as a Colonel, celebrated his 90th birthday a few days after she wrote to me. As I knew the names of most of the people in the photograph, I was wondering who the officer was. Somehow, the energy went out to the Cosmos and my question was answered. Thanks Liz for naming the face.

I sometimes wonder who or what is pulling the strings in the Cosmos, a point I make in the book.

Robert

KINGS AND SPECIAL
PEOPLE ALONG THE PATH

Rashid Karami – Lebanese Prime Minister and political leader. Held office eight times as PM between 1955 and 1987. In the Guinness Book of Records, he held the distinction of the "world's most democratically re-elected Prime Minister." On June 1st, 1987 he was killed when a bomb planted under his helicopter exploded.

King Faisal II of Iraq. On July 14, 1958 General Abdul Karim Kassem and a division of the Iraqi army, marched on Baghdad and overthrew the monarchy. Faisal and his uncle, Emir Abdullah, were killed in the brief fighting, while Prime Minister Nuri es-Said was later butchered in the streets. Iraq became a republic.

Saud bin Abdul Aziz, better known as King Saud of Saudi Arabia. After an internal power struggle within the Saudi Royal Family, Saud gave in and agreed to abdicate on 28 March 1964. After living in Geneva and various other cities, he died in Athens, Greece, on February 23, 1969, after suffering a heart attack in his sleep.

Hussein bin Talal, better known as King Hussein of Jordan, guided his country through forty years of the Arab-Israeli conflict. Born 14th November 1935 in Amman, he was educated in Egypt and at the British Military Academy at Sandhurst in England. At age fifteen, he was almost killed when his grandfather, King Abdullah, was assassinated in Jerusalem on July 20th 1951. He assumed the throne at eighteen in 1953. He reigned forty-six years and wrote his autobiography "Uneasy Lies the Head." On 7 February 1999 in Amman, Jordan, King Hussein died of complications related to non-Hodgkin's lymphoma.

Larry Burrows, (1926 – 1971) British born news photographer, started his career as a "tea-boy" at Life's London office in 1942. Shortly after, he started photographing conflicts in the Congo, a variety of Middle East countries including Cyprus, Lebanon, Suez War, Egypt and finally Viet Nam. He died February 10th 1971 when the helicopter in which he was travelling, was blown up over Laos. Larry's incredible portrayals of war in pictures can be viewed in the book "Larry Burrows: Vietnam" published by Alfred A. Knopf.

Joe Alex Morris Jr. The Middle East was his journalistic home for 25 years. He covered it for United Press International, the New York Herald Tribune, Newsweek, and finally the Los Angeles Times. In February 1979, Morris and other western journalists were in Tehran, covering one of the final events of the overthrow of the Shah of Iran. In a clash at an Iranian airfield on February 10th between forces loyal to the government and those committed to the Ayatollah Khomeini, Morris was struck in the chest by a bullet. He was 51.

His Beatitude, Makarios III, Archbishop and Ethnarch of the Orthodox Church of Cyprus and the first president of the Republic of Cyprus, 1959-1977. In 1959 he accepted independence for Cyprus and was elected president, with a Turkish vice president. Twice re-elected, he fled Cyprus following an attempted coup by Greek Cypriot National Guard (1974) who made Nicos Sampson president for eight days. Despite a subsequent invasion by Turkey and the establishment of a separate Turkish Cypriot state in the north, he resisted partition of the country. He died August 13th 1977 and is buried near Kykko Monastery in the Troodos Mountains.

Nicos Sampson (December 16, 1935 – May 9, 2001) For eight days, he was the de facto president of Cyprus that succeeded Archbishop Makarios, President of Cyprus in 1974. Sampson was a journalist while being a member of EOKA, which rose against the British colonial administration. In 1960 and the formation of the Republic of Cyprus, he entered journalism and publishing and printed a series of stories on how he had executed various Britons. He eventually became a Member of Parliament. Following the coup of 1974 by the Greek Military Junta, he was appointed President. Following the Turkish invasion of Cyprus on July 20th, he resigned. He was sentenced to twenty years in prison for abuse of power. He became the only person convicted and maintained he was a victim of a set-up and cover up, which to date has never been proved or dismissed. He was exiled to France, where he was given medical treatment for poor health. He returned to Cyprus in 1990, and was pardoned the remainder of his sentence in 1993. He died of cancer May 9th 2001.

Sir Charles Hepburn-Johnston, British diplomat. Served as Ambassador to Jordan 1956-1959. He then became Governor and Commander-in-Chief of Aden and High Commissioner for the Protectorate of South Arabia 1959-

1963. His last post was High Commissioner to Australia 1965-1971. During his retirement, he translated Pushkin's novel in verse Eugene Onegin from the Russian, preserving its unusual Onegin stanza form. The translation was published by Penguin Classics in 1977. He died in London April 23rd 1986.

Additional Note: Charles Johnston wrote two other books based on his experiences as a diplomat. "The View from Steamer Point: Three Crucial Years in South Arabia," and "The Brink of Jordan" which is an interesting picture of politics in the Hashemite Kingdom.

Iacovos (Jacko) Iacovides, publisher of the Cyprus Mail English language daily newspaper in Cyprus. As the war ended, Jacko had a vision and he published the first edition on November 2nd 1945. It cost one piaster or half a cent in today's prices. He was every bit a publisher and a journalist. His newspaper chronicled Cyprus through its darkest days through to the sunlight of a new country. When Jacko passed away in November 1988 his son Kyriakos assumed the publisher's chair and at the time of writing the newspaper is sixty-five years old.

David Hand, Animator and Animated Motion Picture Producer. DH started with Walt Disney and was technical director for such classics as "Bambi" and "Snow White." In 1945, J. Arthur Rank commissioned him to start Gaumont British Animation at Moor Hall, Cookham, U.K. A total of nineteen cartoons were produced by 1950, when the Rank Organization facing economic difficulties, generally, closed Moor Hall. The Cookham films were honored in the Festival of Britain, and David Hand was presented to the then Queen of England, who later became the Queen Mother. Since that time, the films have been declared to be Historical Documents. For his work in directing or supervising over 21 films for Disney, several of them Academy Award winners, David Hand was awarded in 1984 the Winsor McCay ANNIE (The Academy Award of the Animation Industry). In 1994, The Walt Disney Company bestowed their highest award on him by proclaiming him to be a "Legend of Disney." The award was posthumous. On Sunday, October 25th 1986 an Associated Press story out of San Luis Obispo, California carried the headline: "Bambi director dies at 86." It quoted Frank Thomas, one of the "Nine Old Men" of Disney, as remembering David Hand for his "energy, drive and determination." Right on!

BIBLIOGRAPHY
SOME BOOKS TO MULL OVER

This bibliography comprises a list of books that focus on the various countries in which the author lived, worked and studied.

ENGLAND

TWO THOUSAND YEARS OF MIDDLE WHARF: History of Maidenhead in Verse, by Bridget Hole.

THE LOST JOY OF RAILWAYS: A Nostalgic Journey Back to the Golden Age, by Julian Holland

CYPRUS

BIITER LEMONS by Lawrence Durrell, a personal view of the last years of Colonial Cyprus.

APHRODITE'S REALM by Robin Parker. An Illustrated Guide and Handbook to Cyprus.

GRIVAS: Portrait of a Terrorist by Dudley Barker.

LEGACY OF STRIFE by Charles Foley. Cyprus from rebellion to civil war

EXPLORING CYPRUS: Land of Eternal Beauty, by Renos G. Lavithis

JORDAN

THE BRINK OF JORDAN by Charles Johnston. Events in Jordan and the Arab World.

UNEASY LIES THE HEAD: Autobiography of H.M. King Hussein of Jordan

THE DEAD SEA SCROLLS DECEPTION by Michael Baigent.

O JERUSALEM by Larry Collins and Dominique Lapierre.

LEBANON

A WALK IN THE MOUNTAINS by Ralph Izzard. Lebanon before the 1958 civil
war.

LEBANON: A HOUSE DIVIDED by journalist Sandra Mackey

ADEN

THE VIEW FROM STEAMER POINT: Three Critical Years in South Arabia, by
Charles Johnston.

BRITISH FORCES BROADCASTING SERVICE

THE LINK WITH HOME by Alan Grace. Sixty Years of Forces Broadcasting

THIS IS THE BRITISH FORCES NETWORK by Alan Grace. BFBS in Germany.

BRITISH COLUMBIA

KAMLOOPS: A History of the District up to 1914 by Mary Balf

JOURNEY FANTASTIC, with the Overlanders to the Cariboo, by Vicki Metcalf

NEW MEXICO (Taos & Santa Fe)

LORENZO IN TAOS by Mabel Dodge Luhan (D.H. Lawrence in Taos)

HYPNOTHERAPY

HYPNOTHERAPY by Dave Elman. Summation of Elman Theories and
Techniques.

THE WIZARD WITHIN, The Krasner Method of Hypnotherapy by Dr. A.M.
Krasner

MY VOICE WILL GO WITH YOU, The Teaching Tales of Milton Erickson, MD

GLASTONBURY

THE GLASTONBURY ZODIAC: Key to the Mysteries of Britain by Mary Caine

KING ARTHUR'S AVALON: The Story of Glastonbury by Geoffrey Ashe

THE DRAMA OF THE LOST DISCIPLES by George F. Jowett

THE NEW VIEW OVER ATLANTIS by John Michell

NEW LIGHT ON THE ANCIENT MYSTERY OF GLASTINBURY by John Michell

COSMIC TEACHINGS

A GUIDE TO MEDIUMSHIP AND PSYCHICAL UNFOLDMENT by E.W. and M.H. Wallis

COSMIC CONSCIOUSNESS by Richard Bucke

HUMAN ENERGY SYSTEMS by Jack Schwarz

I AM by Jean Klein

IN SEARCH OF THE MIRACULOUS by P.D. Ouspensky. Teachings of Gurdjieff.

LIFE IN THE WORLD UNSEEN by Anthony Borgia

PERSPECTIVES by Paul Brunton. The timeless Way of Wisdom.

THE NOTEBOOKS OF PAUL BRUNTON: MEDITATION by Paul Brunton

TO BE HUMAN, by J. Krishnamurti

THE MYSTIC PATH TO COSMIC POWER by Vernon Howard

THE BOOK: ON THE TABOO AGAINST KNOWING WHO YOU ARE by Alan W. Watts

WHISPERING WINDS OF CHANGE by Stuart Wilde

WISDOM OF THE MYSTIC MASTERS by Joseph Weed

YOGI PHILOSOPHY by Yogi Ramacharaka

Lightning Source UK Ltd.
Milton Keynes UK
171032UK00001B/7/P